The Japanese Have a Word *for* It

The Complete Guide to Japanese Thought and Culture

Boyé Lafayette De Mente

PASSPORT BOOKS
NTC/Contemporary Publishing Group

Library of Congress Cataloging-in-Publication Data

De Mente, Boyé.
    [NTC's dictionary of Japan's cultural code words]
    The Japanese have a word for it : the complete guide to Japanese thought
and culture / Boyé Lafayette De Mente
       Passport books.   p.   cm.
    ISBN 0-8092-8316-9
    1. Japan—Social life and customs—Terminology.   2 Japanese
language—Terms and phrases.   I. Title.
DS821.D467   1997
306'.0952—dc21   97-34017
                                                           CIP

Other Books by Boyé Lafayette De Mente

Japanese Etiquette & Ethics in Business
How to Do Business with the Japanese
Japanese Secrets of Graceful Living
Japanese Business Dictionary
Reading Your Way Around Japan
Everthing Japanese—An Encyclopedic Reader on Things Japanese
Japanese Influence on America
Discover Cultural Japan
Japanese in Plain English
Korean Etiquette & Ethics in Business
Lover's Guide to Japan
Business Guide to Japan—Opening Doors and Closing Deals!
Survival Japanese
Japan Made Easy

Cover: Ogata Korin, *Iris Screen*. Nezu Art Museum, Tokyo, Japan.
Bridgeman/Art Resource, New York.

Originally published as *NTC's Dictionary of Japan's Cultural Code Words*

This edition first published in 1997 by Passport Books
A division of NTC/Contemporary Publishing Group, Inc.
4255 West Touhy Avenue, Lincolnwood (Chicago), Illinois 60712-1975 U.S.A.
Copyright © 1994 by Boyé Lafayette De Mente
Printed in the United States of America
International Standard Book Number: 0-8092-8316-9

   5 6 7 8 9 0   DSH/DSH   0 1 0 9 8 7 6 5 4

GUIDE TO KEY CULTURAL THEMES

For the reader's convenience, I have cross listed entries under themes that are central to Japanese culture. All entries that touch upon the theme of "loyalty," for example, are listed numerically. The reader can therefore explore a theme more thoroughly by reading the related entries.

Communication Styles: Thinking and Feeling 22, 36, 49, 70, 71, 97, 107, 116, 143, 145, 151, 158, 160, 169, 173, 175, 185, 187, 228

Conflict 6, 22, 58, 78, 89, 113, 122, 123, 125, 128, 157, 174, 198, 206, 223

Culture and Customs 32, 65, 68, 75, 101, 131, 138, 149, 150, 151, 166, 180, 182, 201, 224

Determination and Spirit 13, 17, 26, 56, 65, 88, 109, 117, 120, 121, 122, 127, 129, 130, 143, 153, 156, 181, 184, 186, 195, 203, 213, 227

Direct vs. Indirect 4, 33, 103, 141, 144, 151, 163, 168, 212, 218, 228, 229

Etiquette and Role 1, 11, 14, 37, 50, 67, 77, 88, 102, 115, 124, 131, 141, 147, 149, 168, 171, 192, 200, 207

Family 14, 118, 136, 193, 222

The Foreign Element 17, 25, 47, 52, 55, 65, 112, 179, 209, 226

The Group (In and Out Groups) 27, 44, 52, 61, 76, 78, 90, 123, 177, 195, 209, 230

Guests, Customers and Service 9, 29, 62, 84, 119, 146, 160, 202, 217

Harmony, Consensus and Cooperation 2, 4, 8, 10, 13, 90, 92, 118, 137, 162, 174, 176, 190, 201, 214, 220, 221

Honor and Shame 7, 13, 66, 69, 89, 92, 113, 139, 159, 197, 229

Imitation and Innovation 46, 61, 74, 80, 81, 95, 106, 133, 135, 156, 164, 183, 210, 215

The Individual 45, 76, 78, 79, 101, 106, 128, 134, 153, 167, 177, 179, 203, 213, 217

Influence and Persuasion 7, 19, 24, 40, 60, 77, 82, 83, 85, 115, 116, 119, 133, 141, 145

Leadership, Loyalty and Obligation 3, 35, 39, 56, 109, 124, 129, 199, 211, 219, 222

Love/Dependence 5, 115, 148, 172, 193

Parties and Meetings 28, 30, 37, 53, 57, 96, 98, 104, 106, 165, 178, 205, 216, 220

Quality, Process and Perfection 10, 20, 23, 34, 42, 59, 65, 99, 117, 121, 136, 151, 152, 156, 182, 183, 208, 215

Rank, Role and Structure in the Company 26, 31, 41, 44, 48, 54, 63, 64, 72, 75, 91, 93, 105, 110, 111, 114, 139, 167, 187, 190, 191, 192, 193, 202, 211, 212

Risk and Caution 58, 86, 134, 142, 153, 221, 225

Starting and Maintaining Relationships 12, 50, 51, 57, 62, 94, 125, 127, 132, 140, 146, 170, 171, 188, 200, 218

Strategic Entertaining 16, 73, 83, 96, 102, 108, 132, 154, 161, 171, 178, 187, 189, 194, 226

CONTENTS

Contents

Contents

Contents

Contents

ACKNOWLEDGMENTS

I am greatly indebted to "Old Japan Hand" friends and colleagues Shichiro ("Mike") Ohshima, Tadashi Shimao, Tadashi Tsuchida, Masao Tazuke, Glenn Davis, Fred T. Perry and Joseph Schmelzeis, Jr. for their constructive comments on both the concept and contents of this book. I also owe special thanks to my editors, Thomas A. Heenan, president of Heenan & Associates and an education-language specialist with extensive background in Japan, for evaluating the word entries and making many improvements in the text, and to NTC Publishing Group editor Kathleen Schultz for putting it all together in an attractive and readable form—Boye Lafayette De Mente.

FOREWORD

For centuries the Japanese used their language as a primary barrier in their battle to keep foreigners at a distance, to prevent them from learning about the inner workings of Japanese society and to ward off foreign influence. This political and economic use of the language eventually became the official policy of the government and for a long period in Japan's history the teaching of Japanese to foreigners was regarded as a serious crime against the state.

This attitude made it very difficult, and sometimes dangerous, for early foreign residents of Japan to develop any significant ability to understand and speak the language. It also contributed to the belief among the Japanese that the language was so different and so difficult that foreigners were incapable of learning it.

By the beginning of the 1990s, however, there were thousands of Japanese-speaking foreigners in the country, some of them very conspicuous as entertainers, diplomats and businessmen. But many Japanese have continued to be surprised, and sometimes disconcerted, by encounters with Japanese-speaking foreigners.

The highly stylized, minutely structured nature of Japanese culture that developed over the centuries molded the language to fit and sustain the social and political system that evolved. The psychology of the system became imbued in and expressed by the language to a degree seldom seen in other cultures.

As time passed virtually every aspect of Japanese thought and behavior came to be described by a specific word that was pregnant with meaning. Like a single life cell, each of these words, when fully extrapolated, contained a blueprint of a key segment of the Japanese way.

Because of the special nature of the Japanese language, key words are in fact the *madoguchi* (mah-doe-guu-chee) or "windows" to an understanding of the way the Japanese think and behave—despite the changes that have occurred in Japan in recent generations and are occurring still on a daily basis.

Many Japanese still strongly feel that when foreigners gain a knowledge of their language it is as if outsiders have mastered a code that reveals their innermost secrets—something that makes them very uncomfortable. They see it as a threat to both the country's unique culture and its sovereignty. Fortunately, more internationally-minded Japanese favor foreigners learning the language.

As more and more foreigners do acquire the ability to communicate well in the Japanese language it will surely contribute to fundamental changes in the way the Japanese perceive themselves and the outside world. It goes without saying (to use a common Japanese expression) that it will also contribute to even more significant changes in how effectively foreign businesspeople, political leaders and others deal with their Japanese counterparts.

The aim of this book is to provide a short-cut to understanding—and using—some of the most provocative and important elements in Japanese attitudes and behavior as expressed in their cultural "code words."

Boye Lafayette De Mente
Tokyo, Japan

1

縦 社 会

Tate Shakai

(Tah-tay Shah-kie)

"The Vertical Society"

Author Lafcadio Hearn (who later was to become famous as one of the first Japanologists) went to Japan in 1890 to write a series of articles for his publisher, Harper & Row. Fascinated by the distinctive character of the Japanese and the sensually beautiful artifacts of their culture, Hearn declared that living in Japan was like being in some kind of paradise, and he decided to take up permanent residence.

Hearn's infatuation with Japan lasted for several years. Like so many Westerners before and since, he was hypnotized by the facade of seemingly perfect order throughout the society, dazzled by the exquisite personal manners of the Japanese in all walks of life, overwhelmed by the hospitality they typically showered on foreign guests, and titillated by the unabashed sexuality that permeated their daily lives.

It was not until Hearn voluntarily gave up his status as a "foreign guest" to become a naturalized Japanese, and began to be treated more as a Japanese than as an honored visitor from abroad, that he realized the vast difference between life in Japan on a foreign pedestal and the life imposed upon the Japanese themselves by their distinctive society.

Nearly one hundred years later sociologist Chie Nakane coined the term *tate shakai* (tah-tay shah-kie), or "vertical society," in an attempt to explain the peculiarities of Japanese society in general and the attitudes and behavior of individual Japanese in particular. By "vertical society" she meant a society in which the people were ranked in a descending order, from the emperor down to the lowest individual.

In traditional, hierarchical Japan, the essence of society was a clearcut delineation between all individuals based on their social class, rank, sex, and age. Everything flowed from the mandatory observance of one's position in society—the use of the language, etiquette, dress, education, occupation—even sexual pleasures.

People had to know their proper place in society and abide by a multitude of laws and customs that had been sanctified and ritualized by the ages. It was these precisely followed patterns of behavior, plus the stylized

1

hospitality that goes with catering to superiors with absolute power, that gave Hearn his glimmerings of a heaven on earth.

Any understanding of the attitudes and behavior of the Japanese today still must begin with recognition of their individual place in the *tate shakai*, specifically including the obligations and limitations that control their behavior because of their position in the overall hierarchy, which, again, is based on rank, sex, age, education and group affiliation.

Most Japanese still today act and react, to varying degrees, according to patterns of thought and behavior that were established generations ago and remain an integral part of the schools, the companies, the professional organizations and the government, where the "vertical society" is alive and well.

Foreign businessmen and government officials must take the *tate shakai* factor into consideration in any dealings they have with Japan. It is not appropriate, for example, to attempt to involve higher executives at larger firms in the early steps of negotiating relationships with Japanese companies. That is a function which is reserved for lower- and middle-level management.

If you go into a Japanese company at the level of president, vice president, director or general manager, it is customary for your contact to bring in the appropriate level of management to interface with you and your people. Most staff work in Japanese companies is done at the *ka cho* or "section chief" level.

和

Wa
(Wah)

"Holy Harmony"

The Japanese have been virtually obsessed with the concept of *wa* (wah) or harmony since the dawn of their civilization. Their fixation on *wa* may have derived from their native religion, Shinto, but whatever its source it permeated their culture and affected every aspect of their lives.

A deep-seated reverence and need for harmony played a key role in the development and use of the Japanese language, in the daily etiquette of the Japanese, and in all the crafts and arts of their culture.

In fact, Japanese philosophy, ethics and etiquette were based on the fundamental principle that harmony took precedence over all other matters—even though the concept, when put into practice, was often at odds with logic and common sense.

Over the centuries, however, the religious-like commitment to harmony surely contributed far more to the lives of the Japanese than it took away. Today its legacy is among the cultural influences that make present-day Japan such a formidable economic power.

Harmonious relations between the government and business, and between labor and management, are distinctive features of the Japanese system. The same customs and rules of harmony are paramount in the management of companies, and are a vital part of the consensus and group approaches to the whole process of business.

Westerners who become involved with Japanese for any business or official purpose quickly learn that the maintenance of *wa* still takes precedence over expediency; that everyone and everything must wait until the demands of *wa* are met.

A thorough understanding of the role of harmony in Japanese life provides some, if not all, of the insights needed to understand the Japanese approach to business negotiations and management and why Japanese invest so much time and money in nurturing cooperative relations with suppliers and customers.

Foreign businessmen wanting to establish and cement relations with Japanese companies can make points by emphasizing their understanding and appreciation of *wa* in Japan's corporate culture and in society at large. Thereafter they can enhance their chances of success in dealing with Japanese by incorporating obvious *wa*-actions into their strategy and tactics.

These actions include copious exchanges of information (being sure they get as much as they give), having frequent face-to-face meetings on both an official and social basis, doing personal favors for key individuals (including lower-ranking managers who do all of the staff work and will eventually replace the higher-ups), and deliberately introducing a significant cultural element into relationships with Japanese associates—music, literature, art, handicrafts.

One area where *wa* is often the most important in dealing with Japanese is in one's manner of speaking, including choice of words, tone of voice, and so on. The Japanese are extraordinarily sensitive to such things, while the typical Westerner is not. Westerners are forever using words and manners that grate on Japanese nerves—words that suggest an inflexible attitude, an aggressive manner, or insensitivities of various kinds.

Much of this problem results from the fact that English and other Western languages simply sound "hard" and "blunt" to the Japanese because they have been conditioned to use and expect "soft, vague" language. Westerners also regularly use such terms as "you must understand," "I know," "we know, for example, that...," "take my word for it," and so on—all of which may sound aggressive or arrogant, especially because they are usually expressed in a strong, confident voice.

Overcoming this problem requires both insight into the Japanese mind and skill in speaking without offending, but also without appearing obsequious or insincere.

3

義 理

Giri

(Ghee-ree)

"Living with Unending Obligations"

Japan's traditional society was one of the most tightly structured social systems ever to develop in any country. There was a precise, proper manner for speaking and behaving at all times, in everything from how one entered and left a room to how one addressed a junior, an equal or a superior. Even minor deviations from the prescribed behavior were subject to serious sanctions.

This social system was enforced by an absolute feudal power over a period of many generations, eventually permeating and shaping the culture, and becoming not only the standard by which all behavior was judged, but also synonymous with one's identity as a Japanese.

For this system to work smoothly without the constant use of outside force, it had to have a philosophical and moral base so that people believed it was the right way to behave. This foundation was primarily provided by adaptations from the precepts of Confucianism, including obedience and loyalty to one's parents and superiors.

The immediate sanction brought to bear on all Japanese to force them to conform to both the subtle and blatant demands of their social system was shame. Shame played the same role in Japan that sin and the fear of God's revenge did in Christianized societies. The Japanese feared shame and sought to avoid it at all costs, which sometimes included the sacrifice of their lives.

The overall control factor in interpersonal relations in Japan was summed up in the word *giri* (ghee-ree), which translates as "obligation, duty, justice." The Japanese were bound at birth by specific kinds and degrees of obligation to themselves, to their parents, their siblings, and to all others who touched their lives, particularly those whose actions resulted in some kind of benefit to the individual, such as teachers, mentors, employers, doctors, and so on.

Expressed in Japanese terms, the people were duty-bound to avoid any kind of shame because of *giri* they owed to themselves, to their parents and extended family, to their employer and to others on up the social and economic chain. They were obligated to return favors or otherwise balance them out with some kind of service or sacrifice.

They were also obligated to do their best in any endeavor they undertook because to do less would bring shame upon themselves, on their families and on Japan as a national entity. When Japanese athletes failed in international competition because they seemingly did not do their utmost, all Japanese felt that they had been dishonored.

In feudal days, *giri* to one's lord could require one to commit suicide in the prescribed ceremonial manner. Today *giri* is defined as the duty one has to fulfill social obligations. This no longer includes the sacrifice of one's life, but it often includes such drastic actions as resigning from a high executive position to take responsibility for a company-related mishap.

Since the final demise of the feudal system in Japan in 1945, the traditional sense of shame has weakened substantially, but among the older generations it remains a primary moral force. Among the ordinary obligations that come within the domain of *giri* are sending and giving gifts, attending such functions as weddings and funerals, and avoiding actions that would harm anyone's reputation.

The various *giri* rituals must be observed in the right manner and spirit to be acceptable. Doing them in a casual or flippant manner is called *giri ippen* (ghee-ree eep-pane), literally "fragmentary giri," but figuratively "giri without heart." In a recent case of this type, several school girls killed one of their classmates who failed to show proper sincerity at the funeral of one of the girls' mothers.

I have built up substantial *giri* with many Japanese over the years by doing them unsolicited favors. Individual foreign businessmen as well corporations can do the same thing. By the same token, you can also incur *giri* by accepting favors that you do not quickly return.

Favors that generally cannot be returned, such as those provided by teachers and parents, last a lifetime and may grow in proportion to the success of the individual.

4

建 前　本 音

Tatemae/Honne
(Tah-tay-my/Hone-nay)

"Facade vs. Reality"

Japanese concern with interpersonal harmony led to the development of a system of behavior that included careful control of facial expressions and body movements, and a highly stylized form of indirect, vague speech designed to avoid commitment or friction of any kind.

This system required the Japanese to maintain, and balance, two worlds. One consisted of reality or *honne* (hone-nay)—their true thoughts and intentions—and the other of a facade or *tatemae* (tah-tay-my)—a screen created to maintain the appearance of harmony and serve as a ploy until the other party revealed their own position.

Presenting a false front and jockeying for advantage is a tactic that is certainly well-known and commonly used in the West, but it pales in comparison with the practice in Japan, where it was institutionalized, ritualized and sanctified to the extent that it became the only acceptable behavior.

While the cultural conditioning that made the *tatemae/honne* system an integral part of the Japanese character has significantly weakened in recent decades, it is still the normal pattern of behavior among the majority of middle-aged and older Japanese.

The *tatemae/honne* system often becomes a crucial factor in encounters between Japanese businessmen and politicians and their Western counterparts because there is a natural tendency for Westerners to immediately lay all of their cards on the table not only as a goodwill gesture but also because they believe it is the best way to reach a fair, speedy agreement.

Unfortunately, this gesture often puts the Western side at a disadvantage because the Japanese side either cannot or will not respond in kind. On many occasions, they cannot respond openly and fully because their cultural conditioning makes it impossible. On other occasions, they knowingly and gladly accept the advantage that has been presented to them, and make the best possible use of it.

Westerners should not regard the *tatemae/honne* factor as a minor cultural quirk that the Japanese can easily dispense with when they are given the incentive to do so, or as something that can be easily overcome by the force of logic and persuasive powers. Generally speaking, logic and forceful persuasion are not effective in Japan because they are regarded as cold, calculating and self-serving.

Since the Western side cannot expect their Japanese counterparts to completely change their cultural stripes on notice for the Westerner's benefit, the best that Westerners can do is to adapt their own strategy and tactics to contend with the reality of the situation and proceed point by point, going from *tatemae* to *honne* in each case.

Contending with the *tatemae/honne* factor in Japanese behavior naturally adds substantially to the amount of time it takes to do business in Japan, and makes patience and persistence absolutely essential. And this is one of the reasons why the Japanese practice of having lower-ranking managers do all of the preliminary staff work on projects makes so much sense as far as they are concerned.

Top Japanese executives behave more or less like the presidents of countries. They go in to sign contracts after the negotiations have been completed and the documents drawn up by subordinates.

甘え

Amae
(Ah-my)

"Indulgent Love"

An expatriate foreign businessman who had lived and worked in Japan for more than twenty years once commented to me, "The longer I am involved with the Japanese the less I understand them!"

The same lament—or words to that effect—is still a common reaction among Westerners who have had substantial experience in Japan and yet repeatedly find themselves surprised and frustrated by the seemingly irrational behavior of their Japanese co-workers and business associates.

Simply stated, the reason why Westerners are often confused and frustrated by Japanese attitudes and behavior is that, in traditional Japanese culture, the guidelines for interpersonal relationships are based on principles that are different, and sometimes diametrically opposed, to the philosophy and psychology that prevails in the West.

The bedrock principle underlying traditional, idealized Japanese behavior is summed up in the word *amae* (ah-may), from the term *amaeru* (ah-my-rue), meaning to presume upon another's love or indulgence.

To properly receive or react to expressions of *amae* requires that individuals repress all selfish instincts and behave toward other people as mothers do toward beloved children—treating them honestly, generously and kindly, regardless of the circumstances.

In the idealized *amae*-filled world that was the prevailing ethical goal in traditional Japan, people could totally depend upon each other without fear of being cheated, disadvantaged or embarrassed in any way. *Amae* incorporated the concepts of absolute dependence and absolute trust in all human relations.

Of course, this *amae* morality was not followed perfectly by the average Japanese at any time during the country's history, but it was prevalent enough that it permeated the culture and set the standard for behavior that is still a key factor in Japanese society today.

Present-day Japanese who were raised in the traditional culture (generally, those born before 1960 as well as many born in more recent years and raised in rural environments) cannot feel at ease with other people until they have established an *amae*-type relationship on the basis of common experiences, common fears, common goals.

This helps explain why it is difficult for individualistic, independent outsiders to understand the Japanese, and why it takes such a long time for foreign businessmen to establish effective relationships with their Japanese counterparts.

Developing an *amae*-based relationship with Japanese is a special challenge for foreign businessmen, but is not as difficult as it might first appear. Basically it means being very careful and deliberate in developing a strong personal relationship before trying to consummate business deals. This involves eating and drinking together, playing together, exchanging gifts and other tokens of friendship, and participating in the various passages of life that are meaningful to everyone—attending weddings, graduations, funerals and the like.

The goal is to put the relationship on a personal basis so that the Japanese will presume that in any business relationship they would not be taken advantage of or let down in any way—that the relationship would take precedence over cold, hard business considerations.

As my colleague Joe Schmelzeis notes, *amae* allows a person to make unreasonable requests ("I have no credit history, but can you give me a Gold Card? Green isn't good enough"). Honoring such requests can win you major points, which you may be able to draw on in the future.

There are innumerable daily examples of *amae* in action that often strike Western businessmen as being totally irrational if not downright bad business. These include maintaining supplier and distribution relationships that are no longer viable and, moreover, accepting whatever economic disadvantage such behavior might entail as being a part of their debt to society. It also greatly limits their options in establishing new relationships with unrelated companies.

6

犠 牲 者

Giseisha

(Ghee-say-e-shah)

"The Victim Syndrome"

The *amae* or "indulgent love" concept in Japan's traditional culture has been both a blessing and a bane to the Japanese. On the one hand, it encouraged a quality of personal relationships that would befit angels. On the other hand, it conditioned them to have such high expectations of each other and everyone else that they were constantly being disappointed.

One of the results of these highly honed expectations was to give the Japanese an overwhelming tendency to become utterly dependent upon others for their mental well-being, causing them to suffer from a severe *giseisha* or "victim" syndrome when this dependency was threatened or ended.

Recent changes in Japan have significantly eroded the influence of the *giseisha* mentality, but enough of it remains to be easily discernible in the attitudes and behavior of the average middle-aged and older Japanese.

Nowadays, the *giseisha* syndrome is most often triggered when a person, a company or a country on whom individuals have been passively dependent, does something—or fails to do something—that they feel is against their interests.

Having been "victimized," whether by action or inaction, knowingly or unknowingly, the victim feels compelled to take revenge against the offending party, and will thereafter spend considerable effort in that pursuit.

About the only method that outsiders can use to avoid precipitating an outbreak of the *giseisha* syndrome is to carefully control the expectations of everyone involved in any situation—to precisely detail what it is they propose to do and how they are going to do it, and to make very clear the limits of the obligation they are incurring.

Americans in particular are prone to exaggerate their abilities and their intentions, a tendency which leads to unreal expectations in the first place. When they fall short of their promise, or fail to meet Japanese standards which are often different, the problems that arise are exacerbated.

One of the reasons why such situations often become much more serious than the foreign side anticipates is that in relationships with a Japanese or Japanese company there are no natural limits to what the Japanese can ask of you or expect of you.

The Japanese tend to see the relationship as giving them total access to one's knowledge and technology, and one must be very diplomatic in setting and maintaining limits on what and how much to give. Any show of reluctance to provide full access to whatever they want will be regarded as unfriendly, unwarranted behavior if the limits have not been specified in advance.

One of the techniques foreigners can use to counter the effects of the *giseisha* syndrome is to deliberately ask their Japanese counterparts dozens of carefully crafted questions during all stages of their negotiations, especially at the beginning.

Many foreigners inadvertently set themselves up for a *giseisha* backlash by giving the impression that they are bringing much more to the table than they are asking credit for, thereby inviting the Japanese side to presume upon their generosity. This is a part of the over-sell syndrome which afflicts many Westerners in their attempts to deal with Japanese.

顔

Kao
(Kah-oh)

"Keeping Your Face Intact"

While morality in the Christianized countries of the West (generally speaking) grew out of principles that incorporated the concepts of individuality and personal responsibility for one's own actions, Japanese morality emphasized group responsibility and the suppression of individuality.

In the West, one could behave in an outrageous manner, insult people and otherwise act like an uncivilized savage, but so long as he did not break well-understood principles of conduct by committing such acts as theft, assault or murder, he was relatively safe from prosecution by the law, and was privileged to defend himself personally if someone took umbrage at his behavior.

In Japan, on the other hand, how one spoke and behaved in the sense of manners was equated with morality, and failure to conform to a highly refined system of personal conduct could lead to disastrous results. In other words, morality in the Japanese context of things could involve something as simple as a properly performed bow, which was <u>visible</u> for all to see.

Because manners and morality were often the same in Japan, it was much more difficult for the Japanese to conduct themselves in a moral fashion at all times. They became excessively sensitive to infractions of the established etiquette and much more concerned about making mistakes and "sinning" against someone, as well as being "sinned" against.

Japanese came to regard any error on their part or any "immoral" behavior toward them by someone else as a blemish on their *kao* (kah-oh), or "face." In addition to exercising extreme caution in their behavior, that is, conforming as precisely as possible to the demands of their detailed rules of etiquette, it also became characteristic for them to avoid risking error by not taking the lead in things, by remaining noncommittal, by speaking in vague terms, and so on.

The Japanese were just as concerned about their "face" being damaged by slights or insults from others as they were about its damage from sins they themselves committed. If the slight was perpetrated out of callousness or arrogance, and especially if it was premeditated, the only way it could be expiated was through a suitable act of revenge.

But the demands of Japanese etiquette made overt response to such incidents both difficult and dangerous. In the old days, some samurai who became involved in matters of face would resort to duels. Most people resorted to some kind of intrigue to exact their revenge covertly.

Present-day Japanese, particularly those who have been directly influenced by exposure to Western attitudes and manners, are generally less thin-skinned than their predecessors, but face is still of vital importance to everyone, and must be taken into consideration at all times.

In a business context, the compulsion to maintain face continues to manifest itself as very cautious behavior by individuals, continuation of the consensus approach to decision-making, and conformity to the highly stylized etiquette that makes up the framework of Japanese morality.

The importance of "face" in Japanese culture is indicated by several common expressions based on the word *kao*: *kao wo tateru* (kah-oh oh tah-tay-rue), "save face" or "prevent disgrace;" *kao wo tsubusu* (kah-oh oh t'sue-buu-suu), "lose face;" *kao ga hiroi* (kah-oh gah hee-roy), "have a wide face," that is, be well-known; *kao wo tsunagu* (kah-oh oh t'suu-nah-guu), or "tie up face," meaning to nurture one's contacts; and so on.

This last point, nurturing one's contacts, is a vital issue where foreign companies are concerned. One of the most frequent complaints voiced by Japanese about foreign, and in particular American, companies is that rather than establishing permanent offices in Japan, they send over a steady stream of different people. The Japanese feel very insecure when they are forced to deal continuously with "new faces" and are much less apt to make serious commitments to such companies.

Foreigners dealing with Japanese in private or business matters should be aware that any kind of personal or professional criticism may be taken far more seriously than what was intended. Other face-damaging "sins" often unwittingly committed by inexperienced foreign businessmen include not seating a Japanese guest in a chair or place that is appropriate for his status, paying special attention to a low-ranking member of a group because he or she speaks English, embarrassing a person by undiplomatically pointing out that something he has just said is not accurate, not accompanying high-ranking guests to the door or elevator or their car when they depart, not expressing thanks for significant favors, and failing to perform some task as promised or expected and not apologizing for it.

8

遠 慮

Enryo
(Inn-rio)

"Holding Back"

For more than a thousand years morality and etiquette in Japan were so pervasive and powerful that their influence created one of the most stylized and regimented cultures the world has ever seen.

On the one hand, the philosophy and psychology of the Japanese, manifested in their arts, crafts and lifestyle, represented one of the most admirable cultures ever devised. At the same time, it also had an inhumane aspect that stifled the individuality and creativity of the Japanese and held them in harsh bondage to the state.

Conforming to the minutely prescribed manners and lifestyle required by this formidable culture was so demanding that it was necessary for the Japanese to develop ways of coping that would reduce the dangers they faced in the event they made a mistake, offended someone, or created any kind of controversy.

One of the most important of these coping methods, which eventually became an integral part of Japanese behavior, was known as *enryo* (innrio), or "holding back," being reserved, noncommittal, "considering from a distance"—a characteristic in which the Japanese still take extreme pride.

In casual social encounters, practicing *enryo* is, of course, often highly prized and praised. But in international business, politics and other professional situations, it is almost always a serious detriment to understanding and effective cooperation.

Japanese businessmen are acutely aware that their custom of "holding back" is exactly opposed to the Western way of "holding forth," and that this cultural idiosyncrasy is often a serious handicap when they are negotiating with Westerners in situations where they must play by Western rules.

When they are operating on their home turf, however, or when they have the upper hand and can control how the game is to be played whatever the location, they are masters at using *enryo* to draw their opponents out and maintain the advantage.

In fact, Westerners can almost always be depended upon to quickly put themselves at a disadvantage in their dealings with the Japanese by being too forward and forthright. Because we cannot stand silence or reticence, we often immediately reveal our position and technology in our eagerness to fill the vacuum.

A partial solution to this problem of communication styles is for the Western side, at the beginning of any discussion, to request that their Japanese counterparts dispense with *enryo ("Go-enryo naku"),* so that the talks will be on a level playing field—and then good-humoredly remind them any time they appear to be reverting to form.

Generally speaking, Japanese are more impressed with people who talk the least, who make their point by their manner rather than by their mouth. The more the Japanese respect a person, the more they will do for him or on his behalf without being directly asked. All so-called "Big Men" in Japan have to do to get extraordinary things accomplished is to subtly let people know what it is they desire.

The power of "Big Men" in Japan comes as much from their moral virtue as from their political or financial power, if not more so. They are perceived as having no selfish motives, and therefore whatever they wish is seen as desirable and something that should be done.

9

お客さん

O'kyaku-San
(Oh-k'yahk-Sahn)

"The Honorable Customer"

Any explanation of Japan's emergence as a leading economic power in the 1970s and 1980s must include the element of etiquette—as incongruous as this might first seem. So much of the character and psychology of the Japanese is reflected in the country's traditional manners that they cannot be viewed separately.

Over nearly half a century, I have also noted that no aspect of reading or hearing about the Japanese way of doing things can provide outsiders with an understanding and appreciation of the essence of Japanese behavior. That is something that comes only as a result of direct personal experience, of physically, emotionally and spiritually absorbing the essence, over a period of several years.

Further, this absorption does not happen automatically, even with intimate, long-term association with the Japanese. It is knowledge and understanding that must be wanted, must be cultivated; and the student of the Japanese Way must be exceptionally sensitive and receptive to the form, process and nuances of Japanese etiquette to achieve true understanding.

Many foreigners spend decades in Japan without letting their own cultural shields down long enough for the subtleties of Japanese etiquette to penetrate their prejudices. They may have surface knowledge of Japanese manners, but they do not learn their philosophical or psychological foundations—and therefore cannot correctly interpret Japanese behavior.

One of the key facets of Japanese etiquette is bound up in the word

O'kyaku (Oh-k'yah-kuu), which means "honored guest," but is also used in reference to customers. (The *san* adds the meaning of Mr., Mrs. or Miss.) The importance of this point is that the Japanese have traditionally treated business customers as honored guests, with a level of service that transcends monetary concerns.

There are a number of historical reasons why the Japanese treat guests and customers with such extraordinary courtesy and a kind and degree of service that is usually associated with high social rank and power. In their hierarchically arranged society, where superiors generally had virtually unlimited power over inferiors, deference, extreme politeness and service were often the basis for survival.

People on every level of the hierarchy were conditioned—and required—to treat their superiors in a highly deferential manner, to anticipate and fulfill their every whim—all following a precisely prescribed etiquette and form that was often detailed in manuals and had the force of law.

Within this general hierarchical structure was a specific class division that separated the people into two distinct groups: the elite samurai ruling class, and the common people.

The meticulously trained and formal-minded samurai not only set the etiquette standards for the entire country, they were also in charge of enforcing them. When the arbiters of good manners are armed warriors who are authorized to use their swords to enforce the rules, politeness and a servile attitude become second nature.

Thus an extreme propensity for politeness and service was ingrained in the Japanese over a period of more than a thousand years as an integral part of their social and political systems. Proper behavior—that is, Japanese etiquette—took precedence over principle.

The language of the country gradually changed to conform to the demands of etiquette, and thereafter played a key role in transmitting the etiquette system from one generation to the next.

In today's Japan, the concept of *O'kyaku* has weakened but it is still a conspicuous and positive facet of Japanese life, adding flavor and color, and giving the Japanese an edge over less mannered people.

型

Kata

(Kah-tah)

"Acting Like Ants"

British foreign correspondent David Powers, who spent many years in Tokyo, once compared covering Japan with covering the Sahara Desert. "It may always look the same, but the grains of sand are moving," he said.

Powers' comparison of Japan with a desert of sand was an insightful and provocative analogy that must, of course, be taken with a grain or two of sand. He went on to add that in order to understand Japan, one had to distinguish among the moving "grains" to determine what really represented change and what was just movement.

Part of the apparent enigma—and strength—of the Japanese is their cultural homogeneity—the similarity in their attitudes and behavior. When this is added to their racial homogeneity, they do indeed present a formidable image of programmed purpose and power—an image that social critic Michihiro Matsumoto likens to a swarm of ants.

The Japanese owe their cultural similarities to a process of behavioral conditioning that spanned scores of generations over a period of more than a thousand years, and included philosophical and spiritual beliefs as well as every conceivable aspect of their physical behavior.

The philosophical and spiritual side of this behavioral conditioning was based on a combination of Shinto, Buddhist and Confucian precepts. The physical side of the programming was based on a precise set of "cultural molds" called *kata* (kah-tah), which, in this case, means "form" and the mechanical process of doing things.

There was a precise *kata*, or way, for doing everything, from sleeping, sitting, eating, dressing and bowing to performing various kinds of work. Every Japanese, from infancy on, was meticulously conditioned in the exact physical actions prescribed for these and all other common functions.

There was only one correct way to perform each of these actions. Deviations were not allowed. Because everyone was conditioned to follow the same etiquette in their personal behavior, and the same form and process in their particular work, the overall behavior of the Japanese became homogenized to a degree seldom seen in other societies.

Japan's *kata*, also often referred to as *do* (doe) or "way," probably had their genesis in the numerous religious rituals that were so much a part of Japanese life from the earliest times. This was followed by adoption of a strict master-apprentice approach to teaching all of the industrial crafts and arts that made up the society's lifestyle.

The use of absolutely prescribed forms and processes became epitomized in such martial arts as *ju do* (juu doe), *aiki do* (aye-kee doe), *karate do* (kah-rah-tay doe), and *ken do* (ken doe), and in such aesthetic arts as *cha do* (chah doe), "the way of tea," and *sho do* (show doe), "the way of calligraphy."

Kata-ized behavioral conditioning is still practiced in Japan's public schools, in the training programs of many larger corporations, and in many aesthetic pursuits, but it is much less strict and much less pervasive than it was prior to the introduction of a more democratic approach to life in 1945.

By the beginning of the 1980s most Japanese had begun to question the value of a system designed to turn them all into clones of each other, pointing out that it prevented them from developing individual creativity and from being able to relate and communicate effectively with the outside world.

It is obvious that the *kata*-ized behavioral conditioning of the Japanese is diminishing rapidly, and that it will continue to decrease. But its influence is such that it will be a significant factor in both the character and personality of the Japanese for the foreseeable future.

*For more on *kata*, see *JAPAN'S SECRET WEAPON. The Kata Factor*, by the same author Also published as *Behind the Japanese Bow*

挨拶

Aisatsu

(Aye-saht-sue)

"Paying Proper Respect"

To understand the nature and importance of etiquette in Japan it helps to think of the whole society as one giant charm school in which a very carefully prescribed militaristic form of interpersonal behavior is the norm for personal conduct, particularly within organizations and companies where it is often rigidly enforced.

There are, in fact, very strong elements of both a military and charm-school type of training in the behavior of the Japanese—to the point that Americans and other Westerners, with their far more casual and informal manners, are often ill at ease in meeting and associating with Japanese.

One facet of Japanese etiquette that is very important for foreign businessmen to understand and assimilate is the *aisatsu* (aye-saht-sue). While translated as "greeting," *aisatsu* entails much more than what this English term suggests. It incorporates serious social as well as business obligations that are essential to fulfill at the right time and in the right way in order to maintain favorable, effective relationships.

The proper fulfillment of *aisatsu* obligations requires that businessmen have regular personal contact, that special occasions be acknowledged through personal visits, congratulations and/or gifts, and that all of these be done in a stylized manner that has been sanctified by centuries of usage.

One of the most important occasions calling for *aisatsu* occurs right after the New Year holidays, at which time *aisatsu mawari* (aye-sot-sue mah-wah-ree) or "round of greetings," is a strongly entrenched custom. Salesmen visit their accounts, and managers and executives visit their vendors, suppliers and bankers to acknowledge their business and support during the year just ended and ask that they continue their patronage during the new year.

Because of the *aisatsu* custom, very little work is done in most Japanese offices for the first two or three days following their reopening after New Year's. On a higher managerial level, appointments are made for most *aisatsu* visits to make sure the right people are in their offices. Lower ranking people, including salesmen, however, often visit their main clients and contacts without advance notice.

The most common of the institutionalized *aisatsu* phrases used at the beginning of the new year is: *Saku nen chu wa taihen O'sewa ni nari-mashita. Mata kon nen mo yoroshiku O'negai itashimasu* (Sah-kuu nane chuu wah tie-hane Oh-say-wah nee nah-ree-mah-sshta. Mah-tah kone-nane moe yoe-roe-she-kuu Oh-nay-guy ee-tah-she-mahss)—which means, "We are deeply obligated to you for your patronage and help last year, and extend our deepest gratitude. We ask that you please continue doing business with us this year."

Failure to perform the expected *aisatsu* ritual, with its precise behavior and language, can be a major slight. Performing the ritual properly is a conspicuous sign of sensitivity to the feelings of the recipients, of goodwill and of gratitude. It shows that the individual making the rounds is sincere, appreciates the relationship and, by extension, is dependable and deserving of the business.

Other universally recognized occasions calling for formal *aisatsu* visits include when an important contact is promoted or suffers a death in the family, and when a son or daughter marries. Courtesy visits are also vital when first establishing a relationship with a Japanese company and to mark such important events as personnel changes on a managerial or executive level.

It is not proper to actually discuss business during an *aisatsu* visit. This is one of the many occasions in dealings with Japanese on which one's real intentions are left unsaid, not only because everyone already knows what those intentions are in the first place, but also because the Japanese prefer to keep relationships of all kinds on as much of a personal basis as possible.

The more personal elements one can bring into play in a business relationship with Japanese, the greater the chances of success.

12

ご 縁

Go-En

(Go-Inn)

"The Honorable Relationship"

Buddhism, imported into Japan from China some 1500 years ago, had a profound effect on the way the Japanese view human relationships, personal as well as business. Unlike Christian philosophy, which taught that all relationships should be based on humanized principles of love and respect on one hand and fear of God's revenge on the other, Buddhist philosophy took a cosmic approach and taught that relationships were a matter of cause and effect.

In the idealized Christian context of things, relationships could be founded quickly and simply on the basis of universal principles—irrespective of other considerations. The rich and the poor could be friends. There were no inherent or contrived barriers preventing people from socializing with each other or engaging in business if they desired to do so.

While this Christian philosophy seldom functioned at anywhere near its ideal level, it nevertheless provided an ethical and moral formula that was easy to understand and just as easy to use when people wanted to take advantage of it.

The Buddhist approach to human relations tended to make matters complicated, however, and contributed to the creation of a system that required one to consider things on a deeper, much more subtle level before a relationship could be established.

In what often appeared to be an irrational contradiction, the traditional Japanese reaction to new relations was that they could not be established because no relations existed. There had to be some kind of recognized outside connection bringing the two parties together—a go-between or some other third party.

The existence or non-existence of a relationship between individuals or companies, as well as the reason why a relationship exists or the possibility of a relationship developing, are expressed in terms of *en* (inn), which basically means "connection" or "relationship." (*En* is sometimes prefixed with the honorific *go*.)

If there is *en*, a relationship already exists or can be developed. If there is no *en*, there is no relationship and one cannot be developed. In other words, *en* is both cause and effect, and without it nothing happens. *En* plays a key role in determining relationships because of the fundamental desire of the Japanese to avoid adding to the obligations they already have. The obligations they were born with and accrue as they grow up, go to school, get a job and go to work are so oppressive that the idea of adding new ones is profoundly disturbing to them.

Refusing to establish *en* because no *en* exists would prevent the creation of highly desirable personal relationships such as marriage, as well as greatly curtail business expansion. So the Japanese came up with a subtle way of circumventing the problem: instead of accepting or making new contacts directly, they expand on existing relationships—using them, or requiring that outsiders use them, as go-betweens.

When Western businessmen without extensive experience in Japan encounter this characteristic Japanese reaction, they are likely to disbelieve what they see and hear, and then be confused and frustrated by their inability to fully accept the rationale behind such behavior. To the logical-minded Westerner, refusing to do business with a company because you have no relations with the company just doesn't make sense. It therefore behooves the Western businessman to find ways in which he can convert from a no *en* situation—*en ga nai* (inn gah nie)—to having *en*—*en ga aru* (inn gah ah-rue). Developing the required *en* must be done through respected third parties over a period of time.

This underlying principle of all relationships in Japan is the reason why intermediaries, marriage arrangers and business go-betweens flourish.

13

大和魂

Yamato Damashii
(Yah-mah-toe Dah-mah-she-ee)

"The Spirit of Japan"

After the United States forced Japan to end its long age of isolation in the 1850s and open its doors to foreign visitors and commerce, the

Japanese were dismayed to discover how far they were behind the Western world in terms of industrial and military might.

The Japanese resolved then that they would overcome their material and technological shortcomings by making use of their extraordinary traditions of persevering in the face of all obstacles until victory was theirs.

Eventually, someone came up with the national slogan *Wa Kon! Yo Sai!* (Wah Kone! Yoe Sie!), or "Japanese Spirit—Western Learning," that became the battle cry for the transformation of Japan from an agricultural society into a major world power.

This special Japanese spirit had long before been enshrined in the national consciousness as a key part of the Imperial system and national polity. Known as *Yamato Damashii* (Yah-mah-toe Dah-mah-she-ee), or "Spirit/Soul of Japan," the concept evolved during the earliest centuries of Japan's existence.

Yamato is the original Japanese name for their country, and is written with the same ideograms used for *wa* (wah), or "harmony." A literal translation of *Yamato Damashii* could be "Spirit of Harmony."

In present-day Japan, spirit, often expressed as "guts" in everyday parlance, still plays a major role in Japanese lives. It is still believed that having "guts" is the key to success in any endeavor, but particularly so in business and professional sports. Spirit, in fact, takes precedence over talent in the eyes of many.

In professional sports, Japanese managers drill their teams to exhaustion day after day after day—not to enhance their ability (which in fact suffers when the training is overdone) but to give them "guts"—the will to play until they drop.

Japanese business managers prize employees with guts—meaning those who will undertake any task, whether or not they know anything about it, and simply never give up until they succeed or ruin themselves trying.

This samurai syndrome is one of the most conspicuous of the traits that have helped make the Japanese such formidable competitors in business. The typical Westerner will go only so far and then walk away from a job or task that proves unduly difficult. Not so the average Japanese. They will work harder and longer, and will sacrifice more of themselves and their lives.

The concept of spirit is instilled into the Japanese from childhood as an integral part of their culture; as an essential ingredient in their identity as Japanese. Failure to demonstrate extraordinary spirit (in pursuit of a sanctioned goal) is regarded as shameful and un-Japanese.

Because of the enormous pressure on all Japanese to conform to the established image of national identity, any failure by a Japanese to demonstrate an acceptable level of spirit is, in fact, regarded as shaming the whole country.

Foreign businessmen should keep this cultural factor in mind when evaluating potential Japanese employees. The best workers are often not the flamboyantly aggressive ones, but the quiet ones who burrow in and do not know how to give up.

They are also more often than not among the majority who do not speak English or any other foreign language.

14

さ ん

San
(Sahn)

"A Little Word With a Big Role"

The Japanese language is far more culturally oriented, or "culturally pregnant," than English. By this I mean that it is far more important to the Japanese that the language be used in a culturally correct manner.

For centuries the Japanese were totally conditioned in an etiquette system that required the most careful and precise use of the language in informal as well as formal situations.

Society was divided into precise levels of inferiors and superiors based on class, sex, age, position and kinship, with each level—as well as variations within levels—requiring a specific language made up of the right words, with the right endings, and, of course, the right tone of voice.

Japanese were so thoroughly programmed in both the physical and verbal etiquette making up the country's social system that the slightest deviation was noticeable, and made the people extremely susceptible to reacting negatively to any variation from the very high norm.

The "correct" use of the language was not just a cultural skill that indicated one's level of education or natural talent, or gave one a social or economic advantage. Using the language at a level that was acceptable for the circumstance at hand was essential for staying out of trouble.

Social changes in Japan since 1945 have greatly reduced the intensity and duration of the language programming undergone by the Japanese, but it remains a conspicuous element in their attitudes and behavior, and continues to be an important factor in the attempts of foreigners to learn and use the language properly.

One of the Japanese terms that often trips up the novice in Japan is *san* (sahn), that ubiquitous little word that seems to be attached willy-nilly to people's names, company names, and sometimes titles as well.

The *san* we are talking about here means "Mr., Mrs., Ms., Miss" and something like "esquire" when it is attached to a company name (other *san* in the Japanese language mean "three, a crosspiece, confusion, child-birth, brilliant, mountain").

Japan's traditional etiquette required an extraordinary degree of formality and politeness that precluded referring to people, including family members, just by their names. People were called by their title, by their title plus *san,* or by their name plus *san.*

Using *san* in addressing people became so deeply embedded in the cultural system that it was done without thinking, as if the term was a required addition to a person's name and had little or nothing to do with personal feelings or the relationship between the people concerned.

Thus it came about that parents habitually add *chan* (chahn), the diminutive of *san,* to their children's names, and children add either *san* or *chan* to the words for mother, father, older or younger brother or sister, grandmother, grandfather, aunt and uncle.

Younger Japanese are gradually giving up the habit of addressing each other as *san* in informal situations, using either first names, nicknames or last names, as Americans do. But in formal situations and in the business world in today's Japan, the last name (or title) plus *san* remains the rule. *Sama* (sah-mah), a highly honorific form of *san,* is used primarily in personal references—to someone else's spouse or children; not in business situations.

A key point: one <u>never</u> attaches *san* to one's own name—a very conspicuous mistake often made by foreigners. For example, I introduce myself as "De Mente desu" (De Mente dess), or "I am De Mente," but <u>never</u> as "De Mente *San* desu." Another honorific suffix used often by men in place of *san,* usually superiors to long-time subordinates and among close male friends, is *kun* (koon), a term that apparently came into use to distinguish males from females.

———————— 15 ————————

油を売る

Abura wo Uru
(Ah-buu-rah oh Uu-rue)

"Oiling Your Way Through Life"

In 1960, during the heyday of Japan's rush to economic glory, I committed a heresy by writing that not all Japanese worked hard, that huge numbers of white collar employees in thousands of companies did very little if any real work during the course of a day.

In addition to deliberate over-employment in many companies, I said that neither the vaunted Japanese system nor famed Japanese spirit inspired all workers to perform at their maximum. On the contrary, I noted, the system made it inevitable that a large percentage of white collar employees in any company would be low producers.

There are several fundamental reasons why so many Japanese office workers are unproductive. In the first place, a portion of the members of any *ka* (kah), or "section" (the basic unit in Japanese companies), are new employees who are still in a learning stage. This phase may last for a year or more because they are mostly left on their own to learn by observing and gradually absorbing the knowledge they need to make a real contribution.

The deeply entrenched custom of rotating employees from section to section and department to department, usually every two or three years, eventually ends up with individuals having broad-based backgrounds in the overall activities of the companies, but during the ongoing process a number of workers in any section or department are always in the learning stage, substantially reducing the productivity of the unit.

It is common for employees with absolutely no knowledge or experience in marketing, for example, to be transferred to the marketing department and placed in positions where they are the contact point for activities going on in the department.

Outsiders, particularly foreigners, dealing with Japanese companies are regularly put at a disadvantage by having to develop relationships with new, inexperienced people in charge of their product or service area.

Most workers in Japan are still hired directly from schools. They are not hired for specific jobs or even departments within a company. They are brought in en masse and then divided up among the various sections by body count—the way an army might draft new recruits and assign them to empty slots, without putting them through a specialty training process.

Despite rigorous screening, Japanese companies still end up with employees who fail to perform for one reason or another—often because no attempt is made to place them in positions that suit their personalities and preferences. Employees who are in jobs they like and are good at are routinely transferred to other areas, leaving them disgruntled and frustrated.

Given the highly structured form and management style in Japanese companies, office workers get a pretty good idea of what their future with the company is going to be within a few years. Many of those who realize they are not going to reach the higher levels of management begin coasting. Their primary motivation is to keep quiet and stay out of trouble.

These and a variety of other factors, some personal and others involving the practices of individual companies, result in a significant percentage of Japan's office workers becoming skilled at *abura wo uru* (ah-buu-rah oh uu-rue), or "selling oil"—a saying that comes from the days when peddlers used to roam the streets selling rapeseed oil for use in lanterns.

Since everyone needed oil for their lamps, the peddlers didn't have to work very hard, so the profession became synonymous with being lackadaisical and lazy. One way to identify "oil sellers" is that they are often the friendliest and best-liked people in the office. They go out of their way to be pleasant and upbeat to everybody.

Another equally well-known historical reference to workers who have easy jobs is *Toyama no kusuri* (Toe-yah-mah no kuu-sue-ree), or "Toyama medicine." Toyama, one of the prefectures on the main island of Honshu (Hoan-shuu), was the fief of the Maeda clan during the long Tokugawa Shogunate (1603–1868).

The clan became famous—and wealthy—from manufacturing herbal medicines and selling them through a nationwide network of itinerant peddlers. The peddlers would leave a box stocked with medicines at every household. Thereafter once or twice a year they would return to collect for any of the medicine that had been used, and to restock the box.

This system of selling continued into modern times, and became associated with a type of merchandising that required no training or experience and little or no effort. Over the generations *Toyama no kusuri* became synonymous with "easy job" or "easy sale."

It also became common for *Toyama no kusuri*-type salesmen to extend various kinds of "special services" to their customers to maintain their loyalty. These services included such things as bringing them news, giving them gifts, acting as baby-sitters, and so on.

It is fairly common for the accounts of foreign businessmen dealing with larger Japanese companies to end up in the hands of "oil sellers." When this happens about the only recourse the foreign businessman has is to diplomatically cultivate relationships with other members of the same section as well as related sections, and get their support in encouraging the "oil seller" to be more productive and, in worst-case scenarios, themselves lend a hand.

赤 提 灯

Aka Chochin

(Ah-kah Choe-cheen)

"Going to an Entertainment District"

When I first arrived in Japan in the late 1940s, the redlight districts for which the country had been noted for centuries were still flourishing. These districts ranged from small sections sandwiched in between residential areas and shopping streets, to Tokyo's large and elaborate *Yoshiwara* (Yoe-she-wah-rah), which during its heyday had been known as the "Nightless City."

Many of these redlight districts, particularly those outside of the large industrialized cities, were still very traditional in their decor. The houses were Japanese style with *tatami* (tah-tah-me) reed-mat floors and sliding doors, made of rice paper, separating the rooms. In some of them the women wore only kimonos.

One of the most distinctive features of some of these traditionally styled courtesan quarters was the festooning of streets (Atami and Gifu especially come to *my* mind) with paper lanterns, called *chochin* (choe-cheen), which have long been associated with eating, drinking and night-time revelry in Japan.

Chochin, but not redlight districts, are still very much a part of the night-time scene in Japan. Large red paper lanterns, *aka chochin*, (ah-kah choe-cheen) remain the sign of *nomi ya* (no-me yah), or "drinking places," that mostly serve sake and beer, along with one or more varieties of Japanese-style food.

Drinking places marked by an *aka chochin* are patronized by blue and white collar workers, plus anyone else who appreciates a laid-back, casual atmosphere, unpretentious surroundings and low prices. Some of the most popular of the *nomi ya* are those that continue the tradition of welcoming new arrivals with shouts, and yelling out orders in a special argot associated with tradespeople in old Japan.

The red-lanterned *nomi ya* represent a part of old Japan that has survived into modern times. They offer an opportunity for foreign visitors to step back in time and enjoy a special "Japanese" ambience that is especially pleasing.

One of the most effective—and least expensive—ways to both get acquainted with and enjoy the company of lower- and middle-ranking Japanese business associates is to invite them to a *nomi ya*. This is a sign that you not only do not consider yourself above patronizing such a place, but enjoy the common pleasures that are so important to the Japanese.

Businessmen who reside in Japan, as well as those who visit from abroad, would be well advised to identify and become familiar with two or three of the more popular *nomi ya* and make a point of taking their Japanese associates there fairly often. This, again, demonstrates a type of sensitivity to Japanese culture that is very meaningful and often far more beneficial to a relationship than formal business meetings.

Foreign businessmen should keep in mind, however, that this level of socializing with their Japanese counterparts should not be utilized in the first stage of establishing a relationship, particularly when dealing with higher-up managers. That stage is better served by using more formal and prestigious restaurants and lounges.

As always, there is a fine line between what is viewed as good and acceptable in Japan, and what has the reverse effect. When in doubt, the best recourse is to ask an experienced third party for advice.

──────────────◆ 17 ◆──────────────

憧れ

Akogare

(Ah-koe-gah-ray)

"Unfulfilled Yearnings"

First-time Western visitors to Japan, especially those who are there for pleasure, are generally so impressed with the people, the service and other amenities that they are lavish in their praise—often to the point of sounding like sycophants.

Even hard-headed foreign businessmen and politicians are frequently so overwhelmed by a combination of the stylized etiquette of the Japanese and their ignorance or misunderstanding of the Japanese culture that they behave in an unbecomingly obsequious manner that includes effusive praise for the most ordinary things.

In earlier times this infantile-like flattery greatly confused the Japanese because the artifacts of their culture were so common to them that they had long ago lost any special meaning, and their meticulous etiquette was so demanding, demeaning and often inhuman that to them it was a prison that confined their spirits as well as their bodies.

Far from being impressed with their own things and behavior, the isolated and unworldly Japanese had an intense longing to see and experience non-Japanese things—a feeling expressed in the term *akogare* (ah-koe-gah-ray). As their limited contacts with the outside world grew, so did their yearnings to see and experience new, foreign things.

It was not until modern times, in fact, that all the praise smothered onto the Japanese by unwitting foreigners began to have a positive effect in the sense that they began to believe at least a part of it—and to feel superior because of it.

But this new belief did not weaken their long-repressed *akogare* for experiences that would transport them beyond their own overly specialized, inward-looking culture. After the first narrow gates in the walls surrounding Japan were cracked in the 1850s, their fascination with foreign things helped transform their society in just a few decades.

Akogare has continued to be an important element in the make-up of the Japanese down to the present time, and is a major force in entertainment, in the communications media in general, in their eating habits—in fact, in all facets of their business world.

Foreign businessmen who have succeeded in Japan owe much of their success to the still powerful *akogare* feelings of the Japanese—to what amounts to an obsession to experience the new, the strange, the foreign.

Entertainment and travel are the most conspicuous of the Japanese industries that are fueled by the *akogare* syndrome. Since the 1960s, some of the most popular TV programs have been those featuring the sights and sounds of the world outside of Japan, and they, in turn, encouraged the long repressed desires of the Japanese to travel abroad.

However, the yearnings of many internationally-minded Japanese go beyond material things, beyond ways of thinking and behaving. In their *akogare* makeup is a strong desire for understanding and acceptance by people whom they respect—and in some ways admire and envy. They do not want to be regarded as different or as outsiders.

These people are turned off by foreigners' behavior that makes them feel like exotic curiosities, not only because it puts them in a category that makes it impossible for them to be fully accepted on their own merits, it also often has a strongly patronizing flavor.

A significant percentage of the foreigners who heap fawning praise on Japanese artifacts and customs are apparently not aware that artifacts and customs of similar antiquity, artistry and quality exist in many other countries.

灰汁（あく）が強い

Aku ga Tsuyoi
(Ah-kuu gah T'sue-yoe-ee)

"With a Little Lye in Your Bones"

For generations in Japan the individualistic, aggressive type of person was a misfit, and in most ordinary situations was not tolerated. One of the few occupations open to such people was as revolutionary-minded priests whose harangues could be ignored if they were not too persistent. If they went beyond a certain point, however, they were apt to be shortened by a head.

Japanese antipathy toward aggressive people acting on their own was a natural result of their emphasis on consensus and group-behavior. Any other kind of behavior was considered immoral and a direct threat to the security and survival of the group.

One of the best-known and often-repeated mythological stories about the divine ancestors of the Japanese and the gods who created the Japanese islands has to do with a god, *Susanoo no Mikoto*, who broke ranks, behaved in a rudely aggressive and individualistic manner, and earned the wrath of the whole pantheon of gods and goddesses. He was subsequently sent into exile.

While a number of historical Japanese heroes became heroes because they took an individualistic stance and stood up for the rights of others, they almost always paid for their actions with their lives. Individualistic behavior was thus seen as admirable only under very special circumstances, and the person concerned had to be willing to sacrifice everything.

The more common morality tales in the Japanese experience are those of people sacrificing their individuality and their own interests for the sake of a group—their family, their village, their clan or their country. This, in fact, was the core of Japan's traditional culture—the basis for the national polity of the country.

In the traditional Japanese context, the more cultured and refined a person, the less aggressive, the less individualistic he would be. The passive, cooperative personality was glorified as the ideal human being. People who displayed self-assertive tendencies were often described as *aku ga tsuyoi* (ah-kuu gah t'sue-yoe-ee), or "being strong in lye." Lye, in this case, refers to the astringent sap found in some plants and is something that has a very harsh taste.

The opposite of the *aku ga tsuyoi* person is one from whom all of the lye has been extracted—an *aku no nuketa hito* (ah-kuu no nuu-kay-tah ssh-toe). In other words, a person who is kind, generous, puts the welfare of others before himself, and goes out of his way to help people without any expectations of gain.

As often the case in Japanese psychology, however, there is a fine line between having too much *aku* and too little. A person with no *aku* at all is so spiritless, so passive, that he is incapable of helping himself, much less anyone else, and is looked down upon.

Most Japanese still recoil in the face of overtly aggressive behavior, considering it arrogant, thoughtless, selfish and so on. The challenge facing

Westerners, who are often conditioned to have lots of lye in their personalities and therefore tend to clash with Japanese ideals, is to settle on a degree of self-confidence and self-reliance that comes off as having "fighting spirit," which, in contrast, the Japanese admire.

19

天下り

Ama Kudari

(Ah-mah Kuu-dah-ree)

"Descending from Heaven"

In ancient Japan the emperor was both the religious and secular leader. Eventually it came to be taught that he was a direct descendant from one of the gods who, according to myth, had created the islands. While his ministers did not claim similarly divine origins, they spoke for the "son of heaven." Since they held office in the Imperial Court, their position cloaked them in a "heavenly" aura.

This image of the government as being so far above the common people that it was equated with heaven was passed on from one generation to the next and is alive and well in Japan today. Nowadays, however, the importance of this identification with heaven primarily applies to vice ministers, the career bureaucrats who actually run the bureaus and agencies of the government, and not to the politicians appointed as ministers.

During the course of their thirty-two to thirty-five year tenure in a particular ministry, the vice ministers build up a network of commercial and government relationships. These networks include their own classmates and alumni brothers in the same and other ministries, those in outside companies, and the many other government officials and company managers they have dealt with over the years.

The vice ministers naturally have a cadre of assistants and junior officials in their departments who are beholden to them. Their number-one assistants, as they reach the appropriate age, almost always replace the vice ministers when they retire.

The key difference between the Japanese system and comparable systems in other countries is that in Japan, group orientation and group obligation result in retired vice ministers retaining considerable influence with the ministries they have retired from.

This chain of influence continues for as long as the retired vice ministers live. They are not given a gold watch and forgotten. They are not resented or cut off by their successors who one day will follow them into retirement. They are able to continue using the relationships they so carefully nurtured during their careers.

Because of the influence retired bureaucrats retain with their old ministries and agencies, they are much in demand by commercial companies that have dealings with the same government entities. The more important and powerful the bureaucrats before their retirement, the more likely they are to have been offered and to have accepted top-level executive positions with major companies well before their retirement date.

Leaving a high-level government job and going into private industry is known in Japan as *ama kudari* (ah-mah kuu-dah-ree) or "descending from heaven." The primary connotation of the term is that life for a top-level bureaucrat is both safe and soft, and leaving such a position for the hurly-burly of the commercial world is like coming down from the clouds.

Japan has laws stipulating a gap between the time a bureaucrat retires and joins a commercial firm, but generally all this means is that the individuals concerned do not "officially" join companies until the required amount of time has passed.

20

行灯

Andon

(Ahn-doan)

"Lighting Up Mistakes"

In its original meaning, an *andon* (ahn-doan) is a portable lantern made of tough paper stretched over a bamboo framework. It was used in Japan for centuries to light up the way for people who had to come and go at night. One of the parts I like most in Japan's period samurai films—the famous *chambara* (chahm-bah-rah)—are squads of firemen or policemen running at night at high speed behind *andon* carriers, who both clear and light the way for them.

Andon were also traditionally used to light up the streets of redlight districts and the precincts of shrines when the latter were staging night-time festivals. Still today, when the Emperor leaves or returns to the Imperial Palace in the evening, Tokyo policemen carrying electrified *andon* line the streets of his passage, presenting a nostalgic scene that links today's Japan with its past.

The use of the word *andon* in its present business context reveals yet another aspect of the surprising turn of events in Japan that has both mystified and frightened foreign businessmen who must compete with the Japanese. When the Japanese at Toyota came up with the startling concept of allowing assembly line workers who spotted defects to stop production by pulling on a cord (as if turning on a light), they decided to call the practice *andon*.

At first, the idea of an ordinary worker being able to stop a whole assembly line by merely pulling on a cord was heresy to most Western engineers and factory managers. The sheer common sense of the concept is fairly readily admitted now, but the system is still not fully accepted outside of Japan.

That Japanese manufacturers invented the *andon* system is surprising in that it represents a total reversal of the traditional Japanese custom of avoiding individual responsibility, of behaving as a group, and of taking action only after a clearcut consensus has been reached within the group concerned.

In fact, in other situations in present-day Japan it is still the rule rather than the exception that mistakes of all kinds are allowed to pass unmentioned and uncorrected because the individuals who spot them don't dare to call attention to them. In many instances, doing so would be a serious insult and would result in equally serious consequences.

Thus the creation of the *andon* system was a conspicuous departure from the cultural norm by Japanese managers and workers, and was another occasion in which the behavior of the Japanese caught outsiders off guard—in this case with a type of thinking and action that was as alien to Western manufacturers as it had previously been to the Japanese.

Obviously, use of the *andon* system has profound implications that go well beyond the assembly line in a factory, where a worker might stop the line because of an error made by another worker. The practice impacts on the heart of the designing, engineering and management processes because many of the problems encountered on the line are due to failures in these processes, not to errors made by individual workers.

Western managers who have since attempted to implement the *andon* system in their own plants have learned, often to their chagrin, that it entails much more than a mechanical, cord-pulling stop on their production track. They have learned that it is a part of a whole philosophy of management that begins with the product concept itself, and intimately involves the relationship between management and labor.

When all things are said, however, the *andon* system is nothing more than common sense—as simple as turning on a light so you can see what you are doing and where you are going.

21

青田買い／青田刈り

Aota Gai / Aota Gari

(Ah-oh-tah Guy / Ah-oh-tah Gah-ree)

"Plucking the School Virgins"

Married couples wanting to adopt children often refuse to consider older kids, particularly if they have lived with other families. Their rationale is that such children would have developed attitudes and habits that might very likely be incompatible with their own standards and ways.

This same rationale was traditionally a primary factor in the hiring policies of larger Japanese companies. They simply would not consider employing anyone who had worked for another company, and some companies would not hire anyone who had taken time off after graduating from school to travel or engage in any other kind of personal activity.

During the 1950s and 60s, this prejudicial hiring policy extended to graduates of Japanese universities who went to the U.S. or elsewhere for postgraduate studies abroad. The idea of hiring people who had been exposed to foreign influences was especially alien to many Japanese companies.

The standard procedure for larger Japanese firms was to hire new employees only once a year, directly from high schools or universities, during their senior years. This system came to be known as *aota gai* (ah-oh-tah guy), which was an old term that referred to wholesalers or brokers buying rice on the stalk while it was still green.

Another version of *aota gai* was *aota gari* (ah-oh-tah gah-ree), which meant harvesting the rice crop while it was still green. In both cases, the connotation was that while the new recruits were unspoiled because they were "green," companies were also taking a big gamble that the recruits would turn out all right once they matured.

The *aota gai* system of hiring is still commonplace in Japan, but it is no longer the only system used. By the mid-1970s the increasingly technical orientation of Japanese industry, growing competition for highly skilled employees, and the movement of more and more Japanese operations abroad forced companies to change their personnel practices and begin hiring outside of domestic schools; even to begin cautiously to hire foreigners.

Most Japanese companies, no matter how international their image at home or abroad, are still not comfortable with non-virgin Japanese employees. Generally speaking, this now has less to do with company policy than with objections and resistance from "pure" company employees who resent outsiders coming in and taking up managerial or executive slots the old-timers feel belong to them.

Given the factional nature of the typical Japanese character, newcomers entering a larger, long-established firm find it difficult or impossible to win full acceptance by company groups. Many say that even after twenty or more years they still feel like interlopers.

The situation regarding foreign employees of Japanese companies, at home or abroad, is even more sensitive. Even the most enlightened and international Japanese company seems unable to fully accept or treat foreign employees as they do their Japanese employees. The few exceptions, and these are certainly outside the pale of regular employees, are top-ranked foreign executives, usually CEOs, who are enticed to take over the foreign operations of Japanese companies for high salaries and extraordinary perks.

Immediate communications problems are often at the top of the list of the complaints foreign employees voice about Japanese companies: the Japanese executives assigned abroad are often not fluent in the language of the host country and few foreign employees speak any Japanese at all. A second factor is that Japanese managers do not ordinarily give ongoing explicit directions to their staffs. They expect them to learn what they are supposed to do and how to do it by observing, by interacting with their group, by osmosis—which often is impossible in a foreign setting.

This situation tends to leave foreign employees frustrated and feeling like they are being left out, and used. This suggests that Japanese companies with operations abroad may have to go back to the *aota gai* system to staff their foreign plants with young people right out of school, and train

them in the Japanese way from the beginning—if they choose to continue
their traditional style of management.

足元を見る
Ashimoto wo Miru
(Ah-she-moe-toe oh Mee-ruu)

"Looking for a Weak Spot"

Prior to the massive introduction of Western technology into Japan in
the 1870s and 80s, virtually all land travel in the country was by foot. Pas-
senger transportation was limited to man-carried palanquins and horseback, and these modes were strictly reserved for members of the imperial
court, the shogun and clan lords' courts, other ranking members of the
samurai class and official messengers.

As early as the 8th century A.D., Japan had a network of roads that
fanned out from the Imperial capital of Kyoto to all the provinces, cities,
towns and villages in the country. The roads were maintained by the government to facilitate the transportation of rice and other produce, and
make it easier for tax collectors and other government officials to travel
about in the performance of their duties.

The roads that connected the capital with the main provincial regions
of the country were known as *do* (doe), or "circuit" roads, and the term
eventually became synonymous with highway. After Kamakura became the
military capital of Japan in 1192, the *To Kai Do* (Toe Kie Doe), or "Eastern
Seaboard Road," between Kyoto and Kamakura became the most used and
most famous highway in the nation.

Japan's last shogunate (the Tokugawa, 1603–1868) had milestones
placed every *ri* (about 2.3 miles) along the roads. The Tokugawa Shogun
also had post stations, where horses and crews were maintained, established along all of the major highways. There were 53 such stations on the
To Kai Do, which then connected the shogunate headquarters in Edo
(Tokyo) with Kyoto.

As the peaceful decades of the Tokugawa era passed, the circuit roads became busy thoroughfares, with constant streams of messengers, clan lords and their entourages, gamblers, peddlers, priests, masterless samurai, shogunate officials, spies and ordinary people on pilgrimages to distant temples and shrines, passing to and fro.

Those going to distant destinations were on the road for several weeks at a time, walking forty to fifty miles a day. The standard footwear for trips of more than a few hundred yards were open thong-type sandals made of straw. The sandals protected only the bottom of the feet, and were good for only a few days or weeks of walking at most. Higher class and more affluent people normally wore finely woven form-fitting socks for further protection, and changed their sandals often.

Thus it was possible to determine a great deal about the social and financial position of a person by *ashimoto wo miru,* or "looking at their feet."

But there was an even more important reason for looking at and being able to "read" the feet of a person during Japan's long shogunate period (1192-1868). During this era Japanese society was dominated by the famed samurai warrior class, whose primary weapon was the sword.

Samurai developed swordfighting into an art that made them among the most dangerous and feared foes ever seen. The more skillful of the swordsmen were able to "read" their opponents' feet—based on how they stood and moved—making it possible for them to judge their strengths and weaknesses, to anticipate their moves and take advantage of any weak points they had.

Ashimoto wo miru is still a commonly heard term in present-day Japan, but it is now associated with looking for weaknesses in businesses and businessmen, and taking advantage of them. There is a general sense that it is an unfair tactic, but that feeling does not prevent it from being a routine business ploy.

————————————— 23 —————————————

当り前の品質

Atarimae no Hinshitsu

(Ah-tah-ree-my no Heen-sheet-sue)

"Quality Taken for Granted"

By the mid-1960s the Japanese had pretty much overcome the reputation they had of being capable only of copying foreign products and producing low quality goods—a reputation that had, in fact, primarily resulted from the policies and practices of foreign importers buying from Japan, rather than from the inclinations and experience of the Japanese.

For close to a thousand years prior to the forced opening of Japan to the West in the 1860s and 70s, Japan's work force consisted of highly skilled craftsmen so meticulously and thoroughly trained in the master-apprentice system that masters were commonplace in all the crafts and arts making up industry.

As the generations passed during this long historical period, the standards of quality that were acceptable in the various arts and crafts became higher and higher. Quality was not confined to the visible portions of a product, no matter how common it was. Quality extended to the back, the bottom and the insides of a product as well.

When Japan was suddenly pressured into opening its borders and ports to foreign traders in the mid-1800s, it wasn't long before the traders were taking advantage of the manual skills and extraordinary abilities of the Japanese to learn and duplicate technical processes brought in from the West.

These old-line traders were quickly followed by importer-buyers who were not as interested in quality as they were in low prices and high profit margins. The training and talents of the Japanese, nurtured by their own cottage industry system for generations, were quickly debased to satisfy foreign demands for cheaply made exports. Within 20 years, Japan was mass-producing toys, textiles and a wide range of miscellaneous dime-and-variety store merchandise for less critical foreign markets.

Extraordinary circumstances following World War II gave the Japanese an opportunity to break the hold that foreign importers had on their export industry and take full advantage of their cultural traditions for turning the manufacturing process (of whatever product) into an art.

As early as 1960, European engineers took apart a Suzuki motorcycle to find out why it was winning so many international races. Their report: it was as finely made as a Swiss watch. Soon thereafter, Japanese manufacturers in many fields surpassed the standards of Swiss watchmakers.

By the 1970s, the Japanese were the standard setters for the world in most manufactured products—overcoming the 200-year lead of the Western world in two swift decades. What had become routine for them was beyond the capabilities of the majority of foreign companies.

By 1990, the Japanese had begun to refer to their everyday quality standards as *atarimae no hinshitsu* (ah-tah-ree-my no heen-sheet-sue), or "quality that is taken for granted."

Again in keeping with their cultural tradition of never being satisfied with anything below absolute perfection, the more advanced segments of Japanese industry began aiming for a still higher level of quality that would transcend the physical attributes of a product. The consumer electronics industry has probably been the most successful in incorporating this quality into its products, from CD ROM disc players to fax machines. But other industries are not far behind.

Businessmen of the world should take notice.

当 て 馬

Ate-Uma
(Ah-tay-Uu-mah)

"Turning On a Prospect"

During Japan's long feudal shogunate period (1192–1868), ordinary people were not allowed to use horses as draft animals or for transportation. This right was reserved for government officials and the military. Horses therefore played a limited but particularly key role in the lives of the Japanese, so much so that there are numerous references to horses in the culture.

One of the more curious and interesting of these uses had to do with the hundreds of redlight districts that flourished in Japan until the 1950s when they were finally outlawed. When a customer could not pay his bill, a money collector was assigned to follow him home to ensure payment. This bill collector was popularly known as a *tsuke uma* (skay uu-mah). *Uma* means horse. *Tsuke* means an account or bill. The same word with a different origin also means to shadow or follow, as well as attach.

Among the more colorful terms used by horse breeders during this era was *ate-uma* (ah-tay-uu-mah), which meant a stallion that was brought near a mare to get her excited and make her receptive to the stud she was to breed with.

Somehow, someone with a great sense of humor began using the term *ate-uma* to refer to ploys used in business negotiations to find out more about the real intentions of the other side. In this instance, the *ate-uma* could be one or more other companies invited to participate in the negotiations, a decoy plan drafted to draw the other party out, an outsider employed to approach the company surreptitiously to ferret out inside information, or any other device that would give the principal player an advantage.

While *ate-uma* is not heard that often in business conversations, the practice it describes is very common indeed. In fact, foreign businessmen initiating dealings with Japanese should keep in mind that what they regard as ethical behavior is often quite different from what is acceptable to and expected by Japanese. The use of an *ate-uma* certainly comes under acceptable behavior.

It should also be kept in mind that Japanese businessmen are masters at manipulating people by using a subtle but powerful combination of etiquette, hospitality, apparent naiveté and patient persistence. Another aspect of this factor, which often gives Japanese an additional advantage, is that their personalities are generally such that Westerners will typically go out of their way to be accommodating and to help them achieve their goals without objectively analyzing the consequences.

The time-consuming nature of the Japanese process of decision making by consensus, plus their culturally-induced ability to take the long-range view and be patient, dovetails very well with the *ate-uma* concept, which takes time to develop and carry out.

One factor that Westerners might use more effectively as an *ate-uma* is the long-term cultural benefit that Japan will gain from a proposed business relationship, emphasizing Japan's strong desire and often-stated need to further internationalize both its society and economy.

Coming up with a specific idea for some kind of cultural program that can be made a part of the business proposal can play a significant role in convincing the Japanese side that the relationship is desirable.

25

後 味

Ato Aji

(Ah-toe Ah-jee)

"Leaving an Aftertaste"

During most of Japan's history the people lived in isolation from the rest of the world. In the earliest centuries, intercourse with Korea, China and other areas of the nearby Asian continent occurred infrequently and even then did not impact directly on most of the people. Generally, following a period of cultural borrowing and trade with the mainland, there would be gaps lasting for several hundred years.

Despite the primitive level of Japan's native culture when the first wholesale copying from Korea and China began, the Japanese had a strong native character that resulted in their digesting the arts, crafts and philosophies imported from the mainland, then homogenizing them into very distinctive adaptations of the originals.

Because of the strength of their own culture and the view they had of themselves as unique, the Japanese at a very early time had become extraordinarily sensitive to anything non-Japanese, especially the racial and ethnic characteristics of people, and down through the centuries have automatically distinguished between foreign and native things.

This trait is now far less conspicuous than it was as late as the 1960s, but it remains a critical factor in the way the Japanese think and behave in regard to anything or anybody foreign. The term *gaijin kusai* (guy-jeen kuu-sie) or "smelling like a foreigner," is no longer common, but most Japanese continue to automatically divide both people and things into foreign and Japanese classifications.

Foreign things have a different "taste" that Japanese may or may not find palatable. Among those things that are acceptable are apparel, accessories, foods and other consumer tangibles, as well as movies, athletic studios, and music. Those that will leave an undesirable *ato aji* (ah-toe ah-jee) or "aftertaste" include people from any other race or ethnic group, and their unstructured, unpredictable behavior.

This bears a remarkable resemblance to the earliest experiences Westerners had with the Japanese, beginning in the early 1540s when Europeans first discovered Japan, and then again in the latter part of the 1800s when the country was finally opened to the West.

As it turned out, the very first Westerners to visit Japan between 1543 and 1638 (when they were expelled), as well as those who flocked into the country following the downfall of the Tokugawa shogunate in 1867, found the Japanese fascinating, but too different and too difficult to be quickly and easily accepted as fellow kindred spirits.

In contrast to this personal reaction to the Japanese, foreigners fell in love with the products of the country—the ceramics, the lacquerware, the pottery, the paintings, the handmade paper, the exotic silks. Foreigners could relate to the arts and crafts of the country but not to the people who made them.

Now the situation has come full circle. The Japanese love many of the products of the West, but cannot comfortably relate to the people. The difference this time is that the volume of Japanese intercourse with the rest of the world is massive and impacts on the whole population. The country is no longer in a position to close its borders, leaving the Japanese with no choice but to develop a tolerance and appreciation for other people who "taste" different.

バ リ バ リ

Baribari
(Bah-ree-bah-ree)

"Working Like Bees"

Japanese have had a penchant for onomatopoeia since ancient times, and today the dozens of commonly used words in the Japanese language that are based on referent sounds or actions give the language a special flavor.

One of my favorites is *garagara* (gah-rah-gah-rah), which is a rattling or clattering sound, and among other things is used in the term for rattle snake: *garagara hebi* (gah-rah-gah-ragh hay-bee). Another is *girigiri* (ghee-ree-ghee-ree), which means to grind in the sense of grinding something down to where there is very little left, including a price or time.

Baribari (bah-ree-bah-ree) refers to a scratching or crunching sound that includes such things as wadding up a newspaper, a pack of house rats gnawing away inside the walls, and other low-keyed but constant sounds that reflect perpetual movement or action.

Nowadays the most common use of *baribari* is in reference to the manner in which the Japanese work—or are expected to work. The idea being that the typical employer expects them to work like automatons, to the point that their actions generate a kind of scratching sound that is always in the background. This expectation includes the concept that the workers will never stop or give up because something is difficult.

The image invoked by *baribari* is decidedly negative. It is used in relation to feelings of exhaustion and frustration, as well as anger at the company concerned and at the business philosophy that condones and often demands that employees sacrifice themselves on the altar of success.

Sometime around the mid-1980s, when Japan's extraordinary economic success could no longer be denied, health authorities, sociologists and others began to speak out about some of the more inhuman and deleterious effects of the long hours and almost maniacal work-pace that prevailed in many of Japan's manufacturing industries.

These commentators did not place blame for the *baribari* syndrome on management alone. They recognized that a significant part of it was self-induced by the workers and was a symptom of traditional Japanese psychology, which demanded unstinted efforts to perform at higher and higher levels, and to continuously increase production.

In past years a number of other terms had been used to describe the attitude and behavior of typical Japanese employees. One of the more telling of these terms was *moretsu shain* (moe-ray-t'sue shah-een), which was generally translated as "gung ho employees."

The real implications of *moretsu* employees are not fully obvious until you consider that the true meaning of the word is "fury" or "violence." It meant that employees worked at a furious, even violent pace, with no thought of anything else.

Practically none of Japan's post-1960 generations demonstrate such passion for their work, and as they see more and more of the older generation burning out, resentment against the system is growing.

Companies that are known for pursuing or encouraging the *baribari* approach to work are being shunned by a growing number of high school and college graduates. They take it for granted that they have a right to a private life, and that leisure and pleasure are a legitimate part of life.

閥

Batsu

(Baht-sue)

"Keeping the Team Together"

One of the primary characteristics of Japanese behavior since ancient times has been a compelling propensity to form or join exclusive factions or groups, thereafter subordinating most or all of their individual interests to the survival and success of the group.

Anthropologists say this compulsion to belong to groups grew out of the need for cooperation in cultivating rice in small, adjoining irrigated fields. There were no doubt other factors as well, including a system in which each village had to be more or less self-sufficient, a clan system of local government, and the Confucian concept that father-dominated families should be the basic units of society.

But most important of all, in my view, was the fact that throughout Japan's history the rights of individual Japanese were generally not recognized and not protected by either custom or law. Generally speaking, individuals had obligations, but no rights. The principle of rights did not begin to come into play until one was dealing with groups of people, and then only in a very limited sense.

Prior to the ascendancy of militaristic clan leaders and the shogunate system of government in 1192, Japan's emperors had rights granted to them by mythical gods of the past, but even these rights were usurped by the new breed of warrior clans. From that point on until the end of the feudal era in 1868, might was right in Japan.

Given these combined circumstances, belonging to a group was the only practical choice people had, not only socially but economically as well. Anyone who refused to belong to a group or broke with a group, whether it was a family, a farming village, a craft guild or whatever, was subject to being ostracized.

Thus the Japanese became conditioned to group-orientation and group-behavior, eventually getting to the point that they were unable to function effectively as individuals.

Following the end of World War II in 1945, the last of Japan's feudalistic laws were abolished and for the first time in the history of the country, the people were given the opportunity, and the legal protection, to exercise individual rights.

Centuries of cultural conditioning cannot be so quickly or easily exorcised, however, and group-orientation and behavior remain characteristic traits of most formalized activities in Japan, particularly in politics and professional organizations.

Politicians in Japan belong to *ha batsu* (hah baht-sue) or "political factions." Graduates of the same school belong to *gaku batsu* (gah-kuu baht-sue). People who come from the same villages, towns or prefectures may belong to *chiho batsu* (chee-hoe baht-sue). Upper-class families that are related by marriage belong to *kei batsu* (kay-ee baht-sue).

In political affairs in Japan, virtually all dealings must involve one or more of the *ha batsu*. Executive positions in many Japanese companies are dominated by school factions (graduates of the same universities) which naturally favor their own alumnae in business matters.

Strong, able men in present-day Japan, in whatever organization, invariably attract followers who form specific groups of supporters. In exchange for the loyalty and support of these groups, the strong men protect and nurture their factions, making sure that they benefit from the relationships.

Foreign businessmen dealing with Japanese companies, including smaller ones, would be well-advised to diplomatically identify factions within the companies and make a point of working with them, or at least trying to make sure they do not become enemies.

28

勉強会

Benkyo Kai

(Bane-k'yoe Kie)

"He's in a Meeting Now"

Japan's traditional etiquette, which continues to play a vital role in business as well as private life, is so precise and demanding that it results in a type of stylized, formalized behavior that limits the easy and rapid exchange of personal feelings, frank opinions and even the truth if there is any chance it might be controversial.

Because of the ongoing role of this type of etiquette, which originally was fashioned to support the hierarchical structure of personal relations in Japan and to guarantee harmony at all costs, it is difficult and uncommon for a group of Japanese to come together during a normal work period, be totally candid with each other, and make rapid decisions.

The process of decision-making within a company or by a company is further complicated by the fact that a variety of individuals representing different groups, different functions, and generally different perspectives, must reach a consensus before any progress can be made.

These circumstances led to the development of a type of meeting known as *benkyo kai* (bane-k'yoe kie), which literally means "study meeting," and offers a forum for all of the people involved to learn about the proposition at hand, and gradually determine the attitudes and positions of everyone else in the group.

At the onset of a *benkyo kai*, whoever called the meeting or has been placed in charge of it makes an opening statement, briefly describing the topic to be discussed, and explaining how and why it came to be a matter for discussion. Whether the topic originated in-house or is a proposition brought to the company from the outside, the meeting is then turned over to the primary spokesperson for a detailed presentation.

Following the formal presentation, the *benkyo kai* then lives up to its name. Participants ask questions and more questions, almost always using up the time allotted for the meeting, then announce that more time is needed for studying the project and set a date for a second meeting some days or weeks later.

In the meantime, if the proposal originated within the company its chief advocate and any supporters will spend as much time as possible lobbying for the idea among the several section and department managers whose signatures or name seals are necessary for its approval. And, of course, the more successful this lobbying the better the chance that the proposal will remain alive and receive serious consideration.

If the proposal has come from the outside, and there is no one championing it inside the company, its chances of making it through the process are considerably reduced.

Even when the initial response to a proposal has been positive, there are generally at least three formal *benkyo kai* before participants feel they know enough about the topic to begin forming some kind of consensus on what to do about it.

Under the best circumstances, the participants in *benkyo kai* are often unable to achieve at the formal meetings the level of understanding, rapport and commitment that is necessary for them to proceed, and they end up holding one or more informal get-togethers after working hours, in restaurants, bars and geisha inns where drinking is an integral part of the process and they can "forget etiquette" and have frank exchanges. (See *Niji Kai.*)

Where foreign companies are concerned, the *benkyo kai* process often becomes an ordeal that they make much worse. If it is their first contact with a Japanese company it generally takes several meetings for them to establish the personal rapport, trust and confidence that is necessary before the Japanese company will seriously consider doing business with them.

More often than not, the foreign participants in a *benkyo kai* have not done their homework and are repeatedly caught short with questions they cannot answer, including information about their own company and the very proposal they are making. Their preparations also frequently lack the detail and the quality that is expected in Japan.

Foreign companies proposing to do business in Japan for the first time can save themselves a lot of time, frustration and money by engaging the services of consultants who can help them prepare for and maneuver their way through *benkyo kai*.

29

勉 強　　サ ー ビ ス

Benkyo / Sabisu

(Bane-k'yo / Sah-bee-sue)

"Giving Special Service"

Japanese are noted for their skill as merchants, and not surprisingly, since they have been honing their expertise for hundreds of years. The history of the country is rich with traditions of vendors hawking their merchandise at shrine and temple festivals, on village streets, and at stop-overs on the national network of pedestrian roads that came into being more than a thousand years ago.

Traveling salesmen were also a part of the colorful traditions of Japan. During the heyday of the Tokugawa shogunate (1603–1868), salesmen carrying their products in cloth-wrapped bundles slung on shoulder sticks were a common sight on the great walking-roads of the day.

Bargaining over price developed very early in the history of merchandising in Japan, particularly because most of the street vendors and salesmen were working for themselves and could change their prices at will in order to clinch a sale.

When a customer balked at a price, one feature of this bargaining process was for the vendor to offer to *benkyo* (bane-k'yoe) or "study" his profit needs a little more as a method of coming up with a discount. Eventually, when used in this context, *benkyo* came to mean a discount. When a customer said, "*Benkyo shite kudasai*" (Bane-k'yoe ssh-tay kuu-dah-sie), it clearly meant, "Please give me a discount."

Benkyo is still used in this sense today in similar situations (when dealing with street and fair vendors and in some independent retail shops), but not in department stores or retail chain stores, where prices are set by central offices.

Another very common and useful term in Japan that is a bit confusing to foreigners when they first hear it is *sabisu* (sah-bee-sue), from the English word "service" (which refers to good or bad service). In the Japanese context, *sabisu* means either a discount or something that is free.

Things that are advertised as *sabisu* are free. This may be a cup of coffee with a breakfast order, a knickknack given away when you purchase some other item, and so on. Ordinary restaurants in particular often include *sabisu* items as a part of their breakfast and lunch menus. Department stores also often have *sabisu* freebies as part of their promotions.

When a vendor says, "*Sabisu shimasu*" (Sah-bee-sue she-mahss), he means that he will give you a discount—not that he is offering the item free of charge. If you say, "*Sabisu shite kudasai*" (Sah-bee-sue ssh-tay kuu-dah-sie), it means, "Please give me a discount."

Using the word "service" in its English context can also be confusing to Japanese if they are not familiar enough with English to know its meaning. This is especially true if you are speaking in Japanese, and pronounce the word in its Japanized form of *sabisu*. The point to keep in mind is that the meaning changes along with the pronunciation when the word is rendered in Japanese.

Benkyo is also commonly used in business conversations when a party agrees to "study" a situation. In this usage, however, as in any language, an offer to *benkyo* a proposition may also be a polite put-off. If such a promise is in doubt, the only recourse is to follow up later—and very often the most effective follow-up is via a third party to whom the individual or company concerned will be more forthright in their response.

忘 年 会

Bo Nen Kai
(Boe Nane Kie)

"Forget-the-Year Parties"

The tradition that people should start each new year with a clean slate is fairly common around the world, but it has a special significance in Japan where, in keeping with Japanese character, it is more structured and formalized than in most countries.

It is possible that the tradition began in Japan, as it probably did elsewhere, because it provided relief to people who had survived yet another year and who could at least hope for a better year the next time around. But once basic survival in Japan was no longer a serious concern, the tradition took on new dimensions.

One of the more interesting aspects of the cleaning-the-slate custom in Japan is the marking of the end of a year with special parties that are known as *bo nen kai* (boe nane kie) or "forget-the-year parties," which are staged from about the middle of December until near the end of the month.

Bo nen kai parties generally involve co-workers, and in smaller companies are often sponsored by the employees themselves, with each individual chipping in to help pay the cost. In larger companies, each section sponsors its own party, and the section itself may make a financial contribution to help pay the cost of the party, especially if it is held at a restaurant.

One of the aims of forget-the-year parties is to provide an opportunity for employees to wipe the slate clean of all the bad feelings that developed among them during the year. It is a kind of kiss-and-make-up party where everyone eats and drinks to the point of being tipsy and does their best to rid themselves of all the ill-will that has accumulated.

In addition to serving as a means of improving employee relations, *bo nen kai* are also used to help employees forget the failures and frustrations they encountered during the year, and to relieve the effects of stress engendered by the very competitive nature of the Japanese system.

Most *bo nen kai* are held at restaurants that have large banquet rooms for groups. In smaller firms and shops, the parties may instead be held on the premises after working hours have ended. Parties held at restaurants generally last longer than those held on company premises, and tend to be noisier and a lot more fun.

Some time after the drinking begins, managers usually say a few words of praise and encouragement, but the formal aspects of the parties are kept to a minimum and the emphasis is on purging pent-up emotions.

Participants in the parties are usually aggressive in pouring drinks for each other, both to encourage everyone to drink freely and as a symbol to those they do not particularly care for, or had some kind of run-in with, that all is forgiven.

Foreigners involved with Japanese companies as customers or suppliers are frequently invited to attend *bo nen kai.* When this occurs it is important for them to keep in mind that they are under a strong obligation to drink enthusiastically and make merry. Not drinking and not participating in the merry-making during this kind of gathering (unless you have a medical or physical excuse) is a cultural no-no.

The final stages of many forget-the-year parties held at restaurants are marked by singing, usually in solo performances but sometimes in duos as well. Performers belt out their favorite tunes with all the gusto they can muster, doing their best to imitate professional singers.

Foreign participants who want to really raise their stock with the group will do their best to make like Frank Sinatra or some other well-known entertainer. The better you can actually sing the higher your stock will go, but the effort is the most important thing. And, of course, foreigners who hold *bo nen kai* should invite their Japanese friends and associates.

When the party begins to break up, participants bow to each other and intone a traditional year-end saying, *Rainen mo yoroshiku onegai itashimasu* (Rye-nane moe yoe-roe-she-kuu oh-nay-guy ee-tah-she-mahss) or "Please favor me/cooperate with me again next year."

──────────────── 31 ────────────────

部 長

Bu Cho
(Buu Choe)

"He Is Best Who Does the Least"

Japan's company culture can probably be best described and understood by comparing it to the typical military culture, with its precise levels of enlistees and officers, its clearly established ranks, and its protocol.

In general terms, individuals with no more than high school educations make up the blue-collar and low-level white collar class of workers—with little or no chance of going beyond the "enlistee" level. University graduates automatically become "officer candidates" who are slated for managerial positions as their seniority and experience build up.

For the first eight or ten years, university graduates remain in the "officer candidate" category without specific rank. They are then promoted to *kakari cho* (kah-kah-ree choe), which means "someone in charge" and is usually translated as "chief clerk."

The next promotion, about ten years later, is either to *ka cho dairi* (ka choe die-ree), "deputy section chief," or to full *ka cho* or "section chief," depending on the company. The biggest jump in middle management is the next step, from *ka cho* to *bu cho* (buu choe) or "general manager of a department." In some companies there is an interim rank of *bu cho dairi* or "deputy general manager of a department."

While the length of time spent in each of these ranks varies a bit with the company, in the typical firm promotion to the rank of *bu cho* comes when the chosen manager is between the ages of 48 and 50.

The rank of *bu cho* in a larger Japanese company is similar to the rank of full colonel in the U.S. Army or Marine Corps, or that of vice president in a major company as far as prestige and benefits are concerned. The similarity, however, generally stops there: in terms of authority and activity there is virtually no comparison.

A *bu cho* does not manage his department in the Western sense of the term. He does not spend his time developing strategy or tactics, giving orders or overseeing the activities within his department. Plans and tactics are developed by the *ka cho* and their staff. Day-to-day instruction and direction required by the staff are also provided by *kakari cho* and *ka cho*.

It often seems to the outsider that the typical *bu cho* has no duties at all, except to attend meetings. *Bu cho* approve or disapprove of plans prepared by the section chiefs in their departments; they act as advisers to their *ka cho* and as mentors to those who one day will replace them as department heads.

Bu cho are responsible for the morale of the people in their departments. This includes interacting with them on a private social level (such as helping to arrange marriages, attending weddings and funerals) and taking part in social functions sponsored by their departments.

Bu cho also coordinate the activities of their departments with other departments in the company, and represent their companies in relations with other firms and organizations, including government ministries and agencies.

Foreign businessmen attempting to deal with Japanese companies should be aware that they cannot limit their contacts to the *bu cho* level, although having the goodwill and support of department managers is essential. In early as well as ongoing relations with Japanese companies, the keys to success are almost always in the hands of the *ka cho*.

Traditionally, accepted conventional wisdom in Japan stated that the less the *bu cho* did—the less they interfered in the activities of their subordinates—the more smoothly their departments would run. The rationale for this attitude was that the employees knew what they were supposed to do and how to do it. Therefore it was not only unnecessary for *bu cho* to "manage" their departments; any attempt to do so was regarded as arrogant and insulting.

Increasing use of complicated technology and the need for highly skilled and experienced individuals in many Japanese companies today has strengthened the position of *bu cho* in technically-oriented firms, but the feeling that *bu cho* should set an example, mediate when necessary and act as a godfather at all times is still very strong.

32

文 化

Bunka

(Boon-kah)

"Culture as a Two-Edged Sword"

There are probably no people on earth who are prouder of their culture than the Japanese. At the same time, a growing number of Japanese are preaching that in order to survive as a people and a nation, the country must deliberately give up much of its culture because it is a serious obstacle to their dealing effectively with the rest of the world.

The ambivalent attitude the Japanese have toward their famed *bunka* (boon-kah) or "culture" is a relatively new thing. It results from the fact that they must now react daily to the influence of other cultures that are fundamentally different from theirs, and also to the negative reaction of other people to facets of their culture that in the past they prized the most.

Japanese culture was nurtured in seclusion over a period of many thousands of years. There were no invasions that brought in other cultures by force. Until the mid-1850s the Japanese chose what they wanted to import from abroad. When the country took its first short steps out of the past in 1853, it was a tribal society politically, and a primitive society technically, but it was one of the most socially and aesthetically sophisticated nations in existence.

Philosophically, the Japanese were steeped in Buddhism, Confucianism and Shintoism. Their lifestyle was based on a minutely-structured social system in which a highly refined etiquette had the status of morality. The crafts that provided their homes, furnishings, appliances and decorations had been raised to the level of fine arts. Their understanding and appreciation of beauty, and of how to make it an integral part of their lives, was unsurpassed.

Over the centuries the nature of their culture, from their language and cuisine to their architecture and arts, had become so powerful and pervasive that it set them apart from all other people—a circumstance that was to eventually become both a bane and a blessing.

In the late 1950s, after I had been absorbed in the study of Japan for more than ten years, it occurred to me that in many respects the United States was just then approaching the social sophistication that Japan had reached during the latter part of its Heian period some 800 years earlier.

On the one hand, in limited areas, their humanistic values, combined with a basic concern for beauty in all of its aspects, had raised the emotional and spiritual level of life in Japan to a point that it often became intoxicating to newcomers. Yet, there was also a dark side to Japanese culture that often resulted in irrational behavior and sometimes unspeakable cruelty.

As long as the Japanese were at peace, living behind the walls of their own distinctive culture and not faced with relating to other ways of thinking and behaving, their system worked. But the moment a foreign element was introduced, the system became unstable and in extreme instances broke down completely.

Today's Japanese are thus faced with a dilemma. Their culture, with its emphasis on national cohesiveness, group behavior, dedication to meticulous training in industrial skills and a built-in compulsion to succeed and be bigger and better than anyone else, has played a vital role in their emergence as an economic superpower.

But many of the cultural factors that made the Japanese what they are, combined with their lack of experience in communicating, working and empathizing with non-Japanese, are now serious weaknesses. As more and more Japanese realize, in order to maintain good relations with the rest of the world they must put more emphasis on reforming the negative aspects of their culture.

無礼講

Burei Ko

(Buu-ray-ee Koe)

"When Etiquette Is Abandoned"

Japan's news media often report that well over half of all Japanese, from kindergarten age on, are so seriously afflicted by stress that it is a problem of epidemic proportions. Part of this affliction results from the intense pressure on people to work harder and produce more than other people. Stress also results from crowded living conditions, and from worry about financial security during old age.

But the core of the stress syndrome in Japan is found in the attitudes and patterns of behavior the Japanese have inherited from their past. In other words, much of the stress experienced by the Japanese derives from conforming to the demands of their traditional social system—part of which is a tendency to be compulsive about things.

Traditional etiquette in Japan was all inclusive. It covered every aspect of attitude and behavior, leaving virtually nothing to individual choice or chance. Conditioning in the established etiquette, which included the manner of speaking and the vocabulary used, was precise and lifelong.

Conforming to this sternly stylized way of behavior was so demanding that it consumed much of the energy and spirit of the people. Proper behavior, as dictated by the situation, was often more important than substance. Improper behavior was a serious crime against society and the state.

It was practically impossible for people to express themselves clearly and unequivocably about any matter without breaking half a dozen or more of the rules of etiquette.

In order to live within this steel-like web of prescribed behavior, the Japanese had to develop safety valves that would allow them to relieve some of the stress caused by the system, and to refurbish their spirits. One of the ways this was done was to formalize occasions when they could *burei ko* (buu-ray-ee koe), or "abandon etiquette."

Burei ko was not a casual thing that one could announce suddenly when he or she became overcome by the burden of etiquette. It had its own rules and its time and place. Originally, *burei ko* was used by people who wanted or badly needed to have an honest, intimate conversation with someone else. On these occasions a meeting "without etiquette" would be arranged.

As Japan's traditional etiquette and the sanctions enforcing it weakened following the introduction of democracy into the country in 1945/6, the variety of *burei ko* situations was gradually expanded to include such things as company parties and after-hours drinking sessions. Many of the meetings that Japan's political figures and top businessmen hold at geisha inns are *burei ko* affairs.

But even at recognized *burei ko* meetings it is difficult for lower ranking members to completely ignore the seniority and rank of their superiors. While the lower-ranked people will get drunk, push and pull on their seniors, and sometimes complain loudly about the burdens of their work or other things, they nevertheless are careful about keeping their behavior within the prescribed limits.

Foreigners who want to have a heart-to-heart talk with Japanese, regardless of who may be senior, may tilt the odds in their favor by saying something like *"Burei ko de hanashimasho!"* (Buu-ray-ee koe day hah-nah-she-mah-show)—"Let's talk without etiquette."

Whether or not the Japanese will lower their shields and respond candidly and completely, however, will be determined by the overall circumstances. In any event, such talks should be private and at neutral locations.

34

ちょうちん記事

Chochin Kiji
(Choe-cheen Kee-jee)

"Putting a Little Light on the Subject"

When I first began working in the magazine and newspaper publishing field in Tokyo in the early 1950s, I discovered that the editorial department was expected to cooperate in bringing in advertising revenue. In some publications, the editorial departments were little more than adjuncts to the advertising side.

Editorial matter was regularly slanted to build up obligation among potential advertisers. If an advertising prospect did not come through with an ad after a suitable period of courtship, some publishers would reverse their tactics and threaten to publish unfavorable material about the companies.

More likely than not, this pressure tactic worked since any kind of blemish on a company's reputation, even a blatantly manufactured one, could be very serious. The typical reaction in the super-sensitive Japanese marketplace was that a properly managed company would not get itself into such a position.

Money paid out to such unscrupulous publishers did not come out of budgets set aside for advertising. The monies were disbursed from a special fund maintained to pay "social debts"—more or less like protection money paid to racketeers. The same funds were also regularly used to entertain guests, and as a source for usually under-the-table donations to political and other groups.

My introduction to this system came one day when the advertising manager of the magazine I worked for came up to me and asked if I was familiar with *chochin kiji* (choe-cheen kee-jee). I knew that a *chochin* was a lantern made out of heavy paper and bamboo, and that a *kiji* was either a news article or a pheasant, depending on the usage, but I didn't know what he was talking about.

In short order the ad manager said he wanted me to accompany him to potential advertising accounts to interview the presidents or other ranking executives and write *chochin kiji* about their companies. The *chochin kiji*, he explained, would make them look good and feel good, and they would then advertise with us.

The combination of *chochin* and *kiji* was a characteristic Japanese device to say something that is delicate or possibly unpleasant in an esoteric, poetic manner that takes the sting out of it and puts it in the best possible light.

A *chochin kiji* is a newspaper or magazine article that sheds light on the subject in such a way as to make it look good—better than it may really be—much the way that photographers will emphasize a subject's best profile and sometimes resort to air-brushing to eliminate blemishes.

Chochin kiji are still very common in present-day Japan (as they are in the U.S. and elsewhere), in major as well as minor publications. The big difference today is that "lantern articles" appearing in top publications are written by professional writers and designed by skilled art directors. They read and look so good most people accept them as legitimate journalism.

The difference between "real" news and publicity that may appear to be gratuitous is, in fact, often hard to discern, particularly in trade publications. The foreign company in Japan generally needs every advantage it can get. The concept of *chochin kiji* can be very useful in getting publicity for your company or product, but it is advisable to shorten the term to just *kiji* in discussions with newspaper or magazine representatives.

Often the only editorial difference between an unwarranted *chochin kiji* and an interesting news story is the perception of the writer and how the article is written. Businessmen can influence both of these by how they present themselves and their products to Japanese publishers.

——————————————⟨35⟩——————————————

提灯をつける

Chochin wo Tsukeru
(Choe-cheen oh T'sue-kay-rue)

"Following the Leader"

From the dawn of Japan's history down to the opening of the country to the outside world in the mid-1800s, innovation and change were not commonplace. Except for the wholesale introduction of various arts and crafts from Korea and China between 300 and 600 A.D., the cottage-industry-based economy and lifestyle had remained very much the same for hundreds of years.

During the last, long shogunate dynasty, from 1603 until 1868, change was, in fact, repressed by the government and, in many instances, forbidden by law. In many public and private areas, individual thought and independent action were taboo, and there were strict penalties, including death, for deviating from the established norm.

The Japanese were conditioned to obey, to act in groups, and to conform. They became masters at following precise patterns of behavior set down for them, and when there were no exact guidelines for them to follow, they were often at a loss for what to do—and were prone to do something very unexpected or nothing at all.

During the massive economic buildup that occurred in Japan between 1945 and the 1960s, the traditional education and conditioning of the Japanese was an asset of extraordinary value. They labored in unison by the millions, achieving goals that are still unbelievable to much of the rest of the world.

But the robot-like attitude and behavior that was a mainstay of Japan's strength during this extraordinary buildup was being viewed as a handicap by the 1980s. Yet, at the same time, the conditioning and the taboos against independent behavior were still so deeply imbedded in the psyche of most Japanese that individual invention and innovation remained rare.

Still today the follow-the-leader syndrome continues to be a paramount force in much of Japanese society and industry. Few individuals or companies are willing to strike out on their own, to make changes. Most prefer to continue copying the success of others, and base their whole management philosophy on that approach.

This imitation is pretty much across the board, from apparel styles and entertainment to high-tech products and services. The average Japanese businessman still waits for someone else to *chochin wo tsukeru* (choe-cheen oh t'sue-kay-rue) or "turn on the lantern" before undertaking any new venture.

The use of the word *chochin*, which refers to a portable paper lantern that was in use until the introduction of electricity and the light bulb, is indicative of the age of this "follow-the-leader" pattern of behavior in Japan.

It will probably be well into the 21st century before the *average* Japanese businessman will be able to break the cultural bonds that bind him and nurture the gambler's spirit and the entrepreneurial bent that characterize Americans, Germans and other Westerners.

In the meantime, Japanese businessmen will no doubt continue looking to the U.S. and European countries for new ideas and new products, particularly for what they describe as "software" in the recreational and elderly healthcare areas.

36

直 感

Chokkan
(Choke-kahn)

"Intuition Outranks Reason"

In attempts to explain characteristic Japanese attitudes and behaviors, anthropologists and others often note that until the mid-1900s Japanese society was primarily tribal, meaning that it was made up of people who shared a common ancestry, language, culture and name, and generally that it was concentrated in a specific, well-defined region.

During much of Japan's history the "parent" tribe was divided into well over one hundred clans that were ruled locally by clan lords and nationally by the shogunate system of government. There were numerous cultural and linguistic differences among the clans in the outer regions of the country, but most of these differences were minor, and all Japanese had a strong sense of national identity.

With the ascendancy of the Tokugawa Shogunate in 1603, the principal cultural themes represented by the Court of the Shogun in Yedo (Tokyo) and the Imperial Court in Kyoto were gradually spread to the outermost regions of the country. Laws were designed to bring uniformity to society, and to compel it to serve the interests of the shogunate. Customs and crafts developed that further homogenized the Japanese into a cultural monolith.

The lives of the Japanese were so closely intertwined and so ruled by convention, causing them to think and act so much alike, that they often seemed to behave more by instinct than rational thought. The whole educational and economic system of the country was designed to further this herd-like approach to life.

As the slow decades of the mostly peaceful Tokugawa period unfolded, custom and ritual became the principal guidelines for most activities. Behavior in virtually all circumstances was minutely prescribed, and therefore became predictable to an extraordinary degree. Aberrations from "normal," expected behavior were serious transgressions, and were routinely punished. Failure to follow established etiquette in some situations was punishable by mandatory suicide or execution, depending on one's social status.

This degree of cultural conformity and social control reduced the role of independent thought and action, often resulting in *chokkan* (choke-kahn) or "intuition" being dominant in Japanese society. The Japanese "knew" what was right or wrong without applying rational thought.

It thus came about that the use of objective reason in making decisions and settling matters was regarded as cold and often inhuman. Using *chokkan* was better than using reason because more often than not it represented the only culturally acceptable solution.

Japanese society today is far less homogeneous than it was as late as the 1970s, but enough of the traditional cultural conditioning remains in the make-up of the average middle-aged and older Japanese to cause them to first react intuitively to virtually everything that confronts them.

Foreign businessmen dealing with Japanese should keep the *chokkan* factor in mind, and combine it with reason in their attitudes and behavior. They should also keep in mind, however, that the intuitive reaction of older Japanese to foreign concepts and products nowadays is often wrong because it does not always apply to the new Japan.

Many older Japanese, especially those who are in traditional businesses, are simply behind the times. They either are not aware of or deny the extraordinary changes that have taken place in the life styles of the younger generations. They will often turn down the opportunity to sell certain foreign products, claiming that they do not meet the needs or desires of the Japanese, only to have the same products become major successes when introduced shortly thereafter by someone else.

朝 礼

Cho Rei
(Choe Ray-ee)

"The Morning Bow"

During the first two decades after the end of World War II in 1945, while riding to work on elevated trains in Tokyo it was common to see large numbers of employees of Japanese companies engaged in early-morning calisthenics on the rooftops of office buildings and factories.

The sight of hundreds of poorly dressed and scrawny-looking people performing military-style exercises out in the open on cold, windy mornings, ranged from being humorous to shocking to most Western viewers. The experience strengthened the then prevailing stereotype of the Japanese as being something less than intelligent robots.

As an employee of the Japan Travel Bureau during part of this era, I became a member of the stereotypical Japanese. Fortunately (I thought), by that time, my department of JTB was exempted from performing the morning exercises, but we were required to participate in daily *Cho Rei* (Choe Ray-ee)—"Morning Salute" or "Morning Greetings."

Our *cho rei* ceremony was simple and fairly brief. We would all line up facing the manager of the department, bow in unison and call out, "*Ohaiyo gozaimasu*" (Oh-hie-yoe go-zie-mahss)—"Good morning!" The manager would then ask if any of the section chiefs had anything to say. The ceremony ended with a few comments or announcements from the manager, and a mass bow.

The importance of these morning meetings was not in their content but in their form and formality. They were a daily reconfirmation that we were a group of people bound together by our obligations and mutual responsibilities to each other. They also clearly revealed who was absent and who came in late, who had a cold or hangover, and so on.

Cho rei have continued to be a key part of the corporate culture of many Japanese companies over the decades. In some of the more tradition-ally oriented companies, the *cho rei* include inspirational talks and, in some cases, the singing of company songs—a system that strikes many Westerners as being an infringement on human rights as well as personal dignity.

In the idealized Japanese context, company employees are members of a family. The company has as much moral obligation to them as fathers and mothers have to their children. The relationship therefore goes well beyond a company paying employees a wage for their work. Federal laws support the concept that companies have a moral obligation to their employees.

Participating in a *cho rei* is thus a family affair, and singing a company song is singing the family anthem.

Of course, as Japan's younger generations become less traditional in their attitudes and behavior, the automatic acceptance of the "morning salute," and its importance in corporate culture, particularly in new entre-preneurial-type companies, is decreasing.

It is too early to begin counting the *cho rei* out, however, because in the latter part of the 1980s many of Japan's largest and most technically-advanced companies began a systematic program of re-introducing and re-emphasizing traditional etiquette among their employees in a determined effort to salvage some of the most advantageous facets of their cultural heritage.

38

ちょっと一杯やりましょう

Chotto Ippai Yarimasho
(Choat-toe Eep-pie Yah-ree-mah-show)

"Let's Have a Little Snort"

Westerners, with their freewheeling behavior, pride themselves on being able and willing to talk about almost anything, anywhere, anytime, and being as candid or as blunt as the occasion seems to demand—the exact kind of behavior that is diametrically opposed to what the Japanese have traditionally considered desirable and acceptable on most occasions.

Certain facets of Japanese etiquette restrict both their manner of speech and what they say in official, formal settings. Propriety often prevents them from saying directly what they believe, or what they want to say, so they have come up with a number of ways to overcome this handicap. One of the most common ploys is to enlist the aid of third parties as go-betweens.

Japanese businessmen, in particular, will ordinarily go to almost any length to avoid talking about matters that might result in verbal fights—from keeping quiet and ignoring situations, to denying them. In business, this attitude and behavior can result in serious matters becoming worse if the concerned party does not know enough to pursue the subject via other means.

When the Japanese want to talk to someone in business situations where confidentiality is desired, where someone wants to talk about something that is not a recognized and established policy or program, or where complaints are involved, Japanese will typically go out of their way to personalize the setting.

One of the more common practices is to say to someone, "*Chotto ippai yarimasho*" (Choat-toe eep-pie yah-ree-mah-show), which figuratively means "Let's have a drink"—an invitation to go to a nearby coffee shop if it is during the day, or often to a bar if it is at the end of the working day.

Businessmen use the *chotto ippai* custom routinely to have conversations with their counterparts in other sections and departments, and with members of their own department. Bosses regularly *chotto ippai* their subordinates when they want to admonish them.

The use of the *chotto ippai* custom is not always negative or surreptitious. Managers frequently invite their staffs or their colleagues out for a few rounds of drinks after work just to socialize with them without the restraints of formal etiquette, and to nurture relationships.

The conversations that take place at these informal meetings very often result in the development of new company policies and programs, or in decisions being made to scrap proposals or projects that are not working out.

Here again is another facet of the Japanese way of doing things that foreign businessmen can easily assimilate into their practices when dealing with Japanese companies. It will not only make the Japanese more comfortable, it will subtly reassure them that you are a person who can be trusted to do the right thing.

A more literal translation of *chotto ippai* is "just one (glass) full," but this is usually misleading because very few such sessions end with just one drink (unless they are one of those that occur during mid-day at a coffee shop).

Having participated in a great many *chotto ippai* that involved other foreigners who were newcomers to Japan, a little advice could go a long way: over-drinking at such meetings is seen as a character flaw, and does nothing at all for one's image as a businessman.

39

中 元　　歳 暮

Chugen / Seibo
(Chu-gane / Say-e-bow)

"Giving until It Hurts"

In lands ruled by despots, the primary aim of most laws and institutions is to control the behavior of the inhabitants, and to guarantee the power and authority of the rulers. Citizens do not have rights; they have obligations. This is true whether the despots are secular or religious.

In such societies the people must devise a variety of ways to gain and keep the goodwill of those in power, whether god or dictator. In many traditional cultures of this type, women were required to provide sex to the rulers and their surrogates.

The Japanese chose gift-giving (since sex was already a readily available commercial commodity) as their way of establishing and nurturing good relations with those who had power over them in order to protect themselves as well as to obtain needed services and favors.

Gift-giving in Japan began with the gods as recipients, and worked its way downward to the emperor, to court and government officials, and finally to anyone who had the power to use, abuse or aid other people, including teachers, doctors, bosses and landlords.

The gods got their regular array of foods and beverages. Emperors and their henchmen, who were more imaginative in the gifts they coveted, received a variety of things ranging from fish to masterpieces of pottery. Less exalted people also went in for a variety of things, but throughout Japanese history food items and alcoholic beverages have been the favorite gifts, indicating that the gods knew a good thing when they got it.

As time passed, protocol governing the choice of gifts and how they were to be wrapped and presented became so extensive that lengthy manuals were written as guides to gift-giving, and someone in each family was generally charged with responsibility for knowing the rules. Giving the wrong gift, using unapproved wrapping or failing to adhere strictly to the proper protocol in presenting a gift, especially to an arrogant superior, was a very serious failing that could have dire repercussions.

Enterprises catering to the gift-giving custom in Japan flourished. Wrapping paper and gift boxes became works of art. The practice of gift-giving became so deeply imbedded in the culture that when the Japanese were freed from the bonds of feudal servitude they did not end the custom; they elaborated on it.

Gift-giving in present-day Japan has grown into one of the largest and most important commercial segments of the economy. The political imperatives for it have long since disappeared, but it obviously continues to serve social needs in Japan's still very distinctive society.

There are two great gift-giving periods in today's Japan: the first is *Chugen* (Chu-gane) and the second is *Seibo* (Say-e-bow) {both words are often preceded by an "O" as an honorific}. *Chugen,* which literally means central origin or central source, refers to Japan's famous mid-summer *Obon* (Oh-bone) religious festival commemorating the dead, but gift-giving during this period (mid-July) is now totally secularized. *Seibo* refers to the end of the year, and the gift-giving period runs from around December 21 to December 28.

On both of these occasions, the primary purpose of giving gifts follows the historical pattern of repaying favors and acknowledging obligations; it serves as insurance to help guarantee continued goodwill or patronage and as a way to build up obligation for when favors might be needed in the future.

————————————40————————————

仲 介 者

Chukai-Sha
(Chuu-kie-shah)

"The Man in the Middle"

Westerners, particularly Americans, have a variety of cultural traditions that derive from their individualism and from the fact that they have historically enjoyed a great deal of personal freedom and have therefore been willing to accept responsibility for their own acts. This right was recognized by society and usually enforced by governments (but not always by religions).

Society took a different turn in Japan. Very early in the history of the country, individualism became taboo. Personal freedom was either greatly limited or absent altogether. Mass conformity to the dictatorial laws of the land was enforced with cruel sternness, and was often based on the despot's ultimate weapon—collective responsibility.

In addition to proscribing the individual accused of some crime, Japan's feudal laws made the accused's family and sometimes the whole village or clan equally guilty and subject to punishment. One of the most famous historical incidents resulting from this macabre morality involved a farmer named Sakura Sogo who went over the head of the local clan lord in 1653 to complain to the shogun about high taxes and other abuses.

Although the shogunate investigated the man's complaints and found them valid, the reigning shogun, Ietsuna Tokugawa, allowed the local lord to execute the farmer, his wife and their four small children in accordance with the law. (There is a shrine in memory of Sogo and his family just a five-minute train ride from the New Tokyo International Airport.)

Within this kind of social environment the Japanese became very circumspect in their speech and manner. It became second nature for them to do everything possible to avoid confrontations, especially with authority figures, to generally speak in vague terms, and often to say nothing at all in response to questions.

The profound influence this kind of cultural conditioning had on the Japanese is still very much in evidence today, particularly among older people who have not been directly exposed to Western ways. Furthermore, the Establishment in present-day Japan continues to de-emphasize individualism and promote group behavior and group responsibility.

Business in Japan naturally reflects these patterns of behavior. One manifestation that foreign businessmen certainly should know about and take advantage of is the very common use of *chukai-sha* (chuu-kie-shah), or "middle-men," in negotiations and other sensitive matters.

The primary rationale for using middle-men is that neither side has to take a chance on saying something that might be interpreted the wrong way, nor accept any responsibility for any faux pas committed by the middle-men. The *chukai-sha* can also be more direct and candid than either of the two principals (were they to meet face-to-face) and bring pressure against both sides to narrow their differences.

A second rationale for using *chukai-sha* in Japan is that generally they are older men with substantial experience—often they have already had successful careers in government or business and are well-known and highly respected; and they put their prestige on the line in their efforts to work out agreements between their clients.

Where foreign businessmen are concerned, more highly qualified *chukai-sha* are also often able to function as very useful consultants who can advise them on the preparations that should be made prior to beginning negotiations with a Japanese company.

41

大黒柱

Daikoku Bashira
(Die-koe-kuu Bah-she-rah)

"The God of Good Fortune"

Konosuke Matsushita, the founder of the great international Matsushita Industrial Corporation (National, Panasonic, Technics, etc.) who passed away in the 1980s, was considered by many Japanese to be the epitome of the ideal businessman. By any world standard, he was one of the most successful men ever to have lived.

Matsushita was a true Japanese, steeped in the philosophies of Shintoism, Buddhism and Confucianism. He had no formal education in business, and did not follow any of the beliefs or practices that are so dear to the hearts of business school professors. His beliefs and his inspirations were instilled in him by Japan's culture.

Matsushita spent a great deal of his time in solitude, meditating and seeking guidance from what might be called the universal mind or cosmic wisdom. He believed that with effort, everyone could tap into the intelligence of the universe and make use of it to benefit themselves and mankind. He required his executives to regularly engage in meditation.

In fact, however, Matsushita was not an exceptional man in Japan. He was a typical Japanese who succeeded on an extraordinary scale because of the types of products he manufactured and other economic circumstances, not because he had talents or visions that were different from or better than those of most other Japanese businessmen.

Matsushita and thousands of other Japanese businessmen have proven beyond any doubt that their own brand of cultural precepts and motivations are capable of producing highly effective commercial enterprises on a global scale. At this point in economic history, such success is still ultimately a matter of managing as well as maintaining people.

Many Japanese companies have Shinto or Buddhist shrines on their premises, and there is a strong religious (if you will) element in the working philosophy of most Japanese businessmen. International television has shown that the Japanese routinely have new buildings blessed by Shinto priests.

Religious concepts and references are common in Japan's business theories and vocabulary. One of the most interesting terms is *Daikoku Bashira* (Die-koe-kuu Bah-she-rah). *Daikoku* (Die-koe-kuu) is one of the seven divinities of good fortune in the pantheon of Japanese gods, with specific responsibility for the kitchen and for food. *Bashira* (Bah-she-rah) means "pillar," as in the large central pillar that holds up a house.

When the two words are combined they mean something like "The god of good luck pillar," and refer to a product or an individual that is the mainstay or star performer of a company. While always delighted to have a *daikoku bashira,* Japanese companies are concerned when they are dependent on a single "pillar."

Foreign companies operating in Japan should be especially cautious about pinning their future on a single *daikoku bashira,* especially if the "pillar" is a Japanese. The famed loyalty of the Japanese does not generally cross racial or national boundaries, and "star performers" often have no compunctions about leaving foreign enterprises.

About the only effective solution to the problem of losing one's main support is an arrangement that gives them an equity interest in the company that reverts back to the company if they leave before normal retirement.

42

駄目押し

Dame Oshi

(Dah-may Oh-she)

"Making Damn Sure"

Fundamental differences in culture make it inevitable that there will be many differences in the way Japanese and Westerners think and behave. One of the most important of these differences is the way the two groups look at and react to errors or mistakes.

In the social and political systems that developed in Japan, making errors, even though they were unintentional, was a serious transgression. In many instances, the perpetrator was treated as if the errors were deliberate; in some cases, the penalty for such mistakes was immediate execution.

The importance of always being correct in Japan no doubt evolved from a number of sources. One was the minutely defined system of etiquette which demanded—also sometimes on pain of death—that individuals follow the precise forms exactly. The higher the rank and social class of a person, the more detailed and demanding the etiquette that was required.

Training in the traditional etiquette made up a substantial portion of the education of every Japanese, again with special emphasis on those in the upper classes. The training and mode of life followed by samurai families would make the most demanding theatrical role, combined with the discipline of the roughest marine boot camp, pale by comparison.

In this environment not only were mistakes intolerable, but everyone was so sensitized to correct behavior that even the slightest deviations from expected behavior were instantly noticeable.

Another historical factor that made the Japanese particularly sensitive to mistakes, and virtually obsessed with the need to avoid them, was the master-apprentice system in all of the arts and crafts. Apprentices were required to spend up to twenty or more years slavishly imitating their masters until they got to the point that they could perform the necessary actions absolutely correctly.

Penalties for errors in both the crafts and arts were not life-threatening, but, if they occurred regularly, especially after the apprentice had been in training for ten or so years, would be severely dealt with by some masters. These penalties were often worse than physical punishment and ranged from having more years tacked onto the apprenticeship to, in worst-case scenarios, failure to achieve the status of master and thus being relegated to the lower rungs of society.

With this kind of background, making a mistake of any kind or degree is shameful to most Japanese. If the error is conspicuous and involves other people, it can be emotionally devastating. If it happens in a business context it can, of course, ruin one's future. And this is, of course, one of the main reasons why the Japanese system is based on collective rather than individual responsibility.

Altogether, the cultural conditioning of the Japanese has made them very careful, very methodical and very comprehensive in their attempts to avoid making mistakes. The process of trying to avoid errors is known as *dame oshi* (dah-may oh-she), which means "making doubly sure."

Foreign businessmen who have dealt with Japanese on almost any matter are familiar with their compulsion to research and evaluate to the point of seeming preposterous, beyond any measure of reasonableness. They ask questions and variations of the same questions; they ask for additional information over and over.

About the only response to *dame oshi* is to anticipate in advance every possible question and bit of information that might be relevant to the situation, and provide it to the Japanese in a package—keeping in mind that there will surely be other angles, other pieces, that will have to be provided later.

43

花より団子

Dango Yori Hana
(Dahn-go Yoe-ree Hah-nah)

"Materialism Is In!"

Most Japanese throughout the history of the country lived near or below subsistence level. The idea that all people had the right to acquire material goods above and beyond their immediate needs was alien to them. During the long feudal era it was often the official policy of the shogunate government to keep the clans poor so they could not afford to field an army and challenge the power of the central government.

One of the ongoing assignments of shogunate spies was to watch over the economic activities in the various provinces and report any signs that a particular area was accumulating more goods than were needed for survival. When such reports were made, the shogunate would devise some scheme to draw off the extra wealth through a special tax or mandatory contribution to the central government or a government-sponsored project.

There had long been a popular saying in Japan that *Hana Yori Dango* (Hah-nah Yoe-ree Dahn-go), or "Dumplings are better than flowers," (because you can eat the dumplings and only smell the flowers), but this was more of a protest against abject poverty than a philosophy.

At one time in Yedo (present-day Tokyo) during the Tokugawa Shogunate (1603-1868), it became vogue among a large portion of the city's day laborers that it was wimpish, if not un-Japanese, to still have any of their wages in their pockets or in their homes at the end of each day.

It was a matter of pride among this rowdy and boastful segment of Yedo's population to spend their money the day they earned it. This extraordinary phenomenon created lively competition among the city's restaurants, bars and redlight districts to attract these carefree spenders. Girls in the redlight districts were often especially aggressive in their efforts to entice the day laborers into their houses, sometimes descending upon their prey in groups and bodily carrying them in.

As the last of the great shogunate dynasties weakened and ideas began seeping into Japan from Europe and eventually the United States, the government gradually lost its ability to limit the economies of the larger and more aggressive clans.

Clan lords in the distant provinces near the southern tip of Korea and closest to China began engaging illegally in foreign trade, building up their knowledge of Western technology and boosting their wealth. Finally, exactly what the shogunate had feared came to pass. The outer clans rebelled and brought the shogunate down.

Today the Japanese are known for being among the biggest savers in the world—a factor that obviously played a vital role in the astounding growth of the economy from 1946 through the 1980s. At the same time, the wealth accumulated by the country during this period allowed the Japanese to have their *dango* and eat them too.

By the early 1980s, for the very first time in the history of the country, the average Japanese could afford to give vent to their pent-up desires to consume conspicuously, to revel in a degree of affluence that would have made the colorful day laborers of old Yedo envious and proud.

———————————— 44 ————————————

同期

Dohki

(Doe-o-kee)

"Keeping Up with Your Peers"

Conservative Japanese politicians and nationalists are forever pointing out that Japan owes a very significant proportion of its extraordinary economic success and social order to its racial and cultural homogeneity—and for that reason, they say, Japan should not and will not open its borders beyond a token level to refugees or immigrants of any kind.

The protectors of Japan's racial and ethnic homogeneity have a point, of course, as can be seen from the social and economic turmoil resulting from diverse groups in the U.S., England, Germany and elsewhere. Whether or not their position is moral or humane is, of course, another story.

But homogeneity is not always the preventive or the cure-all Japan's protectors often presume it to be. One very conspicuous downside to homogeneity is that it helps to make the Japanese antagonistic and sometimes arrogant toward non-Japanese. It also seriously handicaps the Japanese in their ability to be flexible and innovative in responding to new situations within the context of their own environment. Their commitment to homogeneity encompasses attitudes and behavior as well as appearance.

An extraordinary example of this latter factor is the inability of the Japanese to accept back into the cultural fold other Japanese who have been abroad for a number of years. The changes in the attitudes and behavior of even slightly de-Japanized individuals grate so on the polished sensitivities of the Japanese that they are conditioned to reject even their own people.

In Japan, traditionally, racial and ethnic purity have often taken precedence over alternatives that would have served the Japanese much better. An outstanding example of this is their refusal to accord full citizenship rights to the several hundred thousand ethnic Chinese and Koreans who have lived in the country for up to three or more generations.

On a personal and business level in Japan, the pressure to preserve homogeneity takes a variety of interesting twists and turns. Competition between groups, for example, is the prime directive, but personal competition within groups can be fatal to the career of an individual who outshines his group members.

One facet of the Japanese compulsion to be as one is expressed in the term *dohki* (doe-o-kee), which literally means "same period." In this case, the word refers to individuals in an organization or company who joined the same year and are therefore the same where seniority is concerned.

Same-year employees thus automatically become members of finite groups that maintain their identities throughout their careers. They expect to be given the same assignments—or assignments that are similar in degree of desirability. They expect to be promoted at the same time and otherwise receive the same or similar advantages, perks and so on.

Personnel departments in most larger Japanese companies take the *dohki* relationships seriously, and do their best to keep all of the individuals on the same step of the up-escalator, regardless of their ability, energy or contribution to the company.

This *dohki* management philosophy is one of the reasons why Japanese organizations can count on the loyalty and goodwill of their employees. Up to a point, the employees know they are going to rise to a certain level, and not be embarrassed by falling behind their same-year colleagues in wages or position.

The *dohki* policy ends, however, when managers reach the level of section manager after some fifteen to twenty years of service. Only a chosen few are selected for promotion to head of a department (the equivalent of a vice presidency in Western companies), which usually occurs around the age of forty-eight.

独身貴族

Dokushin Kizoku
(Doe-kuu-sheen Kee-zoe-kuu)

"Living the Life of Riley"

Among the edicts passed by the Tokugawa Shogunate, which ruled Japan from 1603 until 1868, were a series of laws designed to prevent well-to-do merchants from lording it over the socially superior samurai-class of professional warriors who depended for their livelihood upon a fixed allowance from the government.

Although the samurai were Japan's highest class, and merchants were at the bottom of the social list, samurai could not legally engage in any commercial enterprise. This left the field of business, and profit-making, in the hands of merchants.

By the middle decades of the long Tokugawa dynasty, many merchants had become rich. It was against the law, however, for them to dress richly, build expensive houses for themselves or engage in many other forms of conspicuous consumption.

As the decades passed, some of the sons, grandsons and great grandsons of these successful merchants created a variety of ways to enjoy their wealth that were beyond the reach of shogunate control. Some merchants took to wearing expensive silk under-clothing beneath their government-approved robes and sporting sash and pouch fobs carved of precious materials.

Some sons of the wealthy became playboys, spending huge amounts of money in the inns, restaurants and redlight districts of the day, at times vying to see who could spend the most in the shortest period of time.

The shogunate and its laws disappeared well over one hundred years ago, but the number of wealthy merchants and their spendthrift sons and daughters have multiplied by the hundreds of thousands, and now make up one of the most important consumer groups in Japan.

In typical Japanese fashion, this new group of profligate spenders has been given a name: *dokushin kizoku* (doe-kuu-sheen kee-zoe-kuu), or "bachelor aristocrats," and is made up of young unmarried men and women who earn good incomes but still live at home and therefore have few personal expenses.

Among the "bachelor aristocrats," young women are more conspicuous than men. They are inclined to spend larger amounts of money shopping, eating out, and traveling. Because they know these privileges will be drastically curtailed when they marry, they choose to live it up while they can.

By the early 1980s a number of businessmen in Japan, both foreign and Japanese, had picked up on the phenomenon of female "bachelor aristocrats" and had either created new businesses catering specifically to them or had re-tailored segments of their old businesses to take advantage of this rich new market.

By the early 1990s it had become conventional wisdom that new businesses in Japan wanting to guarantee their success had to come up with products and marketing programs that would attract the country's several million female *dokushin kizoku*.

Well-to-do "playgirls" also make up the largest single segment of Japan's individual international travelers, some of them going abroad every year on shopping sprees to such faraway places as Paris and London.

It was young Japanese women who gave both impetus and color to the development of a consumer economy in Japan after the debacle of World War II. Since then, the impact of young women on the life-style as well as the overall economy of Japan has grown stronger with each passing year.

Social prophets now foresee the day when Japanese women will have had their fill of shopping and playing games, and will turn more of their intelligence and talents to the political scene, breaking down the last of the feudal walls separating the government from the people.

46

独 創 性

Dokusosei

(Doe-kuu-so-say-ee)

"Creativity in a Closed Circle"

Japan's pre-industrial economy was based on crafts taught by the master-apprentice technique of training. Apprentices were assigned to master craftsmen for anywhere from fifteen to twenty years and sometimes much longer, and learned by imitating the masters.

This system endured for well over a thousand years, during which time the level of skill developed by successive generations of masters in virtually every craft reached the level of a fine art. From this point on, there was no where else to go: the technology and processes for manufacturing remained the same for generation after generation.

Most of the larger crafts were controlled by guilds. People generally worked in strictly-defined groups in which the emphasis was on doing things the way they had always been done. Anyone who might object to doing things in the traditional manner was likely to be ostracised. Lone individuals tinkering away in an attempt to find new or better ways of doing things were virtually non-existent.

Except in extremely narrow areas, such as improvements in the process of woodblock printing, innovation and invention were rare. The environment simply did not encourage, and in some cases did not allow, the type of experimentation that leads to technological break-throughs.

The social and political systems in Japan were primarily designed to maintain the status quo, and to prevent changes that would create friction and disunity or alter the power structure. During the later centuries of Japan's feudal age, it was against the law, for example, to build bridges across rivers. It was also illegal for local leaders to build new roads or widen old ones, or to introduce new methods of transporting goods from one region to another.

Much of the creativity that did exist in feudal Japan was limited to the more esoteric cultural pursuits, to literature and aesthetic practices, both primarily the province of the upper ruling class of professional warriors and court retainers.

Thus when Japan was opened to the industrialized West in the 1850s and the feudal government fell in the 1860s, originality was a concept that was barely understood and even less pursued. But the Japanese had nearly two thousand years of experience in duplicating processes and products created by other people. Spurred on by foreign importers, they set about imitating Western products with an alacrity and skill that astounded out-siders.

It was not until the 1950s that the topic of *dokusosei* (doe-kuu-so-say-ee) or "creativity" became the subject of serious concern in Japan, but it was to be some twenty years more before Japanese creativity began to replace imported technology.

In keeping with the culturally conditioned background of the Japanese, most creative effort in Japan today is group-oriented and is funded by large companies that have created teams to systematically experiment with new materials and new processes aimed at achieving specific goals.

Generations of experience by Japanese craftsmen in breaking every-thing down to its smallest components, meticulously following prescribed processes, recording the minutest detail, and now tackling everything as a team, has turned out to be a major asset in scientific research in Japan.

Given the accumulated experience and wisdom the Japanese have in combining aesthetics, design and manufacturing, added to their newly found freedom to innovate and invent, Japanese makers have a conspicu-ous advantage in the worldwide competition to come up with a steady stream of new products.

―――――――――――― 47 ――――――――――――

ド ラ イ ウ エ ッ ト
Dorai/Wetto
(Doe-rye/Wet-toe)

"The Wrong Kind of Personality"

Japanese have a highly sensitive cultural antenna with which they measure everything. In most cases, the cultural reading is taken automatically, without any conscious effort. It is a conditioned reflex that they have absorbed both directly and indirectly from infancy on.

The cultural antenna of the Japanese clicks on automatically when they come within range of a non-Japanese. Like a futuristic intelligence probe from *Star Trek,* the antenna gathers in information and provides them with an almost instant readout.

This cultural barometer can be used intentionally, however, and when the Japanese meet foreigners for the first time, they generally turn it on high for an in-depth probe. Having been brought up in a culture that is intuitive and especially sensitive to the slightest differences, the probe picks up on things that are not visible to the non-Japanese eye.

When business relationships are being considered, especially with foreigners, Japanese also deliberately arrange for situations that will lower the foreigners' defenses and allow the Japanese intelligence probe to penetrate beyond the facade of best-behavior. Two of their favorite ploys are nights out on the town drinking, sometimes in the company of hostesses, and golf games.

Among the most important of the measurements the Japanese take of each other and foreigners are their knowledge and use of etiquette in speech as well as in physical behavior, how respectful they are toward others in superior as well as inferior positions, and their overall appearance.

A key reading, and one that often determines the quality and extent of the relationship that develops—if one does—is whether one is judged to be *dorai* or (doe-rye) or *wetto* (wet-toe). *Dorai* and *wetto* are from the English words "wet" and "dry."

In its Japanese context, a *dorai* person is one who automatically applies reason and logic to every situation he confronts, whether it be business or a private matter. To the Western mind this, of course, is the ultimate goal of education and training—to make us reasonable-minded individuals who can think and behave rationally and logically.

To the Japanese, especially to Japanese women, the reasonable, logical person is almost always too objective, too cold for their liking. Their point is that in life two plus two does not always equal four, and that feelings are far more important to a happy, satisfying life than is logic.

To Japanese businessmen, foreigners who pride themselves on their logical, reasonable approach to everything are often the most difficult to deal with and get along with because they are unable to recognize or accept the "human elements" that make up business relationships.

Japanese businessmen who attempt to behave in a purely logical manner are very conspicuous misfits in most companies. They generally find themselves sidetracked from the mainstream and eventually frozen out.

The Japanese businessman who speaks English and becomes a conduit between his company and foreign businessmen is invariably put into an awkward position. On the one hand, he is expected by the foreign side to behave in a logical manner, while on the other hand his Japanese colleagues expect him to give full consideration to the human and unpredictable elements in any enterprise.

The *wetto* person is one who gives precedence to emotions and feelings. He may not be a good businessman at all from the Western viewpoint, but is frequently the most successful type of manager in Japan. He is also often especially popular with women.

48

どさ廻り

Dosa Mawari
(Doe-sah Mah-wah-ree)

"Getting Sent to the Boonies"

Much of the writing done on Japan begins with the solemn pronouncement that "Japan consists of four large islands." Well, actually, Japan consists of five large islands (and hundreds of smaller ones). The "large" island that most writers ignore is *Sado Shima* or "Sado Island," situated in the Sea of Japan some one hundred kilometers off the northwest coast of Honshu (the main island) across from Niigata City.

Far away from the center of Japan, and separated from the main island by a cold and storm-tossed sea, Sado Island became famous as a place of exile for fallen political figures when Emperor Juntoku tried to regain power for the Imperial Throne from the Kamakura shogunate in 1197, and was banished to the distant island.

Sado continued to be the most dreaded of Japan's places of exile over the centuries. Gold was discovered on the island in 1601, and for the next 267 years was worked by convict labor. Some of the island's more famous exiles were eventually allowed to return home, but the vast majority of the convicts did not survive the rigors of their enslavement.

During the early years of Japan's last shogunate dynasty (1603–1868), the underworld of gangsters reversed the two syllables for Sado (Dosa) and used it as a code word to refer to the island. Eventually, second-rate entertainers who could not get regular bookings in Yedo, Kyoto, Osaka or other major cities began touring towns in the outer provinces, referring to their road-trips as *dosa mawari* (doe-sah mah-wah-ree). *Mawari* means "going around" or "touring."

The nuance of the *dosa mawari* entertainment tours was that the entertainers would never make it back to the big city or the big time; that, like the convicts sent to Sado, they were doomed to live out their lives laboring away under wretched conditions.

In more recent decades *dosa mawari* has come to be applied to work assignments outside of the major cities, especially when the areas are regarded as hardship posts. Ministries and agencies of the central government as well as major companies routinely dispatch younger managerial staff on tours of duty in regional offices as part of their training for higher office.

However, when individuals receive two or three regional assignments back-to-back, especially if the re-assignments are not accompanied by promotions, it is often a signal that the employees concerned have been shunted off the main promotion ladder and are being told in very clear terms that their future with the ministry or company is limited.

Not all assignments in the boonies are negative. Quite often exceptionally talented individuals from the head office are sent out to regional branches specifically to help them overcome some kind of serious problem. If they succeed, their careers may be greatly enhanced.

Foreign businessmen involved with Japan frequently find that their favorite contacts in Japanese companies have been dispatched elsewhere. This is one reason why it is advisable to develop good relationships with the assistants and other subordinates in any group.

On the other hand, it also pays not to cut the ties you have built up with staff members being transferred, particularly if they appear to be comers who will be back a few years later. They will appreciate regular contact (because it shows you were not just using them), and will remember your loyalty to them when they do return to the head office.

49

洞 察 力

Dosatsu-Ryoku
(Doe-saht-sue-Rio-kuu)

"Having X-ray Vision"

Given their long history and philosophical base in Shintoism, Buddhism and Confucianism, it is not surprising that the Japanese developed a contemplative culture that was quite different from the more direct-action type of cultures that developed in the West.

Among other things, Japanese culture encouraged the development of a variety of aesthetic and esoteric customs that imbued their lifestyle with a distinctive character and promoted skills that were to set them apart from Westerners.

The better-known of these practices included the tea ceremony, writing poetry, and calligraphy—all of which were designed to develop the aesthetic prowess of the practitioners and help them achieve attunement with the cosmos.

In addition to adding both color and flavor to Japan's culture, Shintoism, Buddhism and Confucianism permeated the lives of the Japanese on every level and in every way, becoming the vehicles by which they were homogenized to an extraordinary degree.

One particular facet of Buddhism that played an especially important role in shaping the Japanese character and personality was Zen, which teaches that enlightenment can be achieved through meditation, self-contemplation and intuition (rather than praying to a god to do it for you).

Japan's professional warrior class, the samurai, made the practice of Zen one of the key parts of their education, applying it to training in such martial arts as the use of the sword. They discovered that mental training was at least as important as physical training in truly mastering any skill.

The ultimate aim of the Zen practitioner was to reach the point where one could instantly "see" the difference between reality and the unreal, between the honest and the dishonest; to become so aware that one could see without the use of the eyes or dependence upon light; and to become so skillful (in swordsmanship or the crafts, etc.) that there was no difference between thinking a thought and achieving it.

Many of the special skills and dedication for which the samurai are famous can be attributed to their adoption of much of the Zen philosophy and way of life. The history of the country is replete with stories of accomplishments by Zen-trained warriors that are so extraordinary they read like fantasies.

Thus it came about that the ideal person in Japan was one who had developed *dosatsu-ryoku* (doe-saht-sue-rio-kuu), or "the ability to see through things, to perceive them as they really are," and this was the standard by which Japanese measured everyone.

This ideal has naturally been carried over into the business world, where practicing Zen is regarded as an important part of executive training. Some corporations send their executives and trainees to private schools that conduct courses in pure Zen as well as in business-oriented practices that are impregnated with Zen. Others are sent to Zen temples that are open to the public at large. It seems that the higher up and more successful a Japanese businessman, the more likely he is to be a Zen practitioner, and the more credence he gives to the cosmic element in human relations.

When top Japanese leaders evaluate younger men for higher positions, and especially when they look for replacements for themselves, *Dosatsu-ryoku* is one of the qualities they look for.

Some Western businessmen become adept at *dosatsu-ryoku* after decades of experience (which usually includes many failures). They might speed up this learning process by taking up the practice of Zen.

——————————————— 50 ———————————————

土足のまま上がる

Dosoku no Mama Agaru
(Doe-soe-kuu no Mah-mah Ah-gah-ruu)

"Putting Your Worst Foot Forward"

One of the things that uninitiated foreigners often do in Japan is wear their street shoes into rooms, houses or inns that have tatami reed-mat floors. It obviously does not occur to them that what they are doing is a serious breach of an important Japanese custom.

When these incidents occur, the Japanese are quick to explain to the foreigners that they must remove their shoes; that in Japanese-style places one wears house slippers on wood-floored hallways and goes sock-footed in *tatami*-floored rooms.

Failure to abide by this long-established footwear custom is known in Japanese as *dosoku no mama agaru* (doe-soe-kuu no mah-mah ah-gah-ruu), or, "going/stepping up (into a house/room) with shoes on"—something that only someone behaving irrationally or engaged in serious violence would ever do.

Wayward foreigners who are informed of this blunder instantly understand where they have gone wrong, invariably apologize, and generally never make the same mistake again. But such is often not the case where other cultural blunders are concerned.

Problems resulting from differences in the way of doing things in Japan are often exacerbated by foreign businessmen automatically presuming that they can behave in their normal way and get a Western-type reaction from the company they have approached simply because the Japanese they deal with speak good or fairly good English.

While having contacts on the Japanese side who speak English (or any other appropriate foreign language) is a major advantage, it generally does not prevent foreign businessmen from having to alter their approach to mesh with the expectations of the Japanese.

Just as inexperienced foreigners often fail to take their shoes off before stepping onto *tatami* floors, they also frequently make mistakes in their first approach to Japanese companies, in making presentations, and in creating advertising campaigns that turn the Japanese off instead of on.

When these things are not done well the Japanese equate such actions with *dosoku no mama agaru*, or "going in with your shoes on."

The usual reason for this common failure is that the foreign business-men do not go far enough in Japanizing their approaches or presentations, in giving them the nuances, the images, the spins that appeal to and impress the Japanese.

Often the cultural mistakes made by newcomers to the Japanese mar-ket are so subtle that they cannot be seen by Western eyes, and just as often—if not more so—the foreign businessmen who were responsible for the errors, and are later told about them, have difficulty accepting the idea that the errors were serious.

It is because of the many subtle and often invisible pitfalls in doing business in Japan that foreign companies entering the market are generally well-advised to employ experienced middle-aged and older Japanese man-agers to help them maneuver across and around the cultural sinkholes that litter the Japanese landscape.

Hiring Japanese managers is itself fraught with danger. It is extremely important that they have unblemished records, and the more successful they have been in their previous careers, the better. In particular, people who respond to "Help Wanted" ads should be carefully screened to weed out the ever-present rejects and failures.

Foreign companies that do not have good, long-standing personal con-tacts in Japan, are usually well-advised to rely on reputable headhunters.

同 窓 生

Dososei

(Doe-so-say-ee)

"Working the School Ties"

One aspect of life in the United States most Japanese find so different and so attractive is the freedom that Americans have to talk to anyone with-out reservations or special protocol, and to make friends with anyone they like, regardless of the individual's sex, age, occupation or background.

In feudal Japan it was generally both socially and politically impossible to make friends and develop close relationships with people who were not members of one's own closed-in, exclusive group.

Each group, on whatever level, was designed to be as self-sufficient as possible. New members were either born into the groups or admitted only at the bottom. Other groups were regarded with suspicion and treated as competitors. Ordinarily there were no open, direct lines of communication between groups—or even sub-groups within larger organizations.

Communication between groups was generally limited and normally restricted to formal contacts that followed an established protocol. The free-for-all kind of social intercourse and communication that characterizes American society was alien to Japan.

The limitations and controls on social behavior in Japan enmeshed people in a web that stifled their natural impulses, and while it helped create a stylized form of life that foreigners on the outside often praised highly, those caught up in the web regarded it as more of a morality play in which their roles turned them into puppets.

Social behavior in Japan is no longer controlled by the government system but it is still fundamentally influenced by the generations of cultural conditioning that went into the making of the Japanese. Japan is still a group-oriented society, and there are still limitations and restrictions on individual behavior.

Because of such prevailing past influences, networking in Japan is almost always limited to specific groups. Often the most powerful of these groups, and one of the few that crosses family, regional and occupation lines, are the *dososei* (doe-soe-say-ee), or "alumnae" groups.

It often seems that the relationships that develop between school mates in Japan are especially intense and long-lasting because school is about the only place where children have the opportunity and freedom to meet and to make friends with whomever they like.

In this sense, schools are a democratizing force in Japanese society, but the concept of equality again ends up being Japanized (group-oriented) rather than universal. School ties often take precedence over human ties.

Dososei ties play a key role in both business and politics in Japan—more so, generally, than they do in other countries because the Japanese still find it very difficult to cross group lines to establish or accept new relationships.

Establishing a business relationship with a non-related firm is an especially complicated process in Japan because such relationships are primarily based on personal rather than business factors. In such cases, one of the best personal connections that one can have in the company is a former classmate and, of course, the higher his position the better.

If you do not have a classmate in the company, the next best thing is an alumnae brother. Many Japanese businessmen keep very carefully-maintained lists of their school mates as their primary source of business contacts.

英語使い

Eigo Zukai

(A-ee-go Zuu-kie)

"The Dangers of Speaking English"

In the mid-1950s in the Shibuya Ward of Tokyo, a young Japanese man was killed by an ax-blow to the head because he was overheard speaking English. His assailant, another young Japanese man, told police that he was so incensed by the arrogance and un-Japanese-like behavior of the victim that he killed him in a blind rage.

This was an extreme example of the very common irrational reaction of many Japanese to hearing another Japanese speak a foreign language—a phenomenon that apparently occurred spontaneously when the first foreigners began arriving in Japan in the 16th century.

Having been geographically and culturally isolated for generations, the Japanese had come to believe that protecting their racial and cultural purity from outside influences was absolutely imperative if they were to survive as a people and a nation.

The Japanese language was immediately seen as one of the primary barriers preventing foreigners from learning about Japan and penetrating Japanese society. Teaching Japanese to foreigners soon came to be regarded as anti-Japanese and therefore traitorous.

By the same token, any Japanese who attempted to learn a foreign language was viewed with suspicion, and in a number of recorded cases was looked upon and treated as a traitor to Japan.

Given this deep fear of foreigners who spoke Japanese and equally strong antipathy toward other Japanese who spoke a foreign language, the Japanese boxed themselves into a dilemma in their dealings with foreigners.

During some of the first official meetings between representatives of the American and Japanese governments, the English-speaking Japanese interpreter was kept hidden behind a screen and was carefully watched by armed warriors.

Japanese attitudes toward their own language and toward foreign languages have changed considerably since the mid-1850s, but the ancient symptoms of language exclusivity mixed with xenophobia are still readily visible in present-day Japan.

Much of the Japanese prejudice against foreign-language speakers today is most likely to be reflected in attitudes and behavior toward those who speak English—simply because it is the foreign language most often encountered in Japan.

Despite the fact that the study of English is mandatory in Japanese schools, and is absolutely essential to the conduct of Japan's international trade and diplomatic relations, the decidedly derogatory term *Eigo Zukai* (A-ee-go Zuu-kie), or "English User," is still frequently used in reference to Japanese who speak English.

A significant percentage of Japanese, particularly among those at a high level in the government, still regard the Japanese language as a defensive weapon in their dealings with the outside world, and still view any Japanese who speaks English as suspect.

They believe, and rightly so, that any Japanese who spends enough time studying English to become relatively fluent in the language will also have absorbed a great deal of the psychology that goes with the language—and to that extent is less Japanese.

Languages cannot, in fact, be totally separated from their cultural base and still be used effectively. Their cultural content is often the main message. Because of this, the study and use of English in Japan, no matter how poorly it is done, is probably doing more to change Japanese behavior than anything else.

Eigo Zukai should be lauded rather than condemned.

宴 会

En Kai

(Inn Kie)

"Reaffirming Japaneseness"

Geographic and social isolation during most of Japan's early history contributed to the development of a totally defined culture that pervaded every aspect of the lives of the people. The philosophical and political base for the country's social system required that the Japanese think and behave in a highly refined, specifically prescribed manner to maintain their place in society.

Membership in Japanese society was therefore not a casual or incidental thing. In addition to racial purity, it required an enormous amount of learning and practice, not to mention extraordinary discipline, in order to conform to the demands of the system and *be Japanese.*

Because being Japanese, in every cultural nuance of the word, was a fine art requiring consummate skill in numerous things, it was necessary for the Japanese to have many ongoing customs and rituals that made it possible for them to continuously reinforce their Japaneseness.

One of the most important and enjoyable of these culture-enforcing rituals is the *en kai* (inn kie) or "dinner party." Nowadays, almost any kind of banquet-style gathering, including Western-style sit-down meals and receptions, may be called an *en kai,* but I am referring here to the ones that take place on tatami reed-mat floors and are conducted in the Japanese manner.

En kai originated centuries ago as parties held at the Imperial Court in Kyoto to celebrate special occasions during the year. From the Imperial Court, the custom spread to the general population. Most *en kai* today are sponsored by companies, professional organizations and government entities. They are staged to celebrate such events as the signing of contracts, as part of company trips, to honor individuals, to mark the gathering of sales executives from around the country, as year-end thank-you parties for customers, and so on.

The importance of the traditional *en kai* is that they provide an occasion for groups of Japanese to come together in a precisely structured and controlled event at which traditional patterns of behavior are exercised and relationships among the participants are confirmed.

The seating, food and drink, speeches, interpersonal behavior and entertainment at an *en kai* are quintessentially Japanese. Virtually all of the etiquette that characterizes the Japanese comes into play. Emotions are released, bonds are tightened, and commitments are reconfirmed.

Purely Japanese-style *en kai* thus serve as a reaffirmation of the Japanese identity and the role that traditional culture continues to play in their lives. Any outsider wanting to see and experience Japanese culture from the inside must participate in and understand the meaning of the *en kai*.

The emotional impact of this special Japanese ritual on foreigners who speak the language well enough to understand what is going on, appreciate the experience for what it is, and willingly participate in the activities is quite extraordinary.

Following an *en kai* it is common for close friends and those with special guests to break up into smaller groups and go to bars or clubs for a *niji kai* (nee-jee kie) or "second party" where the drinking and carousing is more intimate. And the *niji kai* may not be the end of it. Diehards sometimes go on to a third and even a fourth party—*sanji kai* and *yonji kai*.

外 圧

Gaiatsu

(Guy-aht-sue)

"Pressure from the Outside"

Valuable insights can be gained into the anatomy and nature of Japanese companies and Japan as a political institution by comparing them to military organizations and to bureaucracies.

The whole of Japan was administered by an elite class of military families from the beginning of the shogunate system in 1192 until 1868. Following the fall of the shogunate in 1868, a modernized military system continued to exercise most of the power in the country until the end of World War II in 1945.

Both the elite samurai warriors of feudal Japan and the civilian authorities since have administered Japan through one of the most efficient, comprehensive and powerful bureaucratic systems ever devised. The influence of these two systems over nearly one thousand years naturally had a profound effect on the psychology and behavior of the Japanese.

The traditional Japanese penchant for structure, order, precise processes, seniority, rank, hierarchical arrangements and chains of command were all nurtured in these traditional bureaucratic and militaristic environments—and all these characteristics remain a significant part of personal and business relationships in Japan today.

Another traditional facet of Japan's Confucian-oriented military and bureaucratic systems that has survived into modern times is groupism—the overwhelming compulsion for everyone to belong to a specific group that gives them roots and identity.

In order to remain in good standing as group members, individuals must adhere strictly to the policies and practices of their group, allowing it to determine their behavior and control their loyalty.

While the strengths of Japanese style groupings are often self-evident, particularly in the enterprise affiliations in the nation's economy, they also have a number of serious and sometimes fatal weaknesses that are now plaguing Japan both economically and politically.

One of the most conspicuous and serious weaknesses of groupism in Japan, particularly in political and professional arenas, is the inability of members of specific groups to make rapid decisions and to cooperate readily and quickly with other groups.

Part of this inability comes from the extreme reluctance of members and leaders of groups to make commitments and take personal responsibility for positions that others disagree with or that might lead to some kind of embarrassment or failure.

Often the only way a group will move is if it is subjected to *gaiatsu* (guy-aht-sue), or "outside pressure," because this gives individual members as well as the group as a whole an excuse if there is criticism or anything goes wrong.

The *gaiatsu* factor is deeply entrenched in Japanese culture, and is regularly used in politics, professional affairs and business. It is the most prominent in international politics because none of the leading political factions want to be on the unpopular side of trade and foreign affairs issues.

Both foreign companies and foreign governments need to be aware of the role that *gaiatsu* plays in Japan, and need to develop expertise in how to utilize it in their negotiations with Japanese companies and the Japanese government.

55

外 人

Gaijin
(Guy-jeen)

"Hairy Barbarians Today"

The first Westerners of record to visit Japan were three Portuguese traders who were passengers on a Chinese junk that was driven ashore on Tanega Island (some 300 kilometers south of Kyushu) by a storm in August 1543.

There is no indication that the three Portuguese went beyond Tanega; even so, their coming was to have a profound effect on Japanese history thereafter. When the weather calmed and they resumed their voyage to Macau, they had left behind guns, tobacco and venereal disease.

Back in Macau, the Portuguese spread the word that there was an island country off the coast of China, and in no time missionaries and other foreign traders were competing for favors and concessions in Japan.

Not surprisingly, the larger-bodied and often bearded foreigners who first arrived in Japan created a sensation wherever they went. In addition to their appearance, they seldom bathed (some apparently never bathed at all), and in comparison with the meticulously behaved Japanese, their manners were atrocious.

The only thing the Japanese could compare the foreigners with was an early historical myth which said that some mountains in Japan were inhabited by large, red-headed, bearded creatures called *Tengu* (Tane-guu) that had long noses and fiery eyes and sometimes raided nearby villages, kidnapping women and babies. As the myth went, the *Tengu* ate the babies and did to the women what such apparitions would naturally do to females.

In short order, the Japanese labeled the strange newcomers *ijin* (ee-jean) meaning barbarians. As far as the Japanese were concerned, the foreigners lived up to their mythical reputation, causing so much trouble in the country that efforts were mounted to eliminate or expel them. In the 1630s, although the shogunate continued to allow occasional visits by Chinese traders, it had closed the country to all other outsiders except for a small complement of Dutch traders isolated in Nagasaki harbor.

Some 225 years later, the United States forced the Japanese to re-open the country to foreign traders and missionaries. Nationalistic elements in the country began calling this new group of foreigners *keto* (keh-toe), meaning "hairy barbarians." Friendlier elements sometimes referred to Caucasian Westerners as *gaikoku jin* (guy-koe-kuu-jeen), or "outside-country people."

The first community of Westerners to be established in Japan after its re-opening in the mid-1800s was in the small fishing village of Yokohama, some 50 kilometers south of Yedo (Tokyo). The community was isolated behind a high wall on a spit sticking out into the bay.

During the early days of the settlement, Japanese gathered by the hundreds near the wall gates, hoping to get a look at the strange creatures on the inside. It is said that the foreign men were especially attracted to Japanese women, and vice-versa.

It was not until after World War II ended in 1945 that foreigners would more or less officially be called *gaijin* (guy-jeen), an old word meaning "outside person" that had previously been used by Japanese to refer to other Japanese who were not members of their group.

Today *gaijin* is officially used in reference to any non-Japanese, but in general usage it refers to Caucasians (non-Asians). Whether or not it has any derogatory connotations depends upon the user and the circumstance. It retains all of the potency of "Gringo," "Spic," "Honky" and other such labels. Polite forms include *gaikoku no kata* (guy-koe-kuu no kah-tah) and *gaikoku jin* (guy-koe-kuu jeen), meaning "foreign person."

The word *gaijin* is indicative of the extreme ethnocentrism of the Japanese. When they are outside of Japan, they generally refer to the local residents as *gaijin* or "foreigners"—and only occasionally note, usually in a humorous way, that they are the foreigners. They also carefully distinguish between white and black people. A black person is a *kokujin* (koe-kuu-jean), or "black person," first and *gaijin*, or "foreign person," second.

---------------◆ 56 ◆---------------

頑張って

Gambatte!

(Gahm-baht-tay!)

"The Never-Say-Die Syndrome"

Obscenities are among the first words foreigners learn upon visiting or residing in the United States for any length of time because such words are used so much and heard so often. Cursing and using colorful invective, in fact, seems to be an American, if not a Western, tradition. Mexicans, for example, are masters at using profanity, including honking onomatopoetical insults with their car horns.

In Japan, on the other hand, there is a conspicuous lack of curse words and invective in the language. Probably the word that is most often heard by foreigners in Japan is *trasshaimase!* (ee-rah-shy-mah-say), or "welcome!"

Another word that everyone in Japan hears over and over is *gambatte* (gahm-baht-tay) from the word *gambaru* (gahm-bah-ruu), meaning to "persevere, never give up, never say die, do one's best." One might say that *gambaru*-ism is the primary philosophy of the Japanese.

"*Gambarimasu* (gahm-bah-ree-mahss), "I will do my best," or *gambatte,* "do your best," are constantly on the lips of the Japanese in virtually every situation imaginable. The term is used as an encouragement, as a promise, as a dedication, almost as a prayer, and as a battle cry.

When baseball players, golfers, singers, sumo wrestlers, newly elected politicians and others are interviewed they invariably promise to *gambaru.* Well-wishers seeing businessmen off for assignments abroad yell out *Gambatte!* Newly hired employees pledge that they will *gambaru.* Parents are continuously imploring their children to *gambaru* in their school work.

The ritualistic use of *gambaru* can probably be traced in part to the fact that failing or coming in second best is really not acceptable in Japanese culture. In the Japanese context of things, a tie is all right because nobody loses, but the innate goal of everybody in everything is to be number one.

Foreign businessmen who want to "push the right buttons" in their dealings with Japanese would do well to incorporate *gambaru* in its various forms into their vocabulary and use it frequently. The Japanese are especially sensitive to the use of this key word, and respond positively when they hear it. In addition to its surface meaning, *gambaru* is symbolic of the aspects of Japanese culture that the people hold the most dear.

In the not-too-distant past, most Japanese had both a serious inferiority complex and a superiority complex about their culture and their racial origins. While believing themselves far superior to Westerners in matters of the spirit and cultural refinement, they felt inferior to Westerners in technical matters and in physical attributes of race.

Using *gambaru* in its proper context is just one of the many ways non-Japanese can demonstrate a knowledge and an appreciation of Japanese culture, and win valuable points in establishing and maintaining fruitful relationships with Japanese.

Japan's economic success, spurred on by the *gambaru* spirit, has, in fact, resulted in a psychological metamorphosis of the Japanese that hopefully is more positive than negative. Because they are now much less inclined to view themselves as inferior, there should be less chance that they will overreact, as they have in the past, to prove themselves to the outside world.

At the same time, it would no doubt benefit many other people to develop some of the extraordinary *gambaru* spirit that infuses and so relentlessly drives the Japanese.

賀詞交換

Gashi Kokan

(Gah-she Koe-kahn)

"Drinking In the New Year"

Despite astounding changes in the Japanese way of living since the late 1950s (when the first signs of affluence began to become noticeable), numerous traditional customs are still observed by old and young alike. Still today there are aspects of life in Japan that are as strange and as exotic to foreigners as they were to the very first Westerners to set foot in Japan in the mid-1500s.

Japan is a land of Shinto- and Buddhist-oriented festivals. At one time or another during the year most large shrines and temples in the country (and there are over 200,000 altogether) sponsor some kind of festival, with the more famous ones attracting two to three million participants.

There are fertility festivals, naked festivals, chase-out-the-devil festivals, bonfire festivals, autumn festivals, spring festivals, summer festivals, dance festivals, processions-of-the-lords festivals and gods-of-good-luck festivals—you name it, and there is probably a Japanese festival to celebrate it.

My own favorite Japanese festival is the one at the end of the year when temple bells all over the country ring out the old year and welcome in the new one. Some of the greater temples around the country have huge bells with giant wooden logs as clappers. The log clappers are suspended from the ceilings by thick ropes. It takes several people to swing them properly against the bells.

As midnight approaches, teams of young men, often dressed in skimpy loincloths despite the frigid temperatures, take turns crashing the massive clappers into the bells a total of 108 times to signify the elimination of all the evils that beset mankind.

There are numerous other major annual events in the lives of the Japanese that help maintain their links with the past and continue to add a special dimension to the bonds that characterize their personal and business relationships. One of these events is the so-called *Gashi Kokan* (Gah-she Kkoe-kahn), or "Exchanging New Year's Greetings," custom followed by millions of businessmen. *Gashi Kokan* are reception-like events that take place from around the third of January to about the 10th of the month.

The purpose of the larger *Gashi Kokan*, which are generally arranged by industrial associations, is to provide executives of member companies with a convenient opportunity to meet and greet each other in one central location. The events are punctuated by copious toasting with sake and beer, as one participant after another makes a brief speech, then leads everyone in a mass *Kanpai!* (kahm-pie!), or "Cheers!"

Another key activity at the annual *Gashi Kokan* is the exchange of name-cards by people who have never met before or who haven't seen each other for a while and have new cards. Often even old friends will exchange cards in keeping with the spirit of the ritual.

In fact, exchanging name-cards at these New Year's events is such an entrenched custom that they are also known as *Meishi Kokan* (May-ee-she Koe-kahn) or "Name-card Exchanges."

Smaller versions of the *Gashi/Meishi Kokan* are also held in company offices. Businessmen call on each other throughout the midday and afternoon, exchanging greetings and cards, drinking toasts and expressing ritualistic requests for continued patronage during the new year.

Foreign businessmen visiting or residing in Japan should certainly take advantage of these "exchange" receptions to nurture their contacts and build goodwill for the future.

58

下剋上

Gekokujo

(Gay-koe-kuu-joe)

"Losing Your Head"

One technique of political control formalized by the Tokugawa Shogunate shortly after it took over Japan in 1603 was the division of the country's population into four classes—samurai warriors and their families at the top, farmers next, craftsmen third, and merchants on the bottom.

Merchants were ranked at the bottom of the social ladder because they did not produce anything, made money off the labor of others, and were held in very low regard by the Confucian-based Tokugawa shogunate. Farmers were ranked second only as a political sop; not because they enjoyed any special privileges or rights.

The Tokugawa government further reinforced the vertically structured society by carefully specifying ranks at the Shogun's Court and among *daimyo* (die-m'yoe) or provincial lords. The *daimyo* in turn divided their own retainers according to precise ranks. Each village had its headman; each work group had its leader, and so on.

In every group and organization in Japan, regardless of its size or importance, there was a specific ranking from top to bottom, just as in an army. Generally speaking, rank was based on size and wealth in the case of provinces and commercial operations, and on heredity and seniority-in-service where individuals were concerned.

Also, just as in the military, there was a carefully prescribed chain-of-command in virtually all matters, private as well as public, particularly in those having to do with government on any level.

Sanctions against anyone subverting the chain-of-command in any way were strictly enforced, again especially when the matter concerned local, regional or national authorities. If an individual farmer had a complaint about taxes or any other government regulation, he was expected to go to his village chief. It was then up to the chief to take the complaint to his superior, and so on up the chain.

Complaints were, in fact, very common during Japan's long feudal era because when any privileged group of people have power over others they invariably tend to abuse them. History records that with rare exceptions, as when the magistrates or other government officials were men of unusual conscience, Japan's system tended to punish the complainers rather than act on their complaints.

A special term, *gekokujo* (gay-koe-kuu-joe), came into use to describe poor people who went over the heads of their immediate superiors to voice complaints. An act of *gekokujo* took a great deal of courage under any circumstance. The higher up the complainer went, the more dangerous it could be to his welfare.

The more arrogant of the clan lords imposed the death penalty on those who dared to bypass them and go to an official of the shogun or to the shogun himself. But conditions were often so bad that recourse to this potentially fatal action was fairly common.

In contemporary Japan, rank and precise chains-of-command are alive and well in practically every organization in the country, though in smaller companies and organizations there is a growing tendency for young people to ignore them. In larger and more traditional organizations, however, a *gekokujo* can be a major gamble with one's career.

Reluctance to take complaints beyond one's own immediate boss, who is sometimes responsible for the complaint in the first place, is often a serious obstacle to the smooth functioning of business in Japan. Foreign businessmen who try to lodge complaints with Japanese organizations frequently encounter this syndrome.

Personally going over the head of a section chief or department manager can make a serious enemy. If all efforts to deal fairly and justly with an individual in a company or government agency fail, the best approach is to enlist the aid of an experienced third party who has a strong relationship with one or more of their seniors.

———— 59 ————

五月病

Gogatsu Byo

(Go-gaht-sue B'yoe)

"Taking the System Too Seriously"

One of the hallmarks of traditional Japanese behavior is taking things far more seriously than what other people generally regard as sensible or rational. This tendency is often so pronounced that Westerners are mystified by such behavior and question both the values and motivations of the Japanese.

Much of life in feudal Japan was based on abiding by very strict government laws and general rules of etiquette that were life-threatening if disobeyed. It therefore became second nature for the Japanese to take a great many things seriously, whether that was sitting in the proper place and manner, eating the right way, crafting a piece of pottery, wrapping a package, greeting a customer or guest, or checking the quality of merchandise in a store.

Among the samurai, in particular, learning the skills and arts that made up the warrior's repertoire was a formidable undertaking requiring years of training initially, with constant practice thereafter. Among the lower classes, failure to achieve a certain standard of skill in some occupation was tantamount to being a social misfit and brought shame on the individual and the family.

The Japanese social system did not condone a casual, laid-back approach to life. Competition among groups drove them to strive continuously for excellence. A fierce sense of pride, fed by an equally strong fear of failure and shame, drove them on—all qualities that are still readily discernible among most of the population in present-day Japan.

One of the strongest areas of competition in Japan since the end of the feudal period in 1868 is getting into the best schools in the country. Like everything else in Japan, schools are ranked according to precise standards that are generally based on how many graduates go on to other high-ranked schools and ultimately to how many graduates go on to successful careers as top-level government officials and company executives.

So fierce was competition to get into these "fast-track" schools that it spawned a huge industry of commercially operated "cram schools" that do nothing but prep students to pass the entrance exams for the schools of their choice. It also turned millions of young Japanese wives into what was later called "education mamas" because they devoted most of their time to helping (and urging) their children to do their homework, and it created an epidemic known as *gogatsu byo* (go-gaht-suu b'yoe) or "May sickness."

Gogatsu means the month of May, which is one month after the start of the spring semester at Japanese universities, when all the freshmen who passed the examinations have had their first month of university experience. *Byo* means "illness."

Medical authorities say that the annual outbreak of *Gogatsu byo* among university students is caused by the tremendous psychological letdown they experience after having spent the previous thirteen or fourteen years of their lives obsessed with studying for one examination after the other, combined with parental pressure for them to succeed.

Students afflicted with May sickness develop a variety of symptoms. Some can't sleep; others can't eat. Many can't concentrate. Some develop severe stomach pains; others suffer from intense headaches. Some lose confidence in themselves and feel totally inadequate. Every year there are reports of suicides among first-year college students. (Some of these symptoms, says Old Japan Hand Joe Schmelzeis, may be caused by withdrawal from excessive drinking of coffee, tea and other stimulants prior to taking entrance exams.)

One of the more surprising factors about the educational system in Japan is that once students reach university there is little or no pressure on them to even attend class, much less study. Many of them float through the entire four-year experience seldom cracking a book or attending a lecture.

60

胡麻すり

Gomasuri

(Goh-mah-suu-ree)

"Flattery Makes the World Go Around"

The social system that began developing in Japan nearly two thousand years ago was based on an extraordinary degree of formality and ceremony which derived from a number of very specific sources that were to have a profound effect on every facet of life in the country.

Probably the original influence on Japan's distinctive life-style derived from religious rituals having to do with the practice of Shintoism in every household. Other key influences included Imperial Court rituals and ceremonies, primarily adapted from those found in China, and rituals associated with Buddhism and Confucianism (also brought to Japan from China), which were gradually assimilated by the population at large.

Japan's famous samurai warrior class, which usurped political power in the late 1100s and ruled the country by the sword until 1868, put the permeating coat of polish on the social etiquette that was later to amaze and impress visitors from the West.

In keeping with historical precedents that were already nearly a thousand years old, the samurai ritualized their behavior to an extreme degree, making their daily lives into roles as precise and demanding as those in the greatest dramatic plays.

The samurai gradually developed a lifestyle that called upon them to become perfectionists in everything they did. This, and the absolute power they wielded, caused them to become arrogant and demand the most obsequious and circumspect behavior from craftsmen, merchants and farmers who made up the lower classes.

For centuries it was legal for a samurai warrior to instantly kill any commoner who broke one of the more rigid rules of etiquette. (A number of foreigners fell victim to deadly samurai swords in the mid-1800s when the foreigners, out horseback riding, failed to leave the road, dismount, and bow to a passing clan lord.)

Among the samurai class, where conforming to rank and a very severe standard of protocol was even more vital than it was among commoners, the samurai had to develop great skill in speaking in circumlocutions to avoid upsetting anyone, and in using *gomasuri* (go-mah-suu-ree), literally "grinding sesame seeds"* and figuratively "flattery," to cater to the supersensitive egos of those above them.

Samurai-like behavior and the standards of etiquette set by the professional warrior class gradually seeped into the lower classes. Because the samurai enforced their standards by the sword, commoners also were forced to exercise the greatest care in speaking to the upper class, and to be equally adept at flattering them.

*Sesame seeds were traditionally ground in earthenware mortars to make flavoring for foods In the grinding process, the seeds fly in all directions, sticking to the wall of the bowl in "a cringing way "

During the last several hundred years of Japan's feudal history it was against the law for commoners to own or carry weapons or to learn any martial art which might be used to attack the samurai or defend themselves. Their only defense was obedience and their ability to use words.

Given these circumstances, the use of *gomasuri* became a fine art in Japan. Dozens of special words and phrases especially designed to flatter people came into institutionalized use. Probably the most commonly used *gomasuri* word in the Japanese language is *sensei* (sen-say-ee), which means "teacher" or "professor." It is regularly used as a title to address people who do not have academic credentials but have written a book or achieved some degree of status in some profession, from politics to art. Another commonly heard *gomasuri* word is *danna* (dahn-nah), an old term meaning "master." Japanese women, especially those in the nighttime entertainment trades, frequently use the term when they want to flatter males. Honorific affixes and prefixes attached to words and the tone of voice were also key factors in feeding the vanity of others.

Gomasuri is still very much a part of life in Japan today. It influences language usage as well as physical behavior, and is a cultural key in learning how to communicate effectively with Japanese.

61

五 人 組

Go-nin Gumi
(Go-neen Guu-me)

"How Japanese Develop New Products"

Despite massive efforts by Japan's business and scientific communities to emulate Western creative techniques, there is almost always a distinctive Japanese flavor to their efforts—and certainly in some cases this native Japanese element is a plus.

In keeping with Japanese traditions of acting as groups, most of the creative effort in Japan today remains a carefully structured process based on gradual, incremental improvements or changes that evolve out of closely coordinated group activity.

Not surprisingly, much of this incremental creativity takes place in Japan's famous Quality Circles (QC) as a natural outgrowth of ongoing attempts to continuously refine designs, rationalize engineering and simplify the manufacturing process.

The contributions that Quality Circles have made to Japan's economic prowess are recognized world-wide, but what is perhaps less well-known, and may eventually have an even more significant impact on both Japan and the world, is that the same process, motivations and synergy that made the QC concept so powerful is now applied to Creativity Circles (CC).

When it became obvious to corporate Japan and the business-related ministries of the Japanese government that the future will belong to the nations that are the most creative, it was a very short step from Quality Circles to Creativity Circles.

These new dedicated CCs generally have five members—enough to provide a variety of input but not enough to bog the circles down in dialogue and trivia—and are known as *go-nin gumi* (go neen guu-me), or "five-person groups."

Go-nin gumi retain many of the characteristics of Quality Circles. They generally focus on a specific product or potential product areas. But membership in the groups is broader-based, usually including representatives from at least four key areas—engineering, manufacturing, marketing and sales—to give the members a more comprehensive view of the challenge.

Again as in Quality Circles, the *go-nin gumi* approach to improving a product or creating a new one is incremental. When the aim is to improve an existing product, each member makes as many suggestions for refinements as possible over a period of weeks or months. Ideas that are judged to have merit are acted on.

When the flow of suggestions stop, the group steps back and takes a more creative approach. Each member is charged with the task of suggesting totally new ways of achieving the same function—to come up with innovations that would result in advanced or completely different products.

When using the *go-nin gumi* method to create new products from scratch, the first requirement is to identify a desirable function that no other product fulfills. The next step is to select a team of experts from all of the pertinent fields of knowledge and technology to make up the Creativity Circle.

The group researches the subject, then each expert makes suggestions for the technological requirements to achieve the desired function. Finally, all of the pieces are put together.

It is often observed that individually the Japanese make few creative breakthroughs, but their *go-nin gumi* approach to solving specific problems and coming up with new applications for old technology has proven to be extraordinarily advantageous.

An interesting note: the number "five" has traditionally played a key role in Japanese culture, apparently being chosen as the ideal number for spiritual and psychological harmony. All eating sets (plates, bowls) come in groups of five; the basic social unit during Japan's feudal age was five households; laws and other regulations were generally grouped in units of five.

The original five-unit concept was imported into Japan from China in the 7th century, where it had developed during the early years of the Tang Dynasty as an ideal political control unit.

62

ご祝儀取引

Go-shugi Torihiki
(Go-shuu-ghee Toe-ree-hee-kee)

"Boosting the Beginner"

One of the more colorful of the commercial traditions in Japan is the staging of grand-opening ceremonies for new neighborhood businesses. Huge floral displays (now made of plastics), with congratulatory banners, are massed in front of the stores for the first several days.

It has also been traditional for proprietors of new shops to employ groups of musicians known as *chindonya* (cheen-doan-yah) to parade around the neighborhood, playing their very distinctive music and carrying banners announcing the opening of the new businesses. But *chindonya* bands appear to be nearing extinction, and are now rarely seen.

Another tradition long associated with the opening of new neighborhood businesses is very practical. People living in the neighborhood make a point of patronizing the new business as a show of their support—a practice known as *go-shugi torihiki* (go-shuu-ghee toe-ree-hee-kee), or "honorable congratulatory business."

The practice of *go-shugi torihiki* is not limited to neighborhood shops. It long ago spread to businesses of all kinds, and continues to play a significant role in the planning and opening of all new businesses in the country.

Because *go-shugi torihiki* is a deeply entrenched custom, it is not necessary to explain the concept to potential "congratulatory" clients. But when informing larger companies of the scheduled opening of a new business, it is important that the announcement be couched in the proper protocol terms in order to avoid the impression of trying to bring undue cultural pressure on them.

Companies to which one would send announcements about a new business include a former employer, banks with which you have done business, any other company with which you have done business as a customer, and potential suppliers.

It is also customary to give congratulatory customers some kind of gift when they visit the new business, with the value of the gift being determined by the size and nature of the new enterprise. Naturally, the larger and more ambitious the enterprise, the more impressive the gift.

Probably one of the key reasons for the development of the *go-shugi torihiki* custom was the fact that during Japan's long feudal age virtually all new businesses were founded by former apprentices who had finished their training and went out on their own with the support of their families and friends—and often their former masters, who treated them more or less as franchised branches.

A recent variation of the *go-shugi torihiki* custom is the practice among many Japanese stockbrokers to deliberately run up the value of shares in their portfolio on the first business day of each New Year as a special present to their customers.

Both stock buyers and sellers are said to cooperate enthusiastically in this *go-shugi soba* (go-shuu-ghee soe-bah), or "congratulatory stocks," in a united effort to start the New Year off with a bullish boost.

The "congratulatory business" custom in Japan, in all of its forms, is another manifestation of the Japanese preference for taking a personal approach to business, whether or not the approach makes logical business sense. The custom reaffirms the metaphysical aspect of the Japanese way.

Foreign businessmen establishing new enterprises in Japan can also take advantage of the "congratulatory business" custom by making as many contacts as possible prior to opening the business—and as far in advance as possible—then advising all their contacts before the opening that their support will be appreciated. And, of course, these contacts should be companies with which they would like to do business, along with government agencies with which they must have or could use good, cooperative relationships.

———————— 63 ————————

肌に合わない

Hada ni Awanai

(Hah-dah nee Ah-wah-nie)

"Rubbing People the Wrong Way"

One of the best ways to imagine what life was like in Japan's upper classes before the introduction of democracy into the country by American-led Occupation forces in 1945/46 is to think of what it would be like to live on a stage that covered your whole world, playing a role in which everything you said and did was precisely scripted. If you did not follow your script exactly, in behavior as well as dialogue, you would be criticized for even the smallest lapse and punished for more conspicuous departures from your role. Keep in mind also that you could not walk off of the stage or change roles.

Raised from infancy in precisely this kind of society, the Japanese developed extraordinary skill in performing their scripted life-roles. Some of the knowledge and skills passed on to each succeeding generation were consciously taught; a great deal of their role-playing was unconsciously absorbed.

Because of this extreme cultural conditioning in both attitudes and behavior, the Japanese became super-sensitive to the correctness of their own actions as well as the actions of non-Japanese, and automatically measured everything and everybody by these standards.

Although the degree of cultural conditioning in "acting Japanese" has greatly diminished since 1945, enough of the conditioning factors remain in the lifestyle today—from the use of the language and bowing to dozens of other daily, routine actions—that contemporary Japanese continue to have super-thin skins.

As a result of their sensitivity, the Japanese are apt to take offense over minor things, even when no offense is intended, making it very important for everyone to follow prescribed etiquette. Becoming such skilled actors, as is required of the Japanese, also brings with it a highly developed ego. When this ego is bruised, revenge is the only cure.

Fortunately, for the most part, Japanese do not expect foreigners to abide by their role-playing rules. They know their way is very difficult and that it is a skill that results from being born and raised as a Japanese. Yet, no matter how open-minded they are, they cannot help but be rubbed the wrong way anytime they are exposed to non-Japanese behavior—even if the reaction is no more than a feeling of superiority.

When Japanese encounter people or situations that upset them they will commonly say *hada ni awanai* (hah-dah nee ah-wah-nie), or "it (they) does (do) not suit/agree with my skin." This term can be used in reference to a person whose tastes, philosophy or personality you do not like, as well as to a job that does not suit your temperament or aspirations.

Not rubbing Japanese skin the wrong way is a skill that requires considerable time and experience to develop. The best bet for foreigners who are in doubt about proper behavior is to take a page from the book of the Japanese and apologize in advance. Just as they have been conditioned to be sensitive to deviations from their norm, the Japanese have also been conditioned to readily accept apologies (that appear to be sincere), and absolve people of blame.

One of the most common examples of foreign behavior that upsets the Japanese is speaking frankly and directly. At the beginning of business or political negotiations, it is appropriate to say that you want to apologize in advance for any of your comments or manners that appear confrontational or arrogant, that you are not familiar with Japanese etiquette and are just doing your best to communicate as clearly and as fairly as possible.

64

生え抜き

Hae Nuki

(Hie Nuu-kee)

"The Virgin Syndrome"

A combination of many factors including geographic isolation, group-orientation, extraordinarily pervasive cultural homogenization and tribal instincts resulted in the Japanese becoming virtually unable to accept outsiders into their society, much less their home or workplace.

This built-in discrimination was first of all based on in-group exclusivity. If you weren't born into a group or raised in a group from a young age, you could never be fully accepted as a member, regardless of your identity as a fellow Japanese.

Another even more pervasive form of built-in discrimination was based on the Japanese perception of themselves racially and culturally. They were conditioned to discriminate on the basis of perceived differences in beliefs, speech, manners, type of work, and appearance. To be regarded as and accepted as a true Japanese you had to be born to Japanese parents in Japan, think like, talk like and look like the standard Japanese— from having totally black hair to typical Oriental facial features.

In the case of non-Japanese, discrimination was across the board. It was and is still today virtually impossible for the Japanese to accept a racially and ethnically non-Japanese as a Japanese, except in the narrowest legal sense of citizenship—a very recent and still rare phenomenon.

This built-in cultural prejudice was naturally incorporated into the business world when Japan began industrializing in the 1870s and 80s. The only fully acceptable recourse open to all the new companies that began springing up was to hire young people right out of school, bringing them into company groups at the bottom.

As time went by, both this system and the ideology behind it became stronger and more solidified. Eventually, employees who had never worked for any other company came to be known as *hae nuki* (hie nuu-kee), which is probably best translated as "purebred" and is more or less synonymous with "virgin birth."

Hae nuki members of a Japanese company look upon themselves as being both the preferred and elite, and automatically discriminate between themselves and other employees who joined the company after having worked elsewhere. In some cases this discrimination can be serious enough to disrupt the operation of the company.

Prior to the 1980s, job-hopping in Japan was rare among the larger companies because of the *hae nuki* syndrome. With the appearance of labor shortages and the growing need for highly-skilled specialists in many new high-tech fields, employers were forced to begin changing their employment practices.

A practice based on deep-rooted cultural conditioning cannot be eliminated in a few short decades, however, and the *hae nuki* mentality remains a major factor in both employment practices and in-office work management in Japan.

Foreign companies setting up operations in Japan should be aware of the *hae nuki* factor, and do whatever they can to reduce the friction that frequently develops between old employees and specialists brought in from the outside.

Just letting everyone know you are aware of the potential for problems, and that you recognize that senior employees have certain "rights," will go a long way toward minimizing the development of ill will between oldtimers and newcomers.

In addition to this employee-relations activity, it is also wise to have ongoing programs designed to help the new and old employees accept each other. Among the most effective methods of homogenizing employees of new firms is to institute training programs in which the old and new employees participate together. Frequent outside social activities, including *enkai* parties and sports events, also help break down barriers between employees.

65

ハ イ セ ン ス

Hai Sensu
(Hi Sen-suu)

"Taking Quality One Step Further"

One of the facets of Japan's traditional culture that distinguished it from most Western civilizations was an extraordinary emphasis on aestheticism. As much as a thousand years ago Japan's upper classes had raised the study and practice of a variety of aesthetic arts to the level of cults.

As the centuries passed, this pursuit of aestheticism became a central theme in daily life, gradually permeating all of the arts and utilitarian crafts that gave the Japanese lifestyle its quality and flavor.

An appreciation for refinement and sophistication was naturally absorbed by all Japanese in the process of growing up—through the language which was the main carrier of aesthetic feelings; through the utensils and furnishings used in the homes; through accessories, gift items and wrappings; and through a Shinto-derived reverence for natural beauty.

While the primary aesthetic arts for which the Japanese are best known—flower arranging, the tea ceremony, folk dancing, noh and kabuki, along with such highly stylized handicrafts as lacquerware, pottery, painting and calligraphy—continue to flourish today in segments of the population, the overall aesthetic thrust of the culture has diminished considerably.

Yet virtually all Japanese today, and particularly those born before 1960, continue to have a highly developed—and unique—sense of style and sophistication that sets them apart from other people.

Virtually all Japanese are still able to instantly recognize when a product has the qualities that fulfills their innate cultural expectations—and this makes them very discriminating shoppers.

This facet of Japan's cultural heritage is having a growing impact on the marketplace. Until well into the 1960s the Japanese carefully distinguished between Japanese-style and foreign-style products. They did not expect foreign-style products to have the same qualities of refinement and sophistication that were found in Japanese items.

But as time passed and the Japanese themselves began to design and manufacture foreign-type products (as opposed to copying things brought to Japan by foreign importers), it was natural that their cultural background would have a fundamental influence on their design concepts.

Within the span of one decade, Japanese manufacturers blanketed the world with a plethora of products that were superior in quality as well as design.

By the early 1990s, however, superior quality and design alone were no longer sufficient to meet the tastes of a growing number of Japan's more affluent consumers. They had begun to demand that whatever they bought have the same level of exquisite refinement and subtlety that had traditionally characterized Japanese arts and handicrafts.

This new consumer ethic was soon labeled *hai sensu* (hi sen-suu), or "high sense," by the new breed of designers and engineers that introduced the concept into the marketplace.

By definition, *hai sensu* refers to products that are designed and engineered to appeal to the five senses—something that is called "sensory engineering."

In actuality, for a product to be an outstanding example of Japan's new "high sense" ethic it must also incorporate and reflect a sixth sense—one that satisfies an innate spiritual need.

As it happens, Western women are generally more sensitive to the "high sense" qualities that Japanese designers and engineers now attempt to attain, and it may be that they will have to play a leading role in product creation if Western companies are to be competitive with their Japanese counterparts.

66

恥

Haji
(Hah-jee)

"Anything but Shame"

Japanese are famous for a number of things, including the fact that they are one of the few people in the world who traditionally adhered to not one but two religious philosophies—Shintoism and Buddhism.

Unlike Christianity, Islam and various other religious faiths which have violent, vindictive gods, neither of the religions of Japan were based on fear of punishment in this world or eternal damnation in the next.

Christianity in particular created irreconcilable contradictions between the body and the spirit by treating them as separate entities, resulting in a constant conflict between them. The body was of the earth and inherently evil. The spirit (soul) was divine but was damned from the beginning by an original sin inherited at birth. It could be "saved" only by obedience to the church.

In stark contrast to this inhuman concept of religion, Shintoism celebrated both the body and the spirit, with special emphasis on sensuality and fertility. Buddhism advocated controlling human instincts and passions, but was more of a personal philosophy than a despotic method of political control.

While, Christians, Muslims and others relied more on the threat of damnation and punishment by a vengeful god and powerful clergy, who were often the epitome of savage cruelty to believers and non-believers alike, the Japanese resorted to shame as their primary psychological sanction to keep people in line.

However, neither Buddhism nor Shintoism were aggressive religions that sought to force their beliefs on anyone. During most of Japan's long history their priests posed no threat of any kind.

Sin, in the Japanese scheme of things, was failing to follow proper etiquette, which went well beyond good manners to include failure to fulfill one's obligations to parents, teachers, employers, and other superiors. It had nothing to do with a threat to one's soul in the Christian sense.

Generally speaking, conforming to proper etiquette was the Japanese equivalent of being religious. The customs, festivals and rituals sponsored by Buddhism and Shintoism were seen as extensions of the traditional Japanese life-style rather than as religious observances.

When a person failed to behave according to expectations, his own highly honed sense of correct behavior and responsibility, and the knowledge that he had let other people down, brought on feelings of *haji* (hah-jee) or "shame." In extreme cases, the only way one could redeem himself was by committing suicide.

By the same token, if someone else behaved publicly in an unacceptable manner toward a Japanese, particularly if it was perceived as being the result of arrogance or selfishness, the Japanese felt shamed. The only way this *haji* could be expiated was through some kind of revenge.

Because the Japanese were exceptionally attuned and sensitive to a highly stylized form of behavior, inflicting shame or being shamed was a daily danger, and was one of the main themes of Japanese life during the long feudal era (which did not end until 1945).

So rigid and demanding was this life-style that the Japanese loved to travel in order to get away from their daily obligations and be on the road where they would be indulged as guests and could get away with all sorts of rough behavior. In fact, during this period (and sometimes now as well) Japanese travelers were known as being shameless when they were away from home.

The behavioral conditioning that was responsible for Japan's traditional etiquette has decreased dramatically since about 1960, but enough of it remains to keep the etiquette-based culture and the shame syndrome alive and flourishing.

The *haji* syndrome in Japanese culture is of special importance to foreign businessmen, politicians and diplomats. Care should be taken not to publicly criticize employees in public (even though Japanese managers frequently do it with a gusto and ferocity that is shocking to foreigners who are not familiar with the contradictions in Japanese behavior). Singling individual Japanese out for special praise in front of their co-workers often results in envy and ill-will, damaging morale and efficiency.

Japanese politicians and diplomats are gradually developing thick skins, but they do not forget or forgive insults or slights as readily as most of their Western counterparts.

羽目を外す

Hame wo Hazusu
(Hah-may oh Hah-zuu-suu)

"Make Merry or Suffer the Consequences"

Some of the most embarrassing moments of my life occurred during my early years in Japan when I was invited to attend various social events, and, from 1953 on, when I began going with my Japanese co-workers on annual recreational company trips.

On these occasions I was automatically expected to join in the drinking, singing and entertainment-type performances that are traditional in such settings.

My embarrassment was caused by the fact that I could not sing and didn't have the courage to try, could not bring myself to get up on a makeshift stage and participate in humorous skits, and was a modest drinker who did not become rowdy while drinking.

Singing in groups or solo has been a traditional custom in Japan since ancient times. Most Japanese practice singing as a routine matter and develop enough skill that they do not have to be coaxed or coerced into participating in such events. They automatically presumed that I would do the same, and couldn't understand why I refused even to try.

The development of acting ability in Japan is even more basic. Life in Japan, in all of its fundamentals, has traditionally been pure role-playing, requiring extraordinary acting skill. Everyone was (and still is to a considerable degree) "on stage" at all times.

With this kind of cultural conditioning from babyhood, the Japanese generally are not inhibited about performing some kind of dance or acting routine in public as long as it involves something that is "Japanese."

The reason I did not measure up to Japanese expectations in drinking was that I could not make myself "forget etiquette" and behave in an uninhibited, drunken or licentious manner the way the Japanese typically do.

Drinking has traditionally been the one socially acceptable excuse for temporarily abandoning the very strict etiquette that characterizes normal Japanese behavior.

Japanese etiquette was so constraining that it was virtually impossible to communicate clearly and candidly or to reveal one's true feelings or emotions about anything during regular conversations. It therefore became necessary for them to create a special time when they could *hame wo hazusu* (hah-may oh hah-zuu-suu), or "remove the bit" (from the horse's mouth).

Figuratively, without a bit in the mouth one was able to behave freely, to say whatever came to mind and, like a horse turned loose, run around, frolic or what-have-you in a totally unrestrained manner.

Just as the Japanese are conditioned to follow the prescribed patterns of behavior on most non-drinking occasions, when drinking they expect everyone to behave freely, that is express themselves honestly and fully and engage in horseplay and so on.

There is a very strong feeling in Japan that you cannot truly get to know another person until they are drunk, or have drunk enough to forget etiquette, because it is assumed that people never reveal their true character while sober.

I recall, vividly, one of my Japanese girl friends studying me with a puzzled look on her face and saying, "I would really like to see you get drunk!"

But as might be expected, there are rules for drunken behavior in Japan, and one still must know how, when and to what degree to display honest, frank and rough behavior. You still have to know the feelings and be able to predict the reaction of anyone you complain to, and being too honest or too frank with someone who does not share your feelings can be held against you. It is all right to push, pull, fall on or lay on somebody in a non-threatening manner when you are drinking, but genuine violence of any kind is not tolerated.

判子

Hanko

(Hahn-koe)

"Putting Your Stamp on Things"

The Japanese system of writing, based on several thousand complicated ideograms borrowed from Chinese between A.D. 300 and 600, had a far greater influence on the culture of Japan than most other writing systems, particularly those that developed in the West, had on their respective countries of origin.

Because of their complexity and number, the ideograms required several years of intense study and practice to master—making the effort one of the primary crucibles in the development of Japanese abilities and character.

Years of daily practice in drawing the ideograms according to absolutely precise guidelines instilled in the Japanese a high level of diligence, determination and manual dexterity, along with an equally elevated level of appreciation for form, order and beauty.

These traits were passed down from one generation to the next, and played a significant role in Japan's emergence as a leading economic power during the 1960s and 70s. While the number of ideograms the Japanese have to learn now has been reduced to 1,850 (approximately half of what was generally regarded as sufficient during the long feudal age), the system continues to influence both the character and personality of the Japanese—not always for the best.

Use of the compact ideograms, which lent themselves to printing, led the Japanese to develop carved name seals called *hanko* (hahn-koe) that were used in lieu of signatures.

Hanko is more or less the generic term for name seal. One's own personal seal is usually referred to as *mitome-in* (me-toe-may-een). An official seal that has been registered and is used by companies and by individuals to sign contractual documents is called a *jitsu-in* (jeet-sue-een).

There are a number of standard "type" styles used in the making of *hanko*, which means that people with the same names might have identical seals if they inadvertently selected the same lettering. This happened frequently in the past, resulting in the personalizing of type styles for individuals, followed by their registration with the local government.

Because a registered *hanko* is an official signature, it can be used by anyone who happens to have it—meaning that a person can use someone else's *jitsu-in* to sign a contract, borrow money, sell a house, and so on. Naturally, this means that once a seal is registered it must be kept out of the hands of unauthorized individuals.

Some foreigners residing in Japan purchase order-made seals for themselves, sometimes just as unusual collector's items, but sometimes to use for banking purposes and other occasions. A few have their seals registered for use in business.

Having a registered *hanko* is fine if one is willing to take the chance that it might be misused by someone else. Foreigners are generally not expected to have official seals, but I was asked last year by a publisher if I had one (to sign a book contract).

More internationally-oriented companies and individual Japanese began signing instead of stamping some official documents in the 1970s, and the trend to replace *hanko* with signatures is continuing. But in the typical company today, proposals and contracts require the registered seal of an authorized individual in order to be legally binding.

Paintings are generally "stamped" with the artists' *hanko*, as are the works of master ceramicists. The owners of paintings also sometimes affix their seal to the works for identification purposes.

As a historical footnote, in former times the Japanese believed that the lettering style and condition of a name seal could influence one's fate. One example: the broken border of the seal belonging to Hideyoshi Toyotomi (1537–1598), one of the country's most famous warlords, was believed to have foretold his early demise.

─────────────── 69 ───────────────

反 省

Hansei

(Hahn-say-ee)

"Just Don't Get Caught!"

One of the causes of friction between the East and the West is so basic that it goes right to the heart of human conduct, and dramatically illustrates the myriad ways different groups of human beings have created their worlds.

In very broad and general terms, Westerners opted for guidelines based on absolute principles derived from universal concepts, with right and wrong behavior clearly spelled out. In theory at least, the obligation to live by these principles applied to everyone, regardless of how humble or exalted their position might be.

Within this system, being able to distinguish between right and wrong was a relatively simple matter. Every action was supposed to be considered on its own merits, and thus justice could be applied equally to everyone regardless of their economic or social status.

In Japan and much of the rest of Asia, however, the guidelines for human conduct were based on circumstances; on rules or laws established by those in power, and designed by them to sustain and extend their power. Under this system, individuals were not protected by absolute principles. Their lives and their fortunes were in the hands of changeable circumstances, as these circumstances were created by those in authority.

The foundation for behavior in Japan was traditionally a long list of personal obligations to the family, the group, the community, the clan, and ultimately the national government. In order to know what was right, individuals had to know what was expected and what would be approved, not only by their superiors but by their peers as well; something, again, that could change with circumstances.

Within this social context, Japanese behavior was primarily controlled by shame incurred by not fulfilling an obligation—a situation that often left people subject to being misused and abused by those in power and in a position to impose their authority arbitrarily.

Circumstantial ethics also meant that anything you could get by with was all right, and did not leave a sense of guilt.

Under this system, the overruling obligation was the appearance of doing the "right" thing; not actually doing it. Form took precedence over content, and what you saw or heard was often a facade instead of reality.

Morality in the Japanese context became something like a show. The primary concern was not to get caught in doing something that would be criticized or for which you might be punished. Doing something "wrong" was no big deal because there was no sense of guilt.

One of the manifestations of this kind of morality is the practice of foregoing completely or greatly reducing the punishment for crimes when the accused performs *hansei* (hahn-say-ee), admits guilt and expresses regret.

Hansei means to reflect on one's failings or misdeeds, with the idea that this self-reflection will cleanse the individual and result in self-rehabilitation. The individual absolves himself or herself of responsibility for any misbehavior.

The Japanese public, the news media and politicians are constantly calling on others—most often politicians—to perform *hansei*, self-reflect, give up their evil ways and fly right. Individuals who drink too much or do other things that are harmful to themselves or others often make resolutions that they are going to *hansei.*

Hansei is especially important in Japan because it helps make up for a lack of universally applied principles in personal behavior.

腹芸

Hara Gei
(Hah-rah Gay-ee)

"Managing with the Belly"

Westerners are familiar with the idea that intuition often plays a role in behavior, particularly in how we make quick judgements about people whether or not they are wrong. It is not uncommon for some Westerners to claim that their intuition is never wrong. But the use of intuition, or "gut feelings," in determining behavior has never been recognized in the West as a valid or reliable method of decision-making.

In Japan, on the other hand, there has traditionally been widespread belief that the use of "gut feelings" as a guide, and often times the final arbiter in making decisions in business as well as in private life, was both valid and reliable. Those who relied on their stomachs instead of their heads were generally admired and sometimes glorified.

The Japanese called this method of evaluating other people and situations *hara gei* (hah-rah gay-ee) or "art of the stomach."

The use of *hara gei* in Japan was a natural outgrowth of a minutely structured, carefully controlled society in which behavior was prescribed down to the most mundane actions. There were seldom any surprises. Both Japanese attitudes and behavior were controlled to the point that every action was almost always predictable.

Part of this concept derived from the ancient belief that the stomach was the seat of the life force—or *ki* (kee) in martial arts terms. The first rule of all of Japan's martial as well as fine arts is to "center" one's self in the *hara* and thereafter allow the center to control all actions. In feudal Japan this applied as much to Japan's great garden designers and tea masters as it did to samurai warriors. [It is also why the samurai custom of ritualized suicide through *hara-kiri* (hah-rah-kee-ree) or "stomach-cutting" was such a symbolic act.]

Japanese businessmen, as well as military and government leaders, traditionally used *hara gei* in their dealings with other people. They couldn't help it. The action was involuntary. Some used it more than others, and a few prided themselves in making all of their commitments on the basis of their intuitive judgement of the other party.

Hara gei is still a common practice among older Japanese businessmen, but it is gradually losing its validity and importance as traditional patterns of thought and behavior break down, and more and more Japanese behave in un-Japanese ways.

One of the reasons why most Japanese businessmen are generally ill-at-ease in dealing with foreigners is that they are extremely conscious of being on a totally different cultural wavelength, and have no confidence at all in being able to read the "stomachs" of foreigners.

Western businessmen also, of course, depend on their intuition to help guide them in their dealings with other people, including the Japanese, but this can be very dangerous, particularly where the Japanese are concerned, because Westerners tend to be less sensitive to cultural differences and are very likely to misinterpret the signals sent by their Japanese counterparts.

It is very common for foreign businessmen to make vital judgements about both the character and ability of the Japanese on the basis of their skill in speaking English. This gut reaction may be wrong as often as it is right, because (1) the process of learning English generally brings on changes in the personality and behavior of the Japanese that may handicap them in their dealings with other Japanese; and (2) learning English well is so difficult and time-consuming it is sometimes the only skill they have.

71

腹を見せる

Hara wo Miseru
(Hah-rah oh Me-say-ruu)

"Showing Your Stomach"

If a Japanese business associate or acquaintance says, "*Hara wo mise-masu*" (Hah-rah oh me-say-mahss), or "I will show you my stomach," he is not offering to drop his pants and put that portion of his body on display, as the comment suggests to the uninitiated.

Asians have historically believed that the stomach was one of the primary seats of power in the human body, with the result that it has played a variety of roles in the psychological profile of the people, in art, in religious practices, even in clothing.

Japanese in particular associated the stomach with the mind, with courage, spirit, intuition, determination, ability and various other attributes that the Western world generally ascribed to the head or the heart.

Interestingly, virtually all of these references to the stomach related to men, and not to women, perhaps because they involved characteristics and behavior that were regarded as masculine. In committing suicide, for example, women were expected to cut the carotid vein in their throat, rather than perform the self-disembowelment expected of men.

Hara wo miseru (hah-rah oh me-say-ruu) refers to fully revealing one's thoughts (and thus exposing one's self) to the other person, for better or worse. The fact that the *hara* is used in this manner indicates the gravity of a decision.

Having a heart-to-heart talk is frequently referred to as *hara wo watte hanasu* (hah-rah oh watt-tay hah-nah-suu) or "cut open the stomach and talk." In other words, such talk involves holding nothing back—a rare kind of conversation between two people that is generally reserved for top-level executives or military leaders when the topic is of grave importance.

When something goes wrong and a person has no choice but to put up with the situation, *hara wo kukuru* (hah-rah oh kuu-kuu-ruu), or "bundling up the stomach," expresses one's determination to live with it. The English equivalent is "girding up one's loins."

Foreigners should be cautious about attempting to put a conversation or negotiation with Japanese on the stomach level until they have developed a fairly strong relationship. The exception to this rule would be if the foreigner is a "Big Man"—that is, someone on a high level whose character and accomplishments are known to and highly esteemed by the Japanese.

Age and experience are key factors in using the belly in business and personal relationships. Younger people (say below 50) would not ordinarily be credited with enough experience or ability to rely on their stomachs for guidance.

It might therefore be taken as presumptuous for people in their thirties or early forties to suggest "stomach" relationships with businessmen or others who are significantly older than they are. It would not be out of order, however, to inform the other person that he kindled a good feeling in your stomach.

One thing to avoid in Japan is getting the reputation of being a *hara guroi* (hah-rah guu-roy) person—meaning someone whose "stomach is black," and used to describe a person who is treacherous and cannot be trusted.

梯子を外される

Hashigo wo Hazusareru
(Hah-she-go oh Hah-zuu-sah-ray-ruu)

"Left Hanging in the Breeze"

One of my Japanese businessmen friends, who was regarded as a comer in his company (a multi-billion-dollar-a-year manufacturing concern), was sent overseas as manager of a foreign branch. He spent some ten years abroad, during which time he vastly expanded the company's business and became known as one of the most creative and progressive managers in the firm.

During his ten-year sojourn abroad my friend became noticeably Westernized in his way of thinking and acting. Of greater importance to his company colleagues when he returned to Tokyo, however, was that this metamorphosis had naturally entailed the loss of a certain amount of Japaneseness.

Having been abroad for so long and having gained valuable international experience that was of special benefit to his firm at that time, my friend assumed that he would move up in management and be able to make major contributions because of his experience.

But that was not to be the case at all. Despite having powerful allies on the executive level in the company, my friend's tendency to express opinions and make suggestions and proposals based on his foreign experience did not set right with other division managers who saw him as a threat to the closed-in group system that guaranteed their own survival regardless of their ability or contribution.

These managers automatically assumed the role of a cabal whose primary purpose was to neutralize my friend. They did not have to come together to plot their moves and coordinate their efforts. These actions came naturally to each of them in the consensus-building process within the company.

When the senior executives in the company became aware of this situation they took the only step that was really open to them. They promoted my friend to general manager of a new department, but gave him no staff and no authority—a step known as *hashigo wo hazusareru* (hah-she-go oh hah-zuu-sah-ray-ruu), or "removing the stepladder."

Hashigo wo hazusareru is ordinarily used when a company wants to sidetrack a manager whose seniority makes him eligible for promotion, but who, for one reason or another, is regarded as incapable or less qualified than other, more deserving candidates.

In this context, "removing the ladder" from beneath one's feet is not regarded as malicious or unfair, but rather is seen as a way to give the individual a higher post, which means more pay and ostensibly more prestige, while not disadvantaging the company.

On other occasions, however, as with my friend, the system is used to ostracize someone who may be so qualified he makes everyone else look bad. Or he may be too individualistic, or have other qualities that put him out of step with the rest of the well-drilled cadre.

My friend ended his career with this company spending most of his days reading newspapers and magazines, while trying unsuccessfully for a new assignment abroad. He finally chose to be reassigned to a small subsidiary of the parent company where he was able to use some of his talents and energy.

Individuals who have been left dangling are fairly common in larger Japanese companies. If a foreign businessman is introduced to someone who has an impressive title but no staff, it would be wise to discreetly inquire about his standing in the firm. Such inquiries can be directed to close friends or contacts of the individual in other companies, who would most likely be aware of his situation and not be afraid to talk about it. The same insight can also be obtained from the individual's co-workers, but must be handled with considerably more finesse in order to avoid any kind of negative backlash. And, of course, some diplomatic detective work is necessary for either approach.

梯 子 酒

Hashigo Zake
(Hah-she-go Zah-kay)

"Loosening Taboos and Nurturing Ties"

First-time visitors to Japan are always asking old-timers what they should do to really enjoy the flavor of the country, to experience some of the special ambience of the Japanese life-style that goes beyond the tea ceremony and flower-arranging.

One thing I always advise is for newcomers to spend one or more evenings in a popular entertainment district, such as the Ginza in Tokyo, Gion-machi in Kyoto and Shinsaibashi in Osaka, strolling the back-streets and lanes and observing the Japanese at leisure.

In addition to seeing some of the most beautiful women in the country (who work as hostesses in the cabarets and lounges and can be seen going to their places of work between six and seven p.m. and leaving them between 11 and 12 p.m.), visitors will also see tipsied businessmen, always in groups and often with arms linked, making their way noisily from one bar to another.

What our usually amused and sometimes frightened visitors are witnessing is the nightly re-enactment of an institutionalized custom that makes up a vital aspect of Japan's business world—the ritualized drinking and communing after work by businessmen in the country's thousands of entertainment districts.

This group movement from bar to bar (or cabaret to cabaret) is known as *hashigo zake* (hah-she-go zah-kay) or "ladder sake"—one possible connotation being that with each additional drinking spot the revelers get higher and higher. This practice is also known as *hashigo nomi* (hah-she-go no-me), literally "ladder drinking."

To Japan's mighty army of managers and office workers, *hashigo zake* is a socially sanctioned way for them to unwind and communicate with each other after a strenuous day of conforming to an etiquette so strict that it does not allow for complete exchanges of feelings and opinions during the regular workday.

It is customary for managers to regularly invite their own staff members out for *hashigo zake* evenings in order to get to know them better and to reinforce their ties to the group and the company. One of the reasons this is so important is that the Japanese typically do not engage in idle get-acquainted-type of bonding conversations at work.

Managers also regularly invite clients and prospective customers out for drinking marathons. Virtually every foreign businessman who goes to Japan is invited out on the town two, three or more times during every visit, and those who are in-the-know generally reciprocate by taking their Japanese hosts out once or twice—usually to dinner with drinks, as opposed to bar-hopping.

Again, the importance of this custom lies in fact that it is the traditional Japanese way of developing personal relationships, which in turn govern most business decisions. It is possible that a business deal can be arranged with a Japanese company without several *hashigo nomi* sessions, but it is not likely.

Sales companies are among the biggest users of the "ladder drinking" system, using it not only to get personally acquainted with potential customers, but also insidiously to build up strong feelings of obligation so that their targets will eventually feel compelled to give them some business.

A Japanese manager who repeatedly refuses invitations to go out on the town drinking is usually signalling that he has no intention of doing business with the would-be host and does not want to get caught up in the cycle of obligations that are so common in Japan.

変化させる

Henka Saseru

(Hane-kah Sah-say-ruu)

"Getting More for Your Money"

Unlike many ancient societies that have not been able to take full advantage of modern-day knowledge and technology because of their cultural heritage, the Japanese have found that much of their inherited wisdom and many of their traditional ways are applicable to present-day challenges, and provide them with a variety of special advantages.

These culturally transmitted advantages include a highly developed aesthetic sense, a built-in desire for precise, refined forms and processes, exceptional manual skill in accomplishing detailed tasks, and the ability to work together as teams.

One of the more interesting concepts from Japan's past that is imminently recyclable is the idea of conserving materials, space, time and cost through utilizing space and materials for more than one function.

The most conspicuous historical example of this factor is the design of the traditional Japanese home, with its movable and removable interior walls, floors, and furniture. In no more than two or three minutes a room can be changed from a living room to a dining room to a bedroom, and back again.

Adjoining rooms can be converted in seconds to a single larger room simply by removing the interior wall panels. The floors, which consist of uniformly sized *tatami* (tah-tah-me), or reed-mats in wooden frames, can also be changed in a matter of minutes.

In contemporary times the concept of designing things that can be almost instantly transformed into other things first proved a boon to Japan's toy manufacturers, then to film makers who produce animated cartoons for children.

Toy makers came up with a variety of immensely popular robots, trucks, tanks and other things that could be transformed (*henka saseru*/hane-kah sah-say-ruu) from one thing to another in a few movements. Cartoonists created vehicles, tools and characters that could merge to form giants to battle huge enemies or metamorphose into warplanes for air combat.

In the 1980s, Japanese auto makers began experimenting with modular cars that make it possible for owners to change the basic style of the vehicles by removing and replacing body panels. Construction companies began erecting modular buildings that can be easily and quickly added to, reduced in size, taken apart, re-assembled in a different style, or moved to a new location.

The latest and perhaps ultimate use of the concept of combining functions is in merging video, telecommunications and computers to create a variety of futuristic products that are now rapidly changing the way people live and work. These combined technologies include pocket computers, electronic dictionaries, and wristwatch videophones.

Another multiple-technology product in which the Japanese are world leaders are holophones, videophones that include holographically projected, three-dimensional, full-color images of the speakers—right out of *Star Trek*. Once holophones and holo-conferencing systems are widely available, the need for most business travel—and a lot of personal travel as well—will simply vanish.

The Japanese are also hard at work improving computerized translator-phones, which eventually will be able to provide instant voice translations for virtually any language, thereby eliminating the communication gaps that now divide and hinder the people of the world.

There is every reason to believe that the traditional *henka saseru* talents of the Japanese will continue to provide them with special advantages in combining technology to create as yet unimagined products.

肘掛け椅子

Hijikake Isu
(He-jee-kah-kay Ee-suu)

"Chair-Reading vs. Face-Reading"

Between A.D. 400 and 600 Japan borrowed copiously from the culture of China, including the Chinese system of writing, architecture, arts, crafts, city planning, various aesthetic pursuits, and many aspects of the Chinese imperial court system.

One aspect of the Chinese imperial court that especially attracted the Japanese was the system of ranking ministers, other court officials and the members of the aristocracy.

In the Chinese system, rank and position were designated by hairstyles, hats and apparel, and by where the individuals sat during meetings and ceremonies. Differently colored and shaped hats denoted different ranks among court officials.

Seating was one of the key means of distinguishing between the various ranks. The higher ranking the individual, the higher the elevation of the seat, with the emperor himself occupying the top spot. Whether one sat on the left or right of the emperor (or the ranking official) was also of importance.

Distance from the main dais was also another factor in the seating of individuals according to rank, with those of higher rank nearest the seat of power.

The Japanese incorporated much of the Chinese system into their own, with one of the main differences being the scale of the meeting halls and plazas. Those in China's imperial capital were immense. The main plaza could accommodate as many as 100,000 retainers and troops, all arranged in precise rows and blocks.

Interior meeting halls and outdoor plazas in Japan were much more modest in size. The largest halls would accommodate a few hundred individuals, and the largest castle plazas perhaps double that. The Japanese simply did not go in for huge, mass meetings.

Seating is still an important part of the hierarchical structure of Japanese society, in private as well as in public settings. In every home and office there is a seat of honor, reserved for the senior individual present or a guest.

Every meeting place that has seats is always automatically set up so that it conforms to a hierarchical division of those present. The Japanese are very sensitive to these gradations, and just as automatically seat themselves in the areas that are proper for their rank and the occasion.

At meetings involving foreigners who are not familiar with the Japanese system of seating, the Japanese hosts carefully and firmly guide them to the seats deemed proper—sometimes forcefully propelling them to the designated place.

In many Japanese offices it is possible to judge the rank of an individual by the type of chair he sits in. Managers have *hijikake isu* (he-jee-kah-kay ee-suu) or "chairs with arm-rests," while others do not.

The higher-ranking the individual, the larger and more comfortable his or her *hijikake isu* tends to be. And, of course, the larger the chair, the larger the desk has to be to accommodate it.

Directors and those higher up generally have arm-chairs that are upholstered in leather or some similar material and have high back-rests. These chairs are obviously not for working in but for sitting back and thinking.

Since most Japanese managers and their staffs share single, large, very crowded rooms, being able to spot the *hijikake isu* is one good way for newcomers to distinguish managers from staff workers.

76

一人相撲

Hitori Zumo
(Hee-toe-ree Zuu-moe)

"Fighting a Battle You Can't Win"

Sumo, or Japanese-style wrestling, could no doubt be described as the national sport of Japan. It began long before recorded history as a Shinto ritual, and for several centuries remained associated with shrines as a form of divination used to predict the outcome of harvests and invoke the goodwill of the gods.

As time passed, sumo became more and more popular as a spectator sport and less of a religious event. Sponsors began to stage bouts at the imperial court for the benefit of the emperor. At one time during this early age, some fights were to the death.

Following the founding of the shogunate type of government in 1192, subsequent shoguns became patrons of the sport, each maintaining his own stable of wrestlers. Some provincial lords also sponsored sumo teams, much like boxing gyms of today.

Bouts were sometimes arranged between the wrestlers of different provinces, but during most of the long feudal period, sumo remained a kind of private sport that depended upon the patronage of individual lords.

It was not until the beginning of the modern era that sumo became a nationally organized sport, operating on a commercial basis under the auspices of a sumo association. Today it flourishes on an unprecedented scale.

Sumo wrestlers are divided into what might be called a minor league and a major league. Tournaments are held six times a year, and each lasts for fifteen days. Each wrestler fights fifteen opponents in elimination matches.

The wrestler with the least number of losses is the winner of the tournament. In both leagues, each wrestler must take on all comers, regardless of their rank, weight or any other advantage they may have. Thus the lowest-ranking wrestlers are also matched against the highest-ranking champions.

No handicaps are given. The 250-pound novice must take his chances against the 350- or 400-pound champion. This regularly results in younger and smaller wrestlers being over-matched, but constant struggles against superior wrestlers is part of their training.

In keeping with a penchant for symbolism, Japan's business world has adopted the sumo saying *hitori zumo* (hee-toe-ree zuu-moe), or "one-man sumo match," which refers to a small, out-classed wrestler who is taking on a much bigger and stronger opponent, and might as well be wrestling by himself.

In its business context, *hitori zumo* refers to an individual who has taken on a task that he can't possibly achieve on his own, and who can't get anyone to help him because they don't approve of the project, don't like him, or have some other reason for staying out of it.

The *hitori zumo* typically perseveres heroically and often tragically to the bitter end, usually without any sympathy at all from his co-workers on the sidelines, who are more likely to regard him as a fool for not realizing he cannot succeed without their cooperation.

The lesson in this for foreign businessmen is that it is virtually impossible for an individual in a Japanese company, even the president, to run a one-man show; to push through projects that he wants but that the majority of managers do not support.

About the only exceptions to this rule are company owners who are the founders of their firm, still own them, are exceptionally strong-willed, have always done things their way, and primarily employ yes-men who accept their way of doing things.

Put another way, foreign businessmen wanting to deal with most Japanese companies should not base their chances for success on a *hitori zumo*.

保 証 人

Hoshonin

(Hoe-show-neen)

"Your Word Is Not Good Enough!"

Japanese society has traditionally been divided into exclusive groups that were also inclusive. You could not get into a group without either being born into it or joining it at the bottom through a primary passage ritual early in life. Each group also felt compelled to be totally self-sufficient to ensure survival and enhance its possibilities of success.

This compulsion for exclusivity as well as inclusivity led the Japanese to regard all non-group members as either competitors or enemies, and was to have a profound effect on virtually every facet of Japanese society—from how they regarded and treated other Japanese and non-Japanese to how they organized and managed their businesses.

In the business world, in particular, the Japanese penchant for groupism impacts not only on the lives of the Japanese but on the people of other countries as well. The ultimate goal of every company is to be as self-sufficient as possible—to have a vertically-integrated operation that covers as many fields as possible from top to bottom.

This impulse is responsible for the great pre-1945 *zaibatsu* (zie-baht-sue) combines, and for all of the huge groups (Mitsui, Mitsubishi, Sumitomo, Toshiba, Toyota, etc.) that sit astride the world today. Foreign businessmen dealing with Japan soon become aware that each of these great groupings is very much like a sovereign nation within itself.

Japan's grouping syndrome impacts on every level of life in the country, in both personal and business matters. Trust and loyalty are primarily reserved for members of one's own group. Whenever possible, members associate and do business only with members of their own group.

It is a relatively easy matter for one Sumitomo company to do business with another Sumitomo company, but even then an introduction is required. In contrast, it has traditionally ranged from difficult to impossible for a Sumitomo company to do business with a member of the Mitsui group—a situation that began changing in the early 1990s.

Establishing a working relationship between two unrelated companies becomes an exercise in drawn-out diplomacy and negotiations that generally involve building personal bridges slowly and carefully, and gradually breaking down the barriers that separate Japanese companies.

On a personal level in Japan, individuals are often not fully recognized as independent entities who are responsible for their own obligations. Earlier in Japanese history, the individual hardly existed. One identified one's self only in relation to a clan, a family, a company or a shop. One either belonged to a group or was a nobody.

To help overcome the disadvantageous aspects of this deeply imbedded social factor, the Japanese developed the institution of the *hoshonin* (hoe-show-neen) or guarantor. Under this system, people who were willing to be held responsible for the actions of a second party, and, of course, the more prominent they were the better, could become guarantors. Generally these guarantees were in the form of signed documents and were therefore enforceable under the law.

In Japan today there are many situations where *hoshonin* are required, regardless of the position, character, or financial ability of the individual concerned. Some of these situations include when one party is buying something on credit, renting a house or apartment, applying for visas or memberships in various organizations, etc.

Foreigners are more apt than Japanese to run into situations where guarantors are needed because foreigners generally do not belong to any recognized Japanese group and would not be acceptable even if they did because Japanese society is so exclusive that outsiders are never integrated, and are considered temporary residents or visitors at most.

Most foreigners requiring official *hoshonin* depend upon employers, the schools they want to attend, Japanese friends, or contacts they make for that specific purpose—the latter usually being people to whom they have been able to obtain introductions.

78

いじめ

Iijime

(Ee-jee-may)

"Hitting People Who Stand Out"

One of the best-known of all Japanese proverbs is "the nail that sticks up will be pounded down." The reference is that anyone who thinks and behaves in any way different from the historically sanctified Japanese norm will be beaten into conformity.

The hallmark of Japan's traditional culture was near absolute conformity in all things as was humanly possible—including not only attitudes and behavior but appearance as well. Variations that existed, and were sanctioned, were based on differences in class, rank, sex, and age—not on inherent individual character, preferences, or experience.

The motivation behind this cultural imperative was order and harmony, which was inspired not only by political considerations but also by a deeply ingrained spiritual element that typically characterizes ancient tribal-type societies.

Homogenization of the Japanese eventually took on the tone and nature of a religion, with its own sacraments. Conformity was not left to chance. Every individual was deliberately conditioned—physically, intellectually and spiritually—in the attitudes and manners that were established for his or her position and role in life.

This process of mental and spiritual homogenization was accomplished within the context of a meticulously detailed system of physical etiquette that made one's morality visible for others to see. The demand for conformity to the Japanese Way was therefore not just intellectual; it was physical as well.

Because the Japanese were isolated from other people during most of their history, and were ruled for nearly a thousand years by successive military dictatorships that were based on enforcing both political and cultural conformity, they developed an extreme sensitivity to any variation in the Japanese Way.

Any attitude, behavior or appearance that varied even to a minor degree from what they were used to—and automatically expected—was regarded as anti-social and un-Japanese. People guilty of such infractions were invariably punished in some way, ranging from criticism to banishment, or worse.

Japanese history since the end of their feudal era in 1868 is filled with innumerable incidents of serious discrimination against people who looked or behaved in any way different from the traditional Japanese mold, and discrimination remains a serious problem despite the cultural metamorphosis the country has undergone in the meantime.

Much of the prejudicial behavior in present-day Japan comes under the heading of *iijime* (ee-jee-may), or "bullying," and is directed against elementary and high school-age Japanese who have spent time abroad with their parents, been influenced by foreign attitudes and absorbed some non-Japanese mannerisms.

The bullying of these "tainted" young students by "pure" Japanese is so serious that some have committed suicide. Many give up in their attempts to reintegrate into Japanese schools and go back overseas. Others attend special segregated schools built to protect them from such harassment.

Not all of the bullying is done by other students. Complaints against teachers are also common. In schools whose *iijime* against returned students is especially serious, one or more teachers is generally responsible for setting the mood that encourages such behavior.

Given the depth and power of Japanese culture, it will probably be well into the 21st century before the problem of *iijime* disappears.

79

生 き 甲 斐

Iki Gai

(Ee-kee Guy)

"The Joy of Living"

The right to be happy, to deliberately pursue happiness, is a relatively new concept in Japan. Throughout the ages, the only recognized obligation of the Japanese was to serve their families, their communities and their political overlords.

On a personal basis, the primary obligation of the Japanese was to conform to the prevailing etiquette system and obey all of the strict customs and laws of the land—in other words, to stay out of trouble.

About the only early Japanese who were able to deliberately seek happiness as a life-style—in their personal relationships, their hobbies and their recreation—were the leisured families of the Court nobles and ministers in Kyoto's imperial capital, and this was mostly confined to the children and the female members of the families.

Most of the traditional games and aesthetic pursuits associated with imperial and feudal Japan, from poetry-writing, kite-flying and incense-smelling to shuttlecock, originated at the imperial court in Kyoto. They fairly quickly spread to the courts of the provincial clan lords, but it was well into the Tokugawa dynasty in the 1600s before such activities became common among the more affluent townspeople.

That is not to say many Japanese in olden times did not enjoy their lives. They did, but most of those who achieved happiness did so as a result of their success in accomplishing practical things in the arts, crafts, and other professions—not in purely recreational pursuits.

Those who were fortunate enough to live worthwhile lives and be satisfied and happy with what they had achieved referred to whatever it was that made them happy as their *iki gai* (ee-kee guy), or "joy of living."

For older people, an *iki gai* could also be especially accomplished sons or daughters, or, more likely, favorite grandsons to whom they could devote their remaining years.

It was not until the 1960s that Japan became affluent enough for large numbers of ordinary people to begin making choices about their lifestyles, to deliberately choose occupations that made them happy, to develop hobbies and engage in a variety of recreational activities.

But still today most Japanese, particularly adult males, are consumed by their work and either have no *iki gai* or for one reason or another are unable to enjoy either their leisure time or the happiness-producing opportunities that are available to them.

When standing alone or used as the first word in compound phrases, *gai*, pronounced *kai* (kie) for phonetic ease, means "worthwhile, useful, effective." *Kai-sho* (kie-show) is used to describe a person, usually a superior, who is very good at his job. *Kai-sho-nashi* (kie-show-nah-she) means just the opposite.

Japanese men who spend virtually all of their time working, drinking with their office colleagues after-hours and otherwise wasting their lives are often described (usually by their wives) as *kaisho-nashi* (kie-show-nah-she) or "worthless." The same term is also used to describe businessmen whose behavior results in their companies going bankrupt.

Another version of the concept is *kaigai-shii* (kie-guy-she-ee), which refers to a person who is full of life and energy and goes about both work and play in high spirits.

By the mid-1980s, the desire for *iki gai* had become one of the primary forces motivating Japan's younger generations. Its impact on the marketplace resulted in the creation of new industries and greatly enhanced the popularity of imported casual and sports apparel, especially from the U.S.

In fact, it is American-style *iki gai* that most attracts today's Japanese.

80

粋 おしゃれ

Iki / Oshare
(Ee-kee / Oh-shah-ray)

"Keeping Up with the Suzukis"

The Japanese are probably the best-dressed people in the world. They spend more money and more time on their appearance than any other people—and it shows. Their concern for wearing apparel and accessories verges on obsession, and has fueled one of the richest clothing markets in the world.

As always, the Japanese owe their fashion sense and their compulsion for dressing in style to cultural factors that, in this case, included a heavy overlay of political expediency during the long Tokugawa shogunate (1603-1868).

Early in the Tokugawa period the shogunate reconfirmed the old division of Japanese society into four classes—the ruling samurai class, merchants, artisans and farmers—and added more controls to enforce the divisions.

As part of this control system, the shogunate established more precise guidelines for the type of clothing each of the classes could wear as a further means of keeping them separate. Later, the government went as far as setting the dates on which people changed from winter to summer wear and from summer to winter clothing.

In addition to government regulations controlling the dress of the people, each of the some 270 feudal clans had their own crests, worn on the backs and/or sleeves of their outer clothing, to clearly distinguish themselves from other clans. Businesses also had company and employee-uniform logos.

Within the approved types of clothing, there were colors and designs that were worn only by men and others that were worn only by women. There were also colors and motifs that were related to age.

Thus it was generally possible to visually determine the class, clan and rank or occupation (sometimes the actual place of employment) of people by their clothing. In the case of young females, clothing and hair style could also indicate whether or not they were married.

Because of Japan's comprehensive and rigidly enforced etiquette system, these visual signs of class and rank were of vital importance in determining social and official positions quickly in order to avoid using the wrong etiquette toward a higher- or lower-class person.

The Japanese thus became extraordinarily sensitive to wearing apparel because being able to recognize the various classes and ranks, and abide by the dress code, was a matter of political and economic survival.

But as the Tokugawa period matured, affluent merchants and their families began wearing rich under-robes beneath their kimono and sporting expensive accessories as a means of getting around the clothing restrictions. Among this group, *iki* (ee-kee), or refined taste and stylishness, took on added meaning.

It was not until the beginnings of a mass-consumer market in Japan in the 1950s, however, that the style-consciousness of the Japanese was fully unleashed, and over the next two decades the fashion industry exploded.

By the 1970s millions of young Japanese were vying with each other to stay on the leading edge of the latest fashions and earn the coveted accolade of *oshare* (oh-shah-ray), meaning "sharp, smart, stylish, fastidious."

Today the *oshare* syndrome remains a key factor in Japan's apparel industry, influencing people of all ages and classes. Everyone, from students, laborers, office workers and tradespeople to rich socialites, strives for a stylish look that either distinguishes them or identifies them with their particular group.

For high-end imported apparel to succeed in Japan, be it casual, sport or dress, it must also have a specific style that appeals to the finely developed Japanese sense of fashion in whatever look they are trying to achieve.

81

育 成

Ikusei

(Ee-kuu-say-ee)

"Cultivating Seeds of Creativity"

One of the critical factors in Japan's feudal culture was that virtually every facet of the culture, from the economic and political systems to social etiquette, was directly opposed to the kind of thinking and behavior that leads to creativity and change.

But unlike most ancient societies that were isolated from the mainstream of civilizations until recent times, instead of being overwhelmed by foreign influences, Japan has thrived on them—like some sort of time-space rift that sucks up any energy it comes into contact with.

It has, in fact, been one of the ongoing marvels of Japan that the Japanese have proven to be so good at introducing Western ideas and technology into their traditional culture without quickly destroying the strength or flavor of the old ways.

This process of synthesizing and building on Western knowledge has not and does not come easily to the Japanese, however. It is something they have had to strive for with the greatest diligence, and with sacrifices that would have defeated a less determined people.

Western attitudes and ways are generally so diametrically opposed to traditional Japanese experience and expectations that trying to merge the two would be something like joining matter and anti-matter. In the past, the Japanese avoided this explosive potential by keeping the two elements apart, by confining them to their own layered compartments.

Now, as the older, fully Japanized generations die off and the younger, less traditional generations come on line, the layers separating Japanese and foreign elements in private as well as business areas are thinning rapidly and are beginning to blend from the top as well as the bottom.

In addition to this natural fusion of Japanese and foreign ways, there is a deliberate movement that is planned and supported by Japanese who are determined to guarantee that Japan does not lose its momentum in technological competition.

Most of this special group of Japanese are leaders in what for Japan is still a new field—creativity and innovation. They have set themselves the task of teaching others how to break the old taboos that prohibit or severely limit individualistic thought and change, and become original thinkers.

Part of the new teaching to break the old cultural restraints comes under the general heading of *ikusei* (ee-kuu-say-ee), which means "to nurture" or "to grow"—and refers to cultivating new ideas that will hopefully lead to innovations and inventions.

The primary thrust of this movement is to change the restraints on thinking and behaving as individuals; on breaking the taboos that have traditionally prevented candid and complete communication between individuals; and in changing the environment of the workplace to make it more conducive to innovative thinking and acting.

This may sound simple, but it entails discarding attitudes and behavior that are so deeply ingrained in the Japanese that the process represents a total psychological metamorphosis and must encompass large numbers of people on all levels of any company or organization for it to succeed.

It involves the way people dress, the way they interact physically with co-workers and superiors, the manner in which they talk to each other—in fact, all of those things that distinguish the Japanese and give them their cultural identity.

Introducing the concept of *ikusei* into the business world as a means of fostering creativity is therefore a seminal step that will speed up the disappearance of Japan's traditional culture.

82

院政　　黒幕　　大御所

Insei / Kuro Maku / Ogosho
(Een-say-ee / Kuu-roe Mah-kuu / Oh-go-show)

"The Man Pulling the Strings"

In the early years of the 12th century Japan's Emperor Shirakawa set a precedent that was to have long-lasting repercussions. In an effort to weaken the power of the regents and advisers who had been virtually running the government for centuries, he made a concerted effort to regain control of the throne, then retired early, intending to exercise power from behind the scenes.

Emperor Shirakawa's ploy of ruling from behind the scenes became known as *insei* (een-say-ee), which literally means "negative" or "dormant." Unfortunately, his action contributed to a series of drawn-out civil wars that ended with the rise of the shogunate system of government and the relegation of the emperor to a figurehead.

From this period on, however, it became common for the reigning shoguns themselves to retire early to avoid the ceremonial aspects of the office, make decisions on their own, and not have to accept responsibility for their moves.

The residence of a retired shogun who continued to exercise considerable power was known as *Ogosho* (oh-go-show). Over the centuries, the term came to be applied to individuals who remained in the background but were very influential in politics or other fields.

During the early decades of the Tokugawa shogunate, which began in 1603, kabuki and other forms of drama were performed on stages that used *kuro maku* or (kuu-roe mah-kuu), or "black curtains," as back-drops. As time went by, this term also came into use in reference to individuals who held no official post but exercised power from behind the scenes, hidden from view.

While these terms are only occasionally heard today, the situations they refer to are perhaps more common now than they were centuries ago. The most powerful political figures in Japan are invariably former prime ministers and faction leaders, not the current head of government or his ministers.

In Japan's business world there are always two or three figures who dominate the scene. Almost always in their 70s or 80s, and still active as the heads of major companies and national organizations, these outstanding individuals serve both officially and unofficially as spokesmen for Japan.

Generally, these *Ogosho* are so respected that all they have to do to get things done is to make their desires known, often by merely hinting at what they would like to see happen.

In fact, in practically every field of endeavor in Japan—the arts, crafts, literature, medicine, sports—there is an *Ogosho*—an individual who is nationally recognized as the "master" or "the grand old man" who exercises supreme authority because of his mastery and his virtues, not because he possesses any kind of actual power.

Another facet of the "behind the scenes" system that has historically existed in Japan is the role of underworld or gangster leaders. Japan's *yakuza* (yah-kuu-zah), or professional criminal gangs, go back for centuries and yield extraordinary power in the country.

It is often rumored that in recent decades no prime minister has taken office without the specific approval of the top crime lord in the country. The most powerful of the *yakuza* leaders are often referred to as "emperors."

Another term that has recently become vogue to describe people who are outstanding in their fields is *kami* (kah-me) or "god." The top sales manager in a company, for example, is called *serusu no kami-sama* (say-ruu-suu no kah-me sah-mah) or "the god of sales."

There are also "gods of baseball," "gods of advertising," and so on.

83

一杯食った

Ippai Kutta
(Eep-pie Kuut-tah)

"Softening Up the Other Party"

Japanese are famous for the courtesy, kindness and hospitality they extend to visitors and guests. Such behavior is deeply rooted in their philosophical and religious beliefs. Equally important is their tradition of service to others, particularly to superiors and guests.

This tradition of service goes back to the feudal period and the appearance of a political/social system in which catering to the needs, comfort and whims of superiors became an essential part of life. Behaving in an exquisitely courteous manner and providing a level of service Westerners normally associate with royalty became the norm, and was enforced with powerful sanctions.

An edict issued by the Tokugawa shogunate in 1638 was to have a profound and ongoing effect on the role and quality of service in the inn, food and beverage industries in Japan. The shogunate decreed that some 250 of the country's provincial lords would maintain homes in Yedo (Tokyo), keep their families there at all times, and themselves spend every other year in Yedo in attendance at the Shogun's Court.

The same edict prescribed the route each lord would take to reach Yedo, along with how many servants, retainers and samurai warriors the lords would bring in their entourages. The overall number of members in each group was based on the size and wealth of the clan. The larger and wealthier the clan, the larger the entourage. The wealthiest of the clan lords, Maeda, brought over one thousand people with him on his treks to Yedo.

These lordly processions traveled on foot from all over the country, meaning those whose provinces were the most distant were on the road for several weeks each way. Within a decade after the issuing of the decree, Japan had the largest and most efficient networks of inns and roadway restaurants the world had ever seen.

Because these traveling lords and their samurai retainers demanded a highly refined level of service, the hundreds of thousands of people employed in the roadway inns and restaurants became masters at catering to them.

This extraordinary system of lordly processions going to and from the shogunate capital in Yedo prevailed in Japan for nearly 250 years, making the Japanese world leaders in the public inn, food and beverage industries long before they opened their doors to the West.

Given these traditions of service and hospitality, which eventually permeated the whole society, it was natural for the Japanese to incorporate the same kind of behavior into their business relationships. It became a fixed custom that clients and prospective customers would be wined and dined lavishly on numerous occasions.

Ippai kutta (Eep-pie kuut-tah), or "I've eaten my fill," became a commonly heard phrase that quickly took on an additional meaning. In addition to meaning that one's stomach was full, it could also mean that one had been deliberately softened up and taken advantage of in a business deal.

Whether designing or innocent, it is typical of Japanese, and especially Japanese businessmen, to treat visitors and guests with extraordinary generosity, often spending shocking amounts of money on their entertainment.

Even when such entertainment is totally without ulterior aims, it saddles the guest with strong feelings of debt. When the guest is unable to return the hospitality in equal kind, he tends to feel especially obligated and is likely to be less objective and more flexible in his business with the Japanese.

Outsiders dealing with Japan should keep in mind that Japanese are masters at using hospitality as part of their negotiating process. But the outsider who is wined and dined by a Japanese does not have to leave it at that. He can reciprocate and keep the debtor scales balanced.

——————————— 84 ———————————

いらっしゃいませ

Irasshaimase

(Ee-rah-shy-mah-say)

"My Home Is Your Home"

Centuries ago Japanese behavior was formalized to the extent that there was a prescribed way for doing virtually everything. The most important, and therefore the most carefully enforced, of these behavioral patterns involved direct interaction with other people, whether in greetings, introductions, requests, orders, speeches or casual conversation.

Japanese became so sensitized to form and manner that the slightest variation from the highly refined norm was instantly obvious to them, and was often pregnant with meaning that was frequently just as obvious.

One of the more interesting situations with its own etiquette involved travelers on the great walking roads that traversed early Japan (the roads were originally built in the 7th century to make it easier for government officials, including tax collectors, to visit the outlying provinces from the imperial capital of Kyoto).

Not unlike today, there were rules of the road that included such things as giving the right-of-way to horseback-riding messengers and government officials, and completely clearing the road and kowtowing during the passage of a clan lord and his entourage.

On a more mundane level, it was considered impolite to pass anyone without apologizing—an action that was regarded as thoughtless if not arrogant.

One of the most interesting of the etiquette customs that developed early in Japan's history was calling out *irasshai* (ee-rah-shy) or *irasshaimase* (ee-rah-shy-mah-say) when someone entered the vestibule of a home or place of business.

Still today these two words are among the most frequently used terms in the Japanese language (and are ones that newcomers invariably ask about). *Irasshai* means "walk in" or "walk up" as well as "welcome," and is an informal, friendly expression used by tradespeople in traditional restaurants and shops as well as in the country's huge department stores as both a greeting and welcome.

It is customary for all the waiters and cooks in many traditionally styled eating and drinking places to yell out "*Irasshai!*" in a singsong chorus to everyone who enters their establishments. Likewise, the departure of customers from such places is marked by enthusiastic shouts of "thank you" and "come again."

When customers enter a shop that follows this traditional custom they know immediately that it is a place where informality is the order of the day and that they can relax and have fun. Waiters routinely jam strangers together around tables or bars, and it is one of the occasions when the Japanese have traditionally felt free to engage strangers in casual conversation.

Close friends say "*irasshai*" to welcome each other into their homes or elsewhere (a bar or restaurant, perhaps) in the same way that Westerners would say, "Come in! Come in!" It is also used informally among adult friends and to children in the sense of "come with me."

Irasshaimase is a much more polite and formal term used only in the sense of "welcome" or "thank you for coming." It is appropriate for any situation, whether informal or formal.

Proper use of this term and its variations is an important part of the overall etiquette of Japan and is one of the things that foreign visitors and businessmen can easily assimilate, and benefit from, in their interactions with Japanese.

This, in fact, is one of the several areas of Japanese etiquette that I believe foreigners should learn and adopt not only out of respect for the sensibilities of the Japanese, but also because it would add to the quality of their lives.

85

色を付ける

Iro wo Tsukeru
(Ee-roe oh T'suu-kay-ruu)

"Putting a Little Sex into It"

When I was a young, naive fellow of 21 visiting in the house of an 18-year-old Japanese girl friend, her younger sister came up to me one day, showed me a 69-position sex chart and asked me which of the positions I liked best. The hand-drawn illustrations on the chart were in glorious color and left little to the imagination, but they combined riotous sexuality with refined taste in such a way that they definitely had redeeming social value.

This was one of the more memorable of my first experiences with Japanese attitudes toward human sexuality, which, as it turned out, seemed far more advanced and human to me than those I had left behind in the U.S.

It quickly became obvious that the Japanese were not intimidated by their sexuality and for the most part (at least where men were concerned) treated it as the very important function that it is in both a physical and psychological sense.

Another facet of the Japanese attitude toward human sexuality that impressed me was its humorous aspect. They saw the funny side of it honestly and clearly, and reveled in the humor of it—an attitude that will no doubt eventually prevail in the world.

Not surprisingly, the Japanese associated sex with color, particularly with pink and other shades of red, and developed a choice vocabulary that contained sexual references expressed in terms of color.

The word for color, *iro* (ee-roe) became synonymous with sex, and with the addition of a number of suffixes came to mean "ardor," "sensual," "sexually aware" and so on. Adding *ke* (kay), meaning spirit and energy, to *iro* gives the two compounds the meaning of "sexual tinge, sexual interest, desire, inclination."

Iroke tappuri (Ee-roe-kay tahp-puu-ree), for example, means something like "overflowing with sexual desire," and refers to an older woman who tries to stay sexually attractive by using cosmetics and dressing in sensual clothing.

The same term is also used in reference to someone who wants something very badly, such as a junior manager who avidly covets a promotion to manager, and behaves in an especially conspicuous manner in an effort to get it.

Wanting something or being in favor of something without going overboard about it is described as *iroke wo miseru* (ee-roe-kay oh me-say-ruu) or "showing desire" for it. In this case, as in the above, using *iroke* adds a sensual flavor to the expression.

When a young girl begins to bloom into womanhood she may be described as *iroke ga dete kita*, (ee-roe-kay gah day-tay kee-tah), or "a sexual shade has come out." The implication is that she is becoming sexually attractive to men.

On the other hand, a girl who has matured sexually and flaunts her sexuality may be described as *iroke zuku* (ee-roe-kay zuu-kuu), which is more or less the equivalent of "boy crazy."

In a business context, *iro wo tsukeru* (ee-roe oh t'suu-kay-ruu), or "add a little sexy flavor to it," is commonly used in the sense of "sweetening the pot" or "adding a little something special to influence someone" or "doing someone a favor."

A foreign businessman facing an impasse in negotiating with the Japanese might request that his counterparts add a little something to break the deadlock—*iro wo tsukete kudasai*—(ee-roe oh t'suu-kay-tay kuu-dah-sie), or might himself offer to put something else into the pot—*iro wo tsukemasu* (ee-roe oh t'suu-kay-mahss).

86

石橋 を 叩 く

Ishi Bashi wo Tataku
(Ee-she Bah-she oh Tah-tah-kuu)

"The Blind Walk Carefully"

Life in feudal Japan was a precarious proposition. There was great danger from fires; earthquakes and typhoons were common; and the common people were subject to the harsh rule and whims of despotic samurai lords who literally had the power of life and death over them without the restraints of any kind of bill-of-rights.

The social system was such that all Japanese had to exercise extreme care to avoid committing errors of etiquette, making commitments that might not be fulfilled, appearing aggressive or selfish, or displeasing anyone in a superior position in any way.

As the centuries went by, this system conditioned the Japanese to be as noncommittal as possible, to express themselves in ambiguous terms, to avoid new social or political entanglements, to keep a low profile and let others lead while waiting for consensus to gradually emerge from their group before taking any action.

This culturally conditioned attitude continues to have a profound influence on the behavior of most Japanese, and is especially noticeable in business and politics where, nowadays, quick decisions and the acceptance of responsibility are often vital to success.

As Japan becomes more involved in international affairs, the pressure on the Japanese to change their cultural ways is becoming heavier and heavier, and how quickly they are able to adapt will have a significant influence on their ability to stay on good terms with the rest of the world.

Individual Japanese, businessmen as well as bureaucrats, who become known for moving slowly and sometimes avoiding action altogether are often described as *ishi bashi wo tataku* (ee-she bah-she oh tah-tah-kuu) or "tapping the stone bridge."

In early Japan, where wooden and stone bridges abounded, blind people were often observed tapping the bridges with their walking sticks prior to crossing to make sure that the bridges were in good repair and safe to cross.

Ishi bashi, or stone bridges, should naturally be stronger and more durable than wooden bridges. Thus when a person is said to be "tapping a stone bridge," the connotation is that he is especially cautious and is not the type to take any kind of chance.

Most foreign businessmen, diplomats and politicians dealing with Japan have encountered stone-bridge tappers because they are the rule rather than the exception. However, many Japanese businessmen who are not naturally bridge tappers themselves may appear to be so because the system they are a part of precludes them from making fast decisions and reacting quickly. It is usually possible to distinguish, after two or three meetings, between tappers and those who hold back because of the system. Those who would like to move forward more quickly clearly demonstrate their desire to move ahead by their enthusiasm, by explaining the holdups, and by doing everything they can to speed up the process.

Once you have come up against a true bridge tapper about the only recourse you have is to enlist the help of someone else, preferably someone he knows well and trusts and is heavily obligated to, to intervene on your behalf and talk or escort the tapper across the bridge.

Japanese businessmen who will leap across bridges or cross them at a run are still rare. Those that do exist are primarily found in new high-tech companies whose success is based on rapid changes, or in new small companies where they have less to lose. Such men, if they fail, are the kind who will turn around and try again.

87

以 心 伝 心

Ishin Denshin

(Ee-sheen Dane-sheen)

"Using Cultural Telepathy"

Husbands and wives who have lived together compatibly for fifty or sixty years often come to know each other so well they can practically read each other's minds. They are totally familiar with each other's likes and dislikes, attitudes, and behavior. There is even some evidence that people who live together over extended periods come to look more like each other.

These principles—and more—have been at play in Japan for over two thousand years. In effect, the Japanese have been one huge, extended family, deliberately subjected to virtually the same cultural influences for generation after generation.

By "deliberately," I mean that the Japanese did not develop common attitudes and patterns of behavior solely incidentally, as a natural result of being born and raised in Japanese society. Particularly from the early 1600s, Japanese society was minutely structured into classes and occupations, with sex, age and seniority being primary factors in determining acceptable roles for each individual.

All Japanese were carefully and thoroughly conditioned to think and behave in certain ways according to their stations in life. This training began in infancy and included everything from how to eat, how to bow and how to pay proper respect to a superior to how to use a hand-saw if you happened to be a carpenter.

This great cultural crucible thus had the effect of molding the Japanese into one huge family whose individual members were in many ways more alike than a husband and wife who had spent decades together. In the Japanese system, there were strong sanctions against even casual differences.

As a result of this homogenization, the Japanese developed the ability to understand each other with only a few, often cryptic, words, and to anticipate thoughts and actions as if they could read each other's minds. Skill in this kind of "cultural telepathy" was highly prized, especially in leaders and others in positions of responsibility, and was carefully cultivated by them.

This silent form of communication came to be called *ishin denshin* (ee-sheen dane-sheen) or "mind-to-heart communication," with the connotation being that whatever intention or information was communicated in this manner was the truth and nothing but—coming as it did directly from the heart.

The Japanese have traditionally depended on *ishin denshin* for much of their communication—and been turned off by people who, by their standards, talk excessively. In contrast to the Japanese, Westerners are noted for being big talkers, with the result that these two widely differing modes of behavior often clash.

Since Westerners and Japanese are obviously on different cultural wavelengths, it is virtually impossible for either side to tune in on the *ishin denshin* of the other. This means that Westerners should curb their tendency to talk too much (they frequently repeat themselves in an effort to make or carry a point), while the Japanese must learn to talk more and not expect foreigners to pick up on their silent broadcasting.

It does pay, however, for foreign businessmen and politicians to make a point of letting their Japanese counterparts know that they are aware of the *ishin denshin* method of communicating, and that they want to have a mind-to-heart understanding with them.

------------------------------ 88 ------------------------------

自分がない

Jibun ga Nai

(Jee-boon gah nie)

"Life Without a Soul"

It is almost axiomatic that when foreigners visit Japan for the first time they are so impressed with the people that their praise runs off the scale. They typically carry on endlessly about how polite and thoughtful and well-ordered the Japanese are, and how "everything just seems to work!"

While invariably overdone, this praise is well-deserved. The Japanese have created a system that is very impressive indeed. Among other things, I had been riding the trains and subways of Tokyo for more than thirty-five years before I saw the very first graffiti on or near any mode of transportation.

This memorable incident occurred on the Marunouchi Subway Line in 1987. I spotted a scrawled drawing, about the size of the tip of my thumb, alongside one of the doors. The incident was so surprising I took out a notebook and wrote down the date and location. The graffiti itself was the profile of a face. [When my editor, Tom Heenan, himself an old Japan hand, read this paragraph he noted on the side of the manuscript: "It is interesting that (in Japan) even the expressions of a tortured soul are miniaturized!"]

Probably the first thing that catches and holds the attention of newcomers to Japan is the beautifully stylized service routinely provided by the employees of first-class hotels where the visitors stay. The staff in the hotel lounge or coffee shop, for example, behave as if every action was as carefully choreographed as a Broadway play—which is exactly the case.

No one can experience this kind of service and not make comparisons with what they are used to at home. The difference is not subtle. It is like night and day. About the only thing that might compare is the service one would get in the most expensive and exclusive club in London or some other major capital.

Probably the second most impressive thing to newcomers to Japan is the awesome efficiency of its transportation and manufacturing industries, particularly its transportation system because that is the one thing visitors are exposed to daily and extensively.

The precise arrival and departure of train after train on long-distance lines—at ten- to fifteen-minute intervals during busy periods—is enough to convince visitors that the Japanese are an extraordinary people and that there is something missing in their own countries.

But there is a hidden element in the Japanese system that dampens, if not destroys, many of its apparent advantages. This element primarily has to do with the extraordinary regimentation of the people that is necessary to make the system function like a well-oiled machine.

Again using a military example, watching a superbly trained marine regiment go through a series of parade-ground maneuvers is a delight to the eye and can stir the spirit to a level that it soars. But, who would want to behave most of the time like a regiment of marines on parade?

The Japanese also typically praise their system, but at the same time they have traditionally lamented their lack of personal freedom, complaining sadly that *jibun ga nai* (jee-boon gah nie), or "I have no self," meaning they have not been free to be themselves, that they have to suppress their personalities and character to fit rigid molds. This feeling is also sometimes expressed by the term *ji-ishiki ga yowai* (jee-ee-she-kee gah yoh-wah-ee), meaning "my/his/her self-consciousness is weak."

Because of the robot-like character and rigidity of the Japanese system, most Japanese who go abroad feel like they have been let out of a straitjacket, and many of them are never again able to squeeze themselves back into the system after they return to Japan.

While regimentation in Japanese society has diminished drastically since the 1960s, it still prevails to such an extraordinary degree in the school and company systems that the majority of the people are still bound by bonds that prevent them from exploring and developing themselves.

89

自重

Jicho

(Jee-choe)

"Staying Out of Trouble"

I saw and heard my first public altercation between two Japanese in the mid-1950s, after I had been in the country for nearly eight years. That is not to say that the Japanese did not have arguments or get into fights, but it is certainly indicative of the public order that was common in Japan.

For all of Japan's long feudal era (1192–1868) the country was under the Japanese equivalent of martial law. Successive dynasties of shoguns were administered by elite samurai warriors whose roles were hereditary, and who were often corrupted by their power.

During this period, the laws of the land were made and enforced to benefit those in power and maintain the status quo—not to protect or service the people at large. It was, in fact, the policy of some of the shogunate governments to keep various of their laws secret from the people to encourage absolutely circumspect behavior.

Punishment for breaking the laws of the shogunate or the local clan lord were usually severe and swift. There were no jury trials. At best, a local magistrate heard evidence and passed sentence in one brief setting. In some cases death sentences were carried out on the spot, and generally within a few days or weeks.

Cruel and unusual punishments were common. Some of the methods used to dispatch offenders (and enemies) included boiling them in oil, impaling them, anus first, on sharpened stakes, or using them for sword practice. Suicide by slicing open one's stomach, reserved for samurai, would also surely rank as cruel punishment.

In this environment it is not surprising that the average Japanese took great care to stay out of trouble, and that many of the attributes for which the Japanese have long been famous—such as politeness, smiling passivity and obeying orders without question—were polished to the point that they became second nature.

As time passed, the Japanese developed a self-preserving mechanism called *jicho* (jee-choe), meaning "self-love" or "respecting one's self," which was used to rationalize behavior that was designed to keep them out of trouble.

In personal situations, the effects of *jicho* ranged from being positive and laudable to being perverse and sometimes fatal. Individuals with power would sometimes refrain from taking action that could have righted terrible wrongs because they did not want to get involved.

Many of the incidents of ritual suicide that occurred during the Tokugawa shogunate were brought on by a powerful sense of *jicho* that compelled individuals who could not resolve dilemmas to take their own lives out of self-respect.

In contemporary Japan, the concept of *jicho* remains a powerful force in the lives of most people. It is one of the things that makes the Japanese law-abiding, loyal, diligent and hardworking. It is also one of the things that prevents many Japanese from taking risks.

Out of respect for themselves, *jicho*-conscious people will avoid being innovative or taking the lead because failing or being criticized would damage their self-respect. This is frequently a factor in business situations, particularly where international contacts are concerned, because it is common for foreigners to ask for and expect individual initiative and action by their Japanese counterparts.

The key is to deal with the appropriate company section and department managers as groups, not on an individual basis. In other words, the most—if not the only—effective way of developing and maintaining a positive long-term relationship with a Japanese company is to build a network within the company that includes all the section and department managers and their assistants who are, or would be, involved in your project.

In the first stages of approaching a Japanese company it is important to have your initial contact identify and introduce you to the others who will play a role in the relationship—something that they will normally do on their own if they are genuinely interested in your project. The point is that the outsider who is introduced around must be aware of the importance of the introductions, follow them up through business and social meetings, and otherwise do his part to keep everyone in the network informed and positive.

90

自前主義

Jimae-Shugi

(Jee-my-shuu-ghee)

"Self-Sufficiency as a Weapon"

From 1603 to 1868, feudal Japan was divided into some 270 clans that were subordinate to the Tokugawa Shogunate government. All of the clans, and especially those that were the farthest away from the Shogun's Court in Yedo (Tokyo), were governed more or less like semi-sovereign nations.

Trade and travel between the clans were limited and strictly controlled, both by the clans themselves and by the shogunate government. Samurai warriors were stationed at key points along the roads leading to Yedo to check the documents of all travelers going to and from the capital, as well as to inspect all goods in transit.

Transportation modes were also controlled by the central government to prevent potential rebels from being able to quickly move large numbers of troops and military supplies. The overwhelming mountainous nature of the islands themselves, and the distances involved, acted as further barriers to the development of trade and travel.

These factors, combined with the closed-group social and political systems of the country, resulted in every group on every level trying to be as self-sufficient as possible. Survival and supremacy, primarily based on inter-group competition rather than cooperation, was the motivating force that energized individual units.

This propensity to act within tightly controlled groups survived the downfall of the Tokugawa shogunate in 1867/8 and was incorporated into the new industrialized economy that blossomed during the 1870s and 80s.

Companies in basic industries quickly grew into giant conglomerates, with dozens of wholly-owned subsidiaries and affiliated sub-contractors.

In effect, the larger conglomerates replaced the former clans of the feudal period. The Mitsui group, for example, had more than three million employees, and the head of the group was richer and more powerful than any of the clan lords had been before him.

It was the singular Japanese capacity to compete with each other fiercely as groups, while coordinating their efforts on a macro-basis to further the interests and goals of the nation, that made it possible for them to create their first economic miracle.

The built-in compulsion for *jimae-shugi* (jee-my-shuu-ghee), or "self-sufficiencyism," remains a key factor in Japan's political and economic philosophies. There is a natural tendency for every company to continuously expand, first into related fields and then into other areas, with each one of the new enterprises becoming a core company that repeats the process of spawning subsidiaries and tying up sub-contractors.

In this system the Japanese not only gain economies of scale, they also bind together groups that remain competitive but act in parallel, thereby greatly expanding their overall power, just as a series of small computers linked together increases the system's total capacity.

Because this kind of behavior is a pure expression of Japanese philosophy, as opposed to American philosophy, which views such concentrations of power as illegal, the Japanese have a major advantage over their foreign competitors.

Fortunately, in one sense at least, Japan's *jimae-shugi* advantage is not unbounded. It is limited to some extent by the country's dependence upon cooperative interaction with world markets—an area where the Japanese are <u>disadvantaged</u> because of problems resulting from their comparatively poor ability to deal with cultural diversity.

At this time, however, the strength of the Japanese Way outweighs its weaknesses.

———————————— 91 ————————————

事務所の花

Jimusho no Hana

(Jee-muu-show no Hah-nah)

"Female Flowers of the Office"

Historically in Japan, women have had their ups and downs. Prior to the take-over of the government by a military warlord in 1192, women were prominent at the Imperial Court in Kyoto. In addition to reigning as empresses and taking part in politics on other levels, they played significant roles in the arts and literature.

It was women who took the lead in developing the first syllabic writing system for transcribing the Japanese language. It was women who popularized the writing of poetry and made it into a national pastime. It was women who promoted the craft of printing.

Between A.D. 1000 and 1100, Kyoto was one of the literary capitals of the world, and most of the star writers were women. Early in the 11th century, Murasaki Shikibu, a lady-in-waiting at the Imperial Court, wrote the massive *Genji Monogatari* (Gane-jee Moe-no-gah-tah-ree) or "The Tale of the Genji," a historical saga of the rise and fall of the Genji clan, which is generally regarded as the world's first novel.

Another of the greatest literary luminaries of this period was essayist Shonagon Sei, whose works included the famed *Makura no Soshi* (Mah-kuu-rah no Soe-she) or "Pillow Book." Izumi Shikibu was a leading poetess. In fact, much of the culture of the whole Heian period, from A.D. 794 to 1192, was dominated by women.

With the ascendancy of the warrior class in 1192, however, Japan became male-dominated to an extreme degree. For the most part, women were relegated to the status of property, and used as workers and the bearers of children. Marriages were arranged. Love and personal feelings were seldom taken into consideration.

The slave-like position of women in Japan did not change significantly until 1945 when the country was defeated in World War II and the government was democratized by American-led Occupation forces.

Japanese women blossomed during the seven years of the foreign military occupation of the country, from 1945 to 1952. The volume and variety of interaction and intercourse between Japanese women and the

Occupation forces was on an unprecedented scale.

Without the cooperation and efforts of Japanese women, as interpreters, translators, clerks and general workers, the Occupation would likely have been a long, drawn-out disaster. Without the aggressive willingness of Japanese women to work and to change their traditional way of living, the consumer economy that now exists in Japan would have been delayed by decades and might never have developed.

The power of Japanese women today is palpable. They are the leavening in Japanese society; they give it its color and its taste, and are the inspiration for most of the creativity in the country. And yet, they are still treated as second-class citizens in the workplace.

In addition to still being paid less than men and offered only low-rung employment opportunities in most companies, Japanese women continue to be regarded by the male bastion as disposable accessories—beautiful but fragile and temporary.

In a typically poetic way of classifying and symbolizing things, a male Japanese commentator labeled the hordes of young, unmarried women office workers *jimusho no hana* (jee-muu-show no hah-nah) or "office flowers." The connotation of this label is obvious—the young women "dress up" the offices for a short period of time, then their beauty fades and they are discarded.

But this situation has been changing rapidly since the 1980s. Japanese women are naturally more flexible and adaptable than the men, and often more talented as well. These factors, plus a growing labor shortage and their manifest will to fulfill long-suppressed ambitions, are slowly but surely bringing them into the upper echelons of business, science and politics.

92

仁 義

Jingi

(Jeen-ghee)

"Cooperating with the Enemy"

The introduction of Confucianism into Japan, on top of the native Shintoism and Chinese Buddhism, was to have a profound effect on the distinctive social and political systems that today still control most of the attitudes and much of the behavior of the Japanese.

Feudal Japan's famed samurai class of professional warriors, who took control of the country in 1192 and administered the government until 1868, adopted Zen Buddhism and the five principles of Confucianism as the philosophical base for the moral and ethical code by which they ran the shogunate government.

The five principles taught by Confucius were benevolence, righteousness, propriety, wisdom and sincerity. Mencius, who followed Confucius, taught that *jin* (jeen), benevolence, and *gi* (ghee), righteousness, were the basic principles of morality and therefore should be the foundation for all human relations. These two principles became the main pillars of *Bushido*, or "The Way of the Samurai."

The samurai did not stop with *jingi* (benevolence and righteousness), however. They also incorporated wisdom, sincerity and propriety into their personal code. Propriety, in particular, became one of the hallmarks of samurai etiquette, as they developed a style of rigid, formal manners that controlled their behavior totally.

As time went by, Japan's large professional criminal gangs, the notorious *yakuza* (yah-kuu-zah), also adopted the *jingi* principles as their code of honor, but in their case it pertained only to the relationship between gang members and their bosses, not the public at large.

The *yakuza* went on to develop a special way of introducing themselves that was called *jingi wo kiru* (jeen-ghee oh kee-ruu). *Kiru* means to cut or to wear, depending on the usage. In the *yakuza* context, it referred to the special gestures and verbal expressions they used to introduce themselves in a dramatic fashion.

In the beginning, the use of this special *yakuza* way of self-introduction was designed to impress others, and was a matter of pride and sometimes arrogance. Eventually it became a way of paying respect to others, particularly when addressing superiors.

Japan's business world eventually adopted the term *jingi wo kiru* to describe their custom of trying to avoid undue friction in the marketplace by informing competitors in advance of intentions to enter a given field of business.

The phrase is also used to describe the practice of notifying competing companies when one proposes to "steal" employees from them—a practice that is still considered immoral by many people in Japan.

Obviously, the use of *jingi wo kiru* in these two situations confirms that both are still considered gangster-type tactics which require an explanation (and a type of apology) in order to maintain honor.

Not all market competitors, or companies faced with losing key personnel, accept *jingi wo kiru* calls in good spirits. But if the notification is done in a fully professional manner, with all the formality that traditionally characterized the behavior of the *yakuza*, convention generally forces them to go along.

93

人事移動

Jinji Ido

(Jeen-jee Ee-doe)

"Terror in March"

The famed cohesiveness and solidarity that large Japanese companies present to the public, especially the image that foreigners are likely to have of these companies, does not represent the truth and nothing but. A significant proportion of this image is a mirage that looks quite different from the inside.

One of the trends that became especially noticeable in Japan in the 1980s was for university graduates to turn down attractive offers from major corporations and cast their lot with smaller and sometimes entrepreneurial-type companies.

Among the reasons given by these un-Japanese-like mavericks was that they did not want to commit their lives to the hide-bound systems followed by the monolithic giants—that they wanted more control over what would happen to them during their working lifetimes.

This new trend was so unlike traditional Japanese behavior that some social and business commentators began describing it as another milestone in the rapid degeneration of Japan's unique business system.

There is no doubt at all that Japan's traditional way of doing business is evolving into something new that incorporates both Japanese and Western concepts, but the primary characteristics of large Japanese companies are going to remain Japanese for the foreseeable future.

One of the Japanese corporate practices that is unlikely to change any time soon is *jinji ido* (jeen-jee ee-doe), or "personnel shuffling." Part of the Japanese philosophy of training management personnel is that they should receive on-the-job experience in as many key departments as possible to give them a well-rounded perspective of the company and its operations.

This regular rotation of personnel takes place within the head office as well as to and among branch offices and subsidiary companies. Employees are also sometimes "loaned" to closely affiliated companies that are in need of some special expertise.

Movement among departments at the head office or within branch offices does not necessarily create any particular hardship as far as the employees' families and their own personal convenience are concerned, but when *jinji ido* involves transferring to another city, that is another matter.

Wives and children invariably cannot go with their husbands because of housing and school considerations. The separations normally last for at least one year and often end up lasting for several years, resulting in conspicuous strains on workers and their families.

Some postings are recognized as stepping-stones to higher managerial positions, and are generally sought after and welcomed despite the personal inconveniences and problems that almost always arise. Other postings are equally recognized as being dead-ends, and as a clear message that the individuals who receive them have limited futures with the company.

Jinji ido traditionally takes place in March, just before the beginning of the new fiscal year in April (adjustment transfers on a small scale may also be made in October). Thus February and March are always periods of extraordinary tension and anticipation in larger Japanese companies, as individuals eligible for transfer wait for *jirei* (jee-ray-ee), or "orders," from their personnel departments.

The practice of *jinji ido* often has a substantial impact on foreign companies doing business in Japan because it regularly means getting acquainted with new contacts and going through the time-consuming routine of establishing a working relationship with them.

This is another of many reasons why it is advisable to always include assistant section and department managers in dealings with Japanese companies so that you will not have to start over with a totally new relationship if the managers are the ones transferred.

In larger Japanese companies the average manager or executive will go through at least four or five transfers during a 35- to 40-year career; some are transferred every three or four years. The most valued executives are frequently the ones transferred the most often because the companies want to take as much advantage as possible of their skills.

94

人 脈

Jinmyaku

(Jeen-me-yah-kuu)

"Plugged into the Pulse"

The old saying, "It isn't what you know but who you know," probably exists in every society, but there are surely few areas of the world where it is more meaningful than it is in the Confucian sphere of Asia.

Since Confucian philosophy gives more importance to hierarchical relationships between individuals than to the individuals themselves, it is natural that in Confucian societies modes of action based on relationships become the key to personal as well as business affairs.

China and Korea, where Confucianism has survived in its purest form, remain prime examples of relational societies. Japan, which imported Confucianism from China nearly two thousand years ago, is a close second, even though few Japanese are conscious of the origin or roots of their way of doing things.

As they did with everything else they imported from China and Korea, the Japanese adopted Confucianism to fit their own form of feudal military government, with loyalty to superiors taking precedence over all other principles and laws. This helped guarantee the continuation of a social system based on vertical, hereditary ranking.

In the Japanese context, neither individuals nor companies were seen as separate entities with which affairs could be conducted on an impersonal basis. The personal element remained the ruling factor.

Despite the process of Westernization (or internationalization as the Japanese prefer to describe it) that is taking place in Japan, the foundation for private as well as business relationships in Japan continues for the most part to be personal connections, particularly where the Japanese themselves are concerned.

In both private and business matters, the natural reaction of the Japanese is to think in terms of *jinmyaku* (jeen-me-yah-kuu), which means something like "person pulse," but is translated as "line of connections" or "personal connections."

In private or business affairs, *jinmyaku* may include any personal contacts an individual has anywhere, but they are naturally of special importance when the contacts concerned are in positions of authority or influence.

Jinmyaku that are the most prized include relatives, school-mates, business colleagues, and members of the same company, club or other organization, generally in that order.

Interestingly, the use of personal connections appears to be decreasing at a significantly faster pace in international business than in other areas. Japanese recognize that most foreigners do not have local contacts that they can use as connections. They also recognize that business in the West generally does not rely on personal connections.

Having said this, I must add that the only way you can initiate business relations with some Japanese companies is through introductions and guarantees from acceptable *jinmyaku*, and that going through connections remains the preferred and best way to develop business relations with most Japanese firms.

Even when Japanese companies are receptive to direct contacts from foreign firms they have not previously done business with, and may not know, it is a definite advantage to have introductions and the support of *jinmyaku*—so much so that it pays to spend time and resources seeking them out. Of course, the most appropriate *jinmyaku* are people who have some connection with the company concerned—its bankers, university professors who have recommended graduates to the firm, alumnae brothers or sisters in other companies, embassy officials, retired employees, suppliers, important customers, etc.

自 在

Jizai
(Jee-zie)

"Tapping into Cosmic Creativity"

Until quite recently, the Western world did not give serious thought to the relationship between the mind and the body or to the power of the mind to influence and change the functioning of the body. Such ideas were regarded as mystic nonsense.

It has only been in the last generation or so that Western scientists have begun to accept the idea that their concepts of the physical world are only a part of the human as well as the cosmic equation, and that there is much more to life and existence than what meets the eye.

Western scientists still tend to ignore such Oriental practices as Zen Buddhism, which is now being rediscovered by the Japanese as a means of achieving breakthroughs in social as well as technical challenges.

Zen advocates learned long ago that conventional wisdom and judgment almost always obscure reality, and that until one is able to rid oneself of programmed perceptions, one cannot see reality, achieve personal freedom, or transcend the perceived limitations of the physical world.

Zen practitioners also learned that physical skills could be developed to an astounding degree through a systematic program of Zen techniques—and this was one of the reasons why Japan's famed samurai warriors adopted Zen Buddhism as an essential part of their training in the use of the sword and the bow.

The aim of the warriors was to meld the mind and the body to such a degree that they could transform thought into physical reality—that they could achieve perfection in both defense and offense, and therefore be unbeatable.

Zen continues to play a significant role in Japan today, in business as well as in personal pursuits. One of the modern versions of Zen in the world of business is known as *jizai* (jee-zie), which translates as "personal freedom," or being able to think freely without being influenced by custom, conventional wisdom or any other preconception.

Virtually all of Japan's best-known businessmen-innovators practice *jizai* in one form or another, and it is the underlying philosophy of a growing number of think-tanks, the best-known of which is probably the *Jizai Kenkyu Jo* (Jee-zie Kane-que Jo), or "Jizai Research Institute," founded in 1970 by Masahiro Mori, a Tokyo University professor of engineering who was also the founder of the Robotics Society of Japan.

Although the number of Japanese researchers who publicly identify themselves as "*jizai*-ists" is still small, virtually all of them utilize some Zen techniques. Many of the most impressive products developed in Japan in recent years came out of *jizai*-based creative sessions, and all indications are that Zen will become even more important as a creative technique in the future.

In simple terms, *jizai*-thinking involves meditating until one achieves the ultimate truth or reality, which by definition expresses the innermost feelings and aspirations that are common to man. In product terms, this means the ultimate in function, refined simplicity and beauty.

The Jizai Research Institute's Sueo Matsubara explains the *jizai* approach to creativity as an unending process of refinement and recycling, as in reincarnation. Each time the concept or product is recycled it is improved.

Much of the creative activity in Japanese companies is conducted by *go-nin gumi* (go-neen guu-me), or "five-person teams," and is more concerned with refining ideas and turning them into new products than in coming up with really new concepts.

The challenge the Japanese now face is to use their Zen culture to tap into totally new concepts, then combine them with their skill in turning new ideas into successful products.

96

事前協議

Jizen Kyogi
(Jee-zane K'yoe-ghee)

"Talking It Over in Advance"

Japan's *geisha* (gay-e-shah), literally "art persons," became famous around the world as soon as the world got word of them. Naturally the reason for this instant notoriety was that *geisha* were women who specialized in entertaining men. A more meaningful translation of geisha would be "person skilled in the arts of entertaining."

As the story goes, geisha began as relatively low-class entertainers who entertained high-class courtesans during Japan's colorful Tokugawa period, when redlight districts were as common as present-day shopping malls.

When the Tokugawa shogunate began to lose its grip on the country in the early 1800s, the status of courtesans also began to decline. Up to this time, the more famous prostitutes were as celebrated and as sought-after as contemporary movie and music stars.

Top courtesans had their own suites of rooms, their own entourages, and enjoyed all of the prerogatives of wealth and power. It was their patronage of the first "art-persons" that gave rise to *geisha*, and ironically, was to hasten their own downfall as the darlings of the rich and powerful men of the day.

In an interesting twist of fate, male patrons of the leading courtesans began calling in geisha for their own private parties and meetings at well-known *ryo-tei* (rio-tay-ee), or "inn-restaurants."

The geisha of that period were primarily entertainers, but when they were attractive they were naturally sought-after by their male patrons as bed partners as well—extra-marital affairs being fully sanctioned by society—and it was customary for them to eventually become the mistresses of their most desirable suitors.

The institution of the *geisha* flourished. Their schooling became longer and more professional. Legislation was passed requiring them to have licenses. So-called *geisha* houses, which actually were inn-restaurants that called in *geisha* when requested (there was a category of inn that had live-in *geisha*), became the favorite meeting places of politicians, gang leaders and powerful businessmen.

By the turn of the 20th century, Japan's hundreds of thousands of courtesans were on the bottom of the social ladder, and top *geisha* vied with champion sumo and kabuki stars as the celebrities of the day.

During these decades, a significant percentage of all the high-level political and business meetings took place in *geisha* houses. Compromises and decisions were worked out in the secretive world of the *geisha*, where female companionship, good food and a steady flow of sake added an extraordinary ingredient to the affairs of Japan—not to mention the enigmatic flavor that was added to Japan's image abroad.

These behind-closed-doors meetings were traditional in Japan; only the venue had changed. Such meetings were known as *jizen kyogi* (jee-zane k'yoe-ghee), or "advance meetings," usually held in preparation for later public meetings at which the agreements already made were officially announced.

Jizen kyogi are still the normal pattern of business in present-day Japan—although *geisha* houses are no longer the preferred venue except in the case of old-time politicians. Japanese prefer to work out their positions in private, informal settings, and then present an agreeable pose in public.

When foreign businessmen meet their Japanese counterparts at home or in Japan to negotiate and sign agreements, both sides are at a serious disadvantage if they have not had the opportunity to meet informally several times in advance and work out all of the details. Foreign businessmen should take the initiative in proposing *jizen kyogi* in any negotiations with Japanese.

常 識

Joshiki

(Joe-she-kee)

"Japanese-Style Common Sense"

I have often heard Westerners make presentations to Japanese businessmen and government officials that ranged from casual requests and important proposals to impassioned pleas for understanding and some kind of action. In most instances, the presentations were listened to politely enough, and were often acknowledged in such a way that the foreigner got the impression that something positive was going to be done.

These presentations, of whatever nature, made all the sense in the world to the Westerners. Particularly in the case of businessmen, whose proposals were often based on facts and empirical foundations that seemed indisputable. Yet, time and again they failed to get the desired reaction.

On many of these occasions, the Westerners involved were totally perplexed by their failure to "get through" to the Japanese side; and this was after they had discounted all of the possible "understandable" reasons why their proposals or requests were not or could not be accepted—timing, cost, and so on. A common lament was "It's just common sense! Why can't they (the Japanese) understand (and accept)?"

An unaccounted for factor in such confrontations, whether they involve businessmen, politicians or just friends, is often a fundamental difference in what both sides accept as common sense. In Japanese the term for common sense is *joshiki* (joe-she-kee), which literally means "usual knowledge," with the added connotation of "to know well, to discriminate." But, of course, it is the full cultural interpretation that makes the difference and is important.

Every culture has its own common sense, and one may be as different from the other as night and day. To the average American or European, common sense is more or less a matter of objective, rational, logical thought applied to everyday circumstances. To the un-Westernized Japanese, common sense is more of an emotional and sometimes arbitrary reaction to his or her own social environment, and is influenced by sex, age, family background, education, rank and position in a company or other organization.

In the Japanese context of things, naturally enough, to have common sense is to think like and act like other Japanese in the culturally accepted way at the appropriate time. This called-for attitude and behavior may or may not be objective or logical, because it is designed to protect the individual concerned and to sustain his or her position, not to conform to any universal principle.

To be regarded as having common sense, and to be accepted in any purely Japanese group, it is necessary to exhibit Japanese style *joshiki* at all times. Any other type of behavior is generally regarded as un-Japanese, and in more traditional settings can get one ostracized.

When Western businessmen, diplomats and politicians expect a "common sense" reaction from their Japanese counterparts they are often putting them in an untenable position; damned by the Western side if they don't and damned by their own side if they do.

Virtually all Japanese, including those who have not been directly exposed to Western thinking, are aware that there are differences between Western common sense (usually equated with individualism, objectivity and logical thinking) and Japanese *joshiki*, and they recognize that it is an enormous barrier between them and the West.

Westerners should be equally aware of this important cultural difference, and factor it into their dialogue with the Japanese by letting the Japanese know that they know, that they are willing to compromise up to a point, and then give the Japanese a reasonable amount of time to reach a consensus—literally to agree to behave in a non-Japanese way—that makes sense to both sides.

●98●

会 議

Kaigi
(Kie-ghee)

"Talking Things to Death"

The subjective nature of Japanese culture has been responsible for many of the facets of the "Japanese Way" that Westerners find different—the fascinating as well as the frustrating.

One of the Japanese customs that foreigners often find frustrating, and sometimes regard as a malicious ploy to gain an advantage, is their practice of holding what Westerners regard as excessive numbers of meetings to discuss business or other propositions, and to generally drag out discussions over inordinately long periods of time.

Westerners go all out to make rational, logical presentations, as briefly and as concisely as possible. They presume that if a presentation is, in fact, rational and logical, which includes the belief that it makes good sense for both parties, that it will result in a quick, positive response.

But Japanese perception of what is acceptable and desirable, even what is understandable, does not begin and end with objective reasoning. It begins and often ends with a very personal, emotional reaction that takes into account every individual involved in the discussions or who might be involved in the project if it is implemented.

Therefore, the rationale that the Japanese apply to making judgements may differ markedly from the Western rationale, and because Japanese decisions must accommodate a variety of viewpoints not necessarily based on objective thinking, reaching a consensus is much more involved and takes more time.

This is the reason why Japanese hold so many *kaigi* (kie-ghee), or "meetings," why larger numbers of people attend the same meetings, and why the same or similar questions are asked repeatedly by different individuals over an extended period of time.

Westerners do their best to think and talk in straightforward logical terms, while Japanese culture compels Japanese to think subjectively as well as in terms of "fuzzy logic," that is, "logic" that takes unknown, irrational and unpredictable factors into consideration.

Of course, there are many Western-educated and internationalized

Japanese who are fully capable of the two-plus-two-equals-four kind of thinking, and they are often the ones who act as points of contact for Westerners dealing with Japan.

But problems still arise because they frequently face an even greater challenge than Westerners do in making Western-style presentations to their still traditional Japanese colleagues. Their role is sometimes more difficult because they can be subject to severe criticism if their manner or words irritate the sensitivities of their coworkers.

The only practical recourse that Westerners have in planning for meetings with Japanese is to be aware that some if not all of their reactions will be subjective and "fuzzy," and they must be prepared to take additional time and energy to work with, and possibly around, these factors.

All of this is not to say that the Japanese cannot or do not think, plan and act rationally. They certainly can and do, but it is most often done on a group basis and it takes them longer to get there.

And while "fuzzy logic" is complex and takes longer, it often has major advantages in that it incorporates a more holistic approach that turns out to be superior, whether it concerns a product design, an engineering concept or a marketing program.

改 善

Kai Zen

(Kie Zen)

"Nothing is Ever Good Enough"

From the 1860s to the 1960s, the Japanese were primarily known as copiers and producers of cheap, and usually shoddy, merchandise. They were, and in fact still are, masters at copying foreign products. But the reputation they had for churning out low-quality goods during that long century was an aberration, and was diametrically opposed to both their philosophy and character.

During that long and tumultuous century it was primarily foreign importers, not Japanese manufacturers, who controlled the kind and quality of the products the Japanese produced for export.

The typical routine was for American importers to take American-made products to Japan as samples, and instruct their Japanese suppliers to copy them as cheaply as possible. The Japanese themselves were so turned off by the quality of these made-to-order products that they referred to them in very derogatory terms and generally did not buy them for their own use.

Japanese manufacturers, most of whom were small and without experience in international markets, put up with this undesirable situation until they became strong enough to dump the foreign importers they had been dealing with and establish their own sales networks abroad.

Once the Japanese had regained control over their own designing and manufacturing processes, the age-old cultural conditioning that in the past had compelled them to produce the finest possible products began re-asserting itself. Their centuries of experience in producing classic designs and in mastering precisely structured manufacturing techniques was suddenly a new element in international trade.

In keeping with their cultural traditions, the Japanese quickly formalized and ritualized the philosophy and the process of striving continuously to make things better and better. Also in keeping with their custom of identifying, categorizing and labeling things, they called this updated cultural element *kai zen*, and made it an integral part of their export industry.

Kai zen literally means "continuous improvement," and is a concept that has permeated Japanese culture since ancient times. It means, simply, that the Japanese are driven by an innate urge to continuously strive to improve both the form of the things they make as well as the manufacturing technology and process.

The historical factor that gave rise to the *kai zen* concept was the master-apprentice approach that was applied throughout the arts and crafts, from the making of pottery and bamboo baskets to the painting of wall scrolls. As the centuries passed, acceptable standards became higher and higher until finally even the most mundane article was expected to be a work of art.

In stark contrast to this attitude and behavior, people in most Western societies, particularly in recent decades, have been conditioned to accept minimum standards for both products and services—to deliberately stop short of doing their best.

As long as the Japanese continue to emphasize the *kai zen* concept in their lives, and we remain content to aim for and accept production of inferior goods and services, we will be at a serious disadvantage in competing with Japan.

Ironically, the Japanese credit an American, Dr. W. E. Deming, with providing them with the know-how to build quality control into their modern-day manufacturing process. But quality control experts from Western Electric Company, invited to Japan in 1948 to help reconstruct the telecommunications system, deserve some of the credit.

Dr. Deming, a statistical control authority [who was amost totally ignored by American industry until the 1980s], gave a series of lectures in Japan in 1950 when the country was still occupied by the U.S. and its World War II allies. His lectures inspired the formation of quality control circles and a national effort that was to have repercussions around the world.

In 1951, the Japan Union of Scientists and Engineers founded the Deming Prize to be given each year to the company demonstrating the most effective use of quality-control techniques. [It was not until the late 1980s that American companies began to pick up on the concept of *kai zen*, and that it was better to build products without defects rather than ignore them or try to repair them later.]

100

格好いい

Kakko Ii
(Kahk-koe Ee)

"The Essence of Japaneseness"

People who are intimately familiar with the subdued beauty and elegance of traditional Japanese arts and crafts, and with how the Japanese use color and design motifs, can almost always discern the special look and feel that identifies something as Japanese.

This special Japanese essence is one of the things that distinguishes Japan's traditional gardens, lacquerware, dining ware, kimono, fans, wall paper—even its haiku poetry.

One of the characteristics of Japanese design is a strong sensuality that affects the libido as well as the spirit, adding a fourth dimension to its appeal. It is this appeal that attracts Westerners to the traditional arts and crafts of Japan—including those who have had little or no training in aesthetics.

In the past, Japanese designers incorporated this special essence into their work without forethought or plan because it was programmed into them. But their culturally programmed mind-set prevented them from even thinking about building the same essence into foreign-style products.

This mental block began dissolving in the late 1950s and by the 1980s was virtually gone—primarily because extensive exposure to foreign cultures, especially American, allowed the Japanese for the first time to begin looking at their own culture objectively.

Now, this special Japanese essence in product design is one of the most important factors in Japan's export industries. From perfume bottles and electronic items to the interiors of cars, this traditional Japanese design sense adds to the popularity and salability of things made in Japan.

By the early 1990s, the superior quality of Japanese-made merchandise had become a given, and the combination of subtlety and sophistication, based on the traditional Japanese design sense, began emerging as the latest factor in Japan's competition for the world's markets.

This new/old element in Japanese design primarily applies to more expensive and luxury items that are aimed at Japan's new wealthy class who want the custom-made and the unique, and are willing to pay for it.

Items that have this new element, whether made in Japan or imported, are described as being *kakko ii* (kahk-koe ee), or smart-fashionable-stylish, and appeal to all of the five senses, with the added dimension of sex appeal.

One of the chief elements in the development of such products in Japan is the growing influence of women in all areas of business and the marketplace. Previously relegated to innocuous, temporary positions as file clerks, tea servers, "office flowers" or assembly line automatons, Japanese women are finally coming into their own.

The incorporation of "sensual elements" into products by foreign designers and engineers is not entirely unknown, but in most manufacturing areas it has been relatively low on the priority list.

All signs point to the conclusion that foreign businessmen who want to maintain their home markets, much less sell their products in Japan, are going to have to take this "sensual" factor into consideration in their own designing and engineering; otherwise their products face the risk of becoming obsolete.

Just as the Japanese have made a number of mental breakthroughs in adapting their cultural insights and skills to the demands and opportunities of modern-day business, foreign businessmen must make a few mental leaps of their own to stay in tune with the times.

101

隠し芸

Kakushi Gei

(Kah-kuu-she Gay-ee)

"The Importance of Hidden Talent"

Japanese do not like to be caught off-guard in any way for any reason. They are so used to functioning in a carefully structured, closed system that unexpected events (except for sudden gifts or the appearance of an old friend, etc.) cause them to suffer great stress.

Japanese are also exceptionally subject to being shamed, and a great deal of the training and practice they go through is to prevent themselves from losing face as well as to protect the image of all Japanese and the nation itself.

In a country whose culture demanded and produced superbly skilled artists, craftsmen, even common laborers, it was expected that all individuals would also develop some kind of cultural skill to enhance their own lives.

Some of the personal skills pursued by the Japanese were aesthetic or literary in nature; others pertained to games or sports. Since the standards of skill throughout Japanese society were extraordinarily high—whether for sword-fighting or carpentry work—the Japanese approached their personal cultural pursuits with the same dedication and intensity they applied to their professions.

It also became customary for the Japanese to pursue at least one entertainment-type of skill which they could demonstrate in public. More often than not, this was singing or acting, both of which were popular folk-skills that played important roles in the daily lives of the people.

In anticipation of the regular occasions on which they would be asked to sing or act in public, the Japanese developed a custom of practicing in secret to hone a particular talent, which came to be referred to as one's *kakushi gei* (kah-kuu-she gay-ee), or "hidden talent."

The point of this discreet practicing was not only to be able to perform well in public, but also to be better than expected, impress one's audience and receive applause for the effort.

The pursuit of cultural skills in Japan today is no longer a universal practice, but enough of the tradition remains to add a special flavor to the scene. There are schools for virtually everything, from tap-dancing to building log cabins. Young women attend schools to develop the now vogue "Five Skills" that are considered essential for marriage—flower arranging, performing the tea ceremony, dancing, cooking, and driving a car.

Singing continues to be one of the favorite pastimes of all ages, with young people favoring contemporary popular songs, and the elderly more likely to take up *naniwabushi* (nah-nee-wah-buu-she), or traditional folksongs.

Some people practice their chosen *kakushi gei* privately at home; others take lessons from professional teachers, sometimes spending thousands of dollars on lessons and equipment.

Proliferation of the so-called *karaoke* (kah-rah-oh-kay) bars during the 1970s and 80s, where patrons are encouraged to perform on stage to the accompaniment of recorded orchestra music, brought new life to the *kakushi gei* custom. One of the "pollution complaints" frequently voiced in Japan today is about noisy neighbors practicing their routines on booming speaker boxes.

Most foreign businessmen visiting Japan end up in at least one *karaoke* bar before their trip is done, and are expected to perform with gusto if not skill. The wise thing, of course, is to do a little *kakushi gei* practicing of your own before going to Japan (or visiting a local *karaoke* bar with your Japanese colleagues).

Being able to play a musical instrument and sing will make you the hit of almost any Japanese party, whether in a cabaret or on a company recreational outing.

かまとと

Kamatoto
(Kah-mah-toe-toe)

"The Dumb Blonde Act"

When I first went to Japan as a 19-year-old in the late 1940s, I spent a lot of my free time in bars, cabarets and other places of somewhat less repute, fraternizing (as the U.S. military used to describe it) with young, unattached and available women.

I learned a lot about Japanese psychology, customs and idiosyncrasies from these girls. In fact, still today, I believe that the time I invested in Japan's night-life then was far more valuable to me over the years than what an equivalent amount of time (and money) spent at some highly-ranked business school would have been.

Just one of the lessons I learned is sufficient to make my point. It took no great talent and no experience whatsoever to realize very early on that the girls staffing the night-life places I (and hundreds of thousands of other "Occupationaires") patronized so enthusiastically made a practice of pretending to be much less clever and experienced than they really were.

In virtually every bar or club or whatever, there was always at least one girl who claimed to be totally innocent of what goes on between men and women. Often she was so clever at this ruse that the more naive foreign patrons would virtually drool over the prospect of being the one to introduce her to the pleasures of debauchery.

The girl would lead the would-be playboys on and on, and on some more, milking them as expertly as any calf sucks from its mother.

Before long I learned that this kind of girl was referred to as a *kamato-to* (kah-mah-toe-toe), or someone who "feigns innocence," and that the ploy was an ancient, if not honorable, practice in Japan's entertainment trades.

Sometimes the girls would switch their tactics and accuse their male patrons of pretending to be *kamatoto* who were trying to mislead them into believing that they were innocents and not hardened playboys interested only in taking advantage of the girls.

Later I realized that the use of the *kamatoto* tactic was widespread in Japan, and in fact was a significant factor in the business and personal behavior of Japanese.

I found that it was commonplace for people in all walks of life and in virtually every situation to pretend to be naive and innocent and much less knowledgeable and clever than they really were.

Part of this "Japanese" syndrome no doubt derived from genuine humility, which is a well-known Japanese characteristic. Another part derived from their need to keep a low profile and not attract undue attention to themselves (to appear knowing and aggressive would invite criticism or worse).

But another and very significant aspect of the *kamatoto* syndrome as it is utilized by businessmen involves appearing non-threatening as well as naive, thereby getting more input from the other side than would otherwise be forthcoming.

Westerners, and Americans in particular, are especially susceptible to being taken in by a *kamatoto* act. I have been involved in uncountable situations in which the polite manner, passivity and claims of ignorance by Japanese businessmen would turn Americans on as if someone had pushed their "Start" button, and everything they knew would gush out.

Of course, a lot of Japanese businessmen are quiet when confronted by foreigners because they don't speak the foreigner's language well enough to express themselves clearly and comprehensively. In these cases they don't have to pretend to be innocent, but often end up achieving the same result.

Foreign businessmen might benefit by learning to play the *kamatoto*.

考えておきます

Kangaete Okimasu
(Kahn-guy-tay oh-kee-mahss)

"I'll Give It Some Thought"

There is a perfectly good word for "no" in the Japanese language, but it is seldom used. "Yes," on the other hand, is heard all the time. This does not mean, however, that the Japanese do not say "no." They say it often, even if what they have said sounds like "yes" to the uninitiated.

For many generations the Japanese were conditioned to avoid blunt responses, confrontations or friction of any kind. Since "no" is often confrontational and can cause disappointment and ill will of one kind or another, the Japanese do not like to come right out and say it.

One of the most controversial books published in Japan in 1990 was entitled *The Japan That Can Say No*—which not only recognized the reluctance of the Japanese to express themselves clearly, but was also an attempt by writer-turned-politician Shintaro Ishihara to help the Japanese "cure" themselves of the "can't-say-no" syndrome.

To get around saying "no" directly, the Japanese developed the habit of using the negatives of verbs, giving vague responses and sometimes not answering at all.

Traditionally, the Japanese have also been almost as uncomfortable with "yes" (in the English sense of the word) as they have been with "no." "Yes" could, and often did, lead to new commitments and responsibilities, to building up expectations and so on. As a result, "yes" gradually came to be synonymous with "Yes, I heard you," or "Yes, I am listening." It ceased to mean "Yes, I agree" or "Yes, I will," both of which required the use of another expression—*Hai, sansei shimasu* (hi, sahn-say-ee she-mahss), "Yes, I agree"; *Hai, yarimasu* (hi, yah-ree-mahss), "Yes, I will do it."

Thus it happened in Japan that the use of "yes" and "no," and all the substitutions and circumlocutions used in their place, became very subtle, requiring the hearer to be exceptionally skilled in interpreting what the speaker meant.

The main reason for this development was the overriding need to maintain harmony, and the importance of self-preservation. Harmony took precedence over personal feelings, and disharmony could be life-threatening.

While the importance of harmony in present-day Japan has eroded significantly—certainly to the point that life or limb are usually not endangered by its lapse—it still influences behavior on the most fundamental level, especially in the use of language.

A naked "no" is still taboo in many situations in Japan, situations in which Westerners think it not only appropriate, even polite, to say "no," but dishonest or even misleading not to come right out with it.

One of the most common substitutes for "no" in the business world is *kangaete okimasu* (kahn-guy-tay oh-kee-mahss), or "I/we will think about it." Generally, when *kangaete okimasu* is the reaction to the proposal or presentation, it means "I/we are not interested."

Being polite, and wanting to put the best face possible on such meetings (so everyone will continue to feel good), the Japanese side may exude friendly interest and even be positive in their comments, but *kangaete okimasu* is almost always a turn-down.

Another code word for "no," often used before the final pronouncement of *kangaete okimasu,* is *muzukashii* (muu-zu-kah-she-e-), or "difficult." When someone says, "It is difficult"—*Muzukashii desu,* (Muu-zuu-kah-she-e dess)—that really means "It is impossible, it won't work, it's too much trouble, we don't have time to bother with it," etc. Another commonly used expression that is much more direct, and comes as close to being an outright "no" as the average Japanese is capable of, is *chotto muri* (choat-toe muu-ree). *Chotto* means "just a little." *Muri* means, "unnatural, unjust, impossible."

A fairly accurate and acceptable way of finding out if an idea is going to receive serious consideration is to say something like, "What do you think? Is it difficult?"—*Do omoimasu ka? Muzukashi desu ka?* (Doh-oh-moy-mahss ka? Muu-zoo-kah-she dess ka?). If the response is quick agreement, the answer is clear.

104

歓 迎 会　　送 別 会

Kangei Kai / Sobetsu Kai
(Kahn-gay-e Kie / Soe-bate-sue Kie)

"Nurturing Group Bonds"

The Japanese rebuilt their country in just fifteen years following the end of World War II, and in another fifteen years went on to become the world's second largest economic power. This astounding performance earned the Japanese the reputation of being "economic animals"—meaning that like dumb animals they didn't know any better than to work all the time.

It was widely assumed around the world that the Japanese were without humor, and never engaged in frivolous or recreational behavior because, like bees, they were conditioned to do nothing but work.

This image of the Japanese was entirely false. It is true that they worked very hard, especially from 1945 until 1975, but it is not true that they took no time out at all for recreation or frivolous fun.

The idea that the Japanese were basically humorless was spread by people who did not know them, didn't speak their language, didn't associate intimately with them, and generally saw them only from a distance while they were working or involved in some formal activity.

In fact, one of the most important and conspicuous facets of Japan's traditional culture is a fondness for humor—found everywhere; in their poetry, their songs, their theater, their legends, even their myths. The Japanese language itself reflects their love and use of humor.

Except in formal situations, Japanese conversations are peppered with jokes, puns, exaggerations and every other type of humor you can imagine. During their after-work hours they are more likely to engage in strictly good-time activities than are Americans, who habitually talk shop when they are supposed to be having fun.

In fact, the leisure/recreational industry has been one of the largest and most important industries in Japan since the early 1600s, when entertainment districts became the center of public life in all of the urban areas. In the 1950s, during the heyday of Japan's rush to economic glory, there were more people employed in the entertainment trades than in any other single industry.

Every city in Japan today has from a few to dozens of thriving entertainment districts, some of them virtually cities within themselves. Visitors are invariably astounded to discover that there are more night-life facilities in Japan than in any other country in the world.

Even Japan's vaunted business system is not all nose-to-the-grindstone. The custom of *kangei kai* (kahn-gay-e kie), or "welcome parties," is just one of the means by which the working world breaks up the grey monotony of long hours and rigid etiquette.

Kangei kai are thrown when new employees join companies, when transferees arrive from other departments, branches or the head office, and when members return from overseas assignments. In the same manner, *sobetsu kai* (soe-bate-sue kie), or "farewell parties," are held to bid adieu to employees leaving on assignments or retiring.

Both *kangei kai* and *sobetsu kai* are fun parties marked by eating, drinking and intimate communing, some of it ritualistic, designed to strengthen the group-ties of the employees. Celebrations involving higher-ranking managers or executives are frequently held in restaurants or hotels, often involve several hundred people, and may cost dozens of thousands of dollars.

Since departures and arrivals are commonplace in larger Japanese companies, both *kangei kai* and *sobetsu kai* are regular occurrences, breaking up the work-periods and providing employees with fun-times at the company's expense.

105

環境　　快適　　休暇

Kankyo, Kaiteki, Kyuka

(Kahn-k'yoe, Kie-tay-kee, Kyuu-kah)

"Creed of the New Breed"

When I went to work for a Japanese company in Tokyo in 1953, one of the things I had to adjust to was that at 5:30 p.m., the official quitting time, no one stopped working and went home.

On rare occasions one of the women in the office would request permission from the manager to leave around 6 p.m. because of some personal reason, but the regular staff normally worked until 6:30 before leaving. Sub-managers stayed on until the manager left, usually between 7:00 and 7:30 p.m.

I was to learn later that working overtime, particularly by managers, was the custom among virtually all Japanese office employees. The practice was not something new that had come about as an emergency measure to help rebuild the war-shattered economy, however. It had deep cultural roots.

Prior to the widespread introduction of the Western industrial system into Japan in the 1870s and 80s, a working day could basically have any number of hours. Under the old, traditional system, income was not based on working for a specific amount of time. It was determined by personal needs, seniority and other factors.

As Japan's postwar economy recovered and went on to surpass even the wildest imagination, working "overtime" became an amalgamate of loyalty to the firm, a burning sense of service to others, patriotism, and fierce competition among managers wanting to rise as high as possible in the company hierarchy.

For the majority of Japan's managers, working for years without taking a day of official leave-time became a matter of perverse pride. And obviously such behavior made a significant contribution to Japan's amazing economic success.

But by the mid-1980s, this success had bred a new generation of Japanese who had not been conditioned in the psychology of self-denial and self-sacrifice, and, instead, had become addicted to the virtues of pleasure and self-expression.

Among the philosophies preferred by this new breed were those expressed in the terms *kankyo* (kahn-k'yoe), *kaiteki* (kie-tay-kee) and *kyuka* (kyuu-kah), or "environmental influence," "comfortable conditions" and "vacations." Their attitude was that they did not want to work for companies unless they were environmentally responsible, provided comfortable working conditions, and encouraged their employees to take vacations.

The depth of this shift in the thinking of young Japanese was revealed in a 1991 survey by the Ministry of Labor which showed that close to 50 percent of all new male recruits who had joined Japanese companies during the past year were so dissatisfied with their jobs and employers that they wanted to quit. Sixty percent of the women surveyed said they would like to leave their companies.

Today things that used to attract young Japanese job candidates to companies—size, length of time the company has been in existence, type of industry, and so on—are no longer the most important criteria. They are now prompted by strong feelings of social responsibility combined with an equally fervent desire for lives filled with personal satisfaction.

Their advocacy of *kankyo, kaiteki* and *kyuka* will play a significant role as Japanese society continues to evolve. One of the more immediate effects of this new attitude is a tendency for job seekers to look more favorably at foreign companies in Japan because they generally have more enlightened images than Japanese firms.

環境造り

Kankyo Zukuri

(Kahn-k'yoe Zuu-ku-ree)

"Becoming Creative in Bars"

By the early 1980s, many of Japan's most astute thinkers were saying the greatest challenge facing the country was to transform the people from copiers and followers into a nation of creators and leaders—to basically alter the way the Japanese think and behave.

This is a formidable task. From the dawn of Japanese history to the mid-1900s, Japanese life was based on mutual responsibility, mutual dependence, group-think and a precisely coordinated behavior that was designed to maintain political and social order—and, in earlier times, to prevent change.

The country's political, social and economic environment was carefully fashioned to condition the people to function in the manner prescribed by the government and by tradition. Housing and the workplace were designed to foster group-think and group behavior.

When universal education was introduced into Japan in the second half of the 18th century, it too was founded on the principle that all Japanese should think according to precise guidelines set down by the government, behave in exactly the same way according to their station in life, follow orders, and do nothing on their own.

More than a century later this system still prevails, but growing pressure from the business community and some government ministries is bringing about changes. By the 1980s, many Japanese had awakened to the idea that cultural emphasis on homogeneity in thought and behavior could be the Achilles' heel that would undermine everything they had achieved through taking advantage of foreign know-how and technology.

The new buzzwords became original thinking, individual action, creativity—all those things that had been, and in many areas still were, taboo throughout the Japanese Establishment.

Not surprisingly, some Japanese faced the challenge of learning how to become creative with the same astuteness that they brought to importing and using Western technology. Their approach to initiating a revolution in Japanese behavior began with the physical environment. They started designing and furnishing "non-Japanese" style offices that contribute to *kankyo zukuri* (kahn-k'yoe zuu-kuu-ree), or "original thinking," rather than suppress it.

Instead of the typical open areas jammed with desks and people that have traditionally been regarded as both appropriate and necessary for the group-oriented Japanese to function effectively, these new offices have private spaces and special, comfortably appointed nooks where small groups can meet for quiet discussions.

Other pioneers in introducing individuality into Japan began using the country's huge collection of bars, clubs, cabarets, pubs and beer halls as training grounds for this new breed of Japanese. Reason for this was that the Japanese had long ago sanctioned drinking for recreational purposes, and had established after-hours drinking sessions as a time when they could "forget etiquette" and break the taboos that bound them to rigid behavior during the workday.

These advocates of Western-style individualism and innovation realized that the only situation in which they could expect their colleagues and subordinates to open up and be themselves was while drinking in the evenings. They began conducting indoctrination sessions after-hours in drinking establishments, encouraging their fellow workers to shed their cultural restraints and engage in the kind of free-for-all dialogue that stimulates *kankyo zukuri*. A very Japanese solution to a serious problem, this kind of unrestrained dialogue was quickly dubbed "nomi-nication," a hybrid word made up of the first half of *nomimasu* (no-me-mahss), or "drink," and the last half of communication.

感 性

Kan Sei

(Kahn Say-ee)

"The Merging of Reason and Emotion"

One factor that stands out in Japanese life is the role of emotion, which often takes precedence over reason. Not surprisingly, this one Japanese trait has been more criticized by foreigners than almost any other facet of Japanese attitude and behavior.

Foreigners who go to Japan for business purposes, or take up residence there for any purpose, and come face-to-face with typical Japanese behavior across the cultural board are inevitably surprised and ultimately frustrated by innumerable instances when emotion, rather than reason, determines the actions and reactions of the Japanese.

There is perhaps nothing more irritating to the logical-minded Westerner than becoming involved with anyone, much less a whole nation, who does not behave in a "reasonable" manner. To Westerners, people who allow their emotions to direct a substantial part of their behavior are suspect and not to be trusted with anything of importance. When emotionalism goes beyond a very low level we regard it as insanity.

I recall very clearly a time in the 1950s when foreign businessmen living in Japan or visiting Japan on buying trips would complain loudly and frequently that the Japanese were so unreasonable (emotional) that there was no way they could develop beyond producing export products under the direction of foreigners.

Perhaps it was a combination of Shintoism and Zen Buddhism that created the capacity in the Japanese to be at home with both emotion and reason, with emotion as often as not overriding reason. The Zen factor in Japanese thought gives them a considerable advantage in being able to distinguish between reality and the unreal or the imagined. The Zen eye sees beyond the facade to the core of a thing.

But long before the appearance of Zen Buddhism in Japan, the Japanese were steeped in the emotional needs of the body and spirit and had incorporated an extraordinary degree of emotionalism into every facet of their lifestyle, including their arts and crafts.

Now we have the modern-day Japanese utilizing their dual character to give themselves both a creative and a technical advantage in manufacturing consumer products for export—products that have a built-in emotional content that helps make them more desirable to consumers.

This new merger of emotion and reason in designing and building consumer products is known as *kan sei* (kahn say-ee), or "emotional rightness," and refers to how people perceive, react to and use the products. *Kan sei* is also defined as "absolute awareness" of the emotional and rational content of a product.

Again, we have a situation where the Japanese have created a word for an otherwise esoteric concept, and can thus talk about it intelligently, recognize it when they see it, and teach it—all prerequisites to being able to deliberately build it into their products.

In addition to building *kan sei* into their products, the Japanese also use the concept in their advertising campaigns, generally giving more weight to the emotional content of the products than to their utilitarian value.

Westerners wanting to catch up with the Japanese in designing and making consumer-oriented products, much less win the lead from them, must reorient their own thinking and then master the skills necessary to give their products personalities that attract and please the people they want to buy those products.

――――――― 108 ―――――――

カラオケ

Karaoke

(Kah-rah-oh-kay)

"Japanese-Style De-Stressing"

Japan's medical authorities estimate that well over sixty percent of the population suffers from stress—a penalty that is being paid for a fast-paced, mechanized lifestyle that shows very little evidence of slowing down.

Prior to the industrialization of Japan between 1870 and 1895, life for most Japanese, most of the time, was slow and evenly paced by the seasons. About the only serious ongoing source of stress was the pressure to make a living under the strict clan and shogunate systems of government. But life was so basic for the majority that even this does not compare with the pressures existing today.

Furthermore, many of the lifestyle customs that had been traditional in Japan for more than a thousand years helped relieve the daily stresses of living. These customs included taking hot-baths daily at neighborhood bathhouses, where the sexes were mixed and the nightly experience was social as well as sanitary.

Hundreds of thousands of people also took regular advantage of the hotspring spas that dotted the country, and—for the menfolk living in towns and cities—there was virtually unrestricted access to a nationwide network of redlight districts and assignation inns.

The most popular and commonly used of all the distractions from work and daily stress, especially for urban dwellers, were the public eating and drinking places found in virtually every neighborhood, along shopping streets, in local entertainment districts and at stopping stations along the country's network of walking roads.

Living in tiny houses constructed of wood on the outside and paper and straw on the inside, with fragile rooms that were mostly bare spaces, the Japanese spent as much time as possible in public places, eating, drinking, talking and entertaining themselves and each other.

Singing was both a popular custom and profession in early Japan, and played a key role as a recreational activity. Drinking bouts typically brought on exhibitions of singing.

The development of the electronic industry in Japan in the 1950s and 60s was to have an extraordinary impact on singing in bars, virtually creating a new industry and providing Japan's millions of overworked businessmen with a totally new means of relieving stress and expressing their emotions.

The appearance of electronic sound systems hooked up to record players resulted in the proliferation of so-called *karaoke* (kah-rah-oh-kay) bars throughout Japan and, shortly thereafter, in foreign Japanese enclaves as well.

Karaoke is short for "empty orchestra," meaning that the singer performs with an orchestra that is not really there.

This new ingredient in self-expression through singing has added new zest to Japan's already burgeoning night-life. There is probably not one Japanese businessman in the country today who has not been in a *karaoke* bar and done his very best to imitate one or more of the noted Japanese and American singers.

The power of *karaoke* singing, done with maximum sincerity and gusto, is remarkable, and has to be experienced to be believed. I have absolutely no skill in singing, so the first time I got up before a *karaoke* bar audience, I had to be half-drunk and literally dragged on stage by my Japanese host, the president of a major company, who was kind and considerate enough to join me in the exhibition.

Once I was up in front of the crowd and doing my best to carry a tune (I had to read the lyrics from a music book thoughtfully provided by the bar), the rush I got was amazing. It was, in a way, better than sex.

Foreign businessmen who do not know any songs and are contemplating or already doing business with Japanese are well advised to memorize and practice two or three songs, no matter how short or simple the choices might be, as part of their business skills. Japanese sing in English about as often as they do in Japanese, with Frank Sinatra's "My Way" being a favorite.

過労死

Karoshi

(Kah-roe-she)

"Death From Overwork"

Japan's rise from the devastation of World War II to economic prominence between 1945 and 1975 was not without human cost. People cannot work for ten or twelve hours a day six and seven days a week, year after year, without suffering physically as well as mentally.

But during the first three postwar decades no one paid any special attention to the larger than usual number of men in their 40s and 50s who died of brain and heart ailments, most often from acute cardiac insufficiency and subarachnoid hemorrhage.

It was not until the latter part of the 1980s, when several high-ranking business executives who were still in their prime years suddenly died without any previous signs of illness, that the news media began picking up on what appeared to be a new phenomenon.

This new phenomenon was quickly labeled *karoshi* (kah-roe-she), or "death from overwork," and once it had a name and its symptoms were broadcast far and wide, it just as quickly became obvious that Japan was experiencing a virtual epidemic.

According to Labor Ministry statistics there had been only twenty-one cases of *karoshi* in 1987, twenty-nine cases in 1988 and thirty cases in 1989. But a liaison council of attorneys established in 1988 to monitor deaths from overwork estimated in 1990 that over 10,000 people were dying each year from *karoshi*.

At that time, Hiroshi Kawahito, an attorney who was acting as the secretary-general of the *Karoshi Bengo Dan Zenkoku Renraku Kaigi* (Kah-roe-she Bane-go Dahn Zen-koe-kuu Rane-rah-kuu Kie-ghee), or "National Liaison Council of Lawyers on Death from Overwork," said: "The corporate world is hiding behind promises of improved consumer services while partaking in excessive competition, thus victimizing its employees."

Kawahito added that employers generally do not recognize *karoshi* as job-related, and that since the Ministry of Labor supports the efforts of industry to maintain a high growth rate it works against the interests of employees. He accused some Labor Ministry officials of being soft on management because they were angling for cushy jobs with major corporations after they retired from government service.

Yoshinori Hasegawa, vice director of the Chiba Kensei Hospital and a recognized authority on *karoshi*, says that most of the victims of death from overwork had been putting in more than one hundred hours of overtime each month. He said the victims did not receive any overtime pay for their extra work, but were members of the elite managerial class who worked themselves to death "out of a samurai-like pride."

Because of peer pressure to keep up with co-workers, out-do competing groups and increase market-share at the expense of competitors, hundreds of thousands of Japanese managers are caught up in a vortex of psychological pressure that forces them to work at a frenzied pace.

After years of such intense over-work, most managers find that they cannot rest even when they do take time off. They are so wound up that not working leaves them disoriented and suffering from serious stress.

Masaaki Noda, professor of foreign studies at Kobe City University, says it is not difficult to understand why so many of Japan's salarymen work so hard because they have shut themselves off from their families and have no place to go but to work.

課制

Ka Sei

(Kah Say-ee)

"Doing Things by the Numbers"

In his controversial book, *The Enigma of Japanese Power*, Karel Van Wolferen, the Dutch journalist, said that many of the most detrimental aspects of the politics and economics practiced by the Japanese result from what he called "the system."

The Japanese are, in fact, one of the most systematized societies in the world. The whole of Japan's culture is based on precisely delineated and defined systems that begin with the concept and process, and include the manner in which the process is applied, down to the finest detail.

This concern with systems has been both an advantage and a disadvantage to the Japanese. On the one hand, breaking things up into their smallest units and studying them carefully greatly enhances understanding of whatever is concerned. Then devising highly refined processes for making a product, using a product, or manipulating a concept provides for the development of a high level of expertise and quality.

On the negative side, however, dependence upon exact systems to study and to perform tasks, particularly in groups in which individuals are not encouraged to take the lead or accept individual responsibility, can be so stifling that it limits creativity and innovation, and often prevents change altogether.

In Japan's business world, the basic company unit is the *ka sei* (kah say-ee), or "section system." Like a squad in a military company, each section consists of a squad leader, the *ka cho* (kah choe), or "section chief," and anywhere from half a dozen to two dozen or so staff members, depending on the overall size of the company and the role of the section.

Several *ka* together make up a *bu* (buu) or "department," which may vary in size from two or three dozen people to well over one hundred, again depending on the size of the company and the function of the department.

As in a military organization, the *ka* (squad) is the primary work unit—the one that is in the trenches and gets the nitty-gritty work done. But the military analogy breaks down here. The *ka* is far more autonomous and influential in the overall operation of the company than a military squad.

In addition to staff work, the other key function of the *ka* is making proposals for specific actions designed to advance the interests and goals of the firm. These proposals, in writing, are circulated upward from section to department and then to the executive and director level. If they are approved, the plans are initiated.

Ideas for proposals acted on by *ka* may originate on a departmental or executive level in the company, or they may be brought in from the outside at a departmental or executive level and then turned over to the appropriate section for the research and planning. In some cases, the *ka cho* themselves or members of their staffs come up with the idea.

This process is the origin of the "bottoms up" type of management for which Japan is notorious or famous, depending on your viewpoint. In very broad terms, what it means to the outsider wanting to do business with a Japanese company is that section managers, not higher executives, are often the keys to success.

If a section chief does not approve of a proposal, the chances of it getting through the complicated process of consensus-approval are greatly reduced. It is therefore often vital that foreign businessmen dealing with Japanese companies make sure they work closely with the *ka cho*.

肩 書

Katagaki

(Kah-tah-gah-kee)

"Rank Has Its Privileges"

One of the traditional customs in Japan is for special guests at receptions and other public affairs to be distinguished by large, conspicuous floral decorations pinned to the lapels of their jackets. The decorations are sometimes so large they seem to shout out the importance of the people wearing them.

At a recent reception in Tokyo I came across a man in his late twenties or early thirties who was wearing a huge floral-wreathed lapel button that read in Japanese, "I am the most important person here!"

Whoever that young man was, he had a lot of courage to flaunt tradition and strike at the Japanese penchant for emphasizing rank and privilege. Every time I think of that occasion I smile anew, and am reassured that the pretentiousness that has characterized Japanese society for ages is gradually wearing away.

Rank, of one kind or another, is still of vital importance to Japanese, however. Back in the fifties it was common to measure companies by the amount of their paid-in capital. One rather conspicuous incident that I remember well occurred at the end of a large party in a garden-style restaurant in Tokyo.

The chauffeur-driven automobiles of the top corporation executives attending the party were called to the entrance in the order of the size of their firms' capital. Today, companies are much more likely to be measured by the amount of their annual sales and the size of their market share.

Japanese concern with rank evolved from their vertically structured feudal society. People were divided into hereditary classes that were ranked in the order of their social and political standing—although in practice, the top-ranked samurai were frequently the only ones whose privileges and rights really counted.

Each social class was similarly divided into groups by community, occupation, location, size, wealth, and so on. In the family, the father was paramount. Generally, males took precedence over females. Seniority brought with it a certain degree of rank.

One of the key factors in the country's stylized and ritualized etiquette system was strict adherence to rank, including the use of the language in such a way as to distinguish between superiors and inferiors, and to properly indicate and conform to one's own rank.

Rank-consciousness was thus instilled into the Japanese from childhood on—in the way they were taught the language, how to think and how to act. In their system it was constantly necessary to make judgements on what level of language to use when addressing or responding to everyone, particularly strangers.

The wrong choice of language to a high-placed member of the samurai class, or to an especially arrogant samurai of any rank, or to anyone for that matter, could have repercussions that ranged from serious to fatal.

Still today, the Japanese attitude toward rank and title are very similar to that prevailing in strict military organizations. People with rank are addressed by that rank and their names, or just the rank itself. A section manager in a Japanese company is almost always personally addressed as *Ka Cho* (Kah Choe) or "Section Manager." The proper form of address for a company president is *Sha Cho* (Shah Choe), or "President,"—not simply his name.

When talking about people with titles it is customary to refer to them by their last name plus their title: General Manager Kato is "Kato Bucho," President Tanaka is "Tanaka Shacho." In other words, the title comes after the family name. Female employees, and sometimes younger male employees who know managers or the president of their company quite well, will sometimes add the honorific *san* (sahn) to the title as a way of making it more familiar or personal.

The use of familiar forms of address among Japanese businessmen and other professionals—first names or nick-names—has traditionally been absolutely taboo. Men would often address female employees by their first names, however.

This strict conformity to the old way is still the norm in Japan, but Japanese who are bilingual and involved in international business are gradually adopting the Western practice of using first names with foreigners.

Still today when the Japanese introduce themselves they customarily mention only their last names, and the use of first names is generally limited to the young. Even life-long friends, particularly men, revert to using each others' last names after they finish school and enter the business world.

Interestingly, ordinary Japanese could not officially have last names until 1870. Prior to that the feudal government restricted the official use of family names to the royal family, members of the samurai class and to a few commoners who had distinguished themselves as artists or in some other prestigious profession. Unofficially, however, ordinary people had been using last names since the 17th century. The use of family names became compulsory in 1875.

112

Katakana

(Kah-tah-kah-nah)

"Building In a Foreign Flavor"

Americans and other English-speaking people are familiar with the practice of using French words or words from other foreign languages to give a special flavor to advertising copy, product names and literary efforts.

But this practice is limited because of practical as well as literary reasons. Readers often cannot pronounce or understand the foreign terms that are used, and they may resent writers who impose this kind of device on them.

There are no such restraints in Japan. In fact, it is almost impossible to listen to a Japanese conversation for more than a few seconds or read more than a few sentences of almost any kind of contemporary Japanese writing without hearing or running into foreign words.

The Japanese have, in fact, made the addition of foreign words into their vocabulary a national effort. Since the 1950s, hundreds of foreign words—mostly English—have been added to the Japanese language every year, and there is now a thick dictionary of them.

The practice is so prevalent that it has received a kind of official recognition from an organization that keeps track of the words added each year, singles out the most interesting ones and writes them up in a national publication.

But in their usual way, the Japanese do not adopt foreign words as they are. They Japanize them by pronouncing them in Japanese, with the result that native speakers of the language from which the words came can no longer understand them. They are, in effect, new words.

Not only do Japanese who use these new words have to learn their meanings, foreigners who speak Japanese also have to learn them as new vocabulary. Just one example demonstrates the fundamental change that takes place: *miruku* (me-ruu-kuu).

Miruku is the Japanization of "milk," and it is absolutely meaningless to everyone until the meaning is learned.

But the Japanese do not stop with the Japanization of the pronunciation of foreign words. They have a special phonetic system of writing called *katakana* (kah-tah-kah-nah) that is reserved exclusively for transcribing foreign words. (A second phonetic script called *hiragana* (he-rah-gah-nah) is strictly used for writing native Japanese.)

Writing foreign words in *katakana* allows the Japanese to distinguish between foreign and traditional Japanese vocabulary no matter how common the foreign words have become in the Japanese language or how long they have been a part of the culture.

It also makes it possible for the Japanese to add a visibly foreign nuance to their signs, advertisements and other writings simply by rendering them in *katakana*. A few Japanese choose to inject a foreign flavor into their names by writing them in this dedicated script, but this is seen as an affectation and may be regarded as anti-Japanese.

One must also be careful to not overdo the use of *katakana*. Any use beyond single words is likely to appear as a foreign affectation and turn Japanese readers off. Such usage has an exaggerated or caricature image that appears cartoonish.

By the same token, writing a foreign name in *hiragana* in an attempt to add a Japanese flavor does not have the desired effect. To the Japanese, it is simply not right and shouldn't be done.

仇討ち
Katakiuchi
(Kah-tah-kee-uu-chee)

"The Need for Revenge"

One of the hallmarks of Japan's feudal samurai warrior class was a deeply engrained sense of honor that, ideally, was unbounded. Upholding their honor, which for the most part meant absolute loyalty to their lords, was the essence of the code of conduct that distinguished the samurai, and took precedence over life itself.

While this all-encompassing code of honor and the strict mental and physical conditioning it demanded resulted in the samurai becoming paragons of Japan's Confucian culture, it also programmed them to be killing machines in defense of their lords and their honor.

Unfortunately, strife in feudal Japan was not confined to the battle-fields. Constant rivalry among the clan lords made intrigue, spying, kidnap-pings, assassinations and other forms of violence commonplace. Obsessed with the honor of their families and clans, each act of violence called for *katakiuchi* (kah-tah-key-uu-chee), or revenge. *Kataki* by itself means "enemy," *Uchi* means "destroy."

During the long centuries of the earliest shogunates, from 1192 until 1603, acts of *katakiuchi* were socially sanctioned, but were not controlled by the government. In the first years of the Tokugawa Shogunate, which began in 1603, a law was passed prohibiting revenge killings except in the case of the murder of a superior.

However, as the decades of the Tokugawa era passed, the law pertaining to revenge killings was gradually broadened to cover one's parents, older brothers and sisters, and finally uncles as well.

Before setting out to avenge someone's death it was necessary to apply to the local clan government for a "certificate of permission," which was in effect a license to kill that had to be carried at all times.

If the search for the killer required travel, the local lord sent an announcement out to the rest of the country, notifying the authorities that the avenger was on an authorized mission. When the avenger found the killer, he had to inform the local authorities and obtain their permission to proceed. Higher-principled samurai challenged their enemies to a sword fight, which generally took place inside a fenced-in ring, with a government official on hand to witness the event.

Revenge killings became the subject matter for many of Japan's most popular bunraku and kabuki plays, which are still performed today as examples of Japan's traditional culture. Most of the vendetta plays emphasize the tragic aspects of such killings, particularly the sacrifices the avengers—and their families—must make in order to achieve their goals.

While the bloodletting that was characteristic of Japan's feudal age has long since gone, the Japanese are still marked by a strong sense of pride in their country, in their culture, in their Japaneseness—and they feel honor-bound to protect and preserve their independence and uniqueness.

The need for revenge remains a significant part of the character of most Japanese on a private, personal level as well as on a national, public level—but without the sacrificial aspects. They prefer to take their revenge in more subtle ways, without endangering themselves.

Having been weaned on the concept that revenge is a duty rather than a sin, and never subjected to a "turn the other cheek" philosophy, Japanese tend to look upon revenge as a natural right. This, in one sense, gives them an advantage over people who are prone to let others abuse them.

The only defense against a tradition of vengence is to always be forthright and candid in both private and business matters. Japanese are especially skilled in recognizing deception in any form while masking their own intentions and actions.

肩叩き

Kata Tataki
(Kah-tah Tah-tah-kee)

"Getting Tapped on the Shoulder"

Japan's government has come in for a lot of criticism ever since the fall of the shogunate system in 1867/8. Most of the criticism has been based on the same factors that apply to most entrenched bureaucracies—

unresponsiveness to the public, arrogance, and the tendency to grow and become more and more powerful.

But there is one criticism that has traditionally been made of Western bureaucracies that has never applied to Japan's government ministries and agencies. While Western bureaucracies have generally been infamous for the limited ability and low character of their personnel, Japanese bureaucracies have traditionally employed the most talented, loyal, ambitious and honest people in the country.

There are no doubt many reasons for the perceived as well as the actual differences between most Western bureaucrats and Japanese bureaucrats. Among other things, there has always been a tendency for Westerners to see government in general as a necessary evil. The Japanese, on the other hand, have traditionally regarded a strong government as both natural and desirable, and approved of it acting as a guide and a protector.

The high repute of the government in Japan, combined with its power in guiding and controlling the affairs of the country, has always attracted some of the best and brightest men (and more recently, women) from each generation.

The tests that government job applicants must take are very difficult, and only those who score the highest are accepted, further distinguishing them from the annual crop of university graduates who are already outstanding.

Within the ministries and agencies of the government, all bureaucrats have traditionally been promoted on the basis of seniority, but only up to a certain level. From that level on, the weeding out of those who are less capable is as rigorous and ruthless a process as can be.

The end result of this elimination process in the higher levels of Japanese bureaucracy is that those who reach the top, or get anywhere near it, are almost always the best qualified—which obviously explains a great deal of the government's success in helping to coordinate the economy of the country.

Like all bureaucrats everywhere, however, government employees in Japan give job security a high priority, and are protected by legislation that gives them the right to work for as long as they want (whereas most companies have mandatory retirement ages).

To prevent employees from working beyond the age of acceptable efficiency, and from occupying positions that could be handled better by deserving younger staff, the bureaucracy has developed its own Japanese-style solution to the problem—a procedure that is known informally as *kata tataki* (kah-tah tah-tah-kee), or "shoulder tapping."

The implication of *kata tataki* is that individuals who (it is believed) should retire because of their age and diminishing capacity can expect to be approached by a senior who taps them on the shoulder and suggests that it is time for them to pack up and go home.

Candidates for earlier-than-planned retirement are not always tapped on the shoulder, but their superiors let them know discreetly that it would be appreciated if they would "volunteer" to step out. If they agree, it is standard practice to promote them one grade in rank, which means they receive a larger lump-sum retirement allowance and monthly pension.

可愛い

Kawaii

(Kah-wah-ee)

"A Case of Terminal Cuteness"

Observers of the Japanese scene frequently comment on facets of Japanese character that distinguish them from other people—comments that cover a variety of ambiguous reactions.

One facet of traditional Japanese culture that invariably elicits a visceral reaction from Western visitors and residents is a fundamentally illogical element that manifests itself in a variety of ways—some of them quite surprising to Westerners.

General Douglas MacArthur, who served as the Supreme Commander of the Allied Powers that occupied Japan following the end of World War II in 1945 (and was greatly admired by most Japanese), once commented that in dealing with the Japanese it was necessary to treat them as if they were 12-year-olds—a characterization that did not upset the average Japanese because they readily admitted that it was true.

MacArthur was referring to the dual character of the Japanese—the fact that they tend to be philosophical and profound one moment and emotional and illogical the next. In fact, in most areas of Japanese life there is no clear-cut separation between emotion and logical thought. Both elements are necessary for the Japanese in order for them to keep their intellectual and emotional balance.

Still today Western attempts to compel the Japanese to think and behave in a strictly logical manner are almost always met with resistance and failure to some degree. The typical Japanese simply cannot function effectively without the necessary emotional ingredient.

One of the more important facets of the emotional side of the Japanese is a compulsive adoration of baby-like cuteness as expressed in the term *kawaii* (kah-wah-ee). The Japanese are more culturally conditioned than most to react positively to people and to things that radiate the kind of sweet innocence found in infants.

Young women in the entertainment trades will often act *kawaii* as an additional lure in their repertoire of sexual charms. Until well into the 1970s, this was stock-in-trade for all young Japanese women wanting to appear more appealing to men.

In broad terms, Japan's traditional culture looks upon infantile innocence as the ideal character for people of all ages—a feeling that is manifested in a variety of ways from how old-fashioned wives treat drunken husbands to how the cuteness factor is utilized in business.

The cuteness syndrome plays a vital role, and is instantly recognizable, in the advertising industry and in consumer products made for children, teenagers and young women up to the age of 25 or so.

Generally, Japanese—and foreigners who are tuned into the Japanese psyche—can go down a department store aisle of merchandise at a rapid walk and identify which items are Japanese-designed and which are foreign without breaking stride—just by their style and overwhelming degree of cuteness.

A significant percentage of Japan's television commercials are specifically designed around cuteness themes that are on the infantile level. The aim of the commercials is to portray virginal innocence and childish honesty; to reach the viewer on the deepest level of goodness.

Westerner reactions to this infantile-cute factor in Japanese TV commercials are often negative because by Western standards they go too far. Some of the commercials are so cute, so sweet, that they turn foreign viewers off.

The Japanese attachment to cuteness does not appear to be weakening as a result of Western influence. It remains an element in the Japanese marketplace that foreign businessmen need to recognize and consider in their efforts to sell in Japan.

━━━━━━━━━━━━━━ **116** ━━━━━━━━━━━━━━

かゆい処に手が届く

Kayui Tokoro ni Te ga Todoku

(Kah-yuu-ee Toe-koe-roe nee Tay ga Toe-doe-kuu)

"Giving the Best Service"

In societies where government leaders and their minions have absolute power over the people, it invariably happens that the people develop a variety of techniques and customs to stay on good terms with their overlords.

All of the methods designed to appease the "lords of life" and keep them as benevolent as possible naturally entail a significant degree of servile behavior: one's attitudes and conduct required the suppression of one's own ego and individuality.

For the first millennium or so of its existence, Japan was ruled by emperors who had dictatorial powers. From A.D. 1192 until 1945 the country was ruled by what amounted to a military dictatorship. This made a very passive and often fawning type of behavior an integral part of Japanese existence.

Having to constantly appease government officials over a period of some two thousand years was not the end of the Japanese experience in human relations. The entire social system of the country was based on principles of absolute obedience to those in superior positions, and equally rigorous compliance to an etiquette system that further negated individual thought and expression and amplified the need for obsequious behavior.

Thus for centuries the Japanese were physically, mentally and spiritually conditioned to both obey and cater to their superiors. This made it very important for the Japanese on every level of society to become especially skilled at discerning the moods, expectations and goals of their superiors, and to react accordingly in a positive manner.

When viewed from the position of the superior, the ideal person was one who could carry out these obligations in good spirits without any feelings of rancor, of being used or abused. The more successful individuals were in this role, the more "pure Japanese" they were considered to be.

This overall system, which endured for such a long period of time, made the Japanese extraordinarily sensitive to the feelings and idiosyncracies of others and made them equally skillful in *kayui tokoro ni te ga todoku* (kah-ruu-ee toe-koe-roe nee tay gah toe-doe-kuu), or "scratching where it itches."

Both the sensitivity of the Japanese and their willingness to scratch other people's itches have significantly decreased in recent decades, but enough of this traditional behavior remains to make it a factor in most relationships in Japan.

In some cases, the motive for scratching another person's itch is strictly above-board, and even admirable. The Japanese are also conditioned to show, and regularly do show, extraordinary kindness and goodwill toward others without expecting anything more in return than appreciation.

But there are also numerous occasions when the scratching represents an attempt to gain some kind of advantage from the scratchee, particularly when the situation involves a superior or someone in a position of authority or power.

The *kayui tokoro ni te ga todoku* syndrome continues to play a very important role in areas where people continue to be treated subjectively, and according to the relationship they have with the individual concerned. To get fair and equal treatment from doctors, lawyers, teachers and a variety of government officials often requires that they be "scratched" in the right way and the right place.

Much of this special catering today takes the form of gifts and hospitality at restaurants and night spots—in addition to the correct ritualized kind of speech and behavior in soliciting favors and expressing appreciation.

稽 古

Keiko
(Kay-ee-koe)

"Putting on a Cultural Polish"

Any effort to understand the attitudes and behavior of Japanese must include a thorough knowledge of the famed samurai class, which administered the country from 1192 until 1868. The samurai began as professional warriors, maintained by the ruling shogun and by clan lords who, in turn, ruled their own fiefs.

During the first century of the shogunate type of government, the profession of samurai became hereditary. Samurai families gradually developed into an elite upper class that eventually made up some ten percent of the country's population.

As full-time warriors and military administrators, the samurai were paid by their lords (either the shogun or clan lords) in the form of an annual rice stipend which they used to barter for their needs.

In keeping with their professional warrior status, the samurai spent a great deal of their time practicing the arts of war—sword-fighting, the use of the bow, jujitsu and other martial arts. The wives and daughters of ranking samurai were also taught how to defend themselves.

As the peaceful decades of the successive shogunate dynasties passed, the samurai also took up character-building practices, including Zen meditation, the tea ceremony, poetry writing, calligraphy, singing, and playing musical instruments. Samurai women were also required to engage in these latter arts.

With the passing of centuries, the practicing of these various arts came to be known as *keiko* (kay-ee-koe), which originally referred to "the learning of old things" from books.

Keiko thus became an integral part of the lives of the samurai class, gradually seeping down into the merchant and craftsmen classes in the cities and towns, and finally—at least to some degree—into the farming class as well.

In contemporary Japan, *keiko* is used in reference to the practicing of any aesthetic or athletic skill, from flower-arranging to swimming. When the word is preceded by an honorific "O," as in *O-keiko*, it refers to the traditional arts that are now primarily associated with girls and women—flower-arranging, the tea ceremony, calligraphy, learning to play the koto or shamisen, and so on.

Taking singing lessons in secret in order to avoid embarrassment (and impress one's friends) when called upon to perform at social events and in karaoke bars comes under the umbrella of *keiko*.

Many of Japan's larger companies give special allowances to female staff members to take *keiko* lessons. Some companies retain teachers of the more popular arts, and provide in-company classrooms for employees who want to polish their cultural skills.

The cultural heritage provided by *keiko* is one of the things that continues to distinguish the Japanese and add a special ambience to life in Japan—not only for the Japanese but for foreigners as well.

Japanese are very much aware that the ongoing role of traditional cultural skills is one of the things that makes them different from—and as far as many are concerned, superior to—typical Westerners.

Virtually all foreigners who spend more than a few weeks—sometimes as little as a few days—in Japan get into situations where they are caught short by not having any cultural skill that they can demonstrate. There is a useful lesson in this typical failure.

系列会社

Keiretsu Gaisha
(Kay-ee-rate-suu Guy-shah)

"Keeping It All in the Family"

When the Industrial Revolution began in England in the mid-1700s, Japan was a hermit nation, closed to the outside world except for a tiny Dutch trading post isolated on a man-made islet in Nagasaki harbour, and occasional visits by trading junks from China.

When the United States took the lead in the mid-1800s in forcing Japan to end its long isolation from the rest of world, anyone could have been forgiven for presuming that the ultra-conservative Japanese would behave very much like the Chinese, and fight to preserve their old ways.

Even the most optimistic observer of Japan would surely have predicted that it would take the Japanese from fifty to one hundred years to catch up with the West—if the Japanese chose to do so in the first place.

But the Japanese were not like the Chinese. The young samurai warriors who rebelled in the 1860s and ended the long rule of the Tokugawa shogunate made a crucial decision to industrialize the country as rapidly as possible, and "catching up with the West" became a national slogan.

The new Japanese government began a massive program of importing Western technology and hiring thousands of Americans and European specialists to come to Japan to teach and to help implement the new learning.

Starting virtually from scratch in the early 1870s, the Japanese transformed their country in the next twenty years—changing it from a weak agricultural and cottage industry-based economy to a significant economic and military power.

The Japanese were able to go from a feudalistic kingdom of sword-carrying warriors to a powerful industrial nation within just twenty lightning-fast years primarily because the government aided and abetted the country's first crop of business entrepreneurs in creating affiliated groups of companies in the basic industrial areas.

In the first few years of Japan's revolution-from-the-top, Mitsui, Mitsubishi, Sumitomo and half a dozen other *keiretsu gaisha* (kay-ee-rate-suu guy-shah) or "related companies," were already well on their way to establishing the great *zaibatsu* combines which would soon be known around the world.

These huge conglomerates, built around wholly-owned banks, manufacturing operations, trading firms and transportation companies (including shipping lines), just as quickly surrounded themselves with networks of *shita uke* (ssh-tah uu-kay) or sub-contractors.

By the turn of the 20th century, only thirty-two years after the fall of the Tokugawa shogunate, Japan was competing with the U.S., England, Germany and other Western countries for world markets—and one generation later was vying with these same powers for political control of Asia.

Japan's notorious *zaibatsu* combines were ostensibly broken into pieces by the victorious Western Allies at the end of World War II in 1945 because the Allies recognized and feared their power. But as soon as Japan regained its sovereignty in 1952, the groups publicly resumed their pre-war relationships.

In today's Japan these same giant groups, and new ones that blossomed during the postwar rebuilding of the country, remain the primary feature of the economy and must be taken into consideration by anyone wanting to do business on a large scale.

These present-day *keiretsu gaisha* are less formal and less restrictive than their pre-World War II predecessors, but they nevertheless monopolize most of the key areas of the nation's economy. By sheer size alone they control the bulk of the importing of raw materials into Japan, the manufacturing processes in the key industries, the distribution systems, space in retail outlets, and well over 80 percent of the country's exports.

It was not until the late 1980s that companies began routinely crossing *keiretsu* lines to deal with firms in other groups. But still today there many product lines and related marketing systems that are dominated by individual groupings, which effectively prevent outsiders from breaking into these fields in any significant way.

A substantial number of the recent foreign successes in Japan were based on the creation of new wholesaling and retailing systems outside of the *keiretsu gaisha*.

煙に巻く

Kemu ni Maku
(Kay-muu nee Mah-kuu)

"Wrapping People in Smoke"

Japanese are known for being scrupulously honest and for going out of their way to show respect and kindness toward other people—as long as they are operating within the bounds of their own environment, and certain other factors apply.

Numerous historical stories that were traditionally taught to every child in Japan emphasized the extraordinary honesty of the average Japanese. As a former long-time resident of Japan, I have personally experienced their innate honesty and thoughtfulness on numerous occasions.

One of my favorite examples: I spent the night at an inn in the Akabane district of Tokyo, and forgot my raincoat when I left the next morning. Some two years later when I had occasion to visit the same inn, the proprietor recognized me the instant I entered the vestibule, and exclaimed, "Ah, Mr. De Mente, you forgot your raincoat!" She quickly retrieved my coat from a closet, carefully folded, and handed it to me.

Each year, hundreds of tourists visit Japan and forget bags and other possessions on buses, in taxis, at restaurants and other places. These tourists are astounded when the articles are returned to them intact, often by people who went to considerable trouble to find them.

The kindness of the Japanese in their treatment of guests is, in fact, legendary and often so overwhelming that it becomes embarrassing. Foreign businessmen also regularly say that they trust their Japanese partners or clients more than they do counterparts from their own countries.

But there is another side to the Japanese character that often plays a key role in their negotiations, whether in politics or in business. This is a propensity to create false scenarios and present them as factual to the other party, with the idea of gaining some kind of advantage.

Ruses of this type have historically been common in other societies as well, but interestingly, they have been especially common in Japan because peculiarities of the culture resulted in the development of situational ethics as opposed to principled ethics.

In other words, Japanese behavior has traditionally been based on the situation at hand, instead of on hard-and-fast principles. This provides for a much more flexible approach to negotiations and relationships, but it puts the person schooled in absolute principles at a disadvantage.

Creating a fictional scenario, particularly in a business context, is colloquially known as *kemu ni maku* (kay-muu nee mah-kuu), or "wrapping (it) in smoke." When both parties in such a setting are Japanese, it is usually up to the famed "belly feeling" of the smoked-in party to discern the reality of the situation, and negotiate his way through the haze.

Where foreign businessmen are concerned, however, the dangers of being suckered are much greater because they are generally not experienced at reading between Japanese lines. In such cases, there is simply no realistic alternative other than enlisting the aid of a third party who has the necessary experience to recognize a smoke-job and deal with it effectively.

More likely than not, this experienced third party should be a Japanese whose talents are for hire (as a consultant/adviser, etc.). Foreigners who are good at seeing through Japanese smoke screens and leveling the negotiating field are rare.

The famed *tatemae* (tah-tay-my) facade that virtually all Japanese present as the first step in any discussion or presentation is part smoke, and although not necessarily designed to deceive, it often does so when the other party is naive about the Japanese way of doing things.

―――――――――――― 120 ――――――――――――

気

Ki
(Kee)

"That Japanese Touch"

Despite a historical pattern of importing ideas, customs and products from abroad, Japanese invariably alter these imports to fit their own distinctive tastes. It often seems, however, that some of these adaptations are made without reason—just to "Japanize" the import.

But this Japanization process goes beyond an arbitrary whim. There are several vital factors in the essence of Japanese culture that compel them to make changes in things, including many occasions when outsiders cannot see the rationale.

Traditional Japanese culture was so comprehensive, so clear, that it created a virtually universal mind-set that controlled the reactions of the people to everything they saw or experienced. The cultural conditioning imposed upon them was also so pervasive that their reactions became automatic.

This characteristic Japanese mind-set was founded on specific philosophies that covered materials, aesthetics, design and use, which in turn were based on standards that had been elevated to the level of fine arts.

When the Japanese were exposed to any foreign product or idea that did not meet the exact guidelines they had been conditioned to follow, they instantly recognized the difference and felt compelled to reject it or to change it.

Several of the abstract qualities that make the Japanese distinctive are summed up in the word *ki* (kee), which has a variety of related meanings, including "spirit, nature, heart, care, feelings, precaution, mood, flavor and atmosphere," depending on its usage.

Japan's traditional culture has been watered down to the point that in the younger, urban generation it may not be visible at all, especially to foreigners. Enough of it remains, however, to continue influencing their attitudes and behavior in subtle but important ways.

But most Japanese born and raised before 1960 have very much the same mind-set that has been typical for hundreds of years, particularly in identifying and judging the quality and value of non-Japanese things.

Much of the cultural influence that keeps the Japanese traditional in their way of thinking and acting is bound up in the language—in words like *ki*, which is used daily in a dozen or more common expressions.

When something or somebody suits the distinctive Japanese taste, it is described as *ki ni iru* (kee nee ee-ruu), which means it is "agreeable, suitable, acceptable." If something really catches a person's attention, a proper response is *ki ni narimashita* (kee nee nah-ree-mah-ssh-tah).

A person who does not demonstrate an acceptable degree of goodwill, energy and spirit, especially in a work situation, results in his or her co-workers feeling *ki ni kuwanai* (kee nee kuu-wah-nie), or that the person is "distasteful."

Because Japanese are conditioned to react in a very specific way that is frequently at odds with Western reactions, Westerners often have difficulty understanding and accepting Japanese behavior. This is of special concern when Westerners propose to export apparel and food items to Japan.

Since apparel and food are especially subject to cultural sensitivities, it is vital that foreign businessmen wanting to sell such items in Japan find out how they are perceived by the Japanese as one of the first steps in their market research.

Whatever it is, it must please *ki* to be successful in Japan. The only valid method of researching this aspect of marketing in Japan is carefully monitored testing of the products concerned.

This same factor may also apply in varying degrees to foreign-made appliances, furniture and other personal-use items, not only in terms of style, but also in the materials used, the workmanship, and the scale. Foreign businessmen often seem to ignore the fact that Western size standards are substantially larger than those prevailing in Japan.

気が進まない

Kiga Susumanai

(Kee-gah Suu-suu-mah-nie)

"My Spirit Is Not Satisfied"

The Japanese are known worldwide for their ambition, energy, devotion to duty and work, and their willingness to sacrifice their individuality, many of their other freedoms, and personal conveniences to help contribute to the goals of their employers and the country.

Both Japanese and non-Japanese have spent a great deal of time trying to discover and explain the origin of the above traits, and to relate them to the extraordinary economic success the Japanese have achieved despite such handicaps as limited natural resources and a usable landmass that is smaller than the state of Tennessee in the U.S.

Obviously the traits and talents of the Japanese derive from their cultural conditioning, and it is in the nature and exercise of that culture that one will find the answers to what made the Japanese the way they are.

Just as obviously, the cultural conditioning undergone by the Japanese included the spiritual as well as the physical, and no doubt incorporated elements of Shintoism, Buddhism and Confucianism.

From Shintoism the Japanese gained an abiding respect for the nature of the materials they worked with—especially wood, stone and metals. From Buddhism, particularly Zen Buddhism, the Japanese learned how to gain control of their minds and bodies and direct them toward specific goals. From Confucianism, the Japanese learned loyalty, devotion and propriety.

All of this learning and experience came together in their master-apprentice approach to the arts and crafts that traditionally made up their economy, and led to what I have described as the *kata* (kah-tah) factor in a previous book (*Japan's Secret Weapon: The Kata Factor—The Cultural Programming That Made the Japanese a Superior People.*)*

In simple terms *kata* are the cultural molds, the precise processes which the Japanese developed to teach and learn their arts and crafts—their formulas for doing things. As everyone who has spent any length of time in Japan knows, the Japanese have absolutely exact ways of doing things that are mechanically learned, traditionally from infancy.

*This book is now published as *Behind the Japanese Bow*.

One of the factors that I believe grows out of intense conditioning in the *kata* of Japan is a remarkable dissatisfaction with anything less than perfection, an affliction that affects all Japanese raised in the traditional manner. I believe that the reason for the development of this condition is that the goals of the *kata* are total perfection, and no one is finished until it has been achieved.

Of course, perfection in anything is virtually unachievable, therefore fully *kata*-ized Japanese are constantly suffering from *kiga susumanai* (kee-gah suu-suu-mah-nie), or chronic "spiritual dissatisfaction," because of their inability to be perfect at everything they do.

This spiritual discomfort burns in "pure" Japanese like an undying flame, constantly spurring them on to do more and do better, and is surely one of the key factors that has contributed so much to Japan's present economic power.

One of the new worries weighing heavily on the older generation of Japanese is the lack of "spiritual burning" in the younger generations. As the *kata* system of cultural training weakens, the flame of dissatisfaction also weakens and in the youngest Japanese today is no more than a flicker.

While the degree of the robot-like conditioning undergone by the older generations of Japanese is unacceptable to most Westerners, there is something to be said for a less de-humanized system that would still inculcate young people with an understanding of and desire for quality and achievement.

危険 きつい 汚い

Kiken, Kitsui, Kitanai
(Kee-kane, Kee-t'suu-ee, Kee-tah-nie)

"Dangerous, Difficult, Dirty"

When I first took up residence in Japan in the late 1940s, I used to marvel at the patient endurance of the many people who were forced to work long hours at jobs that were often dirty, difficult and dangerous, in order to make a living.

I was especially affected by the sight of rice farmers who spent most of their days bent over in water-filled fields. Some of those who were 55 or 60 years old could no longer straighten their backs and had to live out the rest of their lives doubled over as sad caricatures of human beings.

Another thing that both impressed and amazed me was the sight of students going to and from school in the dead of winter without coats, the younger boys often wearing shorts.

At that time, and continuing on for nearly two decades afterward, most Japanese homes were not heated in the winter. Unlike the neighboring Koreans, who invented a method of central heating more than a thousand years ago, the Japanese built homes and behaved as if they lived in the semi-tropics, inuring themselves to the frigid temperatures that beset the central and northern islands during the winter months.

The once famous *hibachi* (he-bah-chee), or charcoal-burning braziers that the Japanese used in lieu of stoves, were effective only as hand-warmers (or as feet and leg warmers when they were placed in covered floor-pits), and anyone who complained about the cold and spent a conspicuous amount of time glued to a *hibachi* was denounced as a weakling or a sluggard.

Putting up with cold weather was regarded as part of being Japanese, which included being patient, working hard and diligently, and being physically and mentally tough. The ability to endure freezing temperatures was often noted as one of the things that made the Japanese a superior people.

By the 1990s, however, affluence and Westernization had wrought dramatic changes in the lifestyle and the attitudes of most Japanese. For the majority, enduring cold and other hardships was out. For the young in particular, being comfortable and not having to extend themselves to make a living was in.

This social flip-flop among those born in the 1960s and 70s gave rise to a new anti-work attitude that was summed up in the words *kiken* (kee-kane), *kitsui* (kee-t'suu-ee) and *kitanai* (kee-tah-nie)—meaning "dangerous, difficult, dirty," and generally referred to as "the three Ks."

More and more young Japanese began shunning occupations and jobs that came under any of these three headings, resulting in profound pressures that are continuing to force changes in social, economic and political concepts that have long been dear to the Japanese Establishment.

One of the most fundamental of these changes is a gradual acceptance of the idea of allowing some foreign workers into Japan—not only laborers who will accept jobs being shunned by Japanese, but professionals who bring in new technology and foreign experience that will benefit Japan's competitive abilities.

This is unlikely to be a major factor in solving Japan's labor shortage, however, because the government will never expose the country to the kind of racial and social conflicts that large-scale labor migration brings on.

Probably the most important of the changes resulting from the "three Ks syndrome" will be the additional impetus for Japanese industry to automate more and more of the manufacturing, delivering and servicing processes—and in doing so, turn a problem into an advantage that will impact favorably on their ability to make inroads into foreign markets.

帰国子女

Kikoku Shijo

(Kee-koe-kuu She-joe)

"You Can Never Go Home Again"

The first foreigners of record to set foot on Japanese soil were Portuguese traders who were passengers on a Chinese junk that was blown off-course on August 25, 1543, and who took refuge on the little island of Tanegashima south of Kyushu.

This accidental contact quickly led to a rush of foreign traders and missionaries to the main islands. But political and religious intrigue by the newcomers eventually soured Japan's ruling shogunate government on the idea of contact with foreigners.

During the latter part of the 1500s, the government launched a number of pogroms against foreign missionaries and curtailed the activities of the resident traders. In 1635 the shogunate banned all Japanese from going abroad and forbade those who were then overseas from ever coming home.

Four years later the remaining missionaries were expelled and all foreign traders, except for a small complement of Dutchmen, were forced to leave the country. This ban on travel to and from Japan was to endure for more than two hundred years, and was a primary factor in Japanese culture becoming more ingrown and more exclusionary.

By the time the United States took the lead in forcing Japan to re-open its doors to the West in the mid-1850s, foreigners and most things foreign were as exotic and strange to the Japanese as one can imagine.

Despite an eventual decision by the new Meiji government (which replaced the Tokugawa Shogunate in 1868) to invite foreign technicians and professionals into Japan to help industrialize the country, travel abroad by Japanese was to remain severely restricted for almost another century.

It was not until the mid-1960s, following the 1964 Olympics in Tokyo, that ordinary Japanese were allowed the opportunity to freely travel abroad, and it was to be another decade before even the most internationalized individuals began to feel comfortable outside of their cultural walls.

In the intervening decades, hundreds of thousands of Japanese businessmen and their families have spent varying numbers of years abroad on company assignments. In thousands of these families, their children were born abroad and are as much (or more) foreign as they are Japanese.

This phenomenon has presented the Japanese government, the business community and society at large with a problem that is reminiscent of the 16th century when the government decided that intercourse with foreigners was more trouble than it was worth.

A significant percentage of Japanese have not yet been able to overcome the exclusionary nature of their culture, to the point that they discriminate even against fellow Japanese who are *kikoku shijo* (kee-koe-kuu she-joe), or "returnees from abroad."

Very much like Western bigots who have historically regarded someone with one-fourth, one-eighth or even one-sixteenth black blood as black, most Japanese who have never lived abroad distinguish between those who have and those who have not—and regard the "haves" as somehow less Japanese and therefore not worthy of full acceptance back into Japanese society.

This discriminatory attitude is frequently reflected in statements by government spokesmen on the highest level, and is based on the assumption that only a "pure" Japanese can understand other "pure" Japanese, is predictable, can be trusted, and will not cause any kind of friction that would result in upsetting the smooth functioning of society.

Since so many Japanese typically are unable to accept *kikoku shijo* back into the fold, it is easy to understand why non-Japanese foreigners in Japan, including those who are citizens, are never fully accepted.

124

気持ちのしるし

Kimochi no Shirushi

(Kee-moe-chee no She-ruu-she)

"Taking Advantage of Good Manners"

When differences in etiquette are cross-cultural, the potential for problems is, of course, greatly exacerbated—and Japan is an extraordinary case in point.

Most Westerners, Americans in particular, go into some degree of culture shock shortly after their arrival in Japan. The first part of this shock results from their suddenly becoming illiterate as far as most signs and writing are concerned. In addition, they are unable to talk to anyone who does not speak their language.

The second and often more dangerous affliction, which occurs gradually over a period of hours or days, is that the Japanese etiquette system results in most visitors unconsciously suspending part of their ability to respond rationally or critically to what they see and hear.

Another equally serious aspect of the culture shock that strikes most Western visitors to Japan results from what might be called a rebound syndrome. Unable to fully understand or behave in the Japanese way, and misled by the veneer of Westernization that obscures the realities of Japan, many visitors resort to—or revert to—applying Western values and rules, only to make matters worse.

On thousands of occasions, I have seen experienced, hard-headed foreign businessmen behave in a manner that was totally out of character—saying, doing and accepting things that were seriously detrimental to their interests because they did not know how to respond to Japanese etiquette.

These situations often seem innocuous on the surface but they generally set the tone for whatever relationship develops, and much more often than not the advantage goes to the Japanese side.

The dilemma arises because most foreigners are not used to the level or degree of etiquette that is common in Japan, and out of goodwill make an earnest attempt to avoid doing or saying anything that would upset the Japanese.

The only practical way for the Western businessman, politician or diplomat involved with Japan to avoid these cultural pitfalls is to attend one of the better cultural orientation programs that are designed for that purpose.

Most Japanese behavior toward foreigners is automatic and without artifice, and is not intended as a direct challenge or threat. It is the equally automatic and often irrational response of foreigners to unfamiliar etiquette that unbalances the relationship.

At the same time the Japanese are acutely aware of the power of their etiquette and are masters at using it to influence or control responses from other people—particularly other Japanese who are conditioned to react in precisely prescribed ways when faced with traditional manners.

Where foreigners are concerned, Japanese may follow traditional etiquette for any number of reasons—because they don't know how to behave any other way; to show respect; to demonstrate their Japaneseness; to distance themselves; to put the other party at a disadvantage.

One of the usually benign areas of Japanese etiquette is the custom of presenting *kimochi no shirushi* (kee-moe-chee no she-ruu-she), or "feeling/mood gifts," to people they encounter during visits or trips.

These token gifts of goodwill and appreciation are usually small things, like scarfs, wrapping cloths, new little electronic devices, and so on. Japanese travelers, particularly those traveling for business or some professional reason, almost always take along a supply of *kimochi no shirushi* to present to those who do them favors or extend hospitality to them.

Businessmen whose goals go beyond casual relationships and expressions of goodwill often give more elaborate and expensive *kimochi no shirushi*—sometimes to the point that they are embarrassing.

There is a ritualized expression the Japanese use to virtually compel a person to accept a gift when the would-be receiver initially refuses out of politeness or embarrassment: *Kimochi dake desu kara...* (kee-moe-chee dah-kay dess kah-rah...). The phrase literally means "It is only (for) feeling..."

The implication of the phrase is that the giver of the gift is doing it out of feelings of friendship and respect, and that refusing to accept the gift would be tantamount to insulting the giver.

Kimochi no shirushi are, in fact, very effective in expressing thanks and for creating goodwill and building up feelings of debt or obligation. Part of the Japanese scene is returning such gifts in kind to avoid an excessive buildup of obligation to the giver.

125

鬼 門

Ki Mon

(Kee Moan)

"Facing Your Devils"

Of the hundreds of festivals held in Japan each year, one of the more unusual is *Setsubun* (Sate-suu-boon), which takes place on February 3 or 4, the eve of the beginning of spring (according to the old reckoning).

Apparently in the spirit of spring housecleaning, *Setsubun* is marked by ceremonies designed to rid houses and other buildings of evil spirits that bring bad luck and replace them with the spirits of good luck.

Somehow, long ago, beans became the symbol of the evil spirits that come to dwell in homes and other buildings. Today Japanese still get rid of evil spirits inhabiting their homes by tossing beans out through open doors and windows while intoning *Oni wa soto! Fuku wa uchi!* (Oh-nee wah soe-toe! Fuu-kuu wah uu-chee!), or "Out with devils! In with good luck!"

This traditional ceremony dates from ancient Japan when people developed the belief that evil spirits came from the northeast; if any home or building had a door facing that direction, evil ones would rush in and take up residence.

The northeast thus came to be known as the *ki mon* (kee moan) or "devil gate," and led to a taboo against doors facing in that direction. Later, perhaps to balance things, the southwest side of buildings came to be known as the *ura ki mon* (uu-rah kee moan), or "rear devil gate," and that side also became taboo for doors.

Gradually the concept of *ki mon* came to be applied to things you could not master or did not feel comfortable with. Therefore, people who were difficult to get along with became the "personal" devils of other individuals.

Students who are not good at physics, math or some other complicated subject may refer to the subjects as their *ki mon*. An unruly child may be the *ki mon* of a parent. Of course, a parent may be the *ki mon* of a child.

The term is also used in reference to people with whom one has no particular personality conflict, but with whom one always comes out the loser in any exchange. One just has bad luck in any dealings with them.

Ki mon is probably used more often in a business context than in private affairs because of the extraordinary importance of personal relations in the business world of Japan. Being able to establish and maintain good personal relationships with other people is, in fact, the foundation of business.

It therefore becomes especially important that salesmen or managers representing a company be able to get along with and make good impressions on customers, suppliers and other people met in the course of business.

When Japanese come across someone with whom they cannot achieve an effective relationship, and yet the person is important to their company, they will often say to a co-worker: "He is my *ki mon*. Please take care of him for me."

It is usually very difficult for non-Japanese, even those with considerable experience in Japan, to know when they encounter Japanese *ki mon* who do not like them and will not be fully cooperative, because the formal politeness of Japanese toward foreigners more often than not disguises this dislike or distrust from anyone not tuned in to their cultural telepathy.

If a *ki mon* relationship is suspected, about the only recourse is to do what the Japanese do: get someone else to handle the relationship or act as a go-between for you. If the go-between is a Japanese, the suspected *ki mon* may reveal the source or nature of his negative feelings.

記者クラブ

Kisha Kurabu

(Kee-shah Kuu-rah-buu)

"Big Brother Knows Best"

In the latter part of the 1950s when I was editor of a Tokyo-published trade journal covering Japanese products for export, my publisher, Ray Woodside, and I showed up at a news conference called by the president of the Japanese Chamber of Commerce & Industry.

Ray and I were the only foreigners in the large theater-like meeting room and quickly became aware that something had caused a buzz of excitement among the forty to fifty Japanese journalists who were also present. Before we could figure out or ask what was going on, we were physically and forcefully ejected from the hall.

This was my first experience with Japan's notorious *kisha kurabu* (kee-shah kuu-rah-buu), or "press clubs."

I later learned that every major news source in the country—the prime minister's office, government ministries and agencies, industrial and business groups, etc.—on the national, prefectual and metropolitan level, were the exclusive preserve of a specific *kisha kurabu*, and that journalists not members of a club—including other Japanese journalists—were not allowed to attend news briefings by that particular source.

The size and power of the news media determined which publication could put forward candidates for membership in the various clubs. Major news media had a virtual monopoly on key political and business news sources. But some of the less important news sources did hold separate briefings for reporters from smaller publications.

It was well into the 1960s before any of the large group of foreign correspondents stationed in Tokyo began to complain publicly about this extraordinary system. But their complaints were ignored.

It was to be another twenty or so years before a new generation of foreign journalists took up the battle against the discriminatory press club system, by which time Japan had a much higher international profile and was ostensibly more sensitive to foreign pressure.

This effort also failed to break the special relationship that existed between the news sources and the news media. However, after a great deal of negative publicity in international news media, a few of the news sources announced that they would hold separate but equal briefings for foreign journalists. A few of the press clubs also agreed to accept Japanese-speaking foreign journalists as nominal members.

Government and other news source spokesmen rationalized the *kisha kurabu* system by saying that almost none of the foreign correspondents in Tokyo spoke Japanese, so attending the briefings would be meaningless; and, further, that even if they could understand Japanese, being foreigners, they would not be able to understand many of the things the Japanese sources had to say because the cultural framework of Japanese and foreign thinking was so different.

This latter factor, the spokesmen went on, would result in foreign journalists misrepresenting the real situation in Japan, and cause unnecessary and undesirable trouble for everyone concerned.

The *kisha kurabu* system has not changed during the intervening years. Japanese journalists from the major news media still regularly collude with major news sources to control or color the news according to what both sides feel is appropriate for public consumption. Foreign journalists are still mostly on the outside peering in through worm-holes.

気をつかう

Ki wo Tsukau

(Kee oh T'suu-kah-uu)

"Burning Both Ends"

Some time ago one of my foreign friends who had worked in Tokyo for more than a decade was suddenly transferred to New York City. I saw him a year later and asked him if he had had any problems in adjusting to an American environment. He laughed and said that compared to Tokyo, the pace in New York was so slow he had to fight to keep from being bored.

Western businessmen newly arrived on the scene in Tokyo are usually more or less prepared for the high cost of living and doing business there, but they are generally not prepared for the "human" investment they have to make in order to survive and be productive.

Prior to the forced opening of Japan to the outside world in the 1850s and 60s by the United States and other Western nations, life in Japan for most people was pretty much based on seasonal customs and events. Time was not precisely measured and counted in small bits as it is today. People thought and behaved in terms of the natural flow of life.

Japanese culture in general, from personal etiquette to the arts, crafts and recreational activities, was built around a studied, deliberate use of drawn-out time—often with the goal being to achieve a kind of timelessness.

In fact, before Japan was opened to the West, the culture was kept fixed by government policy in a kind of time-warp where nothing was supposed to change—and very little <u>had</u> changed in the previous 200 years.

But when the barriers shutting Japan off from the rest of the world came down, the new Japanese government imported, in one huge package, virtually all of the industrial revolution. Japan went from a feudalistic agricultural society to a modern industrial nation in less than 30 years.

The Japanese achieved this remarkable metamorphosis by unleashing an unbelievable amount of energy and concentrated spirit that seemingly went against the grain of much of their national character. But this act of national will was also rooted in their culture and their character—in those areas that had been suppressed for so long by the feudal government.

Intense economic competition on a sectional and divisional level within companies, on a national and international level between companies, and as a single national entity, became a new ethic that combined with a singular pride to compel the Japanese to work with a frenzy that bordered on obsession.

This same obsessive approach to work was a key factor in rebuilding Japan following World War II—and in bringing on the symptom that in the 1980s came to be known as *karoshi* (kah-roe-she), or "death from overwork."

One of the primary facets of the lifestyle of the Japanese is summed up in the term *ki wo tsukau* (kee oh t'suu-kah-uu), which means "to use energy," in the sense of emotional/spiritual energy, and refers to contending with the highly charged interpersonal relationship system that prevailed in Japan for centuries and remains a powerful influence today. One must constantly be aware of others, making sure that one's own actions do not contravene any of the behavioral taboos.

Many Japanese friends who now live in the U.S. and other Western countries tell me that escaping from the obligations and demands of the Japanese etiquette system is like being let out of a prison that combines rigid thought control with physical control.

Foreigners dealing with non-Westernized Japanese must also contend with this *ki wo tsukau* syndrome. Whether they are in Japan as visitors or residents, they generally must use double or triple the amount of emotional and psychic energy that they would use in their home countries.

For those who are higher strung, ambitious and aggressive, this invisible burden is a serious challenge, and can result in serious mental and physical health problems in a matter of months if they do not learn how to pace themselves and find ways of relieving the stress.

128

交 番

Ko Ban

(Koe Bahn)

"Beware of Rogue Samurai!"

Much of the attraction that Japan has for Japanese residents, as well as for expatriates and foreign visitors, is so subtle that it is virtually invisible. Part of it inheres in the variety of pleasurable feelings connected with the intangible qualities of traditional arts and crafts, and the traditional manners of the Japanese.

Another part of this discreet attraction has to do with feelings of personal security, of feeling safe in your home, in the streets—even in the most disreputable neighborhoods at night—when you are alone.

Many visitors from abroad who live in a constant state of fear in their own homes and cities are quickly suffused with an ecstatic sense of relief when they discover that they can roam the backstreets and byways of the slums and the most notorious entertainment districts of Japan at any hour of the day or night without endangering their wallets or their lives.

But such was not always the case in Tokyo and elsewhere in Japan. In the years immediately following establishment of the Tokugawa shogunate in 1603, the streets of Edo in particular (the shogun's capital and present-day Tokyo) were like killing fields.

For the first time in decades, the huge shogunate armies of samurai warriors were without official enemies to fight and instead were charged with keeping order in the rapidly growing city. One law decreed by the shogunate allowed warriors to immediately kill any common person who behaved in an unacceptable manner.

As the discipline of the samurai degenerated, the more dissolute of them began killing people arbitrarily. Some of them would get drunk, waylay passersby and cut them down just to test new swords or show off in front of their fellows. Some would kill on the slightest provocation simply because they were arrogant and cruel and could get away with it.

Drinking quarrels and encounters between small groups of warriors from different clans constantly led to sword-fights that ended in fatalities.

These killings became so common that they were labeled *tsuji giri* (t'suu-jee ghee-ree), or "street-corner cuttings"—*giri* (or *kiri*) coming from the word *kiru*, originally meaning "to cut" but in this case meaning "to kill" by slashing with a sword.

Finally, in 1628, the shogunate ordered the magistrate of Edo to establish guard posts, called *tsuji ban* (t'suu-jee bahn), or "corner guards," on all the busier street intersections in Edo to try to put an end to the indiscriminate killings.

Soon the provincial lords, who were required to maintain mansions and large retinues of followers in Edo, set up their own *tsuji ban* in the areas where they lived. Ranking retainers of the shogun's court quickly followed suit, establishing "corner guards" in their own neighborhoods to protect themselves and their families. Eventually there were a total of 898 *tsuji ban* in the city, indicating the seriousness of the problem.

As the decades passed, the system of "corner guards" spread throughout the country, finally evolving into very effective city police forces administered by local magistrates, and setting a standard of law-enforcement that was to distinguish them down to present times.

After the shogunate system of government fell in 1868, and cities began establishing Western-type administration systems, the name of the "corner guards" was changed to *ko ban* (koe bahn), which is translated as "police box."

When the American-run Occupation forces took over Japan in 1945, they closed most of the *ko ban* and introduced the American system of patrolling the streets in vehicles. As soon as the Occupation ended in 1952, the Japanese re-instated the *ko ban* system.

In today's Japan, there are two types of police boxes—*hashutsu-jo* (hah-shute-suu-joe), or "dispatch (police box) branches," and *chuzai-sho* (chuu-zie-show), or "residential/neighborhood (police) boxes." The former are larger "boxes" in crowded business districts and are staffed by several officers. The *chuzai-sho*, or "residential police boxes," are small and staffed by one or two officers.

Although the incidence of criminal acts and violent behavior in Japan has been rising gradually since the 1950s, the traditions of law and order established during the latter generations of the Tokugawa Shogunate still prevail in Japan, with the result that *ko ban* policemen spend most of their time helping people find local addresses, and making sure that revelers in the country's thousands of entertainment districts get home at night.

In the meantime, American police forces are beginning to accept the idea that the *ko ban* system is worth emulating.

129

心づかい

Kokoro Zukai

(Koe-koe-roe Zoo-kie)

"The Ideal Human Being"

If all the Japanese in Japan were lined up and asked to describe Americans and other Westerners in one word, the majority would probably come up with "selfish." The reason for this is simple enough. The Japanese were conditioned for centuries to look upon independent, individualistic behavior—the hallmark of Americans and many other Westerners—as selfish, confrontational and disruptive.

This is not to suggest that all Japanese are, or were at any time in the past, completely unselfish, but a very significant proportion of them—at least until around the 1960s—were, in fact, unselfish to a remarkable degree. The number of people who were saint-like paragons of unselfishness appears to have been far greater in Japan than in any Western country.

Westerners generally condone and often times glorify selfishness. The Japanese on the other hand were traditionally taught that selfishness was among the worst of all sins, and there were numerous social, economic and political sanctions to encourage—and often enforce—unselfish conduct.

The ethos of traditional Japan was that the individual should sacrifice his or her own interests—and often his or her life as well—for the benefit of the group. And Japanese history and folklore is filled with accounts of men and women who were inspiring examples of this ideal.

As long ago as the last centuries of Japan's remarkable Heian Era (784-1192), living the selfless life was referred to as *kokoro zukai* (koe-koe-roe zoo-kie), which figuratively means "spirit of the heart."

This spiritual concept of unselfishness became a primary component of Japanese culture, promoted by the triad of religious philosophies that were the building blocks of Japanese society, and used first by the Imperial Court and later the Shogunate government as a pillar of their political control.

The social, economic and political systems that nurtured the *kokoro zukai* factor in Japanese culture changed dramatically in 1868 when the shogunate government fell, and again in 1945 when democracy and other Western concepts were introduced into Japan. But the concept remained alive, and continued to flourish well into the 1960s.

Over the decades since, Japanese's educational system, designed to mold young Japanese into selfless cadre for business and government, has remained the last bastion of *kokoro zukai* conditioning, but it too is losing its hold on the minds of the young.

Most Japanese born after 1970 have learned to equate personal freedom and individuality with selfishness, and their greatest ambition is to fulfill their own personal aspirations, not sacrifice their lives for others. This would seem to portend the death knell of the *kokoro zukai* concept in Japan, but maybe not.

There are at least two factors that might prevent the complete disappearance of *kokoro zukai* from Japanese life. One is an extraordinary nostalgia for the past among older Japanese and a growing trend among some of them to go back to the simpler life style of bygone days. The other is a growing realization among intellectuals and others that Japan should not allow all of its traditional wisdom and ways to disappear.

Westerners dealing with older Japanese can get a lot of mileage out of referring to *kokoro zukai* when describing the kind of relationship they would like to develop with them.

根 性

Kon Jo

(Kone Joe)

"The Importance of Fighting Spirit"

During Japan's long feudal age, the samurai spirit reigned supreme in the country. The courage, fortitude and fighting spirit that have distinguished the Japanese down to modern times was repeatedly displayed in scenarios such as this one:

The samurai defenders of a castle find themselves outnumbered, outfought and facing certain defeat and ignominious death at the hands of their enemy. Just as the enemy gathers for the final assault against the castle, the leader of the defenders, a handsome young man not yet twenty-five, shows himself on the ramparts, and while removing his body armor, calls out his name, rank and lineage in a loud voice. Then, the young samurai takes out his short sword, slices his abdomen open, reaches into the wound, pulls out a portion of his entrails and hurls them at the enemy to show them how a man of courage and honor dies.

The suicide missions of World War II kamikaze pilots, the banzai charges of trapped soldiers on the islands of the Pacific, and the arming of civilians with bamboo spears as the Allied powers neared the home islands of Japan were similar demonstrations of the depth and power of the spirit that has historically been typical of the Japanese.

The West has also had its heroes and men of exceptional courage, but a different philosophy generally prevented them from allowing their courage to destroy them. Once it became absolutely clear that they could not win, no matter how brave or skilled, they would usually surrender.

Japanese, on the other hand, had no ready rationale for surrendering. The more certain their defeat, the harder they fought. Surrendering was not only against their moral code, it was generally prohibited by official regulations.

At the end of Japan's feudal period in 1868, the samurai, freed from shogunate laws that prevented them from engaging in commerce, went into business with the same spirit and resolve that had motivated them as warriors who did not know how to accept defeat.

This spirit was to play a key role in Japan's transformation from a feudal kingdom of sword-carrying warriors into a modern industrial nation in less than thirty years, and was to help remake the nation a second time after its military leaders led it to defeat in World War II.

Today when Japanese managers and executives interview potential employees at schools, one of the main qualities they look for in each individual is *kon jo* (kone joe) or "fighting spirit, determination, tenacity, courage."

This kind of character and personality is given as much weight, if not more, as family background, attendance record, grades, or subjects studied. Just as in feudal times, present-day Japanese generally regard spirit and determination as the most valuable assets a person can have.

In present-day Japan, however, not many young people have an opportunity to display their physical courage and tenacity except in sports, which is one of the reasons why Japanese employers vie to hire successful high school and college athletes. Rugby players are especially prized because theirs is a high contact sport that requires extraordinary strength, stamina and a strong will.

Japanese businessmen particularly value the aspect of *kon jo* that results in employees becoming more determined to succeed as the task gets more difficult. In fact, because of their historical conditioning, adversity invariably brings out the best in all Japanese.

Foreign companies hiring new employees in Japan should certainly consider *kon jo* among the important qualifications.

混浴

Kon'yoku
(Kone-yoe-kuu)

"The Blessings of Mixed Bathing"

Shortly after I took up residence in Japan in 1949 I went to a hot-spring spa in the foothills of the mountains about an hour north of Tokyo. Immediately after checking into the spa inn, I was ushered to one of the baths by my room maid.

When I entered the large, steaming pool-like bath it was empty. A few minutes later the door opened and two elderly ladies, a gang of pre-teen girls and several young women trooped in. They were a bit taken aback at my presence, but not as far back as I was at their sudden appearance.

The newcomers quickly demonstrated all of the aplomb that comes with a two-thousand-year-plus history of mixed-sex bathing with whoever was in the neighborhood, but it took me several minutes to get my own reactions under control.

This was the beginning of my rapid conversion to one of the most delightful and wholesome customs ever devised by any society.

It is said, apparently with some truth, that the Japanese were either the first or *among* the first people to discover the sanitary as well as the social benefits of hot water, and to make it a regular part of their lifestyle.

Not having been saddled with the idea of the human body being a licentious and sinful thing to behold, the Japanese did not associate nudity and bathing with provocative sexuality. For one thing, female breasts were not a sexual turn-on at all in Japanese culture. They thought that the back of the neck was a lot sexier—which explains why women wear their kimonos farther back on the neck than men do.

Japan's national female dress, the kimono, de-emphasizes female breasts by compressing them as flat as possible—not only because their protruding would detract from the smooth lines of the garment but also because they were not regarded as erotic appendages. (Of course, this is one place where the instincts and traditions of the Japanese really missed the boat.)

Anyway, *kon'yoku* (kone-yoe-kuu), or "mixed-sex" bathing in public baths, both in local communities and in hotspring spas, was the custom in Japan until the early 1950s. At that time it was outlawed in *sento* (sen-toh), or public neighborhood baths, as the result of effective politicking by a group of women who got into the Diet following the enfranchising of women in 1946.

The new law ordered all bathhouses to put solid partitions down the middle, dividing them into male and female halves. I remember that for the first year or so, most bathhouses just strung ropes down the middle to separate the sexes. When they got around to constructing partitions, the partitions ended at a small U-shaped service counter, which was placed so a single attendant could collect fees from both male and female bathers.

This arrangement made it possible for taller people to stand at the service counter and have a clear view of most of the other-sex side. I know some foreigners who used to take in large denomination bills so they would have to stand at the counter and wait for their change.

In the intervening decades, younger Japanese, especially young women, have absorbed some of the strained morality of the West, and are now sometimes shy about mixed-sex bathing with strangers or new acquaintances in private home settings. They have no qualms about *kon'yoku* with strangers at resort spas, however.

In fact, scenes of mixed-sex bathing at famous spas are commonplace on national television in Japan. One of the most interesting facets of this custom is that the television hosts for these programs are invariably attractive young women who strip off and join right in—using small hand-towels to discreetly cover their pubic areas while entering the water.

This same etiquette—covering the genitals with a small towel—is the norm in all mixed-sex bathing situations in Japan, whether public or private—a point that foreign businessmen should keep in mind when they are invited to join their golfing partners in a hot bath after the game is over.

交 際 費

Kosai Hi

(Koe-sie He)

"Nurturing Friendly Relations"

In the mid-1950s, soon after I had gone into business in Tokyo as the co-publisher and editor of a weekly newspaper, I became acquainted with the marketing manager of an oil company who said he wanted to practice his English and meet other foreign businessmen living in Tokyo.

For a year or so afterward, this gentleman would invite me and my co-publisher out on the town once or twice a month. We would go to one or two bars, then to a restaurant, and finally finish the night off in an elite Ginza cabaret, where we were entertained by some of the most beautiful and seductive women in the country.

It was clearly understood that the oil man was our host, and that the reason he was able to spend so much money on us was that he was privileged to use the equivalent of $3,500 (an enormous amount of money at that time) on entertaining customers every month.

During that period he did not have enough clients or potential customers to use up his expense account in a more direct manner, and so chose to invest it in polishing his English and building contacts within the foreign community.

I learned that his monthly expense account was called *kosai hi* (koe-sie he), which literally means "expense for friendly relations" or "expense for social intercourse," and is more or less the equivalent of a public relations fund in the Western sense.

This was one of my earliest experiences with the role of personal relations in business in Japan, and the extent to which the Japanese go to develop and nurture them. It was also a very thorough introduction to the vital role that bars and cabarets play in the conduct of business in Japan.

Part of this distinctive Japanese approach to business relationships is a different view of expense accounts. It appeared to me that the Japanese were much more open and honest about recognizing the personal benefits that accrued to managers who were authorized to spend *kosai hi* on entertainment and doing favors for their contacts.

My oil man friend and others confided that the personal benefits they gained from their expense accounts was a form of recompense for hours of overtime they put in each day, and also helped make up for their inadequate salaries.

Despite annual criticism of the expense account system as wasteful and harmful to legitimate business as well as to family relations of the nation's hundreds of thousands of "expense account aristocrats," the system has not only continued over the decades, it has grown in volume and importance to the economy.

Today billions of yen are spent each year by businessmen entertaining outside contacts as well as their own staffs as an integral part of creating new relationships and sustaining old ones. *Kosai hi* is the oil that makes business in Japan operate smoothly.

Japanese treat business relationships the same way that Westerners treat personal friendships, but with a very significant difference. While Westerners tend to develop close friendships in a very short period of time, sometimes in a matter of hours, Japanese normally take months to years to do so.

The only acceptable way the process of developing personal relationships in Japan can be speeded up, even within the customary Japanese time-frames, is through participating in entertainment and recreational activities together.

Today a substantial amount of corporate *kosai hi* goes to pay for golf club memberships and fees.

講 座

Koza

(Koe-zah)

"Sitting on the Throne"

One of the most compelling indictments against Japan's educational system—in fact, against many of the key tenets of traditional Japanese culture—is that the overwhelming majority of people who have achieved outstanding success in their fields as a result of their own individual efforts have virtually all been mavericks and dropouts from society.

It is an ongoing scandal that Japan's brightest young scientists are often thwarted by a system that prevents them from doing original research, and that many of them leave Japan to join foreign universities and private research institutes where they have the freedom to pursue their own interests.

Critics of the system that prevails in Japan say the chief culprits are the basic approach to education which stifles individual thought and initiative, the herd-like tendency of the Japanese to do what everyone else is doing, and overwhelming pressure to avoid individual failure in any project.

Traditionally in Japan the individualist was pressured to conform. If he persisted he was shunned, and if he continued to upset the homogenized harmony of his group or community he was ostracized. The same is still true in Japan's universities, and particularly so in medical and other scientific fields.

In universities, departments are generally ruled by the most senior professors, who run them as if they were their own personal fiefdoms. The department heads are often more like gang bosses than administrators, demanding absolute loyalty from those under them, determining and controlling all activities within the departments, playing the key role in who gets hired and who gets promoted, and so on.

These department heads, called *koza* (koe-zah), or "chairs," are especially prominent in university science programs, where they, in conjunction with lab managers, not only control the research topics and budgets, but also take personal credit for any discovery that comes out of their labs.

Young, ambitious scientists working in these *koza*-controlled labs generally have to wait until they are in their late 30s or early 40s before they can hope to begin working on their own projects. By this time, most of their intellectual curiosity has cooled and they have become so conditioned to the system that they no longer seek to change it.

This system greatly limits the variety and volume of research that is going on in Japanese universities at any one time (since the majority of the younger scientists are forced to work on a much smaller number of *koza*-approved projects) and therefore impacts directly on the country's acknowledged need to encourage scientific creativity.

Because the university professor-controlled system is not large enough to absorb all of Japan's Ph.D. candidates and newly graduated doctors, a significant percentage of them end up in limbo. Unable to find jobs in their fields, their training and talents go to waste—unless they are willing to work without pay in their professors' labs.

In this quintessential Japanese environment, intellectual brilliance takes a backseat to connections, skill in catering to the whims and designs of the *koza*, and ability to play the worst kind of politics.

The *koza* system is also one of the primary reasons why there are very few foreign researchers in Japan. The system is so exclusionary, politically as well as culturally, that introducing an unknown and unpredictable foreign element into it is virtually unthinkable to the typical *koza*.

134

首を賭けます

Kubi wo Kakemasu

(Kuu-bee oh Kah-kay-mahss)

"I Will Stick My Neck Out"

One of the more common methods of executing criminals and enemies during Japan's feudal age (as well as during its 20th century wars), was decapitation with a sword.

In order for this method of execution to go smoothly (at least from the viewpoint of the executioner) it was necessary for the victim to stretch his or her neck out as far as possible to give the swordsman an easier target.

It appears that some of the more fastidious executioners would suggest to their victims that they *kubi wo nagaku shite* (kuu-bee oh nah-gah-kuu ssh-tay), literally, "lengthen their necks."

Sticking one's neck out thus became associated with exposing oneself to danger or taking a chance on something that could have seriously harmful repercussions. And from this connotation grew a number of expressions that are still common today.

Kubi wo kiru (Kuu-bee oh kee-ruu), for example, literally means to "cut the neck," but figuratively refers to being fired from a job. Another variation of this is *kubi ga tobu* (kuu-bee gah toe-buu), which literally means "the neck flies" or, turned around, "the head flies off of the neck."

Kubi wo hineru (kuu-be oh he-nay-ruu), or "wringing the neck," refers to racking one's brain in an effort to solve a serious problem. *Kubi ga mawaranai* (Kuu-bee gah mah-wah-rah-nie) means that one cannot turn his neck, that is, he has no way out of a problem.

Probably the one reference to the neck that foreign businessmen most often encounter is when they ask their Japanese contact or counterpart to figuratively *kubi wo kakete* (kuu-bee oh kah-kay-tay) or "put your neck on the line."

Serious problems often arise when this occurs because the foreign side generally is not aware of how tightly restricted most individual Japanese businessmen are in making decisions or commitments on their own, regardless of their rank or position.

More importantly, any kind of arbitrary or overly aggressive behavior by a Japanese manager, such as pushing beyond a very delicate line for something they want, can seriously damage, or end, their career with their companies.

Both of these reasons for not sticking one's neck out are, of course, directly related to the Japanese practice of reaching decisions by consensus, sharing responsibility as groups rather than as individuals, and avoiding any suggestion of working against the interests of the group for selfish motives.

In past decades larger Japanese companies were noted for seldom, if ever, firing any of their regular full-time employees (they usually had numerous part-time employees and sub-contractors that could be let go instead). But even then, and now as well, companies had a variety of techniques for getting rid of unwanted managers or staff.

One such technique is known as *mawata de kubi wo shimeru* (mah-wah-tah day kuu-bee oh she-may-ruu), or "strangle (someone) with a silken thread."

Silk is, of course, soft and smooth. The connotation in the above usage is that an individual is strangled (forced to leave the company) in such a soft and subtle way that he experiences little pain while gradually being placed in an untenable position.

Given the imagery and strength of expressions based on the neck, foreign businessmen who want to emphasize their commitment to a project with Japanese are sometimes well-advised to *kubi wo kakeru*, or "bet their neck."

————————— 135 —————————

クリエーティビティ

Kurietibati

(Kuu-ree-eh-tee-bah-tee)

"The Japanese Way of Creativity"

In the mid-1800s an American sea captain who had visited Japan a number of times wrote in his journal that "the Japanese will surprise the world." And surprise the world they have, in so many ways that it is now expected as a matter of course.

What remains surprising about their extraordinary development is that historically the Japanese were among the least inventive of all people. Virtually all of the arts and crafts making up their civilization were imported from Korea and China between A.D. 300 and 600.

For the next thousand years, the Japanese refined what they had learned from Korea and China, developing basic crafts into fine arts that were far superior to their predecessors, but creating almost nothing new of their own.

In fact, for most of Japan's famed samurai era, which began in 1192 and ended in 1868, change was taboo. In their efforts to maintain power, the succeeding shogunate governments attempted to maintain the status quo in all things. Emphasis was on revering the past and perpetuating the existing economy and lifestyle. Creativity and innovation were simply not in the Japanese vocabulary.

In the late 1630s, the Tokugawa shogunate took the extreme step of closing the country's doors to the outside world, and for the next 220 years the nation was isolated from the technological revolution that swept the West. As the generations passed, they continued honing their skills in duplicating and improving on ancient crafts.

When the country was again opened to the outside world, the Japanese began copying Western technology and systems in a frenzy of change that was to culminate in their becoming a major industrial power in just thirty years.

However, it was not until the collapse of still feudalistic Japan in 1945 at the end of World War II, and the subsequent introduction of democracy into the country by the United States, that the stage was set for the emergence of the Japanese as creators on a vast scale.

It took the Japanese about thirty years to learn how to convert their historically suppressed imagination and talents into creative energy, and they did so within the context of their traditional group and team behavior; not in the Western way of independent tinkering and researching.

Still today most Japanese innovations and inventions are the result of what is called "cultivated creativity," as opposed to the "spontaneous creativity" that is characteristic in the West. Further, most Japanese inventions are adaptive creations accomplished by teams instead of breakthrough creations by individuals.

In simple terms this means that the Japanese tend to take concepts conceived by others and improve or invent new products based on those ideas, using an approach that marketing specialist/author Sheridan M. Tatsuno calls "creative fusion"—which refers to creation by brainstorming and group interaction.

While Japan's focused group-approach to creativity goes against the grain of individualistic Westerners, it is often far more responsive to human wants and the marketplace, and has resulted in an astounding success rate for new products.

One of the key advantages of Japan's approach to creativity is that it can be controlled insofar as volume and pace are concerned. The results are generally incremental rather than dramatic, but they guarantee a steady rate of progress that builds on itself and eventually becomes more important than hit-and-miss methods.

教育ママ

Kyoiku Mama
(K'yoe-ee-kuu Mah-mah)

"The Mothers of Hell"

The ability of Japanese high school students to score high marks in science and mathematics brought Japan's educational system to the attention of the world in the 1970s. Large numbers of Americans concerned about the level of education in the U.S. heaped praise on the Japanese system, much to the surprise and chagrin of many Japanese.

These overnight advocates of the Japanese approach to education were apparently not aware that most Japanese parents, most of the country's business leaders, and virtually all of the country's elementary and high school students are vehement critics of the Japanese system, claiming that it is the most negative and destructive force in Japanese society.

Japan's modern educational system, introduced shortly after the fall of the feudal shogunate in 1868, was designed by the new Meiji government to turn out perfectly conditioned and homogenized citizens who would be diligent, loyal and obedient to higher authority. Students were not allowed to think for themselves or behave in an individualistic manner.

All learning was by rote memorization. There was no classroom discussion or dialogue between student and teacher. Subject matter was strictly controlled by the government and was absolutely uniform throughout the educational system.

Following Japan's defeat in World War II the American-led forces that occupied Japan from 1945 until 1952 attempted to introduce a number of reforms in the educational system, but about the only thing they accomplished was to eradicate the teaching of emperor worship and the concept that the emperor was a living god.

In the intervening decades, fundamental changes in Japanese society and the economy have resulted in some changes in the educational system as well, but for the most part it remains a feudalistic anachronism that reflects some of the worst in Japan's traditional culture.

Students are still regimented like soldiers. The method of teaching has remained virtually the same. There is very limited freedom of thought among the faculty or the students.

But worst of all, at least as far as students and parents are concerned, is the examination system for entry into the more desirable schools. In keeping with the national propensity to structure everything into hierarchies, all schools are ranked, and generally the only way an individual can qualify for the more desirable jobs and professions is to have attended the "right" schools.

A key factor in selecting out the students who will go on to the preferred schools is a system of entrance exams that students refer to as "Examination Hell." The exams are very difficult, with the worst of them being those for entry into the most prestigious universities.

By the 1970s, competition to get into prestigious schools was so severe that thousands of independent *juku*, or "cram schools," had mushroomed all over the country, with hundreds of thousands of high school students going directly from their regular schools to one of these commercial academies for an additional three or four hours of study daily.

An equal number of Japanese mothers had begun devoting a substantial portion of their waking hours to encouraging, serving and supporting their sons to enhance their chances of success at school and in the examinations. Someone in the news media dubbed these devoted wives *kyoiku mama* (k'yoe-ee-kuu mah-mah), or "education mothers," and the sobriquet stuck.

Not surprisingly, the pressure for students to get on the "right school" track gradually encompassed the elementary school level, and finally kindergarten as well. Since the 1980s, graduates from a small number of elite kindergartens, elementary schools and high schools have virtually monopolized the paths leading to entry into Tokyo University and the other most desirable universities.

The pressure engendered on the youth of Japan by this educational system is now linked with the unusually high rate of suicide among the young.

共生

Kyosei
(K'yoe-say-ee)

"Getting in Harmony with the World"

One of the most common refrains that one hears from the Japanese is that the rest of the world does not understand them, and therefore misinterprets many of their attitudes and much of their behavior.

This Japanese posture is very much like a stern father accusing wayward and unappreciative children of resisting his dictates because they do not understand that what he wants them to do is for their own good.

The problem with this traditional Japanese position is that it almost always ignores the feelings and aspirations of non-Japanese, and is transparently self-serving—a rationale and type of behavior that is certainly not unique to the Japanese, but in their case has been especially conspicuous because they have traditionally chosen not to explain themselves to outsiders.

During most of their history the Japanese were virtually sealed off from the rest of the world—from the early 1600s to the mid-1850s—by strictly enforced laws. They have also traditionally viewed all outsiders as dangerous threats, used their complex culture as a social and economic barrier, and followed a deliberate policy of keeping all segments of their society off-limits to all but native-born, mainstream Japanese.

Because they were isolated for centuries, the Japanese became insular and self-centered to an extreme. They developed a system of etiquette and ethics that, in fact, dramatically differentiated them from Westerners, and were further conditioned to avoid intimate contact with foreigners—all of which made them enigmatic and suspicious to other people.

Despite dramatic changes in both the attitudes and behavior of the Japanese since 1945, most are still "Japanese" in the traditional sense to a degree that makes it difficult or impossible for them to comfortably relate to and communicate with foreigners—and vice versa.

By the mid-1980s, however, virtually all Japanese had come to the realization that they had to speed up the changes occurring in their way of thinking and doing things—that they could no longer remain even partially isolated from the world at large and expect to be accepted as full-fledged members of the world community.

In keeping with their penchant for identifying policies, philosophies and movements with precise labels, this new goal was quickly christened *kyosei* (k'yoe-say-ee), which, by itself, means "symbiosis." A more poetic translation would be "living cooperatively" or "living in peaceful harmony."

Japanese businessmen, politicians and others now routinely refer to the need for *kyosei* between Japan and the rest of the world—meaning that the economies of Japanese and other countries must be integrated; and that the Japanese must learn how to live in harmony with the world at large.

This is not likely to happen any time soon, however, despite a growing understanding of the need for change. The prevailing system is buttressed by an underlying fear of altering a formula that has brought amazing prosperity. More importantly, the system itself is so strongly entrenched in the character and psyche of the Japanese—plus the fact that they do not possess the necessary language and cross-cultural skills to quickly alter their way of doing things—that integration, if it is diligently pursued, can only take place slowly, over decades rather than years.

In the meantime, those dealing with Japan today can enhance their standing and communications with their Japanese contacts by incorporating *kyosei* into their own vocabulary.

間

Ma
(Mah)

"Life in the Slow Lane"

Despite the inroads that modernity has made on the traditional Japanese way of doing things, they still see time as their friend and not their enemy, and continue to use it, in many instances, as if it were unending.

The Japanese concept of time is rooted in the native religion, Shintoism, which began as an animistic practice that was closely tied to the seasons and to the growth and harvesting of crops. The rhythm of life in Japan became intimately related to these natural phenomena, which could not be hurried.

There was a season and a time for virtually everything, so much so that later anthropologists were to describe Japan's whole culture as "seasonal"—from the clothing the people wore, the food they ate, the work they performed, to the recreation they enjoyed.

The distinctive etiquette system that the Japanese developed was based on a studied and stylized form that required precise segments of time so carefully controlled that they became exercises in slow-motion. Abrupt actions became taboo.

The entire lifestyle of the Japanese took on a clock-like precision, with actions and events proceeding at a slow, measured pace. Time was not a race. It was an unending journey that went from one stage to the next, inexorably, and the challenge was to stay in rhythm with it.

Instead of trying to speed things up, it was more natural for the Japanese to try to slow them down. Being able to stop, sit back and savor the passage of time by contemplating the rhythms of nature was regarded as the ideal life.

The introduction of industrialization into Japan in the 1870s and 80s forced the Japanese to subvert much of their seasonally-oriented culture. Boarding and riding streetcars and trains, for example, was totally incongruous with wearing kimono, which made long strides and high steps impossible.

The Japanese use of time still today impacts significantly on their international trade and diplomatic relations. In general terms, they spend a lot more time in considering things and in coming to conclusions than most of their Western counterparts.

One of the traditional Japanese ways of using time to their advantage is to build in or inject *ma* (mah), which means "space" or "time-gaps," into whatever proceedings they are involved in.

In business negotiations, for example, it is customary for the Japanese to literally put time on hold for several seconds to minutes at a time without any kind of announcement or explanation. They stop talking and listening to the other negotiating party; close their eyes and appear to be sleeping or resting; hold little side conversations with each other; go to the bathroom, and so on.

Members of negotiating teams may also disappear and not return, and new members may join the group during the proceedings.

The use of time to "kill" an opponent or negotiating adversary is one of the most effective weapons the Japanese have in attempting to gain the upper hand during business negotiations. See *MAKU SATSU.*

Americans in particular tend to panic when a business conversation stops, and rush to fill up the space with talk that often gives their opponents the edge.

窓 際 族

Madogiwa Zoku
(Mah-doe-ghee-wah Zoe-kuu)

"Bored Men by the Windows"

The lives of lower-ranking members of Japan's famed samurai warrior class, which ruled the country for almost seven hundred years, were generally not made up of luxury or leisure.

Their annual stipends of rice were carefully controlled to provide them with just enough to survive in a genteel kind of poverty. In modern military terms they were on duty twenty-four hours a day, and had to be ready to forfeit their lives for their lords at a moment's notice.

Service to a particular lord was hereditary and bound the individual warrior to his lord for life. Quitting one lord and going into the service of another was rare, and when it did happen it was usually the aftermath of war between the clans.

Because of the exclusivity of the clan system, a samurai who lost his lord for whatever reason would most likely become an outcast who thereafter had to live by his wits.

Masterless samurai came to be known as *ronin* (roe-neen), or "wave men," because following wars between the clans, large numbers of them would roam the country in waves, robbing when necessary to stay alive, hiring themselves out to unscrupulous officials as spies or assassins, etc.

In contemporary Japan, students who repeatedly fail entrance examinations at the universities of their choice and thereafter float around for one, two, three or more years waiting to take the exams again, are also known as *ronin*.

There are several other classes of present-day Japanese who have become "outcasts" in one way or another; either having lost their places and having nowhere else to go, or because society disapproves of their behavior. These people are often classified as this or that *zoku* (zoe-kuu), or "tribe," in order to distinguish them from the rest of the population.

Members of motorcycle gangs who terrorize residents of beach cities and mountain resorts with their reckless, noisy behavior are another type of outcast in present-day Japan. They are known as *boryoku zoku* (boe-ree-oh-kuu zoe-kuu), or "violence tribes."

A large group of Japan's businessmen have been labeled *madogiwa zoku* (mah-doe-ghee-wah zoe-kuu), which literally means "beside-the-window tribe." Generally these are middle managers in their fifties who did not qualify for higher positions and have been shunted off of the promotion ladder to make room for younger people.

The usual custom is to provide these middle-level managers with a larger-than-usual desk and comfortable chair near a window, but not give them any staff or duties to perform. Thereafter, they idle away the years, waiting for the time they reach the firm's mandatory retirement age.

All of the people exiled to the never-never-land of the "window tribe" are not necessarily incompetents and may not have reached their level of competence. They were just moved aside to make room for others to take their turn in the same managerial slots.

It is sometimes difficult in a Japanese company setting to distinguish between *madogiwa zoku* and managers who are still on active duty and playing key roles in the activities of their departments. They also often have larger desks, plusher chairs, sit near windows, and often seem to do very little.

When visitors are shuffled off on members of the "window tribe" it is a sign that the visitors, and whatever proposition they may have brought with them, are not considered important.

窓口

Madoguchi
(Mah-doe-guu-chee)

"Getting into a Japanese Company"

One of my Japanese colleagues once described the typical Japanese company as being something like a giant balloon. He said there were no holes ("doors") in the typical "balloon company" because if there were, all of the air would naturally come out and it would collapse.

My colleague added that when an outsider who is not aware of the true nature of Japanese companies makes an approach, he is usually not able to actually get "inside" because there are no doors in the Western sense of the word.

"The company will typically react very much like a balloon when you press on it," he said. "It will give a little at the point of pressure, but no opening is made, and when the pressure is removed it will return to its former shape without any trace of your attempt."

My friend's comments were made in the context of describing the differences between Japanese and Western firms, and the difficulties usually involved in establishing a successful relationship with a Japanese company.

Figuratively speaking, an outsider cannot walk into a Japanese company and quickly or easily get a genuine, positive hearing, no matter how great the proposition might be. The nature of Japanese management generally makes it impossible for a responsible individual or group of individuals in a company to respond quickly to overtures by outsiders.

There is a precise, lengthy protocol that one must follow, first to get even a toe in the door of a Japanese company, and second, to follow this up with a series of meetings that may or may not achieve the results desired. One of the keys to making a successful approach to a Japanese company is finding what is aptly called a *madoguchi* (mah-doe-guu-chee) or "window" into the company of your choice (there being no open "doors")!

A *madoguchi* into a Japanese company can be either another company that already has a successful business relationship with the company concerned, or a ranking member of the target company, provided you have been able to obtain an acceptable introduction to that person from someone who has some clout with the *madoguchi*.

If your *madoguchi* is an outside firm, a suitable representative of that company will take you into the target company through their "window." If your *madoguchi* is an inside manager or executive of the target company, he will use his own personal "window" to get you through the walls of the balloon.

Japanese companies often prefer that potential new relationships take the outside *madoguchi* approach because they prefer to do business with established vendors that have already proven themselves. Their attitude is that it is expensive, time-consuming and possibly dangerous to qualify and take on new business relationships.

The Japanese reluctance to quickly and easily go into business with new entities naturally has a cultural background. They have been conditioned to trust and deal only with members of their own groups. They have a built-in fear of exposing themselves to new obligations and new relationships that might result in some kind of damage to them personally, or for which they would be held responsible by their colleagues and company management.

Of course, as this syndrome fades, more and more Japanese companies are lowering their defense shields, making their operations more transparent, and welcoming direct approaches by foreign companies.

But on the average, the best and often only way to get something going with a Japanese company is through a *madoguchi*.

Often the best way to find a "window" is simply to ask the company you want to do business with to recommend one of the vendors on their approved list. Banks are another source for the means of possible *madoguchi*. Company profiles in trade directories usually list banks. If the company of your choice is not large enough to be covered by such directories, a diplomatic phone call to the company will usually reveal that information.

Other sources include business associations, chambers of commerce, market research companies, large advertising agencies, and consulting firms.

前向きに

Mae Muki Ni

(My Muu-kee Nee)

"When a Promise May Be a Promise"

Within the narrow confines of the Japanese way of doing things, to respond with an unadorned "no" to a person is almost always regarded as impolite, and in many cases is taken as an outright insult.

Generally speaking, about the closest you can get to saying no without crossing the fine line between what is polite or acceptable and what is rude is to use the negative of verbs and other words.

For example, if someone asks (rather politely), "*Shimasu ka?*" (She-mahss kah?) or "Are you going to do it?" an acceptable reply is, "*Shinai*" (She-nie), "I'm not going to do it."

While the use of the negatives of words is one of the most common ways Japanese have of expressing the concept of "no" in ordinary conversations, formal occasions are another matter altogether.

Formal etiquette in Japan requires the use of specifically polite words and word endings in all circumstances, but especially so when the response is negative.

Because of extraordinary sensitivity to verbal slights and corresponding fear about ruffling the feelings of others, Japanese developed a variety of ways to criticize and say "no" by using euphemistic words and phrases, and by changing the meaning of certain words to fit the circumstances rather than mean what they appear to mean.

One of the phrases that generally means exactly the opposite of what it suggests when used in a business context is *kangaete okimasu* (kahn-guy-tay oh-kee-mahss), or "I'll think about it."

The person who says this may, in fact, give the matter some thought, but the very clear meaning is that he will not do anything about it. Because this is readily understood by the Japanese as a turn-down, another layer of subtlety has been added to the phrase to further stretch the meaning.

This second version is *mae muki ni kangaete okimasu* (my muu-kee nee kahn-guy-tay oh-kee-mahss), or "I will take a forward direction (positive approach) to thinking about it."

Some businessmen who use this version do intend to give the impression that they are really not putting you off—that they actually will give the matter serious thought and that there is hope.

Others add the *mae muki ni* prefix more out of an exaggerated sense of politeness and ostensible goodwill than any serious intention of pursuing the subject. In these instances it becomes just an excessively esoteric form of saying "I'm not going to (or can't) do anything about it, so forget it."

It is virtually impossible to distinguish the true meaning of *mae muki ni kangaete okimasu* without additional input of some kind, either from the person who used the phrase or from someone else.

Where serious business considerations are at stake, it behooves the person making the approach to remain skeptical and to cover himself any way he can—by getting a third party to contact the individual concerned, by approaching others, and so on.

These are some of the subtleties that make doing business in Japan both burdensome and challenging. There is no way to avoid them. The only recourse is to become as knowledgeable as possible about them and to give the other side an easy out that will get both them and you off the hook in a reasonable amount of time.

One "out" is for you to suggest that if they cannot respond within ten days or fifteen days (or whatever) you will assume that the project is not for them. If they are really interested, they will let you know that they are in fact "thinking about it in a positive manner."

前向き姿勢

Maemuki Shisei

(My-muu-kee She-say-ee)

"Feed-Forward instead of Feedback"

Every country is tied to its past by a cultural umbilical cord that includes laws, traditional customs, myths and memories that are colored by religious beliefs, historical events and other odds and ends.

But some people are more receptive to change than others, and for some reason not yet fully understood, the Japanese have turned out to be cultural chameleons, able to ingest, synthesize and adapt foreign concepts and ways to suit their own purposes; able to become stronger with each infusion from abroad.

In fact, it is one of the great ironies of the age that Japan, until recently a small, feudalistic country that was one of the most traditionally oriented, backward-looking nations in the world, is now one of the most forward-looking of all countries, and an economic giant.

Lengthy contemplation as to why this is so leads me to believe that a significant part of the answer might lie in the type of Zen Buddhism that was practiced during Japan's long feudal period.

Japanese Zen taught realism—how to distinguish between reality and fantasy, how to accept what could not be changed, and how to focus mental and physical energy to achieve goals.

When the Japanese were freed from the political and economic restraints of their feudal system of government in 1945, and for the first time in their history had an opportunity to create a totally new world for themselves, they were brimming with more than a thousand years' worth of suppressed ambitions and energy.

The suddenly-released drives that energized and motivated the Japanese carried them forward at startling speed, despite an enormous number of cultural handicaps that were incompatible with their new role as business competitors in the markets of the world.

One of the factors that contributed significantly to the economic success of the Japanese was a complete reversal from their tradition of revering and preserving the past. Virtually overnight they adopted a new religion now expressed in the term *maemuki shisei* (my-muu-kee she-say-ee), which translates as "forward-looking attitude" and incorporates the concept of anticipating, planning and preparing for an efficient, stable high-tech future that stirs the imagination.

This new philosophy is coordinated on a national level by various government ministries and major corporate groups, and on a local level by prefectural agencies and affiliates of the country's huge conglomerates.

The Japanese say their *maemuki shisei* approach to economic planning uses *feed-forward* instead of feedback—which, they add, is the outmoded approach that continuously disrupts and limits the American economy.

In other words, the Japanese say that they anticipate events, plan for them and attempt to control them, while American politicians and businessmen react to events after they occur—with the obvious result that the Americans go from one emergency to another in an unending cycle of ups and downs.

If the Japanese are able to continue expanding and improving their *maemuki shisei* business strategy—and chances are they will—it will give them an unprecedented kind and degree of power over their future, with awesome implications for the rest of the world.

In the past Americans and Europeans have proven themselves leaders in technological breakthroughs. The future may belong to those who prove themselves superior in such commonsense but rare intellectual breakthroughs as *maemuki shisei*.

真 心

Magokoro
(Mah-go-koe-roe)

"Looking for True Hearts"

One of the most important differences between typical Japanese and Western businessmen who are considering a relationship is that Westerners tend to emphasize tangible things—money, technology, products—while Japanese tend to be as concerned, if not more so, about the character and personality of potential foreign partners.

Westerners usually go in and begin talking about products, prices and profits, while the Japanese are generally more interested in the who and why at first, and often give more initial weight to these personal factors than they do to the strictly business side of propositions.

Reasons for this significantly different Japanese approach are, of course, bound up in their culture. During most of Japan's long history, their society functioned for the most part on a moral rather than legal foundation. The few laws that existed were decreed by ruling authorities to protect and preserve the system in power—not to empower or preserve the people.

The people had no voice in government. The only rights that ordinary people had were severely limited, and depended on the character and whims of those in power. Behavior was meticulously prescribed for all of the social classes, and was primarily designed to maintain order and obedience to authorities.

With no body of inherent rights to protect them, the Japanese were forced to rely on a morality based on a mixture of Shinto, Buddhist and Confucian teachings. Rather than legal sanctions, the people depended upon a high level of honesty, integrity, and honor to sustain themselves and their system.

Of course, those in power manipulated this morality to buttress their control over society, but by demanding virtually absolute moral conformity, the governments of the shogun and provincial lords played a vital role in conditioning the people to give precedence to personal ethics and character in all things.

Making business deals with other people and engaging in ongoing business relationships with other companies was first of all a personal, moral thing—not something based only on objective concepts.

Given this situation, it was vital that deals between people, whether business or politics, be based on personal relationships that were carefully and systematically developed in advance, often over an extended time period.

This development process included introductions from mutually known connections, face-to-face meetings, eating together, drinking together, exchanging gifts, and so on. It also included careful scrutiny of the other party's background, weaknesses and strengths.

In evaluating other people, one of the key ingredients the Japanese looked for is expressed in the word *magokoro* (mah-go-koe-roe), which is generally translated as "sincerity," but literally means "true heart."

A person with a *magokoro* is one who exhibits all of the characteristics that have traditionally been attributed to the ideal Japanese—one who meticulously follows the dictates of etiquette, is scrupulously truthful and honest, can be trusted to fulfill all of his obligations, and will make any sacrifice necessary to protect the interests of friends or business partners.

When I first went to Japan in the late 1940s, I routinely encountered people whose honesty, integrity and sense of responsibility were astounding. Over the following decades this traditional Japanese trait has weakened substantially, but it is still recognizable and continues to play a vital role in private life as well as business relationships.

Outsiders who are not perceived as having *magokoro* are unlikely to do well in Japan.

誠

Makoto

(Mah-koe-toe)

"Sincerity Japanese-Style"

Individual words are often a serious obstacle to communicating clear-ly and completely with the Japanese because of cross-cultural differences in their interpretation.

I have participated in hundreds of exchanges between Japanese and foreign businessmen in which both sides made a point of emphasizing the *makoto* (mah-koe-toe) or "sincerity" of their intentions, repeatedly promis-ing that all of their future actions would be equally sincere.

Unfortunately, the parties concerned were talking about entirely dif-ferent things, and despite the effusive expressions of goodwill and obvious good intentions of both sides, it was just as obvious that they were not truly communicating and that their promises of *makoto* would not prevent future friction.

Makoto translates as "sincerity, faithfulness, fidelity," but the "real" meaning of sincerity must be understood in the Japanese context for the foreign side to truly understand not only what they are hearing, but also what the Japanese believe the foreign side is saying.

Being sincere in the Japanese context means that one will faithfully fulfill all of the obligations that are an integral part of the Japanese system: putting the interests of the group first; making no individual or arbitrary decisions; consulting with everyone on all matters; performing all of the personal/social rituals designed to maintain harmonious relations with both inferiors and superiors; etc.

Naturally, the Japanese do not want to do business with any foreigner who appears to be insincere from the first contact, so it is essential that the foreign side behave in as sincere a manner as possible and make the usual verbal commitments to pursuing the relationship with all sincerity.

The challenge for outsiders dealing with Japanese is to find out what specifics the Japanese side is actually referring to—what commitments, from the Japanese viewpoint, the foreign side is expected to make or appears to be making.

Far too many foreign businessmen do not recognize the need to pin their Japanese associates down on every possible detail of a proposed new relationship. They are often so anxious to get a deal that they refrain from asking basic questions about the Japanese company and its intentions.

Some of these foreign businessmen fail to ask questions out of a sense of misplaced courtesy or politeness. But not asking detailed questions of a Japanese company (diplomatically, of course) may be viewed as inexperience, insincerity, or both. It can also be construed as indicating weakness.

The Japanese use their system of formality and highly refined etiquette as one of their main weapons in dealing with foreigners. They are very much aware that this puts most Westerners at a disadvantage because they do not know how to react to such formality and etiquette in a comfortable manner.

Westerners who attempt to follow Japanese etiquette down to the letter often put themselves at an unnecessary disadvantage. Except in the case of small routine politenesses, it is usually much better to stick with a decent level of Western etiquette. If any basic alterations in behavior are to be made, let the Japanese side make them.

黙 殺

Mokusatsu
(Mohkuu-sahtsuu)

"Killing with Silence"

Foreign diplomats, politicians and businessmen dealing with Japan regularly find themselves in situations where their wisdom and foreign experience fails them, and they do not know what to do.

These occurrences almost always result in the rapid buildup of stress and frustrations that often make the situation worse, with the foreign side typically overreacting and making mistakes.

One of the main causes of these frustrating experiences derives from differences in how Westerners and the Japanese have been conditioned to view and use time; and in culturally induced modes of communication.

Many Westerners, particularly Americans, have been conditioned to view time as something like a train speeding down a straight track. The train never slows down or stops, and they have a compulsive, deep-seated need to be on it, moving toward specific goals.

Japanese, on the other hand, have traditionally viewed the time track as a circle, with the train moving slowly and repeatedly passing the same place over a period of time. Slow movement, and sometimes getting off the train altogether, has not filled the Japanese with a dreadful sense of wasting time.

Many of the arts of Japan also incorporated the concept of slowing time or stopping it altogether; of capturing the essence of life in a timeless evocation of nature through poetry, through meditation; or in contemplating art or handicrafts that were refined down to their essence and were therefore timeless.

One of the most common and important time factors in Japanese negotiations or discussions about serious matters was—and still is—the use of time gaps or breaks. The people involved simply stop talking. They may just sit and remain silent (often with their eyes closed), get up and leave the room for short periods, or hold low-voiced side conversations with their colleagues.

Japanese negotiators and others develop varying degrees of skill in using these time gaps to their own advantage—so much so that there is a special term used in reference to the process: *mokusatsu* (mohkuu-saht-suu), which means "killing with silence."

Mokusatsu refers to the idea of "killing" the other party's case or proposition by letting it die in the vacuum of silence.

Americans and other aggressive types are especially susceptible to being tripped up by time gaps because they have been conditioned to abhor vacuums—to jump into any gap in a conditioned reflex to keep the dialogue from lagging or stopping.

Too often the foreign side presumes that the Japanese do not understand the points that were made, or that they have not yet accepted the reasoning of the foreign side and need more convincing.

This presumption regularly leads to hurried repetitions and frequently to on-the-spot revisions or compromises that favor the Japanese.

The proper defense for a *mokusatsu* ploy is simple. Just do as the Japanese do—rest and think, make use of the break to refer to notes, hold private discussions with your own colleagues, and so on. It also pays to introduce your own time gaps, and have control of the ball.

Japanese have traditionally had another advantage over Westerners when it comes to negotiations. The homogeneity of their culture made it possible for them to understand each other to a remarkable degree without the use of words. Generally speaking, they have been so conditioned to think and behave alike that they can, still today, anticipate each other's attitudes and behavior, making it possible for them to leave many things unsaid.

146

名 物

Meibutsu

(May-e-boot-sue)

"Here's a Little Something for You"

During the long period when shoguns ruled Japan (1192–1868), the country was divided into political and economic fiefdoms presided over by local clan lords. Travel and commerce between the fiefdoms was limited and carefully controlled.

Rivalry among the fiefdoms was usually intense. Allegiances shifted back and forth and armed combat between them was common as the power of the shogunate dynasties waxed and waned.

Under these circumstances, each fiefdom tried to be as self-sufficient as possible in all of the basics (a trait that is characteristic of Japan's larger companies today). As the centuries passed, each of the feudal domains developed specialty products that were unique to their regions.

These specialty items came to be known as the *meibutsu* (may-e-boot-sue), or "famous products," of the districts. During the last two centuries of the Tokugawa Shogunate, which were mostly peaceful, travel became fairly common and the *meibutsu* gradually became prized throughout the country.

With the advent of affluence and mass travel in the 1960s, the Japanese began flocking to every nook and cranny of the country, enjoying the scenery, sampling the foods and buying the local *meibutsu* as souvenirs and gifts (*O'miyage*/Oh-me-yah-gay) to take back to families and friends.

Buying *meibutsu* and other gifts during trips is not a casual thing with Japanese. It is a deeply established custom that is part of the protocol of making and nurturing personal relationships with a large network of people who are important to one's economic, cultural and social welfare.

By the 1970s, the manufacture and sale of famous regional products had grown into one of the largest craft industries in Japan, and continues to play a vital role in the travel industry. *Meibutsu* can be found in hotel arcades, at resort inn gift shops, at railway stations, in shops lining streets leading to popular tourist destinations, and in special sections of department stores.

All of Japan's forty-seven prefectures have officially recognized the role and importance of their *meibutsu*, and promote them as part of their economic development activities.

Among the famous products of Tokyo are cloisonne, fans, brocades, pearls, porcelains, lacquerwares, silver ware and woodblock prints. Kyoto is famous for its Nishijin embroidered silk, dolls, fans, woodblock prints, damascene, lacquerware and screens. Nagoya is noted for its chinaware, cloisonne, fans, lacquerware and nearby pearl farms.

Japan's famed Kutani-yaki porcelains come from Kanazawa, which is also known for its silk, kaga dolls and toys. The famous hotsprings resort city of Beppu is equally noted for its bamboo products and wooden items for kitchen and household use.

Many of Japan's mountainous northern districts are famous for wooden dolls called *kokeshi* (koe-kay-she) that are made by farmers during the snowed-in months of winter. The *kokeshi* have cylindrical bodies and round heads hand-painted in motifs that are unique to their region.

Among the popular *meibutsu* from Hokkaido, the northernmost of Japan's major islands, are wooden images of bears, fish and other nature objects carved by Ainu, the descendants of the original Caucasoid race that inhabited the central and northern portions of the islands before the arrival of Oriental Japanese.

More than a dozen areas in Japan are noted for their *sake* (sah-kay), Japan's national alcoholic beverage made from rice. Two of the most famous *sake*-making regions are Nagano in north-central Japan in the middle of the Japan Alps, and Nada, now a district within the city of Kobe.

The Japanese prize the regional *meibutsu* of other countries, and are especially pleased to receive them as gifts.

名 刺

Meishi

(May-e-she)

"You Are No One Without Them"

Meishi (may-e-she), or "name-cards," were introduced into Japan from China, where they were first used by eunuchs serving the Imperial Court. These earliest *meishi** were large in size, and came in the bright colors favored by the style-conscious castrates.

The use of name-cards, however, did not become common in Japan until well after the fall of the Tokugawa shogunate government in 1868. Prior to that time, there was very little travel for business purposes, and generally merchants and craftsmen in the towns and cities knew each other and therefore did not need introductions.

Classes and occupations in Tokugawa Japan were hereditary. The ruling samurai class were prohibited by law from engaging in business, and were not constantly meeting new people as is the case today. In addition, samurai could be identified by their apparel, swords and family or clan crests.

In virtually all circumstances, rank and differences in rank were obvious for all to see and provided the cues necessary for individuals to use the correct level of language and behavior required by the etiquette system.

When the feudal system of classes and prescribed apparel was abolished in 1868, these visual signals disappeared almost overnight. But the Japanese had been conditioned to be exquisitely responsive to class and rank and proper etiquette for centuries, and could not change their behavior so readily.

Following the downfall of the shogunate government, the variety and volume of business and social intercourse in Japan expanded at an incredible rate, creating serious etiquette problems.

There was an easily recognizable gulf of difference between the former samurai and the lower classes in speech as well as general demeanor, but the ex-samurai, who took the lead in establishing new businesses and remaking the economy of the country, desperately needed a quick and easy

---

*My editor, Tom Heenan, notes that the original meaning of the Chinese characters used to write *meishi* is "famous gentleman," and was historically used in reference to regionally famous persons.

way of determining the rank and relative importance of other former samurai in the new egalitarian society.

Meishi turned out to be the solution to this serious problem, and before long had become an institutionalized part of Japan's business world. Instead of basing their identities on family and clan, as had been the tradition, the Japanese of this new era identified themselves by their place of employment and company rank.

Because name-cards played such a vital role in the lives of the Japanese, they were used in a carefully prescribed and formal manner—a custom that has continued down to the present time.

While the format and printing style of today's *meishi* allows for plenty of personal preference, it is still important that they be carried in a card-case or in a wallet, and that they be presented with some formality.

The accepted protocol for presenting a name-card is to hold it with both hands, with the printed side up and "out" so the person receiving it can immediately read your name, title and company or professional affiliation.

Virtually all Japanese who are involved with foreigners or international business in any way have their name-cards printed in both Japanese characters and Roman letters (English) so foreigners can read them.

Besides being courteous, it is also common sense and good business for foreigners dealing with Japanese to have their name-cards printed in both English and Japanese. Among other things, many foreign names range from difficult to impossible for the Japanese to pronounce until they have been phoneticized into Japanese syllables.

見合い結婚

Miai Kekkon

(Me-aye Keck-kone)

"Love by Arrangement"

Confucian concepts imported by Japan from China between A.D. 400 and 600 were to have a profound effect on Japanese family life. Continuity of the family through the male side was eventually given precedence over virtually every other consideration. Ancestor worship became an integral part of the moral foundation for the family unit.

Prior to the ascendancy of Confucianism, Japanese women more or less had equal rights with men and played leading roles in all areas of national life. During the famed Nara Period (710–784) and the following Heian Period (794–1192), there were several empresses. Most of the best-known writers and poets of these two periods were female.

Women were also prominent in the spread of Buddhism in Japan, many of them serving as head abbots of leading temples. Moreover, they led the spread of all of the aesthetic arts which were to become key factors in Japanese culture.

During these heady centuries, women had a choice in whom they married, and those in the upper classes exercised the prerogative of taking lovers. Some of the more powerful and forceful women exercised the right to take more than one husband.

The rise of the samurai warrior class after 1192 and their adoption of Confucianism as their moral code resulted in Japanese women being gradually stripped of the rights they had enjoyed up to that time.

Once the samurai class had become hereditary, perpetuation of the family line took precedence over personal feelings. Marriages became family and political alliances. Women became the chattels of their husbands.

The system of *miai kekkon* (me-aye keck-kone), or "arranged marriages," became the custom, first among the samurai and then gradually among the common people as well. Men could divorce wives virtually at will; women had no such right. Love was seen as a detriment to marriage, and did not enter into the picture.

Prostitution, which had existed in Japan from pre-historic times, flourished in this new Confucian-dominated social system. Virtually all inns served as houses of assignation; some maintained staffs of women to serve as partners for male patrons.

During the last shogunate dynasty (from 1603 to 1868) redlight districts proliferated throughout the country, further degrading the position of women. The limited number of love affairs that did occur during this long age usually involved courtesans and their patrons.

At no time during Japan's long feudal age did young Japanese men and women date in the Western sense. Segregation of the sexes began in early childhood. Thereafter, personal relationships between the sexes were discouraged or prohibited altogether.

It was some ten years after the political and social emancipation of both Japanese men and women in 1945/6 that they began to form personal relations, fall in love and get married, but arranged marriages were to remain paramount for the next several decades.

Today, some thirty percent of all marriages in Japan are still arranged, and the annual decrease in the ratio has slowed down. The reason why such a significant percentage of young men and women continue to depend upon *miai kekkon* (*O'miai*/oh-me-aye for short) is that they are still in the grips of centuries of cultural conditioning. They still do not form close relationships during their teen years and do not have boy friends or girl friends to date once they are in their twenties.

Thus the *nakodo* (nah-koe-doe), match-maker or go-between, remains an important figure on the Japanese scene, not only in marriages but in business affairs as well. In fact, a rapid increase in the number of divorces in the 1980s resulted in a conservative reaction against *renai kekkon* (rain-aye keck-kone), or "love marriages," and an increase in arranged marriages.

身 分

Mibun
(Me-boon)

"Rights Without Responsibilities"

The division of Japanese society into four classes—the ruling samurai warriors, farmers, craftsmen, and merchants (in that order)—was reconfirmed as the law of the land by the newly established Tokugawa shogunate in the early 1600s.

The basic needs of the samurai were taken care of by the government (just as members of the military today are paid for their services so they don't have to work outside). A law was subsequently passed prohibiting them from engaging in any kind of commercial enterprise—primarily to keep them dependent upon the government and therefore loyal to it.

Class and status within the classes became a critical factor in all relationships in Japan. Laws governing the occupations, dress and behavior of all of the classes were precise and, especially in the first century of the era, strictly enforced by the military dictatorship.

It was vital that people keep their class in mind and conduct themselves according to the regulations of the central feudal government and the local clan lord. Their rights were not spelled out. The only real protection they had was to carefully obey all laws, and stay on good terms with shogunate and clan officials.

Because social status was fixed, there was a compelling compulsion for people to be especially sensitive about their class rights, and to complain long and loud if they felt their rights were being ignored.

As time passed and Japan's merchant class began to prosper, the samurai remained locked into perpetual poverty. By the mid-1700s, about all the samurai had was their superior social status. The wealth of the country was in the hands of the merchants.

Despite their wealth, however, the merchants were legally on the bottom of the social order. This made them even more sensitive about their class and their rights, and resentful of anyone above them or anyone who behaved as if they were socially superior.

Class distinctions were officially abolished in 1868 when the shogunate government fell, but the people remained extraordinarily sensitive to social status and their class rights.

In fact, there was no significant change in the social attitudes and behavior of the people until 1945, when a defeated Japan was occupied by the Allied powers following World War II, and the feudal system was finally ended.

A new democratic constitution and a reformed system of law enforcement and justice gave individual Japanese personal freedom for the first time in their history. In this new, heady atmosphere the Japanese were particularly jealous and protective of their new-found individuality.

Their former sensitivity about social status was transferred to their rights as individuals. They became even more compulsive about preventing anyone from taking advantage of them by ignoring their rights.

They remained culturally conditioned to avoid personal responsibility, but they were determined to protect and exploit the rights of their new *mibun* (me-boon), or "social position," which were guaranteed by the constitution.

Many Japanese took this new personal freedom to mean that if they were a clerk, no one could order them to make tea; if they were a truck driver, no one could tell them to do some other kind of work; if they were a student, no one could expect them be something else at the same time.

Most Japanese today are still much more concerned about their rights than their responsibilities—a factor that impacts on Japanese society as well as on Japan's international trade and diplomacy.

―――――150―――――

見え隠れ

Mie Gakure

(Me-ay Gah-kuu-ray)

"What Makes the Japanese Japanese"

During a recent visit to Kyoto I took some friends to the Ryoan Temple to view its famous rock and sand garden. The garden is not very large and, on the surface, is not very impressive. It is what you cannot see that makes it noteworthy.

It is this unseen essence that gives the garden, other things Japanese and the Japanese themselves their special character and, despite the cultural changes since 1945, remains distinctive and important in both a positive and negative way.

Because of the reputation of the Ryoan Temple garden, my American friends made an effort to see beyond the sand, rocks and walls that enclose them. They sat down on the veranda overlooking the small enclosure, along with dozens of other Westerners as well as many Japanese, and contemplated the garden for several minutes.

They knew they were being invited to have a metaphysical experience, and I believe they did; at least on a minor order. And perhaps they got an inkling of what is necessary for a true understanding and appreciation of the essence of the Japanese themselves—what it is that makes them different, distinctive, admirable, enjoyable, mysterious, sometimes seemingly irrational and often totally frustrating to linear-thinking, this-world-minded Westerners.

The Japanese learned a long time ago that what is obvious to the naked eye does not necessarily reflect reality, real worth, or even beauty. They learned to look beyond the surface of things, to the spirit that lies behind or below and is hidden to those who do not have a spiritual eye.

They learned that natural things—things that are a part of nature—promote the flow of spiritual harmony, and for more than a thousand years they tried to achieve that character, that power, in their surroundings—in their architecture, their building materials, their household utensils, their landscaping, their crafts and their arts.

The stone pillars, wooden frames, paper doors and reed-mat floors of traditional Japanese homes, inns and restaurants, with their rustic elegance, exemplified this "something" that gave them their character—a "something" that is referred to as *mie gakure* (me-ay gah-kuu-ray), or "hidden from view."

And just as the Japanese have traditionally attempted to build a hidden quality into their artifacts, they also created a style of etiquette and interpersonal behavior based on common intuition rather than expression. Their attitudes and lifestyle became so homogenized, so structured, that verbal communication was often unnecessary. Being open, frank or blunt came to be rude, dangerous, and even life-threatening. Proper etiquette demanded that they keep their thoughts and emotions hidden from view.

The *mie gakure* essence of life in present-day Japan is weakening rapidly as the old culture is buried beneath layers of concrete, steel, plastic and an infusion of Western ways, but it remains in pockets throughout the country, and is readily recognizable in the behavior of most adults.

Westerners dealing with typical Japanese should be aware of the *mie gakure* factor in Japanese attitudes and actions, and make an effort to overcome the barriers it sets up. A key part of this effort is establishing personal relationships with individual Japanese concerned—a step that is virtually mandatory before either side can transcend its hidden values.

Anyone who wants to fully enjoy Japan, whether businessman or vacationing traveler, must be able to look at the country and the people with a third eye; seeing the essence behind the facade; letting themselves go to revel in the spirit of things Japanese.

It is this "hidden from the eye" essence of Japan that acts as a magnet on many foreign residents, drawing them and holding them to the country.

151

未完成

Mikansei

(Me-kahn-say-ee)

"The Power of Incompleteness"

One of the most conspicuous characteristics of Japanese culture is that it provides for and causes what appears to outsiders to be contradictions in their attitudes and behavior. There are dichotomies in virtually all areas of Japanese life, and this is the fundamental reason why Westerners often have difficulty understanding them and tend to view Japan as an enigma.

Westerners in Japan for any length of time, no matter how coarse and loutish their own behavior, cannot fail to notice basic contradictory elements in Japanese culture.

The examples are almost endless—exquisite politeness is often cancelled out by extreme rudeness; all-encompassing friendliness on one hand coupled with vehement hostility on the other; unsurpassed kindness counter-balanced by abject cruelty; boundless honesty coupled with an equal propensity for deceitfulness.

Some of these contradictions occur only when the established harmony of the Japanese way is disturbed. Other aberrations occur when the situation involves non-Japanese who are not in a "friend" or "guest" category. As long as things are normal by Japanese standards, the positive side of the culture generally prevails.

Treatment of cats and dogs is an exception to the general rule—and is one thing foreign residents continuously harp about. Some people treat their cat and dog pets with as much care as is bestowed upon a beloved infant; others treat them with pitiless barbarism.

On the positive side of Japan's contradictory culture is a deeply embedded sense that nothing physical is ever as good as it could be, and therefore the need and opportunity for improvement is unending.

Physically as well as philosophically, the Japanese look upon the material world as *mikansei* (me-kahn-say-ee), or "incomplete," and not only subject to being improved but demanding it.

Unlike most Westerners who have been conditioned to stop trying once arbitrarily established standards have been reached, there are no in-between acceptable standards as far as the Japanese are concerned. They have been programmed to continuously strive for improvement upon improvement, with no end in sight.

The *mikansei* or "incomplete" concept applies to people as well as things, and is the philosophical foundation for the Japanese attitude toward training and learning—in the arts and crafts as well as in the more mundane areas of work.

In the business world the *mikansei* concept is the heart of yet another Japanese idea that Western businessmen first began hearing about in the 1970s—the belief that manufactured products should be continuously refined and improved. (This is the concept expressed in the equally pregnant term *kai zen* (kie zen), meaning "continuous improvement.")

There is, however, a contradictory factor in the *mikansei* concept that is quintessentially Japanese. In the area of aesthetics—in painting, wood-carving, pottery, even landscape gardening—it is the Japanese way to deliberately stop short of completion; to leave something undone so that the viewer may have the pleasure and satisfaction of mentally completing the imagery.

This subtle merging of the *mikansei* and *kai zen* themes throughout Japanese culture is a strength as well as a charm that distinguishes the Japanese from other people, and is a factor that must be grasped before one can hope to understand—and compete with—the Japanese.

152

魅 力 的 品 質

Miryokuteki Hinshitsu

(Me-rio-kuu-tay-kee Heen-sheet-sue)

"Quality With Sex Appeal"

Despite an almost compulsive practical bent that characterizes the driving force in Japan's recent economic achievements, there is a hidden, metaphysical element to the character of the Japanese that is of equal importance in understanding the Japanese and learning how to compete with them.

The Japanese have not thrown aside all of the spiritual and emotional aspects of life that are generally associated with people whose cultures are ancient. It is still common for the Japanese to "see" more than the physical properties of the products they make.

Shintoism, the native Japanese religion, holds that all things in nature, including trees and rocks, have a spiritual essence of their own. In this philosophy, the apprentice carpenter cannot fully master his craft until he is able to recognize and respect the spirit of the wood used in his trade.

For the apprentice carpenter to achieve the kind and degree of insight demanded by the masters, it was necessary for him to go well beyond familiarization with the grain and consistency of the wood. It required his becoming able to merge himself with the essence of the wood, working with the wood to transform it into a pillar, a table or a box.

Japan's history is replete with master carpenters, calligraphers, potters, painters, landscape designers and others whose work is alive with its own essence, and touches the innermost wellsprings of our being.

Now, Japanese manufacturers of modern-day products, ranging from automobiles to wristwatches, deliberately aim at going beyond physical quality in their products, to imbue them with a transcendental spirit that clearly speaks to the viewer and user.

This new endeavor by Japan's manufacturing industries is designed to make a quantum leap beyond the already very high physical quality of their products to a metaphysical realm. This new level of quality has been labeled *miryokuteki hinshitsu* (me-rio-kuu-tay-kee heen-sheet-sue).

Miryokuteki is a word that is often used to describe a woman who is conspicuously attractive in a sensual, provocative way. In addition to having strong connotations of sexuality, it also suggests a kind and degree of beauty which has an irresistible appeal.

In the Japanese context, *miryokuteki* quality goes well beyond the surface of products. It includes the choice and use of materials making up the product. The concept covers the goal of getting the most out of all of the parts of the product, with the parts creating a harmonious unity that results in both the ultimate utility and beauty. Hundreds of examples of *miryokuteki* products can be seen in any Japanese department store, particularly in the furniture and kitchenware departments. Small hot water heaters that attach to the wall over the kitchen sink are just one example.

Japan's emphasis on *miryokuteki* quality presents a serious challenge to the rest of the world. Not only do the Japanese have the motivation to continuously strive for perfection in their products, they also have the skills to get close to their goals thanks to their cultural heritage.

Foreign businessmen who cannot take an anthropological approach to designing and manufacturing because they simply lack the intellectual skills, or because they stubbornly refuse to give credence to a concept that they regard as going too far, are likely to find themselves falling further behind the Japanese.

Survival and success in business are no longer based on a simple three-dimensional approach, and ironically, it is one of the earth's oldest and most traditional cultures that has taken the lead in creating the future.

153

水 引 取 引

Mizuhiki Torihiki
(Me-zuu-he-kee Toe-ree-he-kee)

"Going After the Bird in the Bush"

Despite not having joined the industrial revolution until the 1870s, more than one hundred years after it started in England, Japan quickly caught up with the industrialized countries of the West in a burst of energy, spirit and talent that was astounding.

Japan repeated the same "miracle" between 1945 and 1970, when it rebuilt its economy from the devastation of World War II, again astounding the world with its accomplishments. And, of course, between 1970 and 1980, Japan went on to become one of the top economic powers in the world.

The extraordinary economic success of the Japanese was more than a "business" blow to the Western world. It was a psychological blow as well. Even though there were glimmerings as early as 1959 that Japan was well on its way to becoming an important economic power, not one business forecaster in the world had any inkling of what the Japanese would accomplish in the following fifteen years.

Westerners have since spent a considerable amount of their time and energy trying to figure out how the Japanese achieved their "economic miracle." There is no single explanation, of course, but the overall process was quite simple.

Much of the answer naturally lies in the cultural character of the Japanese. They were conditioned to take life very seriously, to persevere in whatever they set out to do, to be very hard-working, to sacrifice their own personal convenience in the pursuit of company and national goals and so on.

One particular aspect of Japanese character that contributes significantly to their economic prowess is their patient, methodical approach to things. Japanese have traditionally thought in terms of generations, and conducted their personal lives and businesses accordingly.

Generally speaking, the long-range view taken by Japanese businessmen gives them substantial advantages, particularly over Americans and others who are inclined to think in terms of one year—or even one quarter of a year.

Of course, American businessmen point to the demands of their stock-holders and other economic differences to explain and excuse their short-term approach to management, but such rationalizing does not help them in competing with Japanese.

One simple facet of Japanese thinking and behavior that has played a significant role in their successful penetration of foreign markets is expressed in the term *mizuhiki torihiki* (mee-zuu-he-kee toe-ree-he-kee), which means something like "take a loss in the beginning in order to build a profitable business."

Japanese are, in fact, notorious for under-pricing their exports in order to win market share, then raising their prices to a profitable level later, as well as benefiting from higher-volume production and sales.

For that matter, the huge amounts of money spent each year by Japanese companies on entertainment is primarily aimed at developing new business contacts and nurturing old ones as a means of increasing sales and market share, and could therefore come under the heading of *mizuhiki torihiki*.

Japanese businessmen see nothing unethical or immoral about their *mizuhiki torihiki* approach to expanding their business. It seems to them one of the most logical and practical things they can do.

水 商 売

Mizu Shobai

(Me-zuu Show-by)

"The Business of Pleasure"

The traditional Western image of the Japanese was that they were an unemotional people who were robot-like in their work and behavior, and that recreation played only a minor role in their lives. There was enough truth in this image that it helped obscure the character and personality of the Japanese, and still today gives a warped idea of leisure and pleasure in Japan.

Japan's traditional economy provided only a subsistence-level existence for most of the people, and left little time for recreational pursuits. The lifestyle that developed under the earliest emperors and particularly under their successors, the shoguns, had a military thoroughness and sternness that precluded the development of a casual, happy-go-lucky approach to life.

Yet, life in early Japan was not all work, rigid etiquette and formal ceremonies. There were dozens of annual festivals. Drinking *O-sake*, the traditional rice wine, to mark special events and as a regular indulgence, was commonplace. Banquet-style meals, accompanied by *O-sake*, were also common.

Many of the aesthetic practices, including moon-viewing and cherry blossom-viewing, were party events—with the latter especially marked by drinking and general merry-making. Folk-dancing and singing, in conjunction with various festivals and private parties, were universally practiced.

Establishment of the Tokugawa shogunate in 1603 was followed by a general improvement in the economy, the appearance and rapid growth of hundreds of new cities, and the development of a sophisticated urban lifestyle that included a multitude of public eating and drinking places, baths that featured the sexual services of attractive young women, *geisha* houses and the rapid proliferation and growth of redlight districts.

Within the first century of the Tokugawa era, these new enterprises had become one of the largest industries in the country, and came to be known as the *mizu shobai* (mee-zuu show-by), or "water business," a euphemism for the pleasure trades.

The Japan of the 1700s was described as a bacchanalian paradise by Dutch traders who were required to make annual trips to Yedo (Tokyo) from their tiny outpost in Nagasaki Harbor. The Dutch, who had been allowed to remain in Japan when the country was closed to the outside world in 1638, noted that every inn in every post station on the long journey to Yedo provided female bed-partners as well as room and board.

Japan's "water business" survived the downfall of the shogunate government in 1868, lost a little ground during the prolonged wars on the Asian mainland in the 1930s, and was greatly curtailed during the final stages of World War II in 1944/5. But, with the return of peace in 1945, the *mizu shobai* was the first industry in postwar Japan to make a full and complete recovery.

By 1953 the geisha houses, redlight districts, sex-oriented bathhouses, bars, cabarets, restaurants, assignation inns, love hotels and sundry other pleasure-oriented businesses were thriving as never before—fueled this time by the dollars and pent-up sex drives of hundreds of thousands of American GIs and other Allied military personnel who were there "occupying" the defeated country.

By the end of the 1950s most of the foreign Occupation forces were gone, but their role in supporting the still growing *mizu shobai* had been taken over by foreign importers who were flocking into Japan by the dozens of thousands, and by newly affluent Japanese manufacturers and exporters who were pumping out millions of tons of goods annually for their foreign buyers.

The 1960s were the heyday of Japan's *mizu shobai*, but it remains today one of the top industries in the country. Interestingly, a significant percentage of the young women staffing the thousands of *mizu shobai* bars and clubs in Japan today are imported, usually illegally, from the Philippines, Thailand and other Southeast Asian countries.

物の哀れ

Mono-no-Aware
(Moe-no-no-ah-wah-ray)

"Enjoying the Sadness of Life"

One of the most conspicuous facets of life in early Japan was an acute appreciation for the ephemeral nature of man, his struggles in the face of great odds and the inevitability of his downfall and disappearance.

This Buddhistic philosophy was especially strong in the attitudes and behavior of the samurai warrior class. The nature of their profession required them to be ready and willing to give up their own lives—as well as to sacrifice their families in extreme circumstances—at a moment's notice.

It was this philosophy that led the samurai to liken themselves to cherry blossoms, which, though indescribably beautiful, are as fragile as idle thoughts, wafting away on the slightest breeze.

Much of the poetry of Japan's long samurai age took the philosophy of the impermanence of all things as its theme. Especially before going into battle, it was customary for warriors to compose death poems expressing these feelings along with their farewells. Some, particularly higher ranking officers, would conduct tea ceremonies before battles to compose themselves and to enjoy a last communion with their philosophical and spiritual natures.

The great novels, *Genji Monogatari* (Gane-jee Moe-no-gah-tah-ree), or "The Tale of the Genji," and *Heike Monogatari* (Hay-ee-kay Moe-no-gah-tah-ree), or "The Tale of the Heike," written in the 12th century, were also based on this Buddhistic concept.

In fact, much of the beauty, power and poignancy of all of the literature of early Japan is bound up in the universal truth that life is fragile and fleeting, and that an understanding of this is essential before one can mature and live life fully—with the only pleasures often being those that are extracted from the smallest things.

Recognizing the impermanence of life led the Japanese to develop a special vocabulary for describing the sober and often sad side of existence. One of these terms was *mono-no-aware* (moe-no-no-ah-wah-ray), which means something like, "I will give myself up to grief." Those who have spent time in Japan will recognize the *mono-no-aware* element in Japanese paintings, woodblock prints, movies and television shows. The idea is to evoke the greatest possible feelings of sorrow and sadness, tempered here and there by acts of selflessness and kindness.

Other special terms that reflect the Buddhist theme of life are *wabi* (wah-bee) and *sabi* (sah-bee). *Wabi* is an abbreviated form of *wabishii* (wah-bee-she-ee), which means "desolate" or "lonely," and is regarded by the Japanese as an essential part of both the poignancy and beauty of life. *Sabi* can be translated as "the rust of time," and refers to the beauty that comes with natural aging. To the Japanese, the bleached color of old wood, the gnarled body of an ancient pine tree, moss on a rock, as well as the wrinkled, parched face of an old man or woman represent a special kind of beauty.

One of the primary reasons for the special characteristics of Japan's traditional handicrafts is the subtle quality of *sabi* built into them by their makers—the same quality that in the West is sometimes referred to as an "antique look."

Foreigners seeking to understand Japanese culture, including the general attitudes and behavior of individuals, must have considerable knowledge and appreciation of the *mono-no-aware* factor. It is one of the primary ingredients making up the flavor of Japanese life.

One of the best times and ways to experience the *mono-no-aware* element in Japanese culture is to spend a late fall rainy weekend at an isolated inn that overlooks the ocean or a narrow valley. Looking out over the cold, grey sea or a rain-filled valley from the solitude of your room is bound to remind you that life at best is sweet-sad and short.

156

無 我

Muga
(Muu-gah)

"The Art of Achieving Mastery"

Some time after I took up residence in Japan in the late 1940s I became a dedicated fan of samurai movies—the famous *chanbara* films featuring samurai swordsmen of Japan's long shogunate period (1192-1868).

I was fascinated by the samurai concept, with its code of honor, including ritual suicide as a way of atoning for mistakes and failures, its foundation in metaphysics and aesthetics, and the incredible skills developed by those who followed *bushi do* (buu-she doe), or "the way of the warrior," with extra zeal.

While the *chanbara* films typically exaggerated the skills and exploits of their starring samurai, voluminous historical records attest that the average level of ability of samurai warriors with the sword and the bow ranked them among the most ferocious fighters of all times, and that particularly outstanding individuals achieved unbelievable degrees of mastery.

Chanbara films regularly depicted training sessions, showing how the samurai warriors developed and maintained their extraordinary skills with highly advanced methods that had been discovered in China more than two thousand years earlier.

The secret of the system was that it combined physical with mental and spiritual training, giving precedence to the latter, and that it was a total lifestyle—not just a vocational skill picked up as a way of earning a living.

Chinese, particularly Zen Buddhists, had learned that to achieve mastery of any complex skill, mental training is as important if not more so than physical training, and Japan's samurai made this vital insight the central theme of their schooling in martial as well as aesthetic arts.

The ideal of this Chinese/Japanese approach to mastering any skill was to achieve the highest possible level of physical ability in combination with a mental state of *muga* (muu-gah), meaning "self-effacement" or "egolessness"—a state in which the mind does not interfere with the actions of a trained body.

In other words, if you have trained your body to perform the functions of a juggler, for example, and can achieve a mental state of *muga*, then performing the juggling functions perfectly is as easy as thinking them.

A superbly trained samurai swordsman in a state of *muga* was therefore unbeatable because he could defend himself against any move by an opponent, and perform perfectly any offensive move he attempted. A highlight of many *chanbara* movies occurs when two master, *muga*-minded swordsmen meet and battle to a draw.

In one of the great ironies of Japanese culture, the Japanese of old were fully aware of the power of *muga* and used it extensively in their daily lives. But they used it to maintain the status quo, not to fuel change. For close to a thousand years the Japanese were, in fact, held in something akin to suspended animation until outside political events shattered their isolated world.

In present-day Japan, a growing number of Japanese scientist-engineers are tapping into this ancient Zen Buddhist way of eliminating the ego as a means of releasing creative insight and energy. They believe, and rightly so, that most people are not truly creative because their thought processes are controlled by pre-conceived notions; that they cannot think in new ways because unconventional thinking is blocked by psychological barriers.

If Japan's modern-day businessmen and scientists are anywhere near as successful in using *muga* to enhance their creativity as their samurai ancestors were in using it to hone their prowess with the sword, the world is in for a growing flood of Japanese inventions.

157

むかつき病

Mukatsuki Byo

(Muu-kaht-ski Be-yoe)

"When the Worm Turns"

One of the earliest and most popular Western myths of Asia—propagated as much by Asians as by uninformed Westerners—was that Asians were a passive and peaceful people because of the influence of Buddhism and other non-aggressive religions.

It was and still is true that most Asians are passive and peaceful most of the time, but only when the structure of their traditional social system is intact, when the power of the ruling government is absolute and tolerates no dissent, or when it is benign enough that people tolerate it.

In times when political and social changes occur—usually because of outside influences or because the ruling authorities become excessively abusive in their attempts to maintain or extend their power—then the traditional passivity and peacefulness of Asians falls away, and they resort to violence, often times with a degree of savagery and cruelty that is not common even in societies known for their non-passive behavior.

At least a part of the explanation of why normally passive Asians can and frequently do become shockingly violent is that they have no universal principles or morality to fall back on when there is a weakening or failure of the minutely structured, strictly enforced and situationally determined cultural restraints that normally control their behavior.

The foundations of Japanese, Chinese and other Asian behavior were traditionally based on obedience to authority and conformity to prescribed inferior-superior relationships. When these cultural restraints are broken, there is a tendency for many people to give vent to all of the anger they have suppressed, all of the frustrations they have suffered, by striking out capriciously and viciously. Recent history in Asia is full of such incidents, ranging from the behavior of Japanese troops in China during World War II and elsewhere to the genocidal rampages of the Khmer Rouge in Cambodia.

In present-day Japan, where the whole culture of the nation is undergoing dramatic, fundamental changes, the degree of social violence is growing rapidly.

One of the most peculiar aspects of violence in Japan today is that a significant percentage of it is perpetrated by young girls, usually in their mid-teens. Beginning in the 1970s, police records showed an increasing number of young girl gangs which engage in harrassment, assault and battery, robbery and other crimes.

Some of the most startling examples of violence in Japan today involve youths or young men who suddenly, with only the slightest provocation, go into a rage and beat supposed offenders or innocent bystanders—sometimes killing them.

This type of sudden violence has been given a name, *mukatsuki byo* (muu-kaht-ski be-yoe), which literally means "nausea sickness" or "sick feeling," but is used in the sense of "rage sickness." Incidents of *mukatsuki byo* do not always involve rowdy or punk-type young men. The rage also hits ordinary men who have been drinking, and snap because of some irritation.

Japanese health authorities blame these sudden outbursts of violence on stress created by the country's robot-like educational system, overwork, overcrowding, and a sense of helplessness that sometimes engulfs people and fills them with an uncontrollable rage.

Among the things that have been known to set off rage seizures in men (usually when they are drinking) is hearing other Japanese speak English, either among themselves or to a waiter or bartender.

脈

Myaku
(Me-yah-kuu)

"Taking the Pulse of a Situation"

People who have difficulty coping with the complex nature of personal relations in present-day Japan would really have been in trouble during the Tokugawa Shogunate period. There were so many customs and rules involving proper behavior, particularly toward superiors, that life was like a staged play, with each person having a precise script to follow.

The higher the position of the individual involved in a meeting or discussion, the more detailed and demanding the protocol required for the situation. Relations with the shogun himself eventually became so stylized and illogical that some of the practices defied all reason.

According to historical anecdotes, one of the more esoteric customs that the shogun's physicians developed to watch over his health without breaching any of the taboos involved was a method of checking his *myaku* (me-yah-kuu), or "pulse," from an adjoining room through use of a string wrapped around his wrist.

Myaku is used in a number of compound words referring to the connection between things, such as *jin myaku* (jeen me-yah-kuu), or "personal connections."

The word is of particular importance in Japan's business vocabulary. It is commonly used in reference to business deals or projects that are in doubt, and seem to be on the verge of dying. Depending on the case, the response might be that the deal *myaku ga aru* (me-yah-kuu gah ah-ruu), "has a pulse," or *myaku ga nai* (me-yah-kuu gah nie) "has no pulse."

In the Japanese business environment, whether or not a deal lives or dies often depends more on the personal feelings and interests of particular individuals than on its objective merits. Given the personal nature of management and business relations in Japan, there is invariably a substantial element of politics and patronage involved.

This factor makes it important for Japanese managers on all levels to develop considerable skill in *myaku wo miru* (me-yah-kuu oh me-ruu), or "reading the pulse" of their peers and superiors, not only to protect themselves but to build their own constituencies and advance their career goals.

Japan's reading-the-pulse syndrome impacts on foreign businessmen in a variety of ways. The system makes it difficult to impossible for inexperienced outsiders to evaluate what is going on in a Japanese company because of their inability to read the many "pulse strings" that are involved.

Like master intelligence agents, the Japanese depend upon quietly and doggedly gathering dozens to hundreds of bits of information from numerous sources, then putting them all together to create a meaningful portrait.

In their dealings with foreign companies, this approach results in the Japanese side continuing to ask questions and to probe long after the foreign side believes their Japanese counterparts have all the information they need.

This situation is often further complicated by the fact that the Japanese side will frequently continue to indicate interest and progress all during the long, drawn-out diagnostic phase, even after it becomes clear that the program is in trouble.

The reluctance of the Japanese to come right out and announce that they are not going to pursue a project often leaves the foreign side mystified and frustrated. On numerous such occasions, it seems as if the Japanese side continues the dialogue and facade of interest as a training exercise for their junior managers.

One technique for partially controlling Japan's bit-gathering and pulse-reading system is to ask your Japanese counterparts to write out in advance a list of all of the questions they want answered, and any other information they need to make a decision. This also helps avoid answering the same questions over and over.

無かったことにする

Nakatta Koto ni Suru
(Nah-kaht-tah Koe-toe nee Suu-ruu)

"Pretending It Never Happened"

Cultures that are regarded as primitive by industrialized societies often have highly sophisticated, institutionalized practices for maintaining mental health and providing psychiatric therapy for those who encounter disturbing problems.

While historical Japan downplayed innovative technology to the point that change from traditional patterns of behavior and work were often taboo, the early Japanese were world leaders in developing customs designed to fulfill the emotional and spiritual needs of the people.

These customs included festivals with religious themes, aesthetic pursuits such as programmed sightseeing to areas famed for their extraordinary beauty, and banquet parties at which each individual participated in the activities as a means of relieving stress and strengthening group bonds.

However, these practices and dozens of others that made up the traditional life-style were not sufficient to keep all Japanese on an even mental keel because their ritualized etiquette system was so demanding that it frequently exceeded the ability of the people to cope.

There were often occasions when arrangements or agreements fell

apart for one reason or another. To avoid undue stress and possible recrim-
inations, it became common practice for the parties to the problems to
agree to an annulment—to *nakatta koto ni suru* (nah-kaht-tah koe-toe nee
suu-ruu), or to "nullify" them.

Nakatta is the past tense of the negative *nai* (nie). In this case, the
whole phrase means, more or less, "make it as if it never existed." When
both parties agree to *nakatta koto ni suru*, it relieves them completely of
any obligations or regrets. The slate is wiped clean.

The *nakatta koto ni suru* technique is especially useful in business,
where programs and deals often go sour. Rather than agonize over the failure or hold grudges, the Japanese prefer to eliminate the unhappy experience and forget it.

If there is obvious fault on one side of a failed program or problem, its
full erasure is likely to require profuse apologies and an unspoken understanding that the party at fault will give up some advantage in the future.

Of course, there is a similar cultural ploy in Western societies ("Let's
forget the past and start over again"), but it is not as formally recognized or
as institutionalized as it is in Japan.

Foreign businessmen dealing with Japan for any length of time generally encounter the *nakatta koto ni suru* factor at some time—usually without realizing its cultural significance. Those who are not familiar with its
role and do not have total communication with their Japanese counterparts
tend to regard it as an unethical subterfuge.

Whether use of the "pretend it didn't happen" ploy is unethical or not
often depends on which side the viewer is on. In any event, it can be used
by either side to withdraw from an undesirable situation.

Since foreigners frequently get off on the wrong foot when they begin
trying to do business in Japan, they may want to make use of the *nakatta
koto ni suru* technique and start afresh. It should be kept in mind, however, that it is generally effective only in the early stages of a relationship, and
probably only once with the same party.

Invoking this ploy includes an honest explanation of how the situation developed and a sincere apology, and is generally best handled in an
informal setting, over drinks. If the Japanese side perceives the explanation
as honest and fair, and the apology as sincere, they are conditioned to
accept it and not hold any grudge. In some cases, it strengthens the relationship because it puts it on more personal, human terms.

浪 速 節

Naniwa Bushi

(Nah-nee-wah Buu-she)

"Beware of the Naniwa Bushi Man"

During the latter decades of the Tokugawa Shogunate (1603-1868), street entertainers in the great commercial city of Naniwa (present-day Osaka) specialized in a type of folk singing that became known as *Naniwa Bushi* (Nah-nee-wah Buu-shee), or "Naniwa Tunes."

Naniwa Bushi were especially popular among the common folk because they played on the emotions, taking their themes from loves and lives lost, and extolling the glorified exploits of the *yakuza,* the professional criminal class that had existed in Japan for centuries and often acted as defenders of the common people against unscrupulous samurai lords and officials.

Despite their unsavory activities (gambling, loan-sharking, prostitution and monopolistic control of various areas of industry), the *yakuza* had an all-encompassing code of conduct that gave them a Robin Hood image. Their power was such that they operated virtually undisturbed by government authorities.

In a society where people had few rights guaranteed by law, and in which *yakuza* often represented the ideal character, the popularity of *Naniwa Bushi* spread to the far reaches of the country, becoming a significant influence in the attitudes and behavior of Japan's lower classes.

Businessmen, in particular, liked to model themselves after the character and personality suggested by the songs, especially in their dependence on gut-feelings and their sense of honor and justice in the operation of their businesses.

Not all of the influence of the "Naniwa Melodies" was benign or accepted wholeheartedly, however. Like so many other things in Japan, it had a flipside that partially negated its positive influence. People who were overly emotional and apt to act on the spur of the moment without really considering the welfare of others, were frequently accused of being *naniwa bushi.*

It often seems that as Japanese businessmen grow older there is a tendency for them to become more and more *naniwa bushi* in their attitudes and behavior—that is, to depend more on their feelings and less on objective reasoning.

The results of this *naniwa bushi* syndrome may be good or bad, depending on the circumstances. There are numerous instances when Japanese businessmen (and others as well) will make important decisions that are thoughtful, kind, generous and selfless to an extreme, and often do not make "economic" sense.

On other occasions, their reactions are based on totally irrational emotions that lead them to take actions—or refuse to take actions—that result in serious consequences.

It often happens that Japanese will assume their most admirable *naniwa bushi* face when they encounter foreigners, treating them to a kind and degree of generosity and support that is amazing and impressive.

When this factor is combined with the Japanese traditions of showering guests with hospitality, it can overwhelm a lot of objectivity and common sense on the part of visitors, weakening their defenses and making them more susceptible to cooperating with their hosts.

One of the challenges facing foreign businessmen in dealing with older Japanese is to determine if their reactions, whether positive or negative, are a reflection of the *naniwa bushi* syndrome.

Failure to make this determination can result in the foreign businessman agreeing to something too quickly or giving up too soon, and is another reason why patience and a slow, deliberate pace is recommended for all dealings in Japan.

縄 張 り

Nawabari

(Nah-wah-bah-ree)

"Going Where You Have Face"

Japan's long history of virtual isolation from the rest of the world led to the development of an inward-looking, Japan-fixed mentality that colored the entire lifestyle and contributed to the creation of one of the world's most exclusive cultures.

Among the characteristics of the culture was a precise form and order for all things, from mundane daily actions to the practicing of aesthetic arts. Everything had its time and place. Space was divided according to its use. People were divided according to their class and occupations.

While the Japanese had a special penchant for an ultra refined degree of simplicity in their arts and crafts, they were also noted for designing complex military strategies and devices for both offensive and defensive purposes.

One of the specialties of Japanese architects and landscape designers was creating mazes to confuse and disadvantage potential enemies. Castles in particular had a series of maze-like paths leading from the gates to the inner areas. During peacetime, ropes (*nawa*) were strung along these paths to show the way.

The drawings for these maze-paths, used during the construction phase of castles, came to be known as *nawabari* (nah-wah-bah-ree). *Bari* means "stretching," i.e. "rope stretching." Eventually, the different areas of the construction site, for which different contractors were responsible, were also roped off and called *nawabari*.

Finally, the term came to be used in reference to specific areas or territories, as in areas of political influence or gang territories. Now the whole of Japan is divided into both political and gang-related *nawabari*. There are also sales *nawabari*.

One of the most common uses of the term *nawabari* today is in reference to particular bars or cabarets that are regularly patronized by individuals who regard them as their private domain in the sense that they are well-known there and are treated as preferred customers. When they take someone to one of their *nawabari* hangouts, they insist upon paying the bill as part of their image.

Virtually all Japanese businessmen have their personal *nawabari* drinking places where they have "face," get special service, and, if they are on expense accounts, can drink and walk out without paying (their companies are billed later).

The use of bars and cabarets in this manner is a deeply entrenched part of the Japanese system of nurturing personal relationships with their co-workers as well as their clients and business prospects.

Foreign businessmen stationed in Japan or visiting there regularly should definitely have their own special places where they take Japanese businessmen as their guests. In addition to choice bars (like the Old Imperial Bar in the Imperial Hotel, the lounges atop the Akasaka Prince and New Otani Hotels, etc.), it also pays to know and utilize a number of restaurants.

The best idea where restaurants are concerned is to know and have "face" in several that feature a different kind of cuisine, so you can give your guests a choice of steak, Chinese, French, German, etc., and, of course, Japanese foods.

It is especially impressive for a foreigner to be a regular patron at strictly Japanese-style restaurants, particularly if the restaurants are famous, or exceptionally good.

One of my favorites, which never fails to win high marks from Japanese guests, is *Sasa no Yuki*, in the Uguisudani district of Tokyo on the Keihin commuter train line. The *Sasa no Yuki* is the oldest (over 400 years), largest, and best tofu restaurant in the world—but most Japanese have never been there.

根 回 し

Nemawashi
(Nay-mah-wah-she)

"Revolving the Roots of Business"

Foreigners who become involved with Japanese for the first time are often frustrated by the amount of time the Japanese take to consider new propositions, and the general lack of information about the status of the matter during the usually long, drawn-out process.

This characteristic Japanese behavior, derived from cultural conditioning, has several facets, including group mentality and group commitment, that make it difficult or impossible for Japanese to make rapid decisions as groups or individuals.

Within a vertical structure based on rank, the group orientation of the Japanese in responsibility as well as decision-making functions necessitates a carefully designed and enforced protocol that controls the behavior of individuals.

To make the system function smoothly the Japanese must conduct themselves according to precise guidelines required by their position and rank. This means they must be very circumspect about expressing personal opinions and must especially exercise extreme caution in any attempt to persuade others to accept their judgement.

The use of "cold logic" and verbal aggression in any kind of discussion or negotiation tends to be regarded as "un-Japanese." Such behavior is viewed as being both impolite and immoral in the sense that it is perceived as ignoring the feelings and rights of others.

The process by which the Japanese reach agreement in considering any new commitment or action is known as *nemawashi* (nay-mah-wah-she), which literally means "revolving the roots."

In practice, *nemawashi* refers to holding informal, behind-the-scene discussions, often on a one-on-one basis, among all the key people who would be concerned with or involved in implementing any decision made. In other words, the subject is turned around and around, and is viewed and considered from every angle, before it is brought out into the open as an official or formal proposal.

Nemawashi is both a sounding-board for unofficially testing the response to an idea without exposing or endangering anyone—before making a commitment to pursue the idea—as well as a lobbying mechanism used by an individual or group wanting to get a project through the system.

Use of the *nemawashi* process is fraught with danger, and requires considerable skill. Failure to involve people who feel they should have participated, or bringing in people who are unacceptable to other parties, can destroy the attempt. Any deviation from "expected Japanese behavior" can throw the root-revolving off balance.

It is very important that foreigners who want to deal with Japanese understand the role of *nemawashi* and learn how to use it with considerable finesse. One of the best approaches to use right at the beginning of a relationship with a Japanese company is to go to your main contact on the section-manager or department-manager level—not the highest executive level—and ask them to give you advice on how to proceed.

If you take a humble yet confident approach, and if the individual approves of whatever it is you are proposing, chances are very good that he will become your inhouse adviser. It is vital, however, that you do not compromise or endanger him in any way, so such an approach must be handled unofficially and discreetly.

By Western standards, extraordinary patience is generally required in initiating a relationship with a Japanese company. The larger the company the more people that may be required to approve or disapprove of a new proposal. This process may involve as many as twenty or more managers and executives, and can be especially time-consuming because some of them may be away on business trips or vacations and it would be unthinkable to approve a proposal without their input.

Once a consensus is reached in a Japanese company, however, initiating a new program generally moves swiftly because everyone knows exactly what it is all about and what they are expected to do—just the opposite of what often occurs in American companies.

寝 業 師

Newaza Shi

(Nay-wah-zah She)

"Attacking From a Prone Position"

Martial arts have played an extraordinary role in Japanese life for more than a thousand years. Following the usurpation of imperial authority by a powerful clan lord and the establishment of the shogunate form of government in 1192, the system spawned the appearance and growth of a professional warrior class that soon became hereditary.

These warriors were the famed samurai, who were to eventually make up about ten percent of the population and rule the country by the force of arms for the next 776 years.

As professional warriors, who were regularly called upon to put their prowess with the sword, bow and lance to the test, male members of the samurai class spent a significant proportion of their lives in training to develop and maintain their skills.

Because fighting skills were so important to Japan's ruling class, the martial arts flourished. Each of the arts had their schools and their special techniques. In between wars and minor skirmishes, there were tournaments and exhibitions.

Some of the accomplishments and deeds of outstanding warriors, with sword and bow, are difficult to believe today. The long bow that came into use early in Japan was so powerful that one arrow was sufficient to impale three victims who happened to be caught standing or marching in tandem.

The militaristic nature of the shogunate and clan governments led to the appearance of special groups of men and women who carried the arts of war to their ultimate. Known as *ninja* (neen-jah), these family-clan members were hired by the shogunate and competing lords and bosses as assassins and spies, and to engage in commando-type raids and other secret missions.

The *ninja* developed a wide variety of special weapons, tools, poisons and ruses, and practiced their dark arts so thoroughly that they were among the most deadly and feared agents the world has ever seen. Their particular art was known as *ninjutsu* (neen-jute-sue), which can be translated as "the art of invisibility."

The *ninja* in particular, but practitioners of the more ordinary martial arts (aikido, judo) as well, developed a variety of techniques for turning apparent defeat into victory. One of these techniques was *newaza shi* (nay-wah-zah she), or "attacking from a prone position."

Just as the term suggests, the individual who is already prone or is thrown down uses his feet in a lightning strike that catches his opponent off guard, and when done effectively, incapacitates or kills him.

Newaza shi is also used in a business context. It refers to a negotiating technique in which you seem to be on the ropes and going down to defeat, but suddenly reverse the situation by introducing a new element that catches your counterpart off-guard and gives you the advantage.

Like the mother bird that will fake a broken wing to distract a predator from its eggs or young, Japanese negotiators are known to sometimes put on a weak show to draw the other side out, and then pounce when the time is right.

It takes considerable skill to use this technique effectively, and it may not be wise for the foreign businessman to attempt it unless he is experienced and/or is the one being solicited by the Japanese company.

One thing the foreign businessman who is looking for new Japanese business should definitely do is pace his presentation so that he does not lay all of his cards on the table before getting anything from the Japanese side. If at all possible, the presentation should be crafted on a card-for-card basis.

───────────── 164 ─────────────

二番手商法

Niban-te Shoho

(Nee-bahn-tay Show-hoe)

"The Copycat Syndrome"

Until the 1970s and 80s, Japan was regularly castigated for copying Western products and technology, producing cheaper (and often better) versions of the foreign-made goods, then underselling them in the markets where they were invented or originally manufactured.

The propensity for the Japanese to copy foreign products and improve on them is deeply rooted in Japan's cultural and economic history, and continues today to significantly influence the behavior of the entire business community.

The development of civilization in Japan lagged behind the more advanced societies of the world by some three thousand years. When regular contact with Korea and China began around A.D. 300, Japan was barely out of the Stone Age. Over the next several centuries there was a steady flow of Chinese and Korean imports and technology into Japan.

Each category of merchandise brought into Japan seeded the appearance and growth of Japanese craftsmen who faithfully copied the Korean and Chinese models. The Japanese naturally adopted the same master-apprentice system that existed in China and Korea at that time. Apprentices learned by copying their masters. Innovation was strictly taboo until they went out on their own.

The new imported crafts became hereditary, and as the centuries went by the system produced an ongoing line of masters who continuously sought to improve their methods and materials. The masters produced disciples meticulously trained in their techniques.

Eventually the masters became so skilled in their arts, and their works became so highly refined, that further changes for the better were either impossible or considered sacrilege. The epitome of the desire of most craftsmen was to duplicate the work of famed masters.

In the late 1630s, Japan was closed to the outside world, reducing the flow of imports and new technology to a tiny dribble. Further, it became the policy of the government to discourage innovation and change of any kind.

For the next two hundred-plus years, Japanese businessmen and craftsmen were conditioned to copying the past. Forms and processes had long since been refined to the point that generally there was no impulse for innovation.

With the re-opening of Japan to the world in the 1850s and 60s, and the sudden new flood of foreign imports and technology, the Japanese took full advantage of their skill in copying to implement an industrial revolution in less than one generation.

There was an overriding impulse among Japanese businessmen in all fields to imitate rather than innovate. In the beginning, foreign businessmen brought product samples to the Japanese to be copied. This went on for about one hundred years.

By the 1960s, the Japanese themselves were canvasing the world, looking for new products and technology they could bring home and copy. It was natural for Japanese businessmen to adopt what became known as *niban-te shoho* (nee-bahn-tay show-hoe), or a "second-hand way of doing business."

The inference, of course, is that such businessmen not only copied products, they also imitated the way others (primarily American and European companies) promoted and marketed their goods.

The copycat syndrome remains a significant factor in virtually all areas of business in Japan. Almost every successful product is quickly imitated. New advertising approaches are copied within days or weeks.

One of the reasons why copying is so common in Japan (and elsewhere in Asia) is that the concept of intellectual property rights is not well-developed. Generally speaking, people see nothing wrong about copying someone else's product or technology.

二 次 会

Niji Kai

(Nee-jee Kie)

"The Party after the Party"

Most people visiting Japan for the first time are astounded at the size and variety of the entertainment trades, particularly those that involve eating and drinking. They cannot get over how large and numerous the entertainment districts are; how many restaurants there are; how many bars, pubs, clubs and cabarets there are; and how many people throng these places nightly.

One of the primary reasons for the size and popularity of the entertainment trades in Japan is the role that bars, clubs and restaurants play in business. Japanese businessmen (and politicians) have traditionally circumvented the etiquette obstacles that prevent them from being totally honest, frank and forthright with each other in formal situations by giving themselves permission to "forget etiquette" when engaged in eating and drinking parties after-hours.

When they are unable to reach consensus or make decisions during formal daytime meetings they resort to *niji kai* (nee-jee kie), literally "second meetings," at some favorite restaurant or nightspot. There, after an hour or so of eating, drinking and small talk, participants are able to say what is really on their minds. The more the participants drink and the later it is in the evening, the more candid such meetings tend to become.

Westerners participating in *niji kai* for the first time should not try to rush talk about business, as that upsets the purpose and the mood. The proper approach is to eat and drink heartily, engage in a lot of personal, humorous banter, and bring up business after everyone is feeling good.

There are other occasions when *niji kai* are common, such as after birthday parties and company parties, and following wedding receptions. After a wedding reception it is common for someone to invite the bride and groom and their closest friends to a small, private *niji kai*.

Although the average visitor to Japan is ready to call it a night after eating and drinking for three or four hours, when virtually any large party begins to break up the Japanese host will often invite a small, select number of revelers to a "second party" at a favorite place that stays open well after the regular closing time for bars and clubs.

Niji kai are much more personal and intimate than the first party of the evening, and it is something of an honor to be invited to one. They provide an especially intimate opportunity for the guest to become better acquainted with the host, and vice-versa; to build on a new relationship or enhance one already established.

Many foreign visitors, not being aware of the institutionalized nature of *niji kai*, turn down such invitations out of hand because they don't see the point in spending more time and money drinking, and look upon the idea as overkill.

But this is one of the extra investments that the Japanese make in creating and maintaining close personal relationships with colleagues and clients. It is a conspicuous sign of their sincerity and diligence in doing what to them is the right thing.

If you have a reason for not wanting to be out until 1 or 2 a.m., it is good manners and good psychology to advise your hosts in advance that you have a time limit and must end the evening by 11 p.m. or whatever, and that you look forward to some other occasion when you will have more time.

And just so the uninitiated visitor to Japan will not be surprised, more determined hosts frequently drag their guests to a *sanji kai* (sahn-jee kie) or "third party"—and, yes, there are diehards who, if there is any darkness left, insist on a *yonji kai* (yoan-jee kie), or "fourth party."

のれん

Noren
(No-rane)

"Protecting Your Public Face"

Early in Japanese history, people developed the custom of hanging curtains made of hemp under the eves of their homes to help ward off the hot afternoon sun, and, when they had close neighbors, to serve as blinds. These curtains were known as *noren* (no-rane).

As long ago as the illustrious Heian Period (794-1192 A.D.), Japanese innkeepers, shopkeepers and restaurant operators were hanging the short, split curtains across their doorways to help keep out dust and to block the sun.

By the early years of Japan's last great shogunate dynasty (1603-1868), someone had come up with the idea of dying the *noren* navy blue and putting the name or crest of the place of business on the curtains in white—a custom that quickly became universal.

This step had a natural consequence of helping to promote the names of individual businesses, and linking the image and reputation of the businesses with the names or crests on their *noren*.

Eventually it became the practice for successful business operators to allow their favored apprentices to open their own shops under the same names and using the same *noren*. In some cases, the shop owner helped to finance the opening of the new business and acted as adviser to the new proprietor—very much like today's franchised businesses.

In any event, by the 18th and 19th centuries, there were hundreds of *noren* that had been in existence for centuries, and were well-known throughout the land—including Mitsukoshi, Gekkeikan (sake), Yamamoto-Yama (sea-weed), Sasa-no Yuki (tofu) and Nishikawa (bedding).

By these latter centuries, the more famous of the *noren* were regarded as embodying the reputation of the businesses concerned, and the word for the door-front curtains had become a synonym for "face."

A number of expressions such as "I must protect my *noren* (face);" "My *noren* (reputation) was damaged;" "That *noren* (shop) is very old," became popular colloquialisms.

Traditionally styled *noren* are still used in Japan today by thousands of inns, restaurants and drinking places, adding a nostalgic feature to their decor. The older and the more traditional the place, the more likely it is to have continued the *noren* custom.

Some Japanese, as well as foreign visitors to Japan, buy *noren* to hang inside their homes, over doors to kitchens, open pantries or closets, and so on. The *noren* concept is also used as design motifs in other interior decorations.

Companies with old *noren* that have grown into huge corporations with many branch offices or chain stores no longer use the curtains themselves, but many of them have incorporated their original *noren* into their company logos.

Foreign businessmen can earn a few cultural points by now and then referring to their own company logo or a Japanese company logo as the firm's *noren*, with appropriate remarks about maintaining its integrity and reputation.

Another gesture that makes a favorable impression on a Japanese company is for a foreign joint-venture partner to obtain one of the Japanese firm's *noren* (or have one made up if it is no longer available) and have it prominently displayed when senior executives from the Japanese side visit the partner.

This kind of cultural sensitivity goes a long way in Japan.

抜け駆け
Nuke Gake
(Nuu-kay Gah-kay)

"Going for a Coup"

There are few things that delight the individualistic Westerner as much as personal success, especially when it is in the nature of a victory or coup accomplished quickly over strong competitors.

This same egoistic impulse was traditionally common in Japan as well, but generally was never acted upon except for samurai warriors who were trained in single combat and were often called upon, or forced, to demonstrate their prowess—and even they were forbidden from taking such action on their own.

The most notorious occasions of samurai breaking this taboo and acting on their own involved warriors sneaking out of their camps, stealing into an enemy stronghold and attempting a *nuke gake* (nuu-kay gah-kay), or "coup," of some sort by themselves.

Many such attempts ended in failure, with the wayward warrior losing his life and the enemy alerted. But even when such one-man forays succeeded, they were so much against the Japanese way of doing things that the successful samurai faced punishment by his commander and the anger of his fellow warriors.

Western businessmen who are not familiar with, or do not fully appreciate, the importance of group behavior in Japan often call upon their contacts in Japanese companies to engage in *nuke gake*. Even those who do not specifically ask their Japanese contacts to make decisions or take actions on their own often expect them to do so, and are sorely disappointed when they don't.

The point is, any action that is taken by a Japanese manager (unless he owns the company) without being thoroughly discussed with other managers to the point of consensus is most likely to be regarded as a *nuke gake*, and is likely to have dire repercussions for the individual.

The individual may try something on his own to satisfy his own ego, to glorify himself, to show up his less capable co-workers, or in an unselfish attempt to help the company. And he may be praised by his superiors. But his peers and his subordinates are most likely to regard his behavior as an affront and a threat to them, and thereafter to treat him as an enemy.

In Japanese companies where management is still by consensus, anyone who plays the role of wayward warrior is taking a major gamble that he can survive and move upward without the usual peer and subordinate support. This means first of all that he must succeed in his efforts and must have the goodwill and support of his superiors.

The best of all worlds for a maverick in a Japanese company comes to pass when he succeeds in pulling off some kind of impressive coup, is accepted by senior management as a comer, and attracts followers who want to ride his coattails.

A number of my own close Japanese friends who took such gambles and succeeded in impressing their superiors, but failed to attract followers, were eventually forced to resign from their companies because they could not put up with the ill will and lack of cooperation from their co-workers.

The truly superior person in a Japanese company must exercise both humility and extreme caution in dealing with his colleagues and superiors. He (or she) is usually obvious within a short time, but the outsider must also exercise caution in working with such a person in order not to alienate anyone else in the company.

The accepted way of dealing with this kind of situation is to always include the superior person's subordinates and peers in the dialogue, include them in the eating and drinking bonding sessions, regularly ask their advice, and so on.

168

お茶を濁す

Ocha wo Nigosu

(Oh-chah oh Nee-go-suu)

"Muddying the Waters"

Japanese attitudes and behavior go well beyond what is generally meant when we refer to "etiquette" in English. In the Japanese context of things, etiquette, in the sense of their behavior in private as well as business matters, refers to the whole psychological foundation of the society, covering not only their physical manners, but also their ethics.

Very early in their history, the Japanese developed a comprehensive system of etiquette that was so intimately integrated with their ethics and philosophy of life that manners became equated with morality. Failure to meticulously follow prescribed etiquette was regarded as immoral.

Minor lapses in etiquette in feudal Japan were so serious they could ruin one's life. Flagrant disregard of the prescribed behavior toward superiors was certain to result in heavy punishment if not quick death.

The very stylized behavior demanded of the Japanese also became equated with their national identity. Deviations from the strict standards were regarded as un-Japanese, and as a threat to the immediate group, the community and the nation.

The etiquette standards prevailing in present-day Japan are significantly more relaxed than they were at the end of World War II (1945) when the legal foundation for a feudalistic society was finally abolished. Lapses are no longer life-threatening, but being poorly skilled in traditional manners automatically bars one from many opportunities, and failure to live up to expectations can certainly end a career.

The demands of Japanese etiquette, which include maintaining a facade of cooperative harmony, are one of the reasons why the Japanese have become conditioned to using circumlocutions in their speech, and generally avoid candid, direct responses so as not to be pinned down on anything, or upset anyone.

Most Japanese develop extraordinary skill in *ocha wo nigosu* (oh-chah oh nee-go-suu). *Ocha* means "tea," and *nigosu* means "to stir," so this expression refers to making plain water murky so you cannot see through it—in other words "muddying the waters."

While the term *ocha wo nigosu* itself is not so commonly used, the practice it describes is very common, particularly in business situations. Employees of companies, including managers, are typically inclined to automatically gloss over negative factors in order to put the best possible light on their activities.

Foreigners doing business in Japan must develop a kind of cross-cultural vision that allows them to see through the turbid tea water they are often served. Whether the move is a deliberate attempt to cloud an issue and keep the foreigner in the dark depends on the individual and the matter at hand.

In situations where there is a competitive relationship, or when the Japanese side resents the presence and role of the foreign side, the aim may be to deliberately disadvantage the foreign company. On other occasions, the action may just be an attempt to keep everybody smiling.

The duality of this Japanese trait presents the foreigner with the additional challenge of determining whether or not the muddying of the waters is meant to deceive or just to distract.

About the only positive response to this puzzle is to ask questions, diplomatically and indirectly, from more than one source if possible, until you get a clearer picture of reality.

As a final resort, you can try a very personal approach to your best contact, telling him or her that your credibility and career hang in the balance, that you need to know, unofficially and confidentially, what is really going on.

────────────────── 169 ──────────────────

お 辞 儀

Ojigi
(Oh-jee-ghee)

"From Kowtowing to Bowing"

One of the most conspicuous forms of behavior demanded by China's god-like emperors was the kowtow, which required one to get down on knees and hands, bend over and touch the forehead to the floor or ground—much in the way weaker animals demonstrate submissiveness to more powerful animals.

Japan's imperial court adopted the kowtow from China well over a thousand years ago, and in keeping with their habit of Japanizing imported products and customs, the Japanese further refined this ultimate bow, making it more formal and obsequious than the Chinese version.

Between A.D. 700 and 900, members of the royal family who were assigned as heads of fiefs and shrines in the hinterlands set up their own miniature courts and took the kowtow and other etiquette of the imperial court with them.

Following the establishment of the shogunate system of military government in 1192 and the rise of the samurai class of professional warriors, the courts of the shogun and territorial lords gradually became more elaborate and formal, resulting in the kowtow becoming more deeply embedded in Japanese culture.

Throughout Japan's feudal era (1192-1868), the kowtow was a primary feature of the country's society. People kowtowed to the emperor and other members of the royal family, to court officials, to the shogun and his ministers, to clan lords, and to government officials, including city magistrates.

Failure to kowtow on an occasion when such an action was prescribed was a grave breach of feudal law. On some occasions, as when the entourage of a clan lord was passing, bystanders who failed to prostrate themselves could be cut down instantly by samurai guards.

The end of the shogunate system of government in 1868 also ended the legal status of the kowtow, but it did not disappear altogether. It remained a common practice in formal and special situations involving traditional Japanese style settings up to the end of World II in 1945.

Since 1868, the official greeting in Japan has consisted of the *ojigi* (oh-jee-ghee), or ordinary bow. The deeper the bow, the more formal and meaningful the respect and sentiment it displays.

There is a light bow, a medium bow and a deep bow. The light bow is casual. It is used in relatively informal situations, and by superiors to subordinates. The medium bow is used in formal situations of all kinds. The deep bow is relatively rare, and is primarily used when someone wants to demonstrate an unusual degree of respect, sincerity, gratitude or sorrow.

When Japan's Prime Minister Toshiki Kaifu appeared before Emperor Akihito during his coronation in 1990, he performed a medium bow, graphically demonstrating the change in the Emperor's relationship with the people.

Many Japanese now combine bowing and shaking hands, not only with foreigners but with other more Westernized Japanese as well. There is nothing at all demeaning about bowing, particularly the light casual bow, and there are times when it is more practical than shaking hands.

Foreigners who spend only a few months in Japan often find themselves unconsciously absorbing the custom of bowing, and responding to greetings with both bows and hand-shakes.

Bowing is one of the most used forms of non-verbal communication in Japan, and one of the most important. Besides its use as a greeting and farewell, a light quick bow is also used as a means of signaling someone in a store or office when you want service, or want to ask a question. It is also used to acknowledge that you've understood orders or directions.

お蔭様で

Okagesama-de
(Oh-kah-gay-sah-mah-day)

"The Gods Are Watching Over Me"

While the Japanese are far from being religious in the Christian sense, the primary aspects of their mind-set can be traced directly to the influence of Buddhism, Confucianism and Shintoism—with each of these being paramount in specific areas of their lives.

Japanese attitudes toward human sexuality, in all of its nuances, are mostly derived from Shintoism, which is, in part at least, a sex cult designed to appease the gods of fertility, and which provided justification for the casual and commercial treatment of sex throughout Japan's history.

Confucianism, on the other hand, was the source for the historical stratification of Japanese society, for their addiction to form, rules and precise processes, for their submission to authority and their loyalty to superiors.

Buddhism was the wellspring for the aesthetic and spiritual side of Japanese life. It nurtured the arts and stimulated their passion for beauty and refinement. And it imbued them with a deeply felt sense of the role of fate in human affairs and of the fragility and impermanence of life.

In present-day Japan, many of the traditional facets of Japanese character are masked behind a facade of modernity, and are invisible to the untrained eye. Yet, these traits continue to influence and sometimes control the lives of the Japanese outright.

The manual and intellectual skills that have contributed so much to the success of modern Japan have their roots in Buddhism and Confucianism. The flavor of Japanese life in general remains today a subtle amalgamation of these ancient influences.

For example, the expression *Okagesama-de* (oh-kah-gay-sah-mah-day), which is normally translated as "Thanks to you...," is one of the most common expressions in the vocabulary of the Japanese way, but it is almost always misunderstood by Japanese-speaking foreigners who hear it and use it.

Japanese routinely use the expression when someone asks them how they are, asks about the health and welfare of a family member; or asks how their business is going, and so on.

Not understanding the true meaning of *Okagesama-de*, many foreigners take it personally, presuming that the Japanese, out of politeness and their automatic response to formalities, are actually thanking them.

The misunderstanding arises in the translation of the word. Instead of meaning "thanks to you" in a personal sense, the expression actually means something like the English saying, "thank heavens," or "as luck would have it."

In other words, *okagesama-de* is a vestige of the Buddhist concept of fate in the lives of people. It also refers to the proper and effective functioning of relationships between people. It is a way of implying that these relationships have been properly nurtured and are thriving, and that all is right with the world.

Japanese-speaking foreigners can gain valuable points by using *okagesama-de* appropriately when responding to Japanese friends and business contacts. It subtly notes that you are speaking on their cultural wavelength, and gives a warm, positive feeling to your response.

Japanese are extraordinarily sensitive to the use of their language by foreigners. Learning when and how to use only a few dozen key words such as *okagesama-de* can get you a lot of social and business mileage. Some of these key words:

Itadakimasu (ee-tah-dah-kee-mahss)—An institutionalized expression said just before beginning to eat or drink; and especially appropriate when you are a guest (in which case the expression is more or less directed toward the host). In non-hosted situations, it is used in a rather casual manner as a signal that you are going to start eating.

Gochisosama deshita (go-chee-so-sah-mah desh-tah)—Equally ritualized, this is an expression of thanks to the host after finishing a meal or drinking sessions.

Yoroshiku onegai itashimasu (yoe-roe-she-kuu oh-nay-guy ee-tah-she-mahss)—This is a formalized, ritualized way of saying, "Please help me; please do what you can for me; please take care of it; please do it; please don't let me down," etc. It is a humble petition, and if it concerns something really serious is usually accompanied by a bow.

同じ釜の飯

Onaji Kama no Meshi
(Oh-nah-jee Kah-mah no May-she)

"Eating out of the Same Pot"

The tradition of men who are unrelated becoming "blood-brothers" is apparently common to most cultures, but each generally has its own special twist. In earlier years some American Indians, it seems, took the concept literally. They would cut their wrists or hands, then hold or bind them together for a short while, allowing for a symbolic exchange of blood.

In earlier times in Japan there were several ways men could establish brother-type bonds that would obligate them to each other. One of the simpler bonding rituals was for the men concerned to urinate together. Being invited to piss with a man of higher stature was quite an honor.

The traditional bonding ritual that I most appreciate, however, was for two men to have sex with the same woman on one specific occasion (but not at the same time). There was, naturally, a word for this ritual. It was referred to (rather indelicately, perhaps) as *mara-kyodai* (mah-rah-k'yoe-die), or "brothers of the organ."

This particular ritual is about as intimate as two men can become and maintain their heterosexuality, and was therefore a grave and important ceremony in old Japan.

In new Japan (which has not dispensed entirely with either of the above two rituals), there are more publicly acceptable rituals for establishing close personal relationships and becoming "like family."

One of the most common and popular of these ceremonies is referred to as *onaji kama no meshi* (oh-nah-jee kah-mah no may-she), which literally means "food from the same pot."

The inference of the term is that, like family members, people who have eaten from the same pot are bound together by bonds that go beyond the casual or ordinary business relationship.

Japanese businessmen (and others) regularly use the "food from the same pot" principle in developing and maintaining the close personal relationships that are essential in Japan for doing business and obtaining the goodwill and cooperation of others in any endeavor.

There are, in fact, several Japanese "community pot" dishes that play significant roles in this bonding process—particularly *sukiyaki* (which many non-Japanese are familiar with), *shabu-shabu, mizu-taki* and *oden.*

Creating and sustaining a family-type relationship with a Japanese does not *require* eating pot dishes, however. The same results can be obtained simply by eating together. But the process is more meaningful and effective if the meal is Japanese (*sushi, yaki-tori, kaiseki, tofu,* etc. are all acceptable), and if it is accompanied by drinking—with *sake* (sah-kay) as the first choice, and beer the second.

This ceremonial type of eating and drinking together is even more meaningful if it takes place in a traditional Japanese setting, such as an inn or a Japanese-style restaurant. The ultimate in bonding by eating and drinking together is doing it at an inn with *geisha* in attendance.

On a recent visit to Kyoto, two business associates and I were treated to a dinner party in one of the city's most famous *geisha* districts. The venue was on the second floor, with broad, open windows overlooking a river and a promenade favored by young couples.

The setting was right out of 18th century Japan. The food was delicious, the conversation scintillating, and the rapport warm and soul-stirring. The only odd element in the ritual was that the three *geisha* in attendance were in their late teens and early twenties, and when they were not performing their traditional roles, they behaved like hip teenagers so far removed from the *geisha* image that it was comic.

温情主義

Onjo-Shugi
(Own-joe-shuu-ghee)

"Japanese-Style Humanism"

Foreign businessmen setting up shop in Japan invariably encounter a number of concepts that are unfamiliar if not totally alien to them. Just as invariably, the roots of these unusual or strange new ways can be traced to a fusion of the tenets of Confucianism, Buddhism and, even deeper in the Japanese psyche, their native Shintoism.

In the social philosophy that evolved from these roots, the people at large were both the servants and the wards of their group bosses, their clan lords, the shoguns (after they took over in 1192) and finally the emperor.

There was, in theory, a balance between the allegiance and labor the people owed their superiors, and the care and protection the bosses and lords owed their employees and retainers. The balance was certainly not evenly split—it was accepted that superiors being superior would have more—but there was a point at which the common people would fight for their limited share.

However, the gap between the "haves" and those who got what was left was epitomized by a ruling of the Tokugawa Shogunate (1603–1868) which decreed that Japanese farmers should be left with so little of their produce that "they cannot live, but will not die."

It was not until the end of World War II in 1945 and the introduction of constitutional rights and democratic rule in Japan in the following years that Japanese farmers and industrial workers had any say in who could enjoy the fruits of their labor.

One of the traditional concepts that survived the transformation of Japan from a feudalistic society to a democracy was the idea that employers have a fundamental obligation to guarantee the livelihood of their

293

employees—and that the social security of workers, generally speaking, takes precedence over the profits of company owners.

During their heyday in the late 1940s and the 50s, Japan's labor unions took advantage of the age-old attitudes that employees are like family members who cannot be arbitrarily laid off or fired just because of fluctuations in business, and hammered out life-time employment agreements and other clauses to protect the rights of workers.

These new labor laws and agreements incorporated the Japanese concept of *onjo-shugi* (own-joe-shuu-ghee), or "humanism," which, in practice, refers to a degree of paternalism that goes well beyond the standards of American and most other Western companies.

Onjo by itself means "warm feelings" in the sense that loving parents have warm feelings for their children. And in the Japanese context, company responsibilities to employees approach this personal, intimate level of concern and care.

Of course, not all Japanese companies lived up to this humanistic ideal—or ever did in the past, for that matter. In fact, as business in Japan became more and more competitive, there was a growing tendency for Japanese firms to go to the extreme in ignoring the feelings and personal needs of their workers.

But, the ideal remained intact and the expectations of Japanese employees increased rather than decreased. By the mid-1980s a growing labor shortage had forced companies to dramatically alter their hiring practices. They began competing fiercely for high school and university graduates, offering them previously unheard of perks and improving their working environments. Young people, in particular, now refuse to join companies whose policies or practices ignore the rights of workers to have and enjoy private lives.

Foreign companies desiring to hire fairly large numbers of Japanese are advised to get professional advice on structuring their employment practices—from interviewing, hiring and firing to retirement. There are invisible pitfalls, trip-wires and time-bombs every step of the way that only a certified expert can deal with properly.

パ チ ン コ

Pachinko
(Pah-cheen-koe)

"Overloading the Senses"

The Japanese have long been famous for their ritualized aesthetic practices and for their use of Zen to achieve control over the body and the mind in order to sharpen their senses and manual skills to an extraordinary degree.

One of the primary aspects of Japanese efforts to achieve mental control and physical prowess was the ability to empty the mind of extraneous thoughts, and thereby eliminate physical and mental barriers to a perfect union of concept and action, particularly in the pursuit of fine and martial arts.

These mental and physical exercises that both shaped and defined the culture of Japan had another vital use as well. They served as buffers and as release from the strain imposed upon the Japanese by their rigid, unforgiving etiquette and feudalistic social and political systems.

But since the 1950s, Zen and all of its aesthetic progeny have suffered grievously from the massive industrialization of Japan's economy and the increasing Westernization of the lifestyle of the Japanese. The stress caused by these revolutionary changes is now far more severe and serious than anything experienced in premodern Japan.

Rather than seek a traditional, Zen-related solution for this new kind of stress, however, several million Japanese resort to a method that utilizes the same kind of mechanistic activity that brings on the stress in the first place—the "game" of *pachinko* (pah-cheen-koe), usually referred to as pinball.

The term *pachinko* comes from *pachin* (pah-cheen), an onomatopoeic word meaning "snap" or "click" and originally referring to a type of slingshot that became popular in the Taisho period (1912–26). The *ko* in *pachinko* means "slingshot" or "catapult."

The first commercial pinball parlor to use the name *pachinko*, apparently because the way the metal balls were propelled by a lever reminded the owner of a slingshot, opened in Nagoya in 1948. It is now a multi-billion-dollar-a-year industry, with some ten million regular players.

Found mostly near train stations and entertainment districts, *pachinko* parlors are gaudy palaces of neon signs and row-upon-row of high-backed pinball machines that have built-in chairs for players to sit on.

Players buy small bearing-type metal balls, insert them into the machine and flip a lever to propel each ball to the top of the machine. (Some machines have automated repeat-action levers that shoot balls in rapid succession.) The balls then bounce down through a maze of pegs that surround holes in the face-board. If a ball enters a "winning hole," the player is rewarded with a number of additional balls (usually 15). Winners redeem unused balls for prizes (which for the most part are taken to a near-by "hidden window" and illegally exchanged for money).

The thousands of metal balls being shot simultaneously into dozens or even hundreds of machines creates a cacophony of noise that fills the parlor, and, when the doors are open, permeates the neighborhood. After a few minutes of exposure, the metallic clatter and the bouncing of the balls becomes mesmerizing, sending players into a kind of trance.

Tadao Umesao, head of the National Museum of Ethnology in Osaka and a noted author, says that a *pachinko* parlor is something like a museum. He writes: "In a crowded pinball parlor you don't share the excitement with the person next to you. You sit facing the machine and confront it in solitude."

Most *pachinko* players say they play the game because by totally overloading their senses they are able to "blank out," to forget their problems, themselves and the world at large—a way of relieving stress that is a far cry from the aesthetic practices of an earlier time. Many foreigners who live in Japan play *pachinko*, but usually with far less intensity than Japanese players.

理 解

Rikai

(Ree-kie)

"Take My Word for It!"

It is natural, of course, for people of individual societies to automatically assume that their values and ways of thinking and doing things are the correct ones, and for everything to go relatively smoothly as long as most of them continue to think and behave in the same manner. And just as naturally, problems arise when people encounter others who have different mind-sets and patterns of behavior.

It is also a given that the more powerful and aggressive a country, the more its own differences are going to impact on others, particularly when these differences involve fundamental philosophical matters such as religious beliefs, ethics and morality.

Japan is a conspicuous example of a country with different values and ethics that has suddenly become powerful on a world-wide basis and now, for the first time in its history, is having to deal with both national and international conflicts arising from its unique culture.

Like most nations in the past, Japan first attempted to deal with its cultural differences by forcefully imposing them on others, a course that ended in a devastating defeat that shocked the naive but highly intelligent Japanese into realizing they had to take a different approach in their international relations.

The strength of Japan's traditional culture was such, however, that they could not quickly transform either their character or their behavior. Instead, they were compelled by their culture to utilize traditional skills in attempting to influence the attitudes and behavior of others.

A significant part of this new approach is summed up in the word *rikai* (ree-kie), which basically means to "understand and sympathize with." In actual usage, however, its meaning goes well beyond the point of understanding and sympathy.

In its full cultural context (which doesn't appear in its dictionary definition), to *rikai* means that you <u>accept</u> the other person's viewpoint or actions even though you disagree with his motives and disapprove of his behavior. The point is that you accept his behavior because of other considerations—you know it would inconvenience him or make things difficult, or that it is simply impossible for him to do anything else in the first place.

In effect, to *rikai* means to suspend your critical faculties and moral judgement, and not insist upon the truth, forthrightness or fairness. Interestingly, and perhaps ironically, this is one of the skills necessary for successful cross-cultural adaptation.

Japanese in all walks of life make regular use of the *rikai* factor in their interpersonal relationships. They are forever asking someone to *rikai shite kudasai* (ree-kie ssh-tay kuu-dah-sie), or "please understand (and let me get by with whatever it is I want to do, am doing, or have already done)."

Rikai-ing is especially popular among businessmen and politicians, who frequently add a special spin to it in their international dealings by blaming their behavior on cultural factors that they cannot control. They often take the position that international or Western standards of behavior do not and cannot apply to Japan because of the country's unique culture.

While Western businessmen and politicians normally assume that universal standards of truth and fairness should apply to the Japanese, they are often not in a position to persuade or force their Japanese counterparts to abide by such standards, and end up *rikai*-ing right along with the Japanese.

理屈ぽい

Rikutsu-poi
(Ree-kuu-t'suu-poy)

"Beware of Being Too Logical"

Americans and other Westerners pride themselves on thinking logically and presenting their opinions in a factual manner. You might say this principle is the basis for all business and professional discourse in the West.

It often doesn't work that way in Japan.

On too many occasions to count, I have witnessed individuals and teams of Westerners make carefully reasoned, fact-filled presentations to Japanese businessmen that ended up doing more harm than good.

The presentations did not take into account any of the personal or human factors that are always a part of business relationships; the factual material was far more than anyone could absorb or write down in a usable form; the presentations were too long; and the Japanese side was neither prepared for nor welcomed such hard sell approaches.

Instead of impressing the Japanese side, the presentation reinforced the common Japanese position that foreigners do not do their homework before coming to Japan—in these instances, homework that would have explained to the foreigners that detailed presentations are out of place at first meetings, especially when top executives are in attendance.

Had they done their homework, the newcomers to the Japanese Way would have learned that it is first of all necessary to satisfy the emotional demands of a proposed business relationship before going into the hard facts; and that the key to developing and sustaining a desirable relationship with a large Japanese company is first of all obtaining a go-ahead signal from top-level management, followed by introductions from the executive contact to the appropriate middle-level managers; then developing close, emotion-based ties with the middle managers and thereafter working very closely with them.

They would also have learned that typical Japanese are turned off by someone who always resorts to logic or pure reason to make points or resolve issues; and that the more intelligent and clever people are, the more effort they must make to disguise or downplay their abilities.

Despite growing recognition that people with high intelligence coupled with a strong individualistic bent are vital to the future of Japan, generally speaking, brains still take a backseat to a humble approach, team play and mutual responsibility.

In most Japanese organizations still today, one of the worst things that can happen to people, insofar as cooperation from others and advancement up the ranks is concerned, is for them to get a reputation for being *rikutsu-poi* (ree-kuu-t'suu-poy).

Rikutsu means "logic" or "reason." Adding the intensifier *poi* to it means the person being described is overly logical—does not give any, or enough, consideration to emotional or human factors.

Even though downplaying the importance and role of logical thought is a deeply ingrained cultural characteristic of the Japanese, it does not mean that they do not apply logical reasoning to their work, planning and research efforts. They most certainly do, but only in conjunction with a variety of other elements. The Japanese side, in fact, generally does more research and is far more systematic (logical) than are Westerners in preparing for negotiations and new relationships. The big difference between the Japanese and Western approach is both in the amount and quality of the preparation as well as in the way they view it and use it.

The term "fuzzy logic," created to describe a computer function that can deal with irrational, unprogrammable bits of information, is a pretty good way of describing the kind of thinking preferred by Japanese in all things at all times.

Foreign businessmen and politicians who base their Japan policies on strict *rikutsu*, and what they regard as "facts," will not have an easy time of it.

176

稟議制度
Ringi Seido
(Reen-ghee Say-ee-doe)

"Putting It in Writing"

One of the traits that makes the Japanese a formidable people is an almost obsessive concern with the details of things—with what they commonly refer to as "small things" or "trifles." They habitually focus in on the particulars of anything and everything, and are not satisfied until the last detail is understood and in its proper place.

In fact, it is part of Japan's conventional wisdom that Japanese culture is based on emphasizing small things and making them the center of attention. This propensity is also often credited with being the reason why the Japanese excel at designing and manufacturing small, intricate objects.

The Japanese explanation of this cultural habit is that it was inspired and shaped by the small size of the country and its limited resources. But Japan is not that small when compared to many other countries, and on other occasions the Japanese characteristically think and behave in exactly opposite terms, seemingly obsessed with conceiving and building things that are the largest, the longest, the tallest, or whatever.

More likely, the Japanese concern with details is a result of cultural conditioning that traditionally emphasized the exact process of doing things, formalized those processes until they became second nature, and refined actions and things down to their bare essentials.

Learning how to write the complicated ideograms with which the Japanese language is transcribed has also significantly contributed to their preoccupation with precise, intricate details.

Overall, this holistic approach to things was no doubt one of the factors that prompted the Japanese decision-making process known as *ringi seido* (reen-ghee say-ee-doe), or "revolving proposal system," which involves circulating written proposals to all parties concerned for their consideration.

Prior to the drafting of a *ringi sho* (reen-ghee show), or "proposal document," the person initiating the presentation, usually a lower or middle-ranking manager, discusses it informally with key people who would be involved in its approval and implementation.

After the initiator has covered every detail possible, the document is then circulated to other managers, then on up the executive ladder to directors and finally to the president. All who approve of the proposal signify so by stamping it with their private seal (or in some internationalized companies, by signing it).

A manager or executive may signify partial approval of a *ringi sho* by putting his seal on upside down, indicating he thinks it needs more work. Those who totally disapprove withhold their seals.

Generally, *ringi sho* are not officially circulated until the project initiators have spent a lot of time lobbying and sounding out the reactions of key people. If one or more influential people indicate that they favor a project, its chances of being approved all the way up the line are generally enhanced.

Researching, writing, lobbying for, and circulating a *ringi sho* can obviously be a time-consuming process, particularly when a dozen or more busy people, who are often hard to reach, have to sign off on it.

The *ringi seido* is commonly used in many Japanese companies, and is one of the time-consuming, decision-making processes that foreign businessmen should be aware of in their dealings with Japanese firms.

浪人

Ronin

(Roe-neen)

"Men Without Masters"

Japan's distinctive culture, with its combination of aestheticism, fine art, literature and martial arts, was primarily a product of the famed samurai warrior class that made up some ten percent of the population during the last five hundred years of the feudal age.

The predecessors of the samurai were personal guards at the Imperial Court and in the headquarters of clan lords during the Heian Era (794-1192), when the earliest foundations of Japanese culture were formed.

By the last century of the Heian period, the power of the Imperial Court was in the hands of officials and regents. Aristocrats lived in highly refined luxury and spent their lives in the pursuit of pleasure. The emperors had become powerless, and corruption was rife throughout the country.

A series of rebellions began in 1156. Taira-no Kiyomori, the leader of a famed military family, emerged as the victor in these civil wars and the most powerful man in the country. In the mid-1160s Kiyomori had himself named prime minister, then awarded all the higher government posts to members of his own family.

The glory days of the Taira family lasted only twenty years. Yoritomo Minamoto, another military leader, raised an army and in 1185 destroyed the Taira clan in the battle of Dan-no-ura, one of the most famous battles in Japan's history. Yoritomo then obtained permission from the emperor to establish a network of military guard posts called *shugo* (shuu-go) throughout the country. These guards were in charge of all military and police affairs in their districts.

In 1192, Yoritomo had himself named hereditary shogun and set up a military dictatorship that was to endure for nearly 800 years. The formal name of the new military government was *bakufu* (bah-kuu-fuu), literally "camp office," but it is best known as the shogunate government.

The position of *shugo* soon became hereditary and gave rise to a class of professional warrior families that eventually came to be called samurai. The samurai raised the practice of martial skills to a fine art, setting standards for the use of the sword and bow that have never been surpassed.

As the centuries passed, the samurai developed a system of stylized etiquette that was refined to the point of an art form and became a standard of their morality. They also engaged in aesthetic and literary pursuits with the same exacting standards and passions that they brought to the pursuit of war.

In order to maintain control over the samurai, the Tokugawa shogunate (1603–1868) made them dependent upon the shogunate and clan governments for their livelihood. They were not allowed to engage in outside commercial activities. Membership in each clan was reserved for those born into it.

Thus when samurai lost their positions for whatever reason they became outcasts and were generally forced to accept whatever odd jobs they could find in order to survive. During turbulent periods, when fiefs were confiscated by the shogunate or otherwise broken up, droves of samurai roamed the country, and came to be known as *ronin* (roe-neen), or "wave men."

Many of Japan's most famous kabuki and noh plays, as well as present-day "period" movies, are based on the *ronin* phenomenon. The lone samurai, dressed in a thin cotton robe even in winter and reduced to hiring himself out to unscrupulous officials and gangs, plays the same role in Japan as the rogue Western gunman does in America.

Nowadays, students who fail entrance examinations and cannot enter college, as well as adults who refuse to work for others or are fired and cannot find new employment, are commonly referred to as *ronin*. The connotation of the word today ranges from "maverick" and "drop-out" to "reject" and "outcast."

━━━━━━━━━━━━⬣178⬣━━━━━━━━━━━━

旅 館
Ryokan
(Rio-kahn)

"Succoring Travelers and Conspirators"

During most of Japan's early history (prior to the 1700s), travel for pleasure was rare. Most of the population was too poor to consider such an extravagance in the first place; besides, it was controlled or outright prohibited by the shogunate and clan governments.

Among the most interesting of the few earliest travelers in Japan were priests who, from the 8th to the 14th centuries, made a specialty of seeking out extraordinarily beautiful mountain locations in remote areas in which to build their shrines and temples. These priests often played pathfinder roles similar to early American hunter-explorers who led the way across the American continent.

The Tokugawa Shogunate, however, was to bring about amazing changes in the traveling customs of the Japanese. In 1603 Ieyasu Tokugawa, founder of the dynasty, institutionalized the existence of social classes (established by his predecessor in 1590), set strict rules and guidelines for public behavior, and tightened the shogunate's grip on the country's 270-some clan lords.

In 1635, his grandson and the third shogun in the new dynasty, Iemitsu Tokugawa, decreed that the clan lords would build mansions in Edo (Tokyo), headquarters of the shogunate, keep their families there at all times and themselves spend every other year in Edo in attendance at his court.

All regular travel in Japan was by foot. This meant that the lords and their entourages of retainers, servants and samurai guards had to be on the road for days to weeks, going to and from their fiefs. This resulted in the rapid building of post-stations and inns along all of the major routes leading to Edo.

Within less than a decade, Japan had the largest and most elaborate network of *ryokan* (rio-kahn), or "inns," of any country in the world. These inns ranged from luxury class places (which were reserved for members of the Imperial Court in Kyoto, clan lords and their chief retainers) to "economy class" places (where lower-ranking clan retainers and ordinary travelers stayed).

For the next 200-plus years, these processions of clan lords went to and fro on Japan's great roadways, resulting in dozens of the post-stations becoming towns and cities, and contributing significantly to social and economic changes in the country.

By the early 1700s, the reins of the shogunate had begun to loosen, peace prevailed, and the living standard of the people had begun to rise. As more decades passed, ordinary people began to join the itinerant priests, peddlers, gamblers, displaced samurai and clan processions on the roads, resulting in the building of more *ryokan*.

Like their modern-day descendants, Japan's early *ryokan* provided food and drink as well as lodging, and most of them also functioned as houses of prostitution, providing women for male travelers who wanted to indulge. (The traditional attitude of the Japanese government was that men away from home should not be deprived of sexual release.)

Many *ryokan*, particularly those featuring natural hotspring baths, developed into large, well-known resort complexes. Since Japanese homes and offices were small and basic, it became customary for meetings of all kinds to take place in inns where food, drink and entertainment were available.

Ryokan were especially popular with businessmen, politicians, gangsters and conspirators who wanted privacy for their meetings, along with all of the amenities they offered.

Larger offices, conference rooms and meeting halls now abound in Japan, but *ryokan* in the vicinity of political and business centers continue to thrive, as do those in noted hotspring spa areas.

差 別

Sabetsu

(Sah-bate-sue)

"The Urge to Be Different"

Virtually all "real" Japanese have straight black hair, an epicanthic fold in their eyelids, black and brown eyes, a very slight yellowish tint to their skin, and relatively "flat" noses.

Throughout Japan's early history most Japanese in the same social class and same occupations also dressed similarly or alike. With the advent of the feudal shogunate system in A.D. 1192, this tendency for wearing matching apparel became even more pronounced.

Finally, during the last shogunate dynasty, which began in 1603 and ended in 1868, the government issued various edicts specifying the clothing that the different classes could wear, making it possible to identify the class and often the occupation of a person by their dress. The shogunate, in fact, went as far as to establish the date on which the populace changed from summer to winter clothing and from winter to summer apparel.

During this long period, virtually all Japanese women wore their hair long and straight, and generally wore the same hair accessories. Men's hair styles were also generally fixed, reflecting their class and occupations.

Also, throughout most of Japan's history, there were virtually no fat people and very few people who were exceptionally tall.

All of these things combined made the Japanese look very much alike, and over the centuries conditioned them to be especially sensitive to anybody that did not look like them, or wore any unusual piece of clothing or accessory.

During the last centuries of the feudal shogunate system, the Japanese also became more and more alike culturally; a factor that contributed significantly to strongly nationalistic feelings between 1868 and 1945 that were in part based on these similarities.

During the heyday of Japan's nationalistic period, not looking like or dressing like the mass of Japanese became a matter that was taken seriously by the authorities and many organizations. People who looked even slightly non-Japanese faced discrimination and sometimes worse. Women who had auburn or brownish hair were forced to dye it black. Anyone with any non-Japanese-like feature was suspect.

The Japanese did not begin to break away from their own stereotypical image of themselves as racial and sartorial clones until the country was defeated in World War II and occupied by several hundred thousand lusty Western soldiers and civilians of all colors, sizes, shapes and manners.

Not surprisingly, it was young Japanese women who were the first to begin breaking out of the traditional molds of sameness, adopting Western dress and hairstyles with an alacrity that was astounding to the older generations. Yet more than half a century and several generations later, there are still regular occurrences of discrimination against Japanese, especially children who have anything but black hair and the standard Japanese face. Many older Japanese men still feel it is un-Japanese to wear anything but plain white shirts and dark suits.

By the early 1990s, however, it was obvious that the under-20 generation was well on its way to making the final break with the past. The new buzz word was *sabetsu* (sah-bate-sue), meaning "distinctive" or "different," and indicating an urge—a compulsion, in fact—to rise above others in fashion and style; not just to be on the leading edge of trendy, but to create one's own personal fashion.

This sudden metamorphosis of the young Japanese into colorful fashion butterflies caught Japan's apparel industry, especially importers of foreign fashions, off guard. Sales of many lines that had been making huge profits nose-dived. Many simply disappeared.

More and more Japanese women, and a few young Japanese men, are beginning to add color to their hair. Japan is becoming a brave new world.

It is well worth noting for the Western businessman, however, that most of the Japanese they are likely to come into contact with still regard earrings, necklaces and flashy rings as inappropriate for businessmen—besides being unmasculine.

━━━━━━━━━━━━━━━━━ 180 ━━━━━━━━━━━━━━━━━

さ び

Sabi

(Sah-bee)

"Appreciating the Rust of Age"

One of my Japanese friends with an especially strong philosophical bent frequently makes the point that to understand and live the good life, one must first acknowledge and appreciate death.

His point is obviously well-taken because most of us, notably when we are young, behave as if we have all the time in the world to grow up, outlast our shortcomings and mistakes, and live happily ever afterward.

Buddhism taught the Japanese that life is a fragile thing, and should be cultivated to the fullest because we never know which wind will waft us away. Out of this philosophy (combined with a generous helping of Confucianism) came the concept that age—in all things—is to be venerated.

Respect for age, in things as well as people, subsequently played an important role in Japanese life from ancient times, and although considerably weakened now by the insensitivities of mechanized civilization, it is still a vital factor in Japanese society.

Seniority, pure and simple, still reigns in business and virtually all of the professions in Japan—if not supremely then at least with enough clout that its power will not be threatened any time soon. Preservation of the system is part social/part economic, and it impacts directly on anyone involved with Japan.

There is another aspect of age veneration in Japanese culture that is generally separate from the type of seniority found in vertically structured organizations, and is both benign and positive. This facet, expressed in the term *sabi* (sah-bee), refers to a special kind of beauty that results from aging.

Sabi by itself means "rust," and by extention covers the patina or surface changes that accompany the aging process. Many of Japan's arts and crafts subtly reflect an element of *sabi* right from the moment of their creation—not in the sense that they are antiqued, but in their look of simplicity and naturalness.

The more refined a design, the simpler and more natural it tends to look and the more it imparts a "feel" of antiquity. Japanese examples of *sabi*-imbued products range from lacquered trays and tables to the hauntingly human Hakata dolls of northern Kyushu.

Like the terms *shibui* (she-boo-ee), which refers to a restrained beauty, and *wabi*, which denotes a harmonious tranquility, *sabi* is a key word in the aesthetic vocabulary of Japan—the third leg in a triad of aesthetic principles.

These three principles combined are what give Japan's traditional arts and crafts their "Japanese" look, and since the 1970s have been showing up in Western-type products designed and manufactured in Japan.

The built-in compulsion of the Japanese to incorporate these three aesthetic principles into their manufactured goods gives them a distinct advantage over their Western counterparts.

In contrast to the Japanese, Westerners are culturally conditioned to design products to make them easier and cheaper to engineer and manufacture—not to satisfy very demanding aesthetic principles; and in too many cases, not even to meet the utilitarian needs of their customers.

Until Americans and other Westerners adopt a more holistic view of the world, they are going to be at a serious disadvantage in attempting to compete with the *sabi-*, *wabi-* and *shibui*-trained Japanese.

淋しい　しんみり

Sabishii / Shinmiri

(Sah-be-shee / Sheen-me-ree)

"The Pleasure of Sadness"

Materialism is a new phenomenon in Japan. During most of the history of the country it was a philosophical belief—and the policy of the government—that the ideal state for the masses was one of genteel poverty.

Because the accumulation and overt display of wealth was regarded as immoral, even those who had the means to live ostentatiously and extravagantly generally did not do so, contenting themselves with the highly refined but relatively austere housing, furnishings and daily fare that were standard for those of lesser means.

The Japanese of old were simply not into extravagant material things. They were a "mood" people who took their pleasures in contemplating and experiencing the small, the rare, the natural—in communing with the spirits of things. Worth and accomplishment were measured in terms of manners, knowledge, artistic skills and character—not in material wealth.

Buddhism taught the Japanese that the only eternal and constant reality in life is change, and that birth is a sentence of death. This somber but realistic philosophy imbued the Japanese with an especially strong appreciation of the here and now, a stoic acceptance of the vicissitudes of life and a sense of universal sadness that became an integral part of their culture.

One aspect of sadness that was a conspicuous facet of the traditional Japanese character was expressed in the term *sabishii* (sah-be-shee), which refers to an acute sense of loneliness, of an "ocean of nothingness," which was most common in the fall when the fading and falling of leaves was a powerful reminder of the fate of all things.

Rather than trying to avoid the *sabishii* feeling, the Japanese catered to it, making it into an integral part of their customs, from moon-viewing and insect-hearing to their literature. The feeling encompassed a studied melancholy that the Japanese needed to stay in harmony with each other and the cosmos.

In more recent times, *sabishii* has come to mean little more than the short-term sadness or loneliness that all of us experience now and then, and can be dispelled by a kind word or the appearance of a friend.

Another aspect of Japan's traditional Buddhist-tinged philosophy of man as a victim of fate was expressed in the term *shinmiri* (sheen-me-ree), which can be translated as "serene sadness," or "lonely tranquility."

The *shinmiri* concept in Japanese culture went beyond an ephemeral attitude. It also became an essential ingredient in art, handicrafts, music and literature. In order to be truly Japanese and evoke the expected feelings, a piece of art, a handicraft or a poem had to incorporate the essence of *shinmiri*.

Shinmiri remains a common colloquial term in modern-day Japan, regularly used to express the kind of intimate tranquility and sad contentment that is a key part of the atmosphere of a Japanese-style room overlooking a garden, the ocean, or a mountain ravine—especially on rainy days.

When the Japanese leave the city for the countryside, to spend time in an inn, to climb a mountain, to "bathe in a forest," or to visit some isolated shrine, one of the things they are seeking is a *shinmiri* experience.

Knowledge of the *shinmiri* element in Japanese culture is essential to an understanding of the Japanese, and particularly for an understanding of product designs and graphics that especially appeal to them.

細工

Saiku

(Sie-kuu)

"Small Is Beautiful—and Sells"

Beginning in the late 1950s, the Japanese began to turn out a steady and growing stream of high-tech products that were smaller and more refined than their Western predecessors, with Sony's transistorized radio just one of the most famous examples.

Following that epoch, Japanese designers, engineers and manufacturers continued to expand their designing and engineering techniques, and by the 1970s were flooding the world with their handiwork.

Now the primary thrust of a significant segment of Japan's industrial complex is to create and manufacture new miniature products that will have an even more dramatic effect on the way people think, behave and work. The storage and retrieval of information, and how we communicate, are at the forefront of this new frontier of miniaturization and refinement.

The Japanese owe their prowess in refining and miniaturizing products to their traditional folk arts and crafts, which were so deeply embedded in their lifestyle that the two could not be separated.

Among the traditional Japanese things that were a major part of this world of miniaturization were *bonsai, netsuke* (tiny carvings), *ikebana* (flower arranging), the abacus, folding fans, and their famed gardens.

In all of these arts and more, miniaturization was accompanied by a spiritual and aesthetic content that made each of the creations extremely pleasing to the eye, the sense of touch, and the spirit. They were, in fact, works of art with all of the necessary qualifications.

By the 1990s, the Japanese were using their 1,000-year plus cultural experience to marry new technology with practical needs, and were churning out a flood of pocket computers and other high-tech products that were the results of *saiku* (sie-kuu), which literally means "delicate workmanship."

Figuratively, *saiku* stands for craftsmanship, and refers to things that have been so highly refined and miniaturized that there is virtually nothing extraneous, and in some cases are as close to the essence of things as you can physically get.

All of Japan's traditional concepts and skills that came together to give their crafts and tools their special flavor and utilitarian value are now being focused on new, high technology to create new generations of products that are sweeping the world.

Thus, once again, the Japanese are taking advantage of rare cultural attitudes and skills to meet and deal with the challenges of the present—a factor that sets them apart from other people whose traditions are often obstacles to futuristic applications.

One of the primary challenges facing Japan today is continuing the traditions of the past to the point that the people do not lose their special aesthetic and manual skills—a challenge that, in fact, is not being fully met by families, the educational system or the business world.

This means that as the traditionally oriented and trained generations of Japanese die off, the special cultural advantages that played such a vital role in Japan's economic achievements during the last half of the 20th century will gradually weaken.

In the meantime, the contributions that the *saiku* concept have made and continue to make to Japan's extraordinary economic success contain powerful lessons that the rest of the world should learn and adapt to their own educational and training processes.

再 利 用

Sairiyo

(Sie-ree-yoe)

"Re-Using the Past"

In old Japan reverence for the past was a vital part of the culture and was manifested in many ways, from so-called ancestor worship to extraordinary respect for aged persons as well as for old things, whether natural or man-made.

For long centuries, "revere the past" was also the national polity, influencing virtually every area of Japanese life. It contributed to the preservation of the ancient arts and crafts and the traditional way of life in general. The future was seen as a refinement of the past.

This feeling was combined and reinforced by the small size of the country and its limited resources. Extravagance in the use of space and materials was regarded as immoral. Waste, of any type, was equally immoral. One of the most common words in the Japanese lexicon was *mottainai!* (moat-tie-nie!), or "that's wasteful!"—in other words, "don't waste that!"

Thus the practice of conservation, of getting the most out of everything they used and did, was deeply engrained in the Japanese lifestyle. Recycling, or *sairiyo* (sie-ree-yoe), was the hallmark of Japanese existence.

Sudden affluence in the 1960s and 70s seriously weakened the power and importance of the *sairiyo* ethic. For the first time in the history of the country, people began to throw things away instead of recycling them. Mounds of trash and discards became unsightly reminders of the new times.

But the characteristic Japanese talent for taking old ideas and things and making them better did not disappear. It was simply transferred from traditional endeavors to creating new products out of old ideas and borrowed technology.

Very quickly, the Japanese demonstrated a genius for taking foreign technology and creating new products, primarily by refining basic concepts down to their essence and then producing something new to fill a fundamental demand.

The cultural conditioning of the Japanese gives them an edge in looking at things in a more holistic manner, in discerning possible combinations of things that are less likely to be seen by people whose straight-line thinking is narrowly focused.

Japanese are now involved in a great effort to combine and recycle a wide range of traditional concepts and modern technology. They are aided in this process because—again as in many other areas of creativity and design—there are no taboos or restraints from the past as long as they are dealing with non-traditional products.

Not being limited by conventional wisdom or professional myopia, the Japanese are much freer than most to let their imagination look at product ideas without prejudice. Having been culturally conditioned by Zen concepts to persevere until they reach the heart of things, they often come up with original applications of existing knowledge.

The more new technology that arrives on the scene, the more there is for the Japanese to work with in creating new products based on recycling the knowledge in new combinations.

Looking at Japan today always reminds me of the unending stories, particularly in the U.S., of outsiders arriving in new towns with little or nothing, seeing opportunities that local residents are blind to or ignore, and in no time at all building successful businesses.

The competitive challenge represented by Japan's talent for creating new concepts from old ideas may be benign in one sense, but it is not something that the rest of the world should ignore.

三 昧

Sanmai

(Sahn-my)

"The Power of Mind over Matter"

The Japanese were traditionally taught that spirit—particularly Japanese spirit—could prevail over physical things. One of the most important of the slogans that became popular during the 1870s, when Japan first began industrializing, held that Japanese spirit should and would prevail over Western technology.

Japanese belief that the mind was superior to and could overcome matter had its origins in the contemplations of religious leaders in India, China and Tibet, and eventually became a vital part of the teaching and training of Japan's professional class of samurai warriors from the 13th century on.

History shows· that the prowess for which the samurai subsequently became famous was, in fact, due in large part to their strong emphasis on spiritual training. The accomplishments of Japan's greatest artists, craftsmen and garden designers during its long feudal period were also greatly abetted by spiritual exercise.

At the beginning of World War II in the early 1940s, all Japanese, and servicemen in particular, were still being indoctrinated with the idea that the famed Japanese spirit would win out over the military might of the U.S. and its allied powers.

The early success of the Japanese in their war effort and the extraordinary actions that they took to stave off defeat during the latter stages of the war stand as testimony to the power of spirit, no matter how misplaced its goals.

Historically, spiritual training in Japan came under several headings, including Zen Buddhism, but one of the practices that is of special interest was described by the word *sanmai* (sahn-my), which means "absorption," or "spiritual concentration."

The purpose of *sanmai* training was to eliminate the ego—to lose oneself in spiritual contemplation—and transcend the physical world. The more accomplished one became in achieving a state of oneness with cosmic power, the more power he had over his physical environment.

(On the far-out side, there are contemporary descriptions, by apparently reliable authors, of monks in Tibet who are so accomplished at *sanmai* that they can make themselves and those around them impervious to sub-zero temperatures for hours, or appear as anything they wish; and of Indian yogis who can physically project themselves to distant places.)

Japan's devastating defeat in World War II also crushed the popular belief that mind could triumph over matter, and helped set the Japanese on the road to success via high tech instead of high spirit. But this setback to the famed Japanese spirit was to be temporary.

By the 1970s, the country's rapid recovery from the disaster of the war and equally rapid rise to world-wide economic success had resurrected the Japanese belief in the power of the spirit—especially spirit that derived from updated *sanmai* exercises that emphasize an aggressive approach to business.

By the 1980s, Japanese managers in virtually every area of business had incorporated various kinds of *sanmai* exercises into their management training programs, with some of them emphasizing spiritual training over technical training.

The training program of Japan's oldest and most prestigious department store, Mitsukoshi (founded in 1673), is a classic example of the spiritual element in Japan's traditional business philosophy. Originally put into text form in 1905 by then First Managing Director Osuke Hibi, the Mitsukoshi employee manual emphasized the spiritual element in the employee-customer relationship, and stated repeatedly that no one who failed to live up to the standards detailed in the book could be a Mitsukoshi man.

Among the precepts taught by the Mitsukoshi manual: the employee must at all times be totally sincere and loving to customers, treating them as a devoted son or daughter would treat beloved parents; the employee's attitude must be reflected in the way he stands, the expression on his face, his tone of voice and the vocabulary he uses; if a customer appears worried or unhappy it is the duty of the Mitsukoshi man to cheer the person up; employees must never appear idle but always posed and eager to assist customers; and, the employee must do absolutely nothing that would disgrace his status as an employee of a great department store.

In today's terms, the spirit that is typical of Japanese managers includes a fierce patriotism along with a strong sense of group loyalty and willingness to sacrifice for the common good, perseverance in the face of all odds, and an unbounded ambition to help make their company the biggest and the best—all attributes that contribute significantly to the competitive prowess of the Japanese on the world scene.

爽やか

Sawayaka

(Sah-wah-yah-kah)

"Enjoying Sensual Pleasures"

In the late 1950s, when I was editor of *The Importer* magazine in Tokyo, a substantial percentage of the foreign importers frequenting Japan on buying trips had Japanese girl friends—some of whom were introduced to them by their suppliers.

During the course of several years I interviewed hundreds of these buyers—some of the more important ones two or three times a year—and got to know dozens of them very well. Those whom I knew, and most of the others, were regular customers at such popular hostess cabarets as the Copa Cabana, the Latin Quarter and Club Cherry.

Virtually all of them complained about how difficult and frustrating it was to deal with Japanese makers and exporters, and several of them confided to me that the only reason they persisted in importing from Japan was because they enjoyed the women so much.

These early pioneers in helping the Japanese nurture their postwar export industries were not plowing new ground where mixing sensual pleasures with business was concerned. That was something the Japanese had honed to a fine art over many generations, and used with masterful skill.

But this well-established practice did not begin to suggest the importance of sensuality in Japan's culture, and how it affects everything from architecture and product design to the use of the language. Sensuality, with strongly feminine overtones, had been a vital part of Japanese culture from the beginning.

Japanese emphasis on sensuality was a natural outgrowth of their native religion, Shintoism, which in effect was a cult-like belief that focused on fertility in plants, animals and people—and put the blessings of heaven on the pursuit of sensual pleasures.

Cabaret hostesses continue to be a vital factor in the art of doing business in Japan, but some of the more subtle facets of sensuality are now just as important. One of these facets is in the use of language in advertising and marketing.

Choosing the right words, that is, getting consumers to buy products, requires an intuitive knowledge of what turns the Japanese on—and this is often so esoteric that the foreign advertiser or consumer doesn't understand the message in Japanese ads at all.

Some of these key words are chosen to set a mood that has little or nothing to do with the product concerned. Rather than say something about the product, the words are intended to create feelings of contentment, happiness, or appreciation for the beauty of some scene—and induce the viewer to associate the company and its products with pleasant memories.

One word that has helped make millions of dollars for Coca Cola—and can be understood by foreigners—is *sawayaka* (sah-wah-yah-kah), which combines the meaning of "refreshing" with "sensual pleasure."

The *sawayaka* jingle for Coca Cola very clearly got across the message that drinking a coke was a sexual experience. But the you-can-get-sex-in-a-coke-bottle message was not salacious in its Japanese context. It was the perfect use of a culturally pregnant word to sell a product without being pushy or pretentious.

Foreign businessmen should keep in mind that it is often easier to get the Japanese to buy their goods by setting a refreshing, sensual mood than by describing the attributes of products.

One marvelous example of this was a 4-word commercial promoting an upscale apartment building (called a "mansion" in Japanese) suggested by my editor, Tom Heenan. To wit: "Walking-u gureen, talking-u gureen" (or, "Walking green, talking green").

———————————— 〈186〉 ————————————

関 ヶ 原

Sekigahara
(Say-kee-gah-hah-rah)

"A Fight to the Finish"

Sekigahara (say-kee-gah-hah-rah), a small town in southwestern Gifu Prefecture some two and a half "Bullet Train" hours from Tokyo, is one of the most famous names in Japanese history. In the 7th century, as a military outpost, it became the site of one of the three most important *seki sho* (say-kee show) or "barrier stations" in central Honshu, the main island.

It was not until the year 1600, however, that the little town became a household word in Japan. In that year, Ieyasu Tokugawa, a provincial lord whose primary strength was in the eastern and northern portions of Honshu, met his enemies, mostly from the western and southern provinces of Japan, and defeated them in a great battle known as *Sekigahara no Tatakai* (Say-kee-gah-hah-rah no Tah-tah-kie) or "The Battle of Sekigahara."

Tokugawa went on to capture Osaka and quickly began the process of consolidating his victories. In 1603 he established the Tokugawa Shogunate, headquartered at Edo, now Tokyo, from which he and his descendants were to rule Japan until 1868.

The victory of Ieyasu Tokugawa at Sekigahara was so unexpected, so dramatic, and was to have such a decisive influence on the country for the next two hundred and sixty eight years, that it is now regarded as one of the great turning points in Japanese history.

During the long reign of the Tokugawa Shogunate, Sekigahara remained a key military post on the famous *Tokaido* (Toe-kie-doe), "Eastern Sea Road," that connected Edo with Kyoto. Today it is a small town that is described as a transportation center, but is known for its place in history and for having come to characterize one of the key aspects of Japanese business.

Just as Japan's many clans throughout its feudal history vied with each other for territory, and for political and economic supremacy, modern-day Japanese companies compete with each other for market share, and generally attempt to be as self-sufficient as possible through integration of the manufacturing, distribution and retailing processes, and through affiliations with other companies. In their efforts to increase their market share, and if at all possible to totally monopolize markets, Japanese companies are known to engage in all-out warfare with their competitors; struggles that are commonly referred to as *Sekigahara*.

One of the results of this often cutthroat battling is an array of products that are almost exactly the same but are in fact made by different companies. The more the products look alike, the fiercer the price competition and the more apt the manufacturers are to try to export much of their production in order to make their profits overseas.

It was this *Sekigahara* factor that made Japanese companies such formidable competitors in penetrating markets in the U.S., Europe and elsewhere during the 1960s and 70s. And despite the many negative aspects of this approach to manufacturing and marketing, it played a key role in the astounding productivity and quality control achieved by Japanese industry during those decades.

Although the *Sekigahara* syndrome continues to prevail in Japan in the early 1990s, the Japanese have begun to recognize that this management philosophy is detrimental to the world at large, and could eventually backfire against them. Akio Morita, co-founder and chairman of the board of Sony, took the lead in denouncing all-out market share wars, promoting instead the theme of international collaboration rather than competition. (See *Kyosei.*)

席 次

Seki Ji
(Say-kee Jee)

"Sitting in the Right Place"

Kyoto, the imperial capital of Japan from A.D. 794 to 1868, is a living museum of Japan's past, boasting more shrines, temples, palaces and other historical buildings than any other city in the country.

One of the must-see sights in the ancient city is *Kyoto Gosho* (Kyoto Go-show), or "Kyoto Imperial Palace." First built in 794 for Emperor Kammu, the palace has been rebuilt several times over the centuries following destructive fires, and today provides a provocative glimpse of history across more than a thousand years of time.

My favorite historical building in Kyoto, however, is the *Ni Jo* (Nee Joe), or "Second Castle," built in 1603 to serve as the residence of Ieyasu Tokugawa, founder of the Tokugawa Shogunate, when he visited Kyoto from Edo (Tokyo), where his headquarters castle was located. (It was in *Ni Jo* 265 years later that the edict abolishing the Tokugawa Shogunate was issued.)

Ni Jo is a microcosm of the best of Japanese art and architecture of the 1600s, with sculptures, wood-carvings, metal work, paintings, screens and other treasures depicting the luxurious lifestyle that was enjoyed by the upper class of that era.

My own fascination with *Ni Jo* grew out of mentally picturing it during Ieyasu's heyday, when all of the *daimyo* (dime-yoe), or "fief lords," with their advisers, retainers and samurai guards, would travel to Kyoto from their own castles to attend him in the Great Audience Hall.

In the Great Hall, the shogun would sit on a raised dais at the head of the huge room, with the *daimyo* seated below him in descending order of their rank, in perfect arrangement like chessmen, their hair elaborately coiffured, their voluminous silk kimono and broad shoulder boards making them look much larger than their actual size.

For more than a thousand years, similar scenes of meetings between lords and retainers, officials and audiences, were enacted dozens of times daily throughout Japan. In each case, the participants were carefully attired and precisely seated in accordance with their rank: graphic demonstrations of the commitment of the Japanese to form and procedure.

The elaborate kimono, hairstyles and swords have disappeared from Japan's meeting places today, but Japanese politicians and businessmen continue to hold more meetings than most other people, and the importance of *seki ji* or "seating order" remains undiminished.

In Japanese meetings there is invariably someone who is responsible for seeing that the attendees are properly seated. Regular attendees who know everyone else's rank sort themselves out and take appropriate seats. Newcomers or guests are guided to seats chosen for them.

Foreign guests, regardless of their rank, are often honored by being seated at or near the head table or head of the room. (In Japanese style homes, rooms at inns and in traditionally-styled restaurants the seat of honor is that nearest the *tokonoma* (toe-koe-no-mah), or "beauty alcove," in the room.)

In office meeting rooms, including small cubicle-like stalls that are common in many Japanese companies, visitors are expected to take chairs that are at the head of the room, which is normally the side or area away from and facing the door.

Foreign businessmen who have Japanese guests in for meetings should certainly make a point of directing them to the preferred seats.

In business and other types of formal meetings where negotiations are involved, the top man from the "visiting group" is normally seated in the center of the table opposite the entrance, with his chief aides to his left and right in descending order. The "home team" is lined up in the same order on the other side of the table.

This practice is often not followed by the Japanese side, however, when the meetings are technical and involve several people representing different skills. In such cases, especially if it is a first meeting, about the only way the foreign side can keep track of who is who, and know who the key people are, is to line their name cards up on the table in the order in which they are sitting.

先 輩

Sempai
(Sim-pie)

"Using Your 'Senior' Network"

Very carefully cultivated and continuously nurtured personal relationships are one of the primary requisites for functioning effectively in Japan, particularly in business and the professions. Such relationships, and their maintenance, often mean the difference between success and failure in a variety of enterprises, from obtaining the services of a noted doctor to establishing a new business relationship for your firm.

The most important of these personal relationships are those based on same-group experiences from an early age, including birthplace, school and employment. Common interests and common professions often do not count. The engineer who works for one company is not apt to develop a friendship or network with an engineer who works for another firm. They are more likely to behave like unfriendly competitors and shun each other.

School-mate ties are usually the strongest, particularly if the ties include the entire school experience, from elementary school through university. Individuals within these lifelong bonding groups are linked more or less like blood brothers in the Western sense. Most feel a significant sense of loyalty and obligation to each other.

As is characteristic of Japanese society, these same-experience relationships are hierarchical, with the junior, equal or superior status of each individual within the group based on who came first. *Sempai* (sim-pie), or "senior," is the most important word in these vertically arranged relationships. The second-year student is a *sempai* of the first-year student.

The longer the time-span between the school experience of a *sempai* and a junior, the more significant the relationship becomes. To a recent graduate of Jochi University (Sophia) in Tokyo, I am a *dai-sempai* (die-sim-pie), or "great senior," since I graduated from the same school in 1954. This lengthy seniority entitles me to special respect (and attention) from the much younger junior, but the obligation goes both ways. If I am in a position to help my much younger fellow alumnus, I am under special obligation to do so.

Same-school graduates who are successful in business and the government form one of the most important and powerful networks in Japan. There are some government agencies and private enterprises in which it is virtually impossible to reach the highest executive levels if one is not a member of the same-school group that presently monopolizes these positions.

Salesmen wanting to establish new client relationships with a company automatically think in terms of whether or not they have a classmate or a school *sempai* in the targeted company. Many university professors emphasize to their students that the most important thing they gain from attendance at the school is membership in the exclusive network of graduates who preceded them.

The exclusivity of the same-group *sempai* system is one of the many factors foreigners (who do not have their own *sempai* network in Japan) should be aware of in their dealings with Japanese. The system can be a help or a hindrance.

Foreign businessmen can often make direct use of Japan's *sempai* system when their Japanese employees or contacts have attended and/or graduated from the same foreign universities they attended—and when they (the foreigners) have attended Japanese universities. Foreign employers also benefit indirectly when their staff members use their *sempai* connections on behalf of the company.

There are a number of partial substitutes for the school *sempai* system that also gives foreigners a leg up. These include memberships in the highly respected Kiwanis and Rotary service clubs, the Young Presidents Organization, and professional associations. Of course, memberships in these groups "work" (to some degree) only on Japanese members of the same groups.

Another of the direct benefits of the *sempai* system is the role that seniors play as mentors. They naturally adopt the mentor role to younger graduates of the same school, readily giving them advice in crucial matters involving both business and personal affairs.

189

接 待

Settai

(Set-tie)

"Partying with an Ulterior Motive"

Japan's traditional culture continues to be both a blessing and a curse, depending on the circumstances. There are virtually no situations involving interpersonal relationships, whether they are with other Japanese or with outsiders, in which the duality of the culture does not come into play and require special consideration.

The politeness and the decorum for which the Japanese are famous do not come cheaply. Both require an extraordinary amount of effort, of psychic energy, and either the suppression of emotions or their generous application. A meeting that is very ordinary by Western standards is typically a major production in Japan. Knowing your lines and your cues is very important.

It is especially trying for most Japanese to meet and deal with Westerners, who behave according to a different set of rules that keep the Japanese guessing and on edge. There is nothing more upsetting, or tiring, to the Japanese than not being able to predict what other people are going to do.

Because of this factor, one of the most useful things foreign businessmen can do to ensure smoother and more efficient relations with their

Japanese counterparts is to prepare very detailed agendas for their meetings, make them available to the Japanese well in advance, and adhere to them as strictly as possible.

Japan's traditional etiquette system was so comprehensive and pervasive that it did not provide for a time-out, when people could just be themselves, during informal and private periods. A Westerner, for example, may conduct himself in a very controlled and rigid manner in a formal setting, but will invariably revert to a relaxed, casual mode once the ceremony is over.

There was, in fact, only one specific occasion when it was permissible for the Japanese to break their rigid rules of hierarchical etiquette and behave in the free-for-all manner that is favored in the West—and that was when they were out drinking after-hours.

This is one of the reasons why it became customary in Japan to hold meetings at geisha houses and restaurant-inns—and why such meeting places have flourished in huge numbers during most of Japan's history. The Japanese learned very early that they simply could not conduct their business and political affairs within the constraints of the etiquette system. (See *Benkyo Kai* and *Niji Kai*.)

In modern times, the infrastructure of eating and drinking places has kept pace with the enormous growth of the economy, and continues to play a vital role in the way the Japanese conduct all of their affairs, particularly business and politics.

Eating and drinking together, subsumed in the word *settai* (set-tie), which is generally translated as "entertainment," is, in fact, the oil of life in Japan. At one time or another, virtually all relationships in Japan involve drinking an alcoholic beverage, and more so in the world of business than anywhere else.

Managers take their subordinates out for drinking sessions as part of their communication and bonding process. Managers hold casual as well as key meetings among themselves in bars, clubs and restaurants as part of their approach to management.

Manufacturers routinely provide *settai* to their suppliers, distributors and retailers. Suppliers and distributors routinely entertain their customers. Salesmen entertain clients, partners entertain each other, and everyone entertains guests.

There is, of course, a precise etiquette in the world of *settai* having to do with seating, pouring and receiving drinks, and, in fact, the degree of drunkenness that is necessary to excuse certain kinds of behavior. Learning and following these rules is one of the challenges, as well as one of the pleasures, of living and working in Japan.

世 話 役

Sewayaku

(Say-wah-yah-kuu)

The Buck Never Stops

Most Westerners have a deep-seated, culturally-embedded yearning for strong, decisive leaders who do not pass the buck and get things done on their own initiative. Because of this visceral fixation, Westerners tend to go off in all directions when left on their own, often unable to come to a consensus or act in unison for the benefit of the whole.

This compulsive need for leaders naturally results in Westerners automatically expecting the heads of Japanese corporations and the Japanese government to be leaders in the full sense of the word. Learning that this is generally not the case at all can be—and often is—an expensive lesson for businessmen and politicians dealing with Japan.

Japan has traditionally been a society made up of thousands of very specific, highly-structured groups that were relatively independent of each other and yet were members of larger groups. Generally, each of these groups was self-managed within the context of the policies and goals of the larger bodies. Also generally speaking, decisions within the unit groups were based on consensus, not on the ideas or orders of single, strong individuals.

Over the centuries, this led the Japanese to abhor individuals who acted in an independent, aggressive manner or who gave orders without considering the views and feelings of others. It also led them, in one way or another, to ostracize such individuals. There were exceptions to this rule, such as gang bosses and founder-heads of so-called one-man companies, but they were and still are rare.

There is no word in the Japanese language that expresses the Western concept of leader—one result of which has been the growing use of the Japanized version of the English word—*rida* (ree-dah)—mostly to deplore the fact that there are so few leaders in Japan.

The very same qualities that Americans and Europeans expect in the heads of companies or governments are almost precisely the ones that virtually guarantee that a Japanese with the same qualities will never reach even a senior executive level, much less become the top man.

The chairmen, CEOs and presidents of typical Japanese companies are not leaders. They are coordinators or facilitators—a role that is described by the word *sewayaku* (say-wah-yah-kuu), which more or less means "one who keeps problems from arising by acting as a conciliator, a go-between."

There is a top man in Japanese organizations, but he is someone who got there because he is good working with people; not because he is the brightest or the most productive. His influence in the organization is based more on his human virtues, his ability to get along with everyone and maintain harmony, than on purely business talents.

The proper role of the top man in Japan is to see that everything goes smoothly by creating an atmosphere in which employees can work together harmoniously and productively, <u>without</u> orders from the top.

Because the heads of Japanese corporations symbolize the reputation of their companies, they take responsibility when the companies do something or fail to do something that results in public outrage. And in the Japanese context of things, resigning from their positions is the highest form of expressing responsibility.

When a situation occurs that reflects badly on the company, the top man has failed in his obligations, and is expected to step down—even though the situation may have been an equipment failure or some other kind of accident for which he has no direct responsibility.

Because Japan's top businessmen and politicians do not "run" their organizations, it is no great loss when they resign. Things generally do not change at all. But the public's need for a scapegoat has been fulfilled.

社 長

Shacho
(Shah-choe)

"The World of the Japanese President"

The Japanese concept of an ideal leader is almost exactly the opposite of what Americans and other Westerners look for, and expect, in their chief executives. In fact, the brilliant, hard-driving, rugged individualist who fights his way to the top in the West, or is chosen by a board of directors because of his intelligence, drive and personal successes, is the least likely to make it to the top in the typical Japanese company.

In the Japanese system of bottom-up management by consensus, the strong-minded, individualistic approach is a serious and usually fatal handicap. Young employees who demonstrate such characteristics are invariably shunted aside—or stifled—long before they reach the executive level.

The Japanese rationale is clear and simple. Strong personalities upset the harmony of the group. They do not passively accept the traditional system of advancement by seniority rather than ability and accomplishments. Their attitude and behavior results in envy, resentment and eventually hate among their co-workers.

Because Japanese managers do not manage by giving orders from a position of authority, the further up they go in the hierarchy, the more important it is for them to be experts in personal relations—in maintaining harmony within their sections and departments.

By the time the Japanese manager reaches the level of *bu-cho* (buu-choe),* which is the equivalent of a vice president in Western terms, he begins to take on the aura and role of a godfather who watches over loyal lieutenants and soldiers who know what they are supposed to do and do it without his direct participation.

The *bu-cho* has almost always worked in several other key departments on his way up and knows the operations of the company from a number of perspectives. He has good personal relations with his same-age managers in other areas, and can call on them when he needs input or help.

He looks after the personal needs of the members of his department, including helping them find marriage partners, and attending weddings, funerals and other special occasions. He spends a lot of time at night in drinking establishments with subordinates, nurturing personal relationships with them and helping them resolve personal as well as business problems.

The directors of a company are almost always chosen from the cadre of *bu-cho* who have demonstrated the most ability in maintaining the management philosophy of the company, based on the prime directive of harmony and group-oriented behavior.

*In written Japanese the characters for department manager, *bu* and *cho*, and various other titles, are written or printed together as if they were one word (*bucho, kacho, kakaricho*, etc.). The first Westerners to use roman letters to phonetically spell Japanese words carried this Japanese practice over into the romanized versions of the titles. Now and then, to help the reader relate the Japanese to English, I have chosen to separate or hyphenate the romanized version of the titles.

Finally, the director who has consistently demonstrated superiority in his ability to inspire loyalty and cooperation among his subordinates and has demonstrated the same qualities in his relations with senior directors and executives during his career, is chosen for the role of *shacho*, or president.

The president of a Japanese company is not expected to "lead" or command like a general. Typically, he does not initiate campaigns or projects or play a direct role in the daily management of the company. His primary responsibilities are to deal with government agencies and industrial relations; to participate in long-term thinking about the company and its industry; to watch over the hiring, training and nurturing of future managers and executives, and to act presidentially in high-level affairs with other companies. Like the president of a country, he often comes into the picture directly only to sign important contracts.

It is rare for a Japanese company president to be removed from office by his board of directors, and his tenure is not based on annual profits. He is not paid the high salary that is common for Western chief executives, but his perks are enormous and he is assured of a life-time income.

192

社員旅行

Shain Ryoko
(Shah-een Ree-oh-koe)

"Breaking Etiquette Barriers"

One of the greatest contrasts between most larger Japanese companies and Western firms, particularly American, is the difference in the behavior of employees. Compared to the loose, casual behavior that typifies American workers, the Japanese are paragons of a highly stylized formality that is totally alien to the American character.

Generally, this meticulously controlled behavior of Japanese employees contributes to a higher level of competence and productivity, and traditionally has been one of the most important advantages the Japanese had over American and other foreign companies.

But formal Japanese behavior in company settings is, in fact, so stylized and controlled that it makes candid communication virtually impossible, and often is as much of a disadvantage as an advantage, particularly in establishing and maintaining relationships with foreign companies.

A growing number of top Japanese managers recognize that free-flowing horizontal and vertical communication among employees is vital to their future, and are resorting to a variety of methods to work around the etiquette barriers.

One of the most common and popular of these etiquette-busting techniques is itself a long-established traditional custom among Japanese companies—the annual *shain ryoko* (shah-een ree-oh-koe), or "company-employee trips."

All employees, executives and managers as well as regular staff are expected to participate in these annual group excursions. In larger companies, the groups are on a sectional or divisional level to prevent them from being too large because one of the key factors in the trips is that participants travel together, stay together, eat and drink together, play together and even sleep together.

Shain ryoko are generally to some famous hotsprings spa for one or two nights. The most important activity is an evening banquet party that begins with a big meal and lots of drinking and banter, then proceeds to humorous skits and other forms of entertainment staged by the employees themselves.

Everyone at the party is expected to make some kind of contribution to the entertainment, either with a solo performance or as a member of a singing or acting group.

Etiquette during the entire trip is very informal, with none of the rigid protocol that prevails in the office. But it is at the party after the drinking begins that virtually all the etiquette barriers come down. Members are allowed to ignore rank.

Much of the banter and joking at these banquet parties has strong sexual overtones, which is especially characteristic of Japanese humor. Now and then there may be brief conversations of a serious nature, but the prevailing purpose of the trips is to allow all levels of employees in the company to share their common humanity in a very personal way.

Employees generally do not use the trips as occasions to criticize their superiors or complain. Such behavior would spoil the mood and the overall purpose. The ultimate goal is simply to get to know and appreciate each other on a personal level—something that cannot be done in the context of the workplace.

Foreign employees of Japanese companies are expected to participate in the revelry during company trips, and should be prepared to make their contribution to the entertainment, no matter how shy they might be. Failure to do so can be taken the wrong way.

社内結婚

Sha-nai Kekkon

(Shah-nie Keck-kone)

"Getting Fixed Up by the Company"

In early Japan, prior to the replacement of the Imperial Court by the feudalistic Shogunate as the seat of power in the 12th century, women played leading roles in both society and the government, including becoming empresses and regents.

The Confucian-oriented Shogunate government put a stop to that, and officially made women subservient to men. It became tradition for marriages to be arranged by parents or third parties. Husbands ruled their households by both law and custom.

Divorce was made illegal. The only way abused or unhappy wives could escape from their husbands was to run away and hide, or, during the latter centuries of the long feudal era, take refuge in designated nunneries.

Men had access to several forms of prostitution, with redlight districts a common feature of towns and cities, while women were expected to remain faithful to their husbands.

There was a fundamental distinction between the acculturation and education of boys and girls—so much so that as late as the 1960s, foreigners in Japan were forever saying that Japanese men and women were so different that they seemed to be the products of different cultures.

In the late 1940s, when I took up residence in Japan, virtually all marriages were still by arrangement. Single men and women did not date. But the Occupation forces (mostly American) were to change all that. Within weeks of their arrival in Japan, many of the foreign troops and civilian personnel assigned to the Occupation had Japanese girl friends.

But it was not until well into the 1950s, after they had been directly exposed to the influence of Americans and other Westerners for ten years, that young Japanese men and women began dating.

Still today there has not yet been a full break from the past. Some one-third of all young Japanese still depend upon their parents, relatives, friends or professional go-betweens to arrange marriages for them.

There are dating banks and other kinds of services designed to bring young men and women together, but at any one time there are still several hundred thousand would-be couples who cannot help themselves.

Because of this major social problem, virtually all of Japan's larger companies encourage their managers to take an active role in match-making for male and female employees in their departments.

Such company-arranged marriages, often among the most successful in terms of compatibility, are known as *sha-nai kekkon* (shah-nie keck-kone)—"in-company marriages" or "in-office marriages." Generally the couples involved work in different departments.

It is not farfetched for managers in Japanese companies to play such a personal role in the affairs of employees. Japanese firms have traditionally been looked upon as extended families, with responsibilities for the social as well as the economic interests of employees.

Japanese employees in turn expect their employers and bosses to be concerned about their personal affairs, and are critical of them if they are not. Such concern is considered part of the overall responsibilities of companies—and is one of the factors often contributing to friction between foreign companies in Japan and their Japanese workers.

The close, often overlapping, relationship between personal time and work time, and between personal affairs and company affairs, is a legacy of Japan's feudal past, when there was no clear distinction between the two areas.

─────────── 194 ───────────

社 用 族

Shayo Zoku

(Shah-yoe Zoe-kuu)

"Japan's Expense-Account Princes"

Larger Japanese companies tend to be operated as clan-like communities, with all of the characteristics—responsibilities as well as privileges—of a strictly run male-dominated family.

For the young man, entering such a company immediately upon graduation from school is very much like being adopted into a new, hierarchically-structured, seniority-based extended family that happens to run a business enterprise. He is expected to serve quietly and faithfully, like a dutiful son, gradually rising in the ranks.

In Japanese companies, as in families, every effort is made to treat members as much alike as possible to prevent envy, friction and disruptions. The regular salary of the president is only about six times higher than that of the first-year employee. Conspicuously visible perks are generally kept to a minimum.

But each employee (in larger companies) knows that the chances of him being laid off or fired are very small,* and the president knows that his income and company benefits will continue for as long as he lives. This guarantee of social security is, of course, one of the primary factors in the famed diligence and loyalty of Japanese workers.

One aspect of Japanese management that plays a key role in the Japanese economy and society in general is its personal nature, particularly in its virtually complete dependence on interpersonal relationships between managers and their subordinates, between co-workers, and in inter-company relationships with clients and suppliers.

Most of this personal interplay within and between Japanese companies is financed by expense accounts assigned to managers. It takes place at night in bars, cabarets, pubs and restaurants, and is the main reason Japan has such a large night-time entertainment industry.

*A significant percentage of the employees of larger Japanese companies are temporary employees, and are subject to being laid-off or terminated on short notice. All larger Japanese companies also make substantial use of sub-contractors that can be cut off at will, thereby providing the companies with cost-free cushions during business slow-downs.

Altogether, Japanese companies spend several billion dollars each year on these employee and customer relations activities, funneling most of this amount into the system through managers, and giving rise to a group of several hundred thousand men who are known as *shayo zoku* (shah-yoe zoe-kuu), or "the expense-account tribe."

Shayo by itself means "company business," giving the whole expression the connotation of "people spending money on company business."

Managers in Japanese companies are authorized to spend a certain amount each month, with the amount generally depending on their position and rank as well as the size, profitability and type of company. Sales managers are often authorized to spend larger sums because of the nature of their work.

From the 1950s through the 1970s, it was most common for managers of larger, well-known companies with expense accounts to first make themselves known to a number of favored night spots and restaurants, which thereafter would invoice their companies directly for their bills. Often all these people had to do to establish a charge account was to hand over one of their name-cards.

Managers of smaller, unknown companies, however, usually had to patronize a place several times and become personally known before they were extended charging privileges.

Increased affluence in the 1980s led to some managers paying for their business entertainment out of their own pockets, and later being reimbursed by their companies. Now, many businessmen use company or personal credit cards to charge their official entertainment expenses.

Shayo zoku continue to make up the biggest spending segment in Japan's world-famous night-scene.

195

社 是　　社 訓

Sha Ze - Sha Kun

(Shah zay - Shah kuun)

"Instilling Company Spirit"

It has traditionally been of vital importance to the Japanese that they belong to some identifiable and viable group, for it was only through a group that they could establish and maintain their identity and place in society.

During Japan's long feudal period (1192–1868), there were a number of institutionalized groups that covered most of the population, including clans, villages, guilds, shops, temples, shrines and households.

In each of these groups, loyalty to the group involved took precedence over individual wishes and concerns, with the degree of loyalty ranging from fierce to fanatical. The large ruling samurai class epitomized loyalty in their behavior toward and defense of their clans and lords.

Loyalty to one's group was not based solely on economic imperatives, it also had deep roots in the philosophical beliefs and social ethics of the Japanese. It was something that had been drilled into them for centuries as the foundation of their society.

When both the social and economic systems of Japan were upended in the late 1860s and early 1870s, changing virtually overnight from a minutely structured feudalistic hierarchy to what legally amounted to a free society, the Japanese automatically transferred their fierce allegiance to the new commercial enterprises that sprang up all over the country.

In terms of both economic and psychological needs, Japan's new commercial companies took the place of the traditional groups. In many respects, the great *zaibatsu* combines such as Mitsui (which had over three million employees during its pre-1945 heyday) took over the role of the clans—a role that is now played by the so-called *keiretsu kaisha* (kay-ee-rate-sue kie-shah), or "affiliated companies," which are the successors to the *zaibatsu*.

Just as the leading clans and houses of feudal Japan had their laws and philosophical guidelines, the new commercial enterprises founded in the early years of the modernization of Japan created their own *sha ze* (shah zay) and *sha kun* (shah kuun).

Sha ze can be translated as "company philosophy," while *sha kun* is more or less the equivalent of "company motto" or "company principle." *Sha ze*, however, are often expressed in short motto-like statements, so it is sometimes hard to distinguish between the two as far as content is concerned.

Generally *sha ze* are expressed in formal language, while *sha kun* may be in either formal or informal language.

Both *sha ze* and *sha kun* are part of the spirit that Japanese companies work to instill in their employees. Some companies require that the company philosophy be repeated at morning meetings, much like a pledge that is part of the opening ceremonies of service clubs such as Kiwanis.

In recent years, some of Japan's larger companies have undertaken to expand on their *sha ze* to make them more comprehensive and meaningful to both employees and the public at large.

One of the reasons for this new trend is that individual Japanese companies no longer want to be lumped together with other Japanese firms in a monolithic "Japan, Inc." image. They say that all Japanese companies are not alike, and they want their own, separate identities.

Training in larger Japanese companies emphasizes spirit and loyalty as well as technical knowledge, adding to the stability and competitive prowess of the firms. Most companies, in fact, put as much or more emphasis on having the right philosophy as on technical training.

渋い

Shibui

(She-buu-ee)

"The Ultimate Beauty"

One of the most conspicuous and positive aspects of Japanese culture is the extraordinary role of aesthetics. It may have been Shintoism, which in a sense is nature-worship, that led the early Japanese to take a holistic approach to beauty and to incorporate it into their lifestyle.

The high aesthetic value of Buddhist art, introduced into Japan between A.D. 400 and 600, was another primary factor in adding the ingredient of beauty to the artifacts of daily life. In any event, by the middle of the golden Heian era (794-1192), virtually all Japanese were imbued with a refined aesthetic sense that influenced every aspect of their lives.

The cultural medium by which aesthetics was translated into tangible products with artistic value was the master-apprentice system in all of the craft industries. Each Japanese craftsman spent years under the tutelage of a master who passed on the technology of the craft—a technology that included the elements of a highly refined beauty as one of the essential facets in all finished products, regardless of their use.

Thus it came about that the porcelains, pottery, baskets, fabrics, wooden boxes, tables, floor mats, paper panels—all the things that the Japanese used in their daily life—were objects of beauty, often qualifying as fine art.

When Europeans first encountered Japan they were amazed at the artistic merit of virtually every mundane object in the homes of the Japanese. One of the more telling historical anecdotes is that Europeans first became acquainted with Japan's now famous woodblock prints because the Japanese used them as wrapping paper when sending their highly prized lacquerwares, porcelains and other handicraft items to collectors in 16th and 17th century Europe. Understandable explanations of "Japanese style" beauty did not become available to collectors or anyone else until Japanese artists and connoisseurs with cross-cultural experience began to delve into the subject in the early 1900s.

Kakuzo Okakura, the great Japanese art authority who wrote the classic *Book of Tea* in the early 1900s, was one of the first to explore the nature and origin of the beauty found in Japanese and other Asian arts and crafts. Soetsu Yanagi, the famed handicraft authority and author of *The Way of Tea*, who died in the 1970s, took the analysis of Japanese beauty to its ultimate. Before his passing, he shared his insights with me, using the terms *shibui* (she-buu-ee), *yugen* (yuu-gain) and *myo* (me-yoe) as the keys to the Japanese concept of beauty.

In Yanagi's terminology, *myo* refers to a special "spirit" that imbues the truly beautiful; a spirit that goes beyond mechanical skill to express a delicate mystery. *Yugen*, explained Yanagi, "expresses both a mystery and subtlety that lie modestly beneath the surface of things" in a delicate but perfect harmony. *Shibui* is a more generic term for Japanese-style beauty. It refers to a restrained, highly refined beauty that epitomizes classic simplicity and also exhibits the qualities of *myo* and *yugen*.

Foreigners immediately recognize the special quality of beauty that makes traditional Japanese products outstanding. Recognizing the quality in products being made in Japan today is not always instant, but the signs are there. They are visible in the basic designs as well as the decorative facets of products.

Obviously, the vital role that the study and practice of aesthetics has traditionally had in Japanese society continues to make a significant contribution to their economy through highly refined product designs and the quality of their workmanship. And just as obviously, it sends a powerful message to foreign companies wanting to compete with Japan.

始 末 書

Shimatsu Sho

(She-maht-suu Show)

"I'm Sorry Sorry Sorry"

Life based on Confucian principles of absolute obedience to higher authorities may be impressively structured and give the appearance of peaceful, happy harmony, but it has a flip-side that is dark and dangerous. Pure Confucianism is predicated on rulers being both wise and benevolent, but this has hardly ever been the case, and when it was it didn't last very long.

The facade of harmony generally presented by Confucian-oriented societies not only comes at the expense of personal freedom, it has historically ended in periodic eruptions of violence that were shocking in their inhumanity and destructiveness.

Even during peaceful times in the Confucian sphere of Asia, people have had to develop a variety of subterfuges to cope with the extraordinary demands of their social systems. In Japan, one of the customs devised to maintain the image of harmonious loyalty and blind obedience to superiors among the samurai class was *seppuku* (sape-puu-kuu), or ritual suicide.

This form of penitence and self-inflicted punishment was deliberately painful and fatal not only to demonstrate the courage and will of the samurai, but also to warn others of the fate that awaited them if they broke with etiquette and traditions.

Because the standards of the samurai were so high, they often could not avoid social or political blunders. Only mitigation by some other socially sanctioned custom prevented these blunders from being regarded as unforgiveable or having unpleasant if not serious repercussions.

The common folk of Japan were not expected to live up to the same standards as the samurai, but they were charged with following a very strict ethic of harmony that required extraordinary diligence and dedication. And like the samurai, they often failed to maintain the exacting standards of the system.

Because it would have been impractical and inhuman to exact punishment for all social infractions, the Japanese system incorporated the concept of instant atonement through institutionalized apologies. Since transgressions of one kind or another were commonplace, apologizing became ingrained in Japanese behavior.

Still today the Japanese are forever apologizing, often for slights or incidents that are minor or imagined, or sometimes in advance in an effort to avoid friction or ill will.

One of the most conspicuous—and useful—of Japan's ritualized forms of apology is the *shimatsu sho* (she-maht-sue show) or "letter of apology," which literally means "beginning and ending writing." Foreign residents in Japan are regularly amazed at how often letters of apology are expected, and how effective they can be in absolving people of quite serious transgressions.

Run-ins with bureaucratic regulations involving such things as licenses, visas, customs forms, traffic violations, even accidents, invariably call for letters of apology. Whether or not the party involved is actually guilty of breaking any law is sometimes irrelevant. Writing a letter of apology that accepts responsibility and expresses regret often ends the affair. If such an apology is not forthcoming, the authorities are compelled to pursue the matter and take some kind of legal action.

Tourists in Japan, foreign residents and visiting businessmen should be aware of the role and power of the *shimatsu sho*, and willingly make use of it when they run afoul of the Japanese system. By the same token, refusing to accept an apology is regarded as a serious breach of etiquette, so it is important for foreigners to be just as willing to accept letters of apology as they are to write them.

198

進退伺い

Shintai Ukagai

(Sheen-tie Uu-kah-guy)

"Pleading Guilty in Advance"

In Japan's traditional society, individual rights were primarily based on one's age, sex and social position. People were not created equal, and class privilege took precedence over all other considerations.

Customs and rules governing the lives of people were based on responsibilities rather than rights. Each of the several classes in Japanese society—nobles (*kuge* / kuu-gay); warriors (*buke* / buu-kay); merchants and craftsmen or "towns-people" (*cho-nin* / choe-neen); and farmers (*Nō*/no)—had their specific responsibilities which were established by government fiat.

This Confucian social system was designed to maintain absolute control over the people while protecting and preserving the political power structure of the shogunate government. Within this system, the emphasis of both government regulations and custom was on each class of people fulfilling their obligations to all levels of government.

Since the aim of the system and its administration was the survival and prosperity of the ruling elite, the interests of the people were secondary and often times not considered at all, depending on the arbitrary whims of the officials in charge.

In this environment, ignoring custom or breaking clan or shogunate laws, even when the indiscretion or action was minor by non-Japanese standards, could be very serious, calling for punishment by the authorities or revenge from an offended party.

Generally speaking, anyone accused of an offense in etiquette or of breaking the laws was treated as if they were guilty until proven innocent. Suspects were often abused and sometimes savagely beaten.

The harshness of the system, and the sure, swift sanctions by which it was enforced, conditioned the Japanese to be extraordinarily circumspect in their behavior and, on the surface, presented a picture of order and harmony.

Staying out of trouble was more than just a moral philosophy for the Japanese. It was a means of survival. In public disputes, for example, it was common for the authorities to treat both parties as guilty until the matter was resolved.

The introduction of democracy into Japan in 1945/6 removed the legal system that supported strict feudalistic conditioning in formalized behavior and unquestioning obedience to laws, but the system was so deeply ingrained in the culture and character of the people that it was to continue virtually unabated for the next two decades and still today remains an important factor in life in Japan.

Most Japanese today will go to great lengths to avoid confrontations of any kind with anybody. They are quick to apologize and to accept responsibility, often for things that are beyond their control and have nothing at all to do with them.

One aspect of this tendency is demonstrated by the custom of *shintai ukagai* (sheen-tie uu-kah-guy), or "resigning in advance." People who are responsible for problems or mistakes that embarrass, or could embarrass, companies, political groups or other organizations, or cause them losses of one kind or another, often hand in their resignation before the matter comes to a head.

In some cases, the individuals concerned turn in written *shintai ukagai* on their own; in other cases they do so at the urging of their co-workers and superiors. In both cases, agreeing in advance to accept responsibility for the problem, and expressing regret, is accepted as partial or complete absolution and significantly reduces any penalty.

This practice particularly applies to high-level business executives and politicians, including prime ministers, and usually results from scandals of one kind or another.

199

信 用

Shinyo

(Sheen-yoe)

"Absolute Trust"

During Japan's long feudal age, which began with the ascendancy of the samurai warrior clans near the end of the 12th century and did not really end until 1945, *shinyo* (sheen-yoe), or trust in relationships between individuals and among groups, was a very serious matter.

Japanese society was arranged in vertically-structured, exclusive groups that competed in a variety of ways with all other groups. Loyalty to one's group was a prime directive. Survival depended upon having the trust and goodwill of fellow group members.

Shinyo was not easy to achieve in feudal Japan. It developed slowly over a long period of self-sacrifice and service to the group, and had to be constantly reinforced. Even a minor slip was enough to destroy years of effort which, once lost, was virtually impossible to regain. Developing and maintaining trust therefore became a vital part of the daily lives of the people.

Much of the behavior of present-day Japanese continues to be based on the development and nurturing of a kind and degree of trust that transcends selfish interests and puts the good of the group above the individual.

It is the kind of trust that makes it possible for the soft-drink industry to put hundreds of thousands of vending machines out in the open, unprotected, and know that they will not be vandalized.

It is the kind of trust that makes it possible for businessmen to engage in business with each other without written contracts and know that no one will take advantage of them.

It is also the kind of trust that Japanese want and need to develop with foreigners before doing business with them.

Americans, in particular, are inclined to separate business and personal considerations. We think more in terms of the product and the price, and presume that their acceptability is all that is necessary to establish a business relationship.

While the process of developing personal ties with a Japanese company is usually drawn-out and costly, it is vital that such relationships be established because the Japanese are not under any social or ethical restraints to treat outside parties fairly if they do not have close personal relations with them.

Generally speaking, all relationships in Japan—business, political and professional—are based on personal considerations, not on principles or the kind of objective reasoning preferred by Westerners—and this is the main reason why lawyers are not nearly as common in Japan as they are in the U.S. Traditionally, business arrangements in Japan were based on verbal commitments backed by trust and loyalty, which, unlike detailed contracts, allows for considerable flexibility in their interpretation and management as circumstances change. Until this fact is recognized and understood, the Westerner attempting to do business in Japan is at a disadvantage.

In some respects, Western businessmen dealing with Japanese have gone from taking a superior approach to taking a supplicant approach. The Japanese abhor both. The superior approach clashes with Japanese businessmen's concepts of themselves and others. The supplicant approach offends their sense of pride in strength, dignity and courage.

Weakness in an adversary or competitor does not bring out compassion in the Japanese. It encourages them to more vigorous action.

紹介状

Shokaijo
(Show-kie-joe)

"Where Did You Get My Name?"

Historically, Japan's minutely detailed social system, including both daily etiquette and work, was so comprehensive and so strictly enforced by custom and law that there was virtually nothing unexpected, unstructured or spontaneous in Japanese life.

The philosophical and ethical foundation for the Japanese way of life, based on a fusion of Buddhism, Confucianism and Shintoism, resulted in the system being personalized and made as humane as possible, but it nevertheless was one of the most demanding social environments ever devised by any people.

Because the demands of daily living were so burdensome, the Japanese became extremely sensitive about someone imposing new demands on them and equally reluctant to add new responsibilities to their already restricted lives.

Japanese therefore developed a number of techniques for avoiding new involvements and responsibilities. One was to simply ignore anything involving strangers or unexpected events such as accidents. This traditional syndrome was so deeply embedded in the Japanese that as late as the 1950s, crowded subways and trains were usually as quiet as tombs.

It was not until the 1970s that children, teenagers and younger Japanese began chattering and carrying on freely when aboard regular public transportation (although school buses and cars reserved for students could be filled with noise).

Another way the Japanese protected themselves, in business as well as in their private affairs, was to ignore anyone who approached them without a *shokaijo* (show-kie-hoe), or "introduction."

Given the extraordinarily personalized nature of all relationships in Japan, business and private, combined with the conditioned reflex to avoid new responsibilities, the Japanese evolved and institutionalized the custom of responding positively only when newcomers came to them with introductions from third parties with whom they had meaningful relationships.

Introductions from respected and valued third parties immediately put new contacts on a personal basis and at the same time also carried with them the strong inference that the introducers were guaranteeing the character and intentions of the people being introduced.

A significant aspect of the Japanese system of *shokaijo* was the fact that the personalized nature of the whole social system made it very important for people to take introductions seriously and accommodate the introducer by extending whatever courtesies or help they could to the newcomers.

When I first began working in Japan in the late 1940s and calling on Japanese companies, virtually the first question I was always asked was "Where did you get my name?" — in other words, who had "introduced" me to the individual and his company.

I quickly learned that if I did not have a *shokaijo* I would be treated courteously enough but nothing else was likely to happen. In those days, an introduction in the form of a letter or a note written on a person's name-card, rather than just a verbal referral, was expected.

Shokaijo are just as important in Japan today, even though the absolute need for them has diminished as the Japanese have become less traditional in their reactions to forming new relationships.

Introductions remain valuable and highly recommended for foreigners wanting to establish new connections in Japan because they continue to be the ideal way for opening new doors and beginning the drawn-out process of establishing the personal relations that are so important in doing business with Japanese.

Introductions by foreigners with friends and business contacts in Japan, particularly if the contacts and friendships are of long standing, are perfectly acceptable. These introductions may involve either other foreigners or Japanese.

201

集団意識
Shudan Ishiki
(Shuu-dahn Ee-she-kee)

"Dealing with Group Consciousness"

In the early 1950s I had the extraordinary experience of appearing as an extra in a number of Japanese movies, along with several other foreigners. The thing I remember most clearly about the experience was how readily and expertly the Japanese extras reacted to the demands of the directors to behave in unison and how difficult it was for us foreigners to act in an acceptable herd-like fashion.

The Japanese extras played the group scenes perfectly, without prompting, much as drops of water in a wave move together smoothly and effortlessly. The foreigners, on the other hand, had to rehearse over and over, and in the end still failed to perform satisfactorily.

One of the most conspicuous facets of traditional Japanese behavior depicted in period films set in the 1700s and 1800s was the degree to which the Japanese players often behaved as groups, not only in their actions but in their comments as well.

Scenes involving a dozen or more employees of an inn, restaurant or shop discussing a problem or making plans were especially revealing. They were all so finely tuned to the same mental wavelength that complete sentences or explanations were unnecessary.

This *shudan ishiki* (shuu-dahn ee-she-kee), or "group consciousness," of the Japanese was deeply rooted in the culture, and derived from the homogenization effects of living for centuries within the confines of a carefully detailed social system that not only controlled actions but thoughts as well.

For generation after generation, the Japanese lived in a closed-in system in which behaving in a non-prescribed way was severely punished. The result of this life-long conditioning to behave in the "right" way programmed the Japanese to such an extent that much of their behavior became mechanical and predictable.

Because enforced behavior that is highly structured has a direct influence on attitudes, and eventually beliefs, the Japanese came to believe that group-behavior was the only moral behavior; that independent thought and action was anti-social. Many of the traits for which they were to become famous resulted from their group orientation.

Despite the dramatic changes in Japan since 1945 (when individual rights were introduced into the country for the first time), cultural programming in group-think and group-behavior remains today a significant factor, first in the school system, and then in the work environment.

Japanese schools are under increasingly heavy fire to eliminate their fixation on the rote learning process and their emphasis on entrance examinations. But the educational establishment is so firmly rooted in the traditional methods that change is at a snail's pace.

Managers in most Japanese companies are equally resistant to rapid change in the old ways. They see the traditional group orientation of the Japanese as facilitating both communication and team-work, and regard these skills as part of the reason for the overall superiority of the Japanese workforce.

The *shudan ishiki* syndrome often exacerbates problems that foreign businessmen have in Japan because they are used to working with people on an individual rather than group basis. They are generally not skilled in dealing with situations where authority and responsibility are diffused throughout a group; where there is essentially no one in charge.

The obvious challenge for the foreign businessman in Japan is to learn how the consensus system of management works, then turn it to an advantage.

202

出向社員

Shukko Sha-in
(Shuke-koe Shah-een)

"Loaning Out Company Employees"

During Japan's long feudal age (1192–1868) the country was divided into fiefs or provinces that were presided over by the hereditary heads of clan-families who generally had achieved power in their areas by force of arms.

Alliances among the 200-plus fiefs shifted with the times and personalities involved, and skirmishes of one kind or another were frequent. Ongoing political and economic rivalry among the clan-families encouraged them to be as self-sufficient as possible.

Both political and economic self-sufficiency thus became a deeply ingrained characteristic of the Japanese—and is a trait that has remained a significant factor in Japan's ongoing history.

The modern-day equivalent of Japan's feudal fiefs are the great industrial enterprise groups that are now called *keiretsu kaisha* (kay-ee-rate-sue kie-shah), or "affiliated companies," instead of *zaibatsu*. The best known of these groups are Sumitomo, Mitsui and Mitsubishi. These three plus some two dozen others are responsible for around half of Japan's total gross national product.

All of these affiliated companies are meshed together to varying degrees by mutually owned stock, interlocking directorships, marriage, school and other connections. One of the additional ways that the core companies in these groups support their subsidiaries and related firms is a deeply entrenched system known as *shukko sha-in* (shuke-koe shah-een), or "loaning company employees."

In this system, the parent companies (and there is normally one in each industrial category) regularly assign members of their own staff to affiliated companies on a part-time or permanent basis.

There are a number of reasons why parent companies assign some of their own staff to related firms. One reason is to aid companies that are in trouble and do not have the financial, engineering or marketing expertise to help themselves. In such cases, experts from the core companies are loaned to the firms in need for set periods of time.

Experts from parent companies may also become *shukko sha-in* when new subsidiaries are established. On these occasions the loaned employees may end up becoming permanent staff members of the new companies—and disappointed and unhappy if the companies remain small and insignificant.

Parent companies also use the *shukko sha-in* system to dump unwanted or excess employees on their subsidiaries and related firms. Unwanted employees who are most likely to be shifted permanently to subsidiaries are section and department managers who have reached or passed the level of their competence, are drawing high salaries, and are standing in the way of younger, more able co-workers. Maverick-type managers are also subject to such transfers.

Also, as part of the training programs of parent companies, younger employees who are candidates for promotion to higher managerial positions are also sent out to subsidiaries and branches as *shukko sha-in*. The aim of the parent firms is to provide future managers with a broad perspective of the core companies and how they relate to their branches and subsidiaries. These assignments are usually for two to three years or more.

Foreign businessmen dealing with large companies in Tokyo or Osaka, for example, can often expand their business through branch offices and subsidiaries by finding out which head-office managers used to work in the regional companies, and enlisting their help in approaching these firms directly.

趣 味

Shumi
(Shuu-me)

"Fulfilling Personal Needs"

Foreigners living in Japan often complain about not being accepted by the Japanese—no matter how long they have been in the country, how fluent they might be in Japanese, or how much they might know about Japan.

The truth of the matter is that if foreigners were, in fact, accepted by the Japanese and treated as if they were Japanese, the majority of them would probably leave the country at the earliest opportunity.

Social and work demands put on the Japanese by their hierarchical society, the still-mandatory group behavior and the limitations placed on individual thought and actions would be more than what most independent-minded Westerners would put up with.

But the same restrictions and obstacles with which the Japanese have traditionally had to live, and which still exercise extraordinary influence over their lives, are also responsible for some of their most enlightened and enviable customs.

Because they have historically been unable to think and behave as individuals, and forced instead to share their labors and their successes with members of their group, the Japanese have had to look elsewhere for personal satisfaction and fulfillment.

This basic human need led to the early emergence of *shumi* (shuu-me), normally translated as "hobbies," as a major factor in Japanese life. In this case, however, *shumi* means more than just "hobby" in the usual Western sense. It also means "taste," in an aesthetic, emotional and spiritual sense.

Denied outward self-expression in their work and relations with others, the Japanese resorted to developing their inner selves through a variety of arts and crafts, from singing, dancing, writing poetry and calligraphy to judo and karate.

The Japanese approach to these skills went well beyond their mechanical aspects. In addition to the necessary physical ability, they aimed for the development of self-control and willpower, and the contentment that comes with mastering difficult challenges.

For many Japanese, *shumi* was their real world, where they went to discover themselves and their relationship to the cosmos—with the result that virtually the entire population developed skills, beyond the demands of their daily work, that contributed significantly to their own lives and to the culture of the country.

Beginning in the 1960s, the Japanese began substituting a variety of modern-day activities for their *shumi* of choice, from photography, golf and hiking to mountain-climbing. But whatever they chose to do, they approached it with professional dedication, making sure they had the best equipment, taking lessons, and devoting a lot of their free time to achieving a high level of proficiency.

Thus the traditions of *shumi* have continued to broaden and strengthen the character of the Japanese, while at the same time making them more capable and productive in their daily tasks that demand will power, dedication and thoroughness.

Westerners visiting and living in Japan are often caught culturally short when they are unable to demonstrate any of the personal skills that the Japanese still take for granted—particularly singing. Businessmen especially regularly get into situations where they are expected to sing.

Western societies have, in fact, been seriously remiss in ignoring the importance of personal skills in the development of mature personalities and character—with the result that millions of people in the U.S. and elsewhere have no talents and no self-esteem.

出 張

Shutcho

(Shuut-cho)

"No One Else Can Help You!"

When the typical American or other foreign businessman goes to Japan he becomes functionally illiterate in the sense that he cannot speak or read the language, and is therefore totally dependent upon people who can understand his language to act as interpreter and guide.

The shock of suddenly becoming culturally dysfunctional is far more debilitating than the inexperienced person can imagine. The effects range from glaring to subtle, and are often the most devastating to high-powered, confident businessmen or politicians who are used to running things in their own countries.

One of the more serious results of culture shock is that the dysfunctional person becomes far more susceptible to being led and misled, to making mistakes and errors in judgement.

Foreign businessmen who do not speak or understand Japanese, but have had substantial experience in Japan, can usually make do despite the linguistic handicap, but they are greatly limited in their efficiency and effectiveness.

Americans in particular tend to give little importance to this cultural barrier as far as its deepest and broadest implications are concerned, and characteristically downplay it or try to get around it by taking an easy way out.

This "easy way out" usually means the foreign company licenses a Japanese firm to utilize its technology in Japan, signs an agreement with a Japanese trading company to handle the project or product from beginning to end, or makes a deal with a company in Japan because someone in the firm speaks English.

Generally, foreign companies that license their technology to Japanese firms do not learn how to do business in Japan, do not become known in Japan, do not develop their own market share, and eventually "lose" the technology.

Foreign companies that tie up with large Japanese trading firms are almost always in a position where they learn little or nothing about the Japanese market and basically remain outsiders—especially if they are involved in consumer goods that do not require any technical follow-up by the foreign side.

The third "easy way out" category—going with a Japanese company for the wrong reasons—can be a very informative and valuable lesson in the long run, but it is almost always expensive and is sometimes fatal.

One of the several reasons why going with a large trading company—or with any Japanese company for that matter—can be disadvantageous is the practice of *shutcho* (shuut-cho), or "business travel." The fact is that in most Japanese companies when the person in charge of your account is out, nobody covers for him or her. Generally, no one will assume any kind of responsibility for making decisions on behalf of the missing person.

The larger the Japanese company, the more likely its section and department managers are to be away from their offices on *shutcho*. One of the major reasons why there is so much business travel in Japan is because of the deeply engrained custom of conducting affairs face-to-face instead of communicating by letter, fax or phone.

Shutcho is common enough in Japan that it is essential to include it as a factor in maintaining effective relations with Japanese companies, in keeping programs moving forward, and in resolving issues that become problems.

It is particularly important for businessmen visiting Japan from abroad to check the travel schedules of their contacts in advance, and to keep in mind that making appointments with new contacts after arriving in Japan can be substantially affected by *shutcho*.

205

送 別 会

Sobetsu Kai

(So-bate-sue Kie)

"Enjoying Togetherness"

Functioning smoothly and effectively in traditional Japanese society was a tremendously demanding challenge that required extraordinary dedication, patience, perseverance and skill.

You could not just be yourself and get by. Being yourself—behaving in an independent, individualistic manner to suit your own character and moods—was not acceptable. Everyone was expected, and to a considerable degree, forced, to behave in the one, acceptable "Japanese" way.

The few people who were so independent-minded that they chose to go their own way invariably became partial or complete outcasts.

Japanese history is filled with stories and anecdotes about people who would not or could not accept the highly stylized social system and the sanctions that were used to force people to conform. Most of those who rebelled against the system, including lovers who were not allowed to marry, generally met tragic ends.

But within the often smothering confines of the Japanese system there were a variety of customs that served as stress relievers, and played significant roles in the overall tone and quality of Japanese life.

Many of these cultural "safety valves" involved aesthetic practices such as the tea ceremony, moon-viewing, listening to the songs of insects, incense-smelling, and celebrating the beauty of cherry blossoms. Writing poetry was also a major cultural activity that took some of the pressure off of people.

Virtually all of these practices have survived into modern times in Japan—and are one of the reasons why many foreigners find some aspects of living in Japan so delightful.

One of the common customs in Japan that I personally find especially enjoyable is the *sobetsu kai* (so-bate-sue kie), or "farewell parties." *Sobetsu kai* are usually thrown by co-workers or private friends when someone is leaving on an extended trip, being transferred to a new location, or retiring.

In the case of smaller, private groups, *sobetsu kai* are usually held in the evening, often at pubs featuring a wide variety of Japanese foods (similar to Chinese dim sum in that the most popular format is to eat small portions of a dozen or more choices), with lots of drinking and banter that goes on until 10 or 11 p.m.

On such occasions, the visitor who enjoys a variety of Japanese dishes, appreciates Japanese culture in general and is fluent enough in the language to participate in the humorous repartee that is part of such gatherings is able to better understand how the Japanese can put up with the more oppressive aspects of their formal, but mostly daytime, etiquette.

When upper level executives of companies and other organizations retire, the *sobetsu kai* generally take place in large well-known restaurants with private rooms or in the banquet rooms of major hotels.

On these occasions, the parties are sponsored by the companies and may be attended by several hundred people. They are carefully organized and orchestrated, with a master of ceremonies who conducts the group through ritualized greetings, speeches and the bestowing of gifts on the retiree.

Larger *sobetsu kai* of this type are very revealing of the Japanese way of acknowledging life passages and continuously nurturing the personal relations that are so important to the smooth functioning of both the society and the economy. But they are not nearly as much fun as the small, intimate parties staged by individuals.

大衆団交

Taishu Danko

(Tie-shuu Dahn-koe)

"The Ritual of Mass Violence"

Foreign businessmen, politicians and diplomats dealing with Japan are often confused by contradictions between the personal and group behavior of the Japanese. The contrast between individual etiquette and group actions is often so shocking it defies Western understanding.

Japanologists and others have been preaching for generations about the importance of harmony in the Japanese Way; about quiet, behind-the-scenes negotiating and compromising to avoid confrontations and achieve consensus.

While all this is absolutely accurate, it is not all of the story. There are regular occasions in the Japanese context of things when harmony is deliberately breached, and extreme violence is the order of the day.

Some of the most obvious of the occasions when peaceful negotiation and compromise are replaced by violence are in confrontations between workers, students, townships or other groups, and opposing groups. Throughout Japanese history such confrontations have been (and still are) regular occurrences.

The long, drawn-out confrontation between radical students (allied with local farmers) and the government against the building of Tokyo's international airport at Narita during the 1970s, 80s and 90s was one of the more conspicuous recent examples.

Japan's annual spring "offensives" by labor unions regularly result in violent street clashes that seemingly give lie to the reputed Japanese preference for peaceful compromise.

But all of these mass confrontations are staged, and follow ritualized patterns of behavior with precise rules that allow for a certain amount of spontaneous action, including violence and deliberate law-breaking.

The most common form of ritualized mass confrontation in Japan, regularly seen in the Diet, in other government assemblies and in private organizations, is described by the term *taishu danko* (tie-shuu dahn-koe), which means "mass bargaining."

Rather than confrontations that pit groups against corporations or other organizations, *taishu danko* conflicts involve groups against specific company executives or government officials who have fallen from grace because of some accident, blunder or behavior that is deemed unfair, disruptive or destructive.

On these occasions, the party presumed to be guilty is called before a mass meeting where he is lambasted with verbal abuse. The raucus crowd goes on to demand that he explain his actions, confess his guilt and accept responsibility for whatever he is accused of doing.

Generally, charges made against individuals in *taishu danko* confrontations result in demands that the accused resign from their positions. Businessmen and others in the private sector who are subjected to "mass-bargaining" attacks by stockholders, customers or members usually do resign, but politicians are more likely to face down their accusers and hang onto their offices.

The *taishu danko* tactic became institutionalized in Japanese society as a last resort for inferiors to discipline or bring down superiors they no longer trusted and could not be loyal to, because they generally had no legal recourse.

Japanese who are involved with foreign companies and organizations in Japan and become disenchanted with a foreign executive or official will not as a rule resort to mass-bargaining (because they presume it won't work). Instead, they use passive resistance and behind-the-scenes maneuvering to bring him down.

玉 虫 色

Tamamushi Iro

(Tah-mah-muu-she Ee-roe)

"Speaking with a Forked Tongue"

Japanese etiquette, which includes physical behavior as well as manner of speaking and what one says, has a number of goals. One has to do with the Japanese preference for carefully defined form and controlled physical movements, and the other pertains to maintaining harmony in an emotional, intellectual and spiritual sense.

The importance of maintaining harmony in Japanese society resulted in the development of a number of intellectual subterfuges to help people avoid making mistakes or inadvertently upsetting others—thereby disrupting harmony.

One of the most common and yet sensitive and intricate of these subterfuges was in the use of the Japanese language. Different levels of the language, based on different vocabulary, word-endings and manner of speech, were used as a key element in conversing with people on different social levels.

The higher the social level of the people being addressed, the more esoteric and stylized the language required in addressing them properly. Learning these higher (and lower) levels of the language was virtually like learning a dialect.

The highest levels of polite Japanese have practically disappeared from normal usage since the end of the feudal period in 1868, but the levels that remain are so different from common speech that they continue to be a special challenge to foreign students of the language as well as to the Japanese themselves.

Japanese who are exceptionally skilled in *kei go* (kay-ee go), or "polite language," are always in demand for formal functions.

The use of the language to maintain harmony went beyond ultra-polite forms, however. It also resulted in the Japanese being conditioned to use ordinary vocabulary in an indirect and often flowery manner that could be taken to mean different things—or nothing at all.

Such usage of the Japanese language contributed to the development in Japan of what I call "cultural telepathy," meaning that the people eventually became so culturally alike that in many instances they did not need to speak, or could talk in vague and sometimes meaningless terms, and still be understood perfectly.

Speech that is deliberately unclear and open to interpretation came to be known as *tamamushi iro* (tah-mah-muu-shee ee-roe) talk. *Iro* means color. A *tamamushi* is a beetle that has metallic-like iridescent bars of golden green on one wing and golden purple on its other wing.

The colors of the *tamamushi*'s wings glow a beautiful blue, green, red, gold or purple, depending on how the light strikes them and the angle of your view. The wings look good but you really can't tell what color they are—thus the application of *tamamushi iro* to gobbledygook.

In Japan the most notorious practitioners of *tamamushi iro* talk are politicians. With them it is not just an ordinary cultural habit designed to help maintain harmony; it is a carefully practiced skill used to keep from making public commitments on anything.

Japanese businessmen are also naturally inclined to use *tamamushi iro* talk in their public comments—unless they are making announcements of decisions that have been reached in advance by consensus. When confronted by questions from foreigners, Japanese businessmen often are not able to say anything specific because they do not have the authority to make decisions on their own.

棚 卸 し

Tana Oroshi
(Tan-nah Oh-roe-she)

"Picking Things to Pieces"

A number of practical factors that impact on business in Japan would probably never occur to the uninitiated foreigner. Among these things are the
narrowness of streets, the fact that most streets in the country do not have
names, and that the addressing system has nothing to do with streets in the
first place.

A significant percentage of the streets in Japanese towns and cities
were not designed for vehicular traffic. They began as pedestrian lanes several hundred years ago, and still today consist of single lanes that will not
accommodate large trucks or two-way traffic.

Historically in Japan, only major national roads were named. Later it
became common for main city thoroughfares to be unofficially referred to
by area names or the name of some activity taking place in the area. When
the Allied military forces occupied Japan following World War II, the
Occupationaires gave English names and numbers to more than a dozen of
the main streets in the larger cities.

When the Occupation of Japan ended in 1952, the street signs put up
by the Allied forces gradually disappeared, and it was not until the 1960s
that Tokyo and other city governments began a systematic program of
assigning Japanese names to key connecting streets.

Still today less than one percent of the streets in Tokyo have names,
and what is even more confusing to foreign visitors is that addresses of
homes and buildings are based on area designations, and have nothing
whatsoever to do with streets. Finding an address, once you locate the
right area, is more or less a process of elimination and can take as much as
an hour or so.

Since so many of Japan's narrow streets will not accommodate large
vehicles, the automobile industry was forced to make small cars and delivery
trucks—and still today narrow streets are regularly listed as one of the reasons why American-made automobiles do not sell in large numbers in Japan.

Another factor that impinges dramatically on business in Japan—and
is closely related to the problem of narrow maze-like streets—is the num-

ber of retail outlets that have to be serviced by wholesalers. Japan has one of the largest number of retail outlets per capita of any country in the world.

Furthermore, virtually none of the outlets, including the largest department stores, have storage space to maintain any substantial amount of stock, and therefore require servicing by wholesalers on a daily basis.

Japan's retail and wholesale districts are therefore beehives of incredible activity, with hundreds of thousands of miniature vans and trucks scurrying about from early morning until late at night.

Because of the miniscule size of most retail outlets and their lack of storage space, *tana oroshi* (tah-nah oh-roe-she), or "taking things off of shelves," came to be equated with taking inventory. *Tana oroshi*, or taking inventory, was an unending process. The literal meaning of *tana oroshi* is "lowering the shelf (so as to take inventory)".

Keeping track of sales and stock in retail outlets was a formidable task requiring meticulous care and attention, which in turn required someone who was a stickler for order, detail and preciseness.

Eventually, *tana oroshi* came to be used to describe criticism, especially nitpicking comments about other people's attitudes, behavior and looks. The term itself is not heard so often today in this context, but the overall cultural conditioning of the Japanese makes them habitual nitpickers.

Japanese consumers in particular are meticulous and thorough in inspecting merchandise. Unlike typical American consumers who tend to ignore minor faults, Japanese shoppers are experts at *tana oroshi*.

他人

Tanin

(Tah-neen)

"Land of Strangers"

When the Japanese are in a crowd, whether it is at work, on the street or aboard a bus or train, they seem to have a special talent for pretending that other people do not exist.

No doubt part of the reason for this phenomenon is that there are so many Japanese crowded into such small areas that for them to continuously acknowledge or be concerned about the presence of others would simply be impossible.

Anyone who has spent time on commuter buses and trains in Japan, literally pressed up against other passengers like canned sardines, can fully appreciate the daily experience of being nose-to-nose to strangers for an hour or more and having to refrain from getting familiar or violent.

But the habit of blocking out the existence of other people goes well beyond Japan's crowded buses and trains. It is a cultural syndrome that grew out of the traditional political and social systems, and has been characteristic of the people for generations.

Japanese are famous for their group orientation and team spirit, but historically they have also been notorious for having little or no sympathy for strangers, including other Japanese who were not members of their group—and particularly for people who were not Japanese.

Open-mindedness and the "Good Samaritan" philosophy did not develop in Japan because of a number of political, social and economic factors. Membership in a group and total dependence on that group took precedence over everything else. All outsiders were competitors at best and enemies at worst.

Each group member was required to suppress his or her own individual desires and put the collective interests of the group first. Involvement in a group was so total that it generally precluded intimate and often even casual, relationships with members of other groups.

For the last several hundred years of Japan's shogunate system of government, members of individual groups were equally responsible for the behavior of other members. Punishment for infractions of the law were often collective. If one man in a village committed a crime, everyone in the village could be and often was punished.

This type of mutual dependence resulted in the Japanese going to extremes to avoid entanglements of any kind with people outside of their group. Anyone not a group member or not directly known was a *tanin* (tah-neen), or "stranger"—someone to be suspicious of and avoided.

While this system greatly enhanced the ability of the Japanese government to control the people most of the time, it also led to sudden outbursts of unrestrained violence when the pressure became too great or was abruptly released for some reason.

On a larger scale, the mutual dependence of the Japanese was also apparently a factor in the fanaticism that afflicted militaristic groups of people when their desires or efforts were blocked by some outside force—

factors that contributed to the outbreak of World War II in the Pacific.

At the same time, it was this traditional dependence syndrome that allowed the Japanese to accept defeat by the Allied Powers in 1945, and switch from a fanatical belligerence to cooperation, even friendship, with the United States overnight. They merely substituted one power group for another.

On a business and professional level in Japan today, this group-related *tanin* syndrome continues to keep people apart. The instant comradeship that is commonplace among newly met engineers, doctors, scientists, salesmen, etc. in the U.S. and other Western countries is generally repressed by most Japanese because they still cannot break the limitations imposed upon them by their group affiliations.

探 索

Tansaku

(Tahn-sah-kuu)

"The Search for New Ideas"

Looking at Japan today, it strains the mind to recall and dwell on the fact that until 1868 the country was still in the Middle Ages—a feudalistic kingdom of warriors and fief lords whose attitudes and ways had not changed significantly for more than seven hundred years.

This extraordinary contemplation becomes more incredible when you consider that from 1868 until 1945 the Westernism and technology that was imported into Japan remained little more than a facade. The essence of Japanese culture remained very much the same as it had been during the long feudal age.

In broad terms, modern Japan dates from 1945, when the changes resulting from defeat in World War II finally saw the end of the sword as the primary symbol of power, and ordinary Japanese at last freed from the bondage of feudalism.

To complete this image of pre-modern Japan, it is essential to add that during most of the country's history it was isolated from the rest of the world both geographically and culturally, with the limited exceptions of Korea and China.

Thus, again in broad terms, when the walls separating Japan from the outside world were battered down in 1945, it was something like exposing a socially sophisticated but still feudalistic society to other people and other cultures for the first time.

In the decades that have passed so swiftly since then, the Japanese have astounded the world with their ability to rapidly incorporate the most sophisticated technology into their industry and lifestyle, and to move beyond imitation to become innovators and creators.

I believe the key reasons for the fantastic success of the Japanese in such a short period of time were a finely trained and tuned intellect that had been stifled for nearly two thousand years by a past-oriented feudalism, a powerful pride, and an unbounded curiosity about the forbidden outside world.

Political and economic freedom in 1945 unleashed the energies and ambitions of the ordinary Japanese for the first time in the history of the country. For the first time they could use their minds, their strength and their diligence to benefit themselves.

For the first time, new ideas were not only permitted; they were encouraged. Within a decade of the beginning of this new-found freedom, the first of Japan's new, innovative products were already on the market. By the 1980s, what had started as a trickle had become a torrent.

The Japanese had combined their feudal-based skills in organization, order and discipline with an imaginative vision of the future and the previously prohibited experience of *tansaku* (tahn-sah-kuu), or "searching/exploring," anything that attracted their attention.

In a complete reversal of their feudal history, which was marked by almost total stagnation, the Japanese today are not only world leaders in their vision of an ever-changing future, they are the most committed to searching for new ideas, and the most focused in their efforts to apply them to creating a better world.

The Japanese commitment to technology *tansaku* is not limited to laboratories in Japan. As incompatible to traditional Japanese culture as it might seem on the surface, their search is global. It recognizes no boundaries, no cultural identity. They are now as obsessed with combing the world for knowledge as they once were in keeping Japan closed off from the outside.

⬢211⬢

単身赴任者

Tanshin Funin-sha
(Tahn-sheen Fuu-neen-shah)

"The Boondocks Bachelors"

Japan's large corporate conglomerates have dozens to hundreds of branch or field offices scattered throughout the country, including some that are in distant, out-of-the-way places with few of the amenities that abound in Tokyo, Osaka and other major metropolitan areas.

One of the key facets of the management training programs of such corporations is to systematically assign young head office and regional office managerial candidates to these branches for two, three, or more, years.

It is also common for the companies to assign especially productive middle-aged managers to local branches as a means of increasing their sales or productivity—or, to help them resolve financial or technical problems requiring more experience than is available among locally hired employees.

Other categories of headquarters personnel routinely sent to the boonies are younger people who can't hack it at the head office, and older middle managers who are being farmed out because they are not qualified, or do not have enough influence, to be promoted to a higher rank.

Employees who are sent out to branch operations on temporary but long-term assignments are known in colloquial terms as *tanshin funin-sha* (tahn-sheen fuu-neen-shah). *Tanshin* by itself means "to be alone" or "lonely," and *funin* means "posting" or "leave for a new assignment." *Sha* means "person." Together they have come to mean something like "business bachelors."

There are well over half a million *tanshin funin-sha* in Japan, and their numbers are increasing yearly as companies expand their operations.

The *tanshin funin* policy of Japan's larger companies is the subject of a great deal of debate because it invariably means that the men who are married cannot take their families with them. The problems associated with finding new housing and their children changing schools are simply unacceptable.

Another factor that works against them relocating their families is that most of them expect to be called back to the head office within a few years, which means they would have to go through the same housing and schooling problem a second time.

The lives of *tanshin funin-sha* and their families are a common theme in Japan's news and entertainment media, with the latter emphasizing what such separations do to husbands and wives, particularly dramatic events that occur when they take lovers and mistresses.

At best, most of the *tanshin funin-sha* are able to function only as part-time husbands, putting in cameo appearances a few times a year. In cities where there are large numbers of them, they have formed clubs or associations that are meant to be support groups to help them put up with being separated from their families and having to take care of their own personal needs.

But for the most part, all these clubs do in the way of supporting their members is to coordinate regular meetings at the same bars, clubs or pub restaurants where they eat, drink and commiserate with each other.

There appears to be no way the problems of the *tanshin funin-sha* in Japan can be alleviated, short of companies eliminating the system altogether, because of the extreme shortage of affordable housing, and the educational system that makes switching schools difficult and rare.

In earlier decades Japanese businessmen posted overseas also almost always went alone. Their problems were compounded by culture shock that was exacerbated to an extraordinary degree by the power and exclusivity of their own culture. But beginning in the 1970s, particularly after the rise in the purchasing power of the yen, they began to take their families with them, and to make greater efforts to break out of their cultural shells.

たらい廻し

Tarai Mawashi

(Tah-rye Mah-wah-she)

"The Royal Run-Around"

The Japanese were conditioned for centuries to do specific jobs according to precise forms and processes, with absolutely no deviations. This training resulted in the gradual development of an extraordinary level of expertise in all of the mundane acts of living, from using chopsticks to mopping floors, as well as in the arts and crafts of the nation's cottage industries.

This same technical and psychological conditioning helped make it possible for the Japanese to convert their cottage industry economy into an advanced industrialized economy in less than thirty years following the downfall of the feudal Tokugawa shogunate in 1868, and to transform their shattered country into one of the world's leading economic powers in a similar period following the end of World War II in 1945.

There was, however, a significant negative factor in the mental robotization of the Japanese. It forced them to sacrifice their individuality and the general quality of their lives on the altar of political ambitions and economic progress.

The mechanization of Japanese society also created the perfect milieu for bureaucratism, providing a foundation for its morality and psychology, and guaranteeing that it would become the overriding factor in all organizations—particularly so in government.

Bureaucracies in all levels of government has been a primary fact of life in Japan for ages, affecting everyone from birth to death. It has, in fact, been the core of the governmental system, controlling both the essence and spirit of government.

About the only recourse the Japanese have had to bureaucracy over the centuries has been to make fun of it with such semi-humorous references as *tarai mawashi* (tah-rye mah-wah-she), which literally means "revolving the barrel."

In early Japan, street acrobat-entertainers performed one of their more popular acts by lying on their backs, balancing a wooden wash-tub on their up-raised feet, and twirling it around.

One point in comparing bureaucrats with *tarai mawashi* is that the bureaucrats move, but like the tub, they just go around and around and never do anything.

Another facet of the *tarai mawashi* reference is that people who go to government and public sector offices are forever getting the run-around; sent from one department to another, sometimes until it becomes ludicrous.

Much of the *tarai mawashi* syndrome in Japan derives from the cultural conditioning of the Japanese to focus totally on their primary job or concern, ignoring everything else, and to go to extremes to avoid exposing themselves to new responsibilities.

Another facet of the problem is a holdover from the recent past, when neither government offices nor private enterprises considered it their duty, or important, for them to provide the public with detailed information about their activities or service.

Their reaction was, in fact, often just the opposite. They tended to consider such information confidential. Until the 1970s, it was frequently necessary to resort to industrial espionage-type tactics to get "public" information out of Japanese companies.

While the situation began improving dramatically in the 1980s, particularly in government services having to do with passports and visas, and in larger commercial enterprises, it remains a conspicuous and often burdensome part of living in Japan.

叩き上げ

Tataki Age
(Tah-tah-kee Ah-gay)

"Pulling Oneself Up by the Bootstraps"

One of the most famous people in Japan's colorful history was a man named Hideyoshi Toyotomi, who was born to a peasant family in 1536 and was the lord of Japan when he died in 1592.

As a youth, Hideyoshi was so intractable and troublesome that his parents finally packed him off to a temple run by tough-minded priests. He was also so ugly he was nicknamed *Ko Zaru*, or "Little Monkey." When he was twelve years old, Hideyoshi ran away from the temple, and some time later laid down beside the road and went to sleep.

A notorious gang of robbers and cut-throats came by while Hideyoshi was asleep and spotted him beside the road. One of the members went over and kicked Hideyoshi just to get a rise out of him. He came up cursing and fighting.

It turned out that the leader of the gang was from the same region as Hideyoshi (they spoke the same dialect), and was so impressed with the young boy's spirit and courage that he made him a member of the gang, later apprenticing him to a blacksmith and then a carpenter.

When he was in his early twenties, Hideyoshi managed to become the sandal-keeper to Nobunaga Oda, an ambitious clan lord who was then trying to unify the divided country and restore the power and prestige of the shogunate.

Hideyoshi so impressed Nobunaga that he was soon put in charge of repairing a war-damaged castle. Shortly afterward he enlisted the aid of his old gang leader to attack and defeat one of Nobunaga's strongest enemies. By the time he was 35, Hideyoshi had his own fief and army. Five years later he controlled the five provinces of Western Honshu.

When Nobunaga was assassinated in 1582, Hideyoshi took over his struggle and by 1586 was so successful he had himself appointed prime minister. By 1590 he was the undisputed master of the country. In 1591, Hideyoshi issued an edict fixing the population of the country into four hereditary classes—samurai, farmers, artisans and merchants.

The first peasant ever to reach the highest pinnacle of power in Japan, Hideyoshi's edict froze social mobility for the next 277 years, effectively preventing anyone else from following in his footsteps.

It was not until Japan's last shogunate dynasty fell in 1868 that the way was again opened for a socially disadvantaged person to achieve political or commercial prominence and duplicate Hideyoshi's feat by becoming a *tataki age*—a person who overcomes tremendous obstacles to pull himself up by his own intelligence, hard work and courage, and achieve great success.

Originally, *tataki age* meant hammering metal into swords or other useful objects. Eventually it was applied to people whose own hard experiences had imbued them with the character and ability to succeed.

Among Japan's *tataki age* of the modern era, the best-known include Konosuke Matsushita, founder of the huge Matsushita conglomerate, and Kokichi Mikimoto, founder of the Mikimoto pearl kingdom—both of whom were born before the end of the 19th century.

There were only a few other *tataki age* during the first half of the 20th century because Japan's social system still did not encourage the entrepreneurial or innovative spirit and the handicaps facing an uneducated, unconnected person remained enormous.

The Japanese system today continues to make it extremely difficult for anyone with only an elementary education and no capital to build a major business, but there are now thousands of establishment drop-outs and people who refused to join the establishment in the first place who are creating new enterprises that may be the giants of the future. *Tataki age* is also used today to refer to individuals who overcome a variety of major obstacles to rise to the top of their companies.

叩き台

Tataki Dai

(Tah-tah-kee Die)

"Punching Holes in Proposals"

In pre-modern Japan, temples and shrines abounded throughout the country and played an important and colorful role in Japanese life. Buddhist temples in particular were conspicuous in villages, towns and cities because of their annual festivals.

Major temples usually held their festivals on holidays, while those at small neighborhood temples generally took place in the evenings on regular work days. Music and folk dancing were an integral part of the events. Larger festivals combined the elements of fairs and outdoor markets, with vendor stalls lining the walk-ways or streets to the temples.

Vendors vied loudly to attract the attention of passersby. In addition to shouting out the names of their wares, some vendors periodically pounded on their display tables with short pieces of wood made for that purpose—a custom known as *tataki dai* (tah-tah-kee die), or "pounding the table."

Still today in Japan there are over 90,000 Shinto shrines and more than 88,000 Buddhist temples—figures that are far down from the numbers that existed prior to the modern era. But they continue to make up an important and picturesque side of Japanese life.

The age-old custom of *tataki dai* also remains, and is frequently seen in front of regular shops that set up sidewalk tables and heap them with merchandise during special sales.

Sometime during the 1960s, the term *tataki dai* moved into the meeting rooms of Japan's business world, where it was adapted to mean the process of considering ("pounding!") proposals—an allusion that would seemingly be more in character with the Western way of doing business.

Despite the image of noisy debate that *tataki dai* might conjure up in the mind of the foreigner, the process in the Japanese context is typically Japanese in that the discussion goes on quietly and deliberately, usually at two or three or more meetings, until a consensus is reached.

A main point for foreign businessmen to keep in mind is that any proposal that they take to a Japanese company will be looked upon as a *tataki dai*—something to be "pounded" into a final shape that hopefully everyone will find acceptable.

In my experience in attempting to act as a bridge between American and Japanese companies, foreign businessmen tend to bring to the table what they regard as a complete proposal, and their best offer.

Invariably the Japanese side does not consider the proposal complete enough to satisfy their requirements. It often seems to outsiders that the Japanese are obsessed with unnecessary details, with things that have nothing to do with the matter at hand.

One of the factors in the persistence of the Japanese to get more and more information about any proposal is that each individual involved in the discussions brings a different perspective to the table, and has to be satisfied one way or the other—before he or she will agree to the proposal, or agree to accept the consensus in spite of any reservations.

It is usually best for the foreign side to come in with a proposal that is preliminary and flexible, and say up front that it is a *tataki dai*. This helps reduce or eliminate any feelings of reluctance or anxiety on the part of the Japanese and encourages them to work with you to hammer out an agreement.

Just letting your Japanese counterparts know that you are familiar with the *tataki dai* concept is enough to earn you some points.

215

手習い

Te Narai

(Tay Nah-rie)

"Hands-On Learning"

One of the advantages that the Japanese have traditionally had over many other people is their extraordinary manual skill in accomplishing complicated, difficult tasks, from the carving of tiny accessories such as *netsuke* (nay-t'sue-kay)—toggles used to secure carrying cords to a kimono sash—to fine carpentry, martial arts, and now, sophisticated electronics products.

This unusual manual skill grew out of a culturally-induced compulsion to refine things, including the mundane actions of living, down to their essence and make them beautiful in their simplicity and functionality.

There were probably many reasons for the development of this compulsive behavior, including religious rituals that were a part of Shintoism, the complex writing system and handicrafts that were imported from Korea and China between the 4th and 6th centuries A.D. and, later, the influence of Zen Buddhism.

Virtually all craft skills in Japan were based on a master-apprentice approach that in some professions lasted for as long as twenty or thirty years. Apprenticeship (for males) began early, generally by the time they were ten or eleven years old.

For the first several years, in most cases, apprentices served their masters as personal attendants, not as assistants. They were expected to learn the intellectual, spiritual and ethical values of the profession by observing and listening. At most they were allowed to clean the tools of the master and make sure they were properly stored when not in use.

Once apprentices had mentally assimilated the attitudes and actions of the masters, and were respectful of the trade and its tools, they were gradually allowed to begin the stage of hands-on experience.

In some of the more demanding arts, such as drawing the intricate ideograms making up the Chinese writing system, masters would sometimes hold the students' hands in theirs, guiding their movements—a custom still practiced in Japan's elementary schools today.

Apprentices were not allowed to deviate from the processes or forms taught by their masters. Any deviation, by design or carelessness, was regarded as the worst kind of insincerity and a character failing.

Thus, for most people, learning in Japan became a two-stage process: watching and then imitating; a method that eventually came to be known as *te narai* (tay nah-rie), or "hands-on learning." During most of Japan's early history, only rare individuals went beyond what they had been taught to introduce innovations into their crafts.

It was not until the ascendancy of Zen Buddhism in Japan in the 12th and 13th centuries, however, that the Japanese way of learning came into its own. Zen taught that the mastery of any skill depended upon achieving a perfect union of the body and the mind.

This required first achieving control of the mind through a variety of Zen exercises, and then combining mind-control with physical practice to the point that the body and mind could act as one. Once this goal was reached, there was no gap between being able to visualize an action or product and accomplishing it.

Today very few Japanese subject themselves to the rigorous discipline necessary to fully meld mind and body in their pursuit of excellence, but enough of the heritage remains in the culture, especially in the educational regime necessary to learn how to draw some 2,000 *kanji* (kahn-jee) characters, that the manual dexterity and overall skill level of the Japanese remain exceptionally high.

手打

Te Uchi
(Tay Uu-chee)

"Sealing Bargains with Claps"

Japanese often comment on the fact that the United States has about forty times more lawyers than Japan. This point is made to demonstrate graphically that there is a fundamental difference in the way the Japanese and Americans conduct their business and private affairs.

When this comparison is made, the inference drawn is invariably that the Japanese way is superior to the American way.

There are several reasons why Japan does not have more lawyers. One of the most important reasons is that during the country's long feudal age, which ended in principle in 1868 but not in practice until 1946, there was no constitution proclaiming and protecting the rights of the people.

In fact, the laws of the land during the feudal age were designed solely to preserve the fief and shogunate governments by severely limiting and controlling the rights of the people. The concept of people being created equal and having inalienable rights was totally foreign to Japan's ruling class.

Rather than living by a body of laws that detailed and protected the rights of people, the Japanese lived by laws and customs based on individuals and classes of people fulfilling obligations to their superiors and their groups.

In this environment, which lasted for more than a thousand years, morality and ethics were generally based on circumstances rather than principles. Thus what was legal and right for one was not necessarily legal or right for others. Justice was not impartial. It looked out sharply for the rights and privileges of those in power.

Contractual arrangements between people and businesses were based on personal commitments founded on integrity, honor and reputation rather than law and written documents. Because all relationships in Japanese society depended upon carefully nourished personal commitments, reputation was of vital importance. Breaking one's word was not done lightly.

There were a number of ways of indicating commitment in feudal Japan, including some that were pretty far out and have already been covered in Entry 171 (having sexual intercourse with the same woman; urinating together). One that has survived into modern times, sometimes in somewhat altered forms, however, is *te uchi* (tay uu-chee), which refers to closing a deal and clapping the hands to signify the agreement.

Te uchi is a ceremonial clapping of the hands, usually thirty times in sets of ten. Each set consists of three rapid claps punctuated by a single clap at the end of the set. The clapping is part of a ceremony that includes toasting with *sake* (sah-kay).

The *te uchi* ritual is now most commonly performed at the end of large meetings to signify goodwill and mutual commitment to the goals of the group, as well as to mark the end of the meetings. In this situation it does not necessarily refer to any specific agreement.

Te uchi is appropriate and often used at the conclusion of larger meetings where there have been specific agreements of one kind or another, such as when groups get together and agree to back political candidates.

As mentioned, *te uchi* normally follows a number of toasts, so the occasions are generally upbeat and stimulating, much in the way that the routines of cheerleaders get spectators revved up to support their favorite teams.

Participating in a *te uchi* ceremony is fun as well as informative, since it is a demonstration of the kind of bonding behavior that is so important in the Japanese system. [The practice apparently evolved from a Shinto ritual in which devotees stand before a shrine and clap their hands several times to attract the attention of the enshrined diety, prior to saying a silent prayer.]

殿様商売

Tonosama Shobai
(Toe-no-sah-mah Show-by)

"Too Big for Your Britches"

During Japan's last feudal shogunate dynasty (1603–1868), the country was divided into some 270 fiefs that were ruled by hereditary clan leaders known as *daimyo* (dime-yoe), or "great names." The *daimyo* were referred to as *tonosama* (toe-no-sah-mah), which translates as "lord," or "honorable lord."

Under the laws of the Tokugawa shogunate, the samurai class, which included the clan lords, their officials and their warriors, were prohibited from engaging in business directly. The *tonosama* and their ministers were therefore unable to gain any first-hand knowledge of commerce.

Generally speaking, the economy was in the hands of merchants who acted as distributors and wholesalers, buying from farmers and other producers, and selling to both common people and the samurai class.

As the decades of the long Tokugawa dynasty passed, more and more of the wealth of the land ended up in the hands of merchants. At the same time, the lords and their samurai retainers, all dependent upon their allotments of rice as the main form of currency, became more and more impoverished.

Merchants, who were legally the lowest of Japan's stratified social classes, envied the lordly samurai and disliked their power and privileges. This led to some of the merchants taking advantage of the inexperience and naivité of the *tonosama* and their retainers in their business transactions with them.

The merchants also resented the haughty attitude and behavior of the samurai, who had been conditioned to disdain money and not to lower themselves by haggling with merchants over prices.

After the clan and samurai systems were abolished in 1868, ending the government stipends as well, the former lords, fief officials and warriors had no choice but to begin earning their own living.

Thousands of the formerly privileged elite went into business, but many of them did not fare well because they were unable to rid themselves of the superior attitudes and behavior that had been so much a part of their lives before their transformation into ordinary citizens.

Since that period in Japan's history, any businessman that looks down on his customers and treats them callously or arrogantly has been accused of trying to be a *tonosama*. Businesses that get the reputation of disregarding the interests and feelings of the public are said to be guilty of operating a *tonosama shobai*, or "lordly business."

Once a company in Japan gets this kind of reputation it is very difficult to overcome. The Japanese take such things very seriously and are generally not forgiving. In extreme cases, the company concerned is forced out of business.

Unfortunately, some of the attributes of foreign businessmen strike the Japanese as being *tonosama*-ish, and whether intended or not, this factor makes it more difficult for them to succeed in Japan.

In broad terms, arbitrary assumptions by foreigners that their way is best and will work in Japan come across to the Japanese as *tonosama shobai*. This may involve anything from management style to brand names and the content of advertising.

Often the differences in style or content are so insignificant to the foreign side that it is difficult for them to understand why something won't work well or at all in Japan. Generally, Westerners are simply not used to the fine-tuned sensitivity of the Japanese to subtle nuances, and are often inclined to discount all or part of what they hear about it.

つまらない物

Tsumaranai Mono

(T'sue-mah-rah-nie moe-no)

"Here's Something Worthless for You!"

One of the aspects of Japan's culture that foreigners encounter in living among and dealing with the Japanese is a variety of attitudes, behavior and things that appear to be totally contradictory—things that may confuse, amuse, fascinate or frustrate the uninitiated outsider.

Some of the more conspicuous examples that appear contradictory to the senses include gardens made totally of sand and rock; trees that are only one or two feet tall and yet are more than a hundred years old; nondescript entryways that give no hint of the size and luxurious appointments of the home, inn or restaurant that lies beyond their doors; room partitions made of sheer, translucent sheaths of rice paper pasted over fragile latticed wooden frames; meals made up of the most common vegetables and seafoods served on tableware that are masterpieces of the lacquerware art; and the practices of using bathtubs for soaking rather than bathing and not wearing shoes into homes.

There are many other seemingly contradictory examples of life in Japan that are on a much more subtle level, and that impact directly and strongly on all personal and business relationships. One of the more important of these is the Japanese penchant for playing down and often disguising their talents and accomplishments, and being critical, sometimes vehemently, of any degree of prideful behavior.

This latter characteristic may be a reaction to the arrogant behavior that marked the sword-carrying samurai class which ruled the country during the long shogunate period from 1192 until 1868, for it was during this period that common Japanese were forced to conduct themselves in the most humble way; constantly apologizing and bowing.

The need for the Japanese in all social classes to avoid attracting undue attention to themselves during the ordinary course of their lives, especially to avoid engendering envy, while at the same time catering to superiors on whom they depended for their livelihoods—and often times their lives as well—resulted in their habitually minimizing their efforts, their accomplishments, the food they served, the gifts they gave.

It became customary for the Japanese to refer to the gifts they gave to anyone for any purpose as *tsumaranai mono* (t'sue-mah-rah-nie moe-no), or "trifling, insignificant, petty, worthless things," despite the real value of the gift concerned.

Using the phrase *tsumaranai mono* in this manner amounts to reverse psychology, however. On the surface it implies that the person receiving the gift is not expected to be impressed or influenced "because the gift has no real value," whereas the intent of the giver is exactly the opposite. By minimizing the gift the giver also protects himself or herself from being considered a cheapskate or someone with no taste if, in fact, the person receiving the gift is not impressed, or worse, is actually insulted by it.

The practice of minimizing all gifts with the *tsumaranai mono* concept is so deeply rooted in Japanese culture that the word *soshina* (so-shee-nah), the literary version of *tsumaranai mono*, is printed on the packaging made for boxing and wrapping gifts, and is especially in evidence during the two great gift-giving occasions—*O'chugen* (oh-chuu-gain) at mid-year and *O'seibo* (oh-say-ee-boe) at year's end.

Foreigners who give gifts to Japanese friends or business associates are advised to follow the *tsumaranai mono* custom, if for no other reason than to make sure that the relationship remains culturally balanced.

鶴の一声

Tsuru no Hito-Koe

(T'sue-ruu no Shh-toe-Koe-eh)

"When the Crane Speaks . . ."

A deep-seated desire for harmony—in the sense of form and order—seems to have been a significant part of Japanese character from earliest times. The country's first "Constitution," promulgated by Prince Shotoku in the 7th century, began with the declaration that harmony was the basis for Japan's culture, and should prevail in all things.

Japanese-style harmony was not just a self-discipline that grew out of some cosmic wisdom, however. It was also a system designed by the government to achieve maximum control of the people and maintain the ruling elite in power—and it was enforced by the sword.

In this Japanese context, harmony took precedence over virtually all other considerations—over feelings, over personal relationships, even over political and economic matters. Decisions were routinely made for the sake of harmony rather than practical sense.

This harmony-driven social system was to have a fundamental impact on every area and nuance of Japanese life, molding the attitudes and behavior of the people to such a degree that it produced one of the world's most distinctive cultures.

The harmonious aspects of life in Japan have traditionally been among the things that appealed most to Westerners—the exquisitely refined etiquette in personal conduct, the mass conformity of the people, the public order—but these sentiments were a reaction to the facade of life in Japan and were often at odds with what was taking place below the surface.

Because the habit of harmony and the sanctions to enforce it were so strong, the Japanese developed a variety of ways to cope with its demands, including behind-the-scenes consensus building, speaking in vague terms, and the use of silence as non-verbal communication.

Despite extraordinary changes in Japan since 1868 (when the feudal shogunate system of government ended), the power of the culture was such that their highly refined traditional manners and politeness still today set the Japanese apart.

All of the methods devised by the early Japanese to help them cope with the demands of harmony have also survived. One that plays a significant role in political and business affairs is known as *tsuru no hito-koe* (t'sue-ruu no ssh-toe-koe-eh), or "the voice/cry of the crane."

Cranes are known as very cautious birds that always post a guard when the flock lands. At the first sign of danger, the guard crane emits a loud cry, warning the flock, which then rises into the air in unison, thereby escaping danger and subsequently living a long life.

Tsuru no hito-koe refers to any group of people trying to reach a decision, but bogged down by an impasse, calling in an outside person of standing and authority to hand down a decision that all can—or must—accept.

In a company situation, the "voice of authority" may be a senior manager, a director or—more likely—the president. In such situations, the "crane" will usually make the decision that reflects the will of the majority in the group, thereby ensuring that most of those involved will agree with the decision, while at the same time giving those in the minority an out because it takes the matter out of their hands.

Foreign businessmen can make use of this cultural technique in a number of ways. If, for example, a negotiating team gets itself boxed into a corner and cannot alter its position without losing face, it can call in a senior executive to approve of the change.

220

打ち上げ

Uchi-age

(Uu-chee-ah-gay)

"Giving Success a Big Hand"

Japan imported the technology for making fireworks from China in 1543. Their manufacture quickly became a hereditary craft that was monopolized by a few families who subsequently made revolutionary improvements in both the technology and design concept, turning it into an art.

The variety and complexity of the firework designs became more and more sophisticated, eventually reaching the point where the makers could create recognizable scenes in one huge burst. The Japanese called their fireworks *hana bi* (han-nah bee), or "flower fires."

The fame of the "flower fires" became so great that the shogun's court began inviting the families to stage competitive exhibitions of their work on the grounds of the shogun's castle.

These castle displays were finally banned, however, because of the danger of fire, and the event was moved to the nearby Sumida River. Eventually the exhibits took on religious overtones, and were associated with Buddhist ceremonies to console the spirits of the victims of a great famine and epidemic.

One of the most famous of the stories connected with the annual fireworks exhibit involved a master of the craft who witnessed a murder. Afraid to identify the killer directly, he re-created the scene of the murder in fireworks, and during one of the mass *uchi-age* (uu-chee-ah-gay), or "shooting up/launching," he shot them into the sky where the killer was revealed for all to see.

The tradition of *uchi-age* fireworks at the Sumida River in Tokyo continued for 223 years, finally ending in 1956, only to be started up again in 1977, with the descendents of the original families still monopolizing the industry.

The party atmosphere that accompanied the annual fireworks displays led to the term *uchi-age* being used to describe celebrations at the end of theatrical performances and other forms of entertainment. These celebrations consisted of the beating of drums, drinking and general merrymaking.

Following this, it became the custom for carpenters and finally workers in other areas of business to stage *uchi-age* when they finished a hard or particularly satisfying project.

Workers and businessmen staging *uchi-age* dispensed with the beating of drums, however, and concentrated on drinking, letting their hair down, dissapating any stress built up because of the project, and cleansing the slate for the next job.

Uchi-age thus became one of the many occasions when the Japanese use drinking as both a stress-reliever as well as an occasion for nurturing goodwill and a cooperative spirit among groups of employees.

While participants are expected and encouraged to forget the stifling etiquette that controls their behavior during office hours, breaking the traditional taboos goes only so far.

Arguments and other kinds of disruptive behavior that might lead to physical violence are still strictly taboo, and are very rare during such celebrations. In more than forty years of participating in dozens of such celebrations, I have never witnessed a disruptive argument or a fight.

Uchi-age parties are another of the institutionalized customs of Japan that foreign businessmen and others can utilize to help establish and maintain good relations with Japanese employees, co-workers or partners.

As always, it pays to let the Japanese know that you are familiar with the *uchi-age* custom—but explain that the party is not just for them but for you also because you appreciate the purpose and value of such celebrations.

―――――――――――――― 221 ――――――――――――――

打ち合せ

Uchiawase

(Uu-chee-ah-wah-say)

"Avoiding Surprises"

One of the principle factors in Japanese and foreign-Japanese relation-ships, whether business or personal, is a precise etiquette and protocol for virtually everything one might say or do—a factor that often confuses and frustrates Westerners in particular because approved attitudes and behav-iors do not necessarily follow logical patterns.

To fully understand and appreciate Japanese etiquette and the Japanese way of doing things in general it is essential to begin with the principle or concept of harmony (*wa*). In the ideal Japanese world, every-thing begins and ends with a harmonious attitude and behavior, and all actions should be designed to fulfill and further this goal.

Apparently long before the beginning of recorded history in Japan, the main "religion" of the Japanese was based on people maintaining a har-monious relationship with the gods, spirits, the physical earth around them, the seasons, and among themselves.

The commitment to harmony was so important to the Japanese that it was the first article in the nation's first "Constitution," promulgated in the early 600s (A.D.) by Prince Shotoku, who served as regent for Empress Suiko.

Obviously, this philosophy of harmony did not preclude violence against competitors or enemies, but even in specific manifestations of vio-lence in Japanese society there was a prescribed manner, and order, for pursuing and contending with violence in a controlled way. .

Even ritual suicide by samurai who disgraced the profession or ran afoul of their lord or the shogunate was an extraordinary example of a care-fully choreographed, harmonious ritual that astounded the first foreigners to view the ceremony.

One of the still very prominent facets of Japanese etiquette is a strong need for and commitment to preventing surprises in business, politics or whatever because such surprises might be disruptive. There are numerous ramifications of this factor.

Among them: the Japanese business custom of refusing to deal with companies or individuals until they have established a personal relationship over a period of time; the practice of carefully researching companies, individuals and markets they are interested in; a preference—and sometimes a requirement—that any new relationship be supported by third party guarantors.

Of course, all of these things are simply good business practices, but the Japanese generally put much more stock in them and take them much further than typical American and other foreign businessmen, who tend to emphasize the deal instead of the participants.

The Japanese practice of preparing in advance for any contingency, and preventing surprising factors from suddenly appearing in the first place, is summed up in the term *uchiawase* (uu-chee-ah-wah-say), which means "to settle" or "arrange in advance."

Formal meetings and deals in Japan are routinely preceded by anywhere from a few to dozens of informal, unofficial preliminary discussions that are designed to obtain more information, to sound out the attitudes of others, to lobby for a project or point-of-view—in short, to achieve consensus.

This *uchiawase* activity is usually time-consuming and often appears to be totally unwarranted to foreign businessmen. It can also be an obstacle to consummating a deal with a Japanese company because it often requires the full endorsement of a dozen or more individuals.

Foreigners who are experienced in Japan make sure they are participants in the *uchiawase* process when it concerns them.

内の会社
Uchi no Kaisha
(Uu-chee no kie-shah)

"Don't Mess with My Sister"

Surface similarities in Japanese and Western companies, particularly in department names, titles and other structural facets or nomenclature, give the impression to outsiders that Japanese and Western firms are very much alike despite the more obvious cultural differences.

These structural similarities regularly lead many Western businessmen to automatically presume that once they get beyond the language barrier (almost always through Japanese who speak their language), dealing with Japanese companies is much like doing business with non-Japanese firms.

This supposition just as regularly leads inexperienced foreign businessmen up to their armpits in quintessential Japanese muck and mire.

There are dozens of invisible but powerful cultural factors at play in Japanese companies that take precedence over the companies' Western-like structure and give them a character and flavor that makes them significantly different from typical Western corporations.

One of the most powerful of these cultural factors is the Japanese concept of a company as a close-knit family that tends to view all outsiders as competitors and/or enemies until a personal relationship is established—and there is a precise protocol and lengthy time factor involved in successfully establishing and sustaining such relationships.

The Japanese company-family concept is, of course, a product of the culture and is a combination of tribal spirit, group orientation and Confucian principles that include familial exclusivity, mutual responsibility and loyalty.

During the last of Japan's feudal dynasties (1603-1868), the people were stratified into specific classes (samurai, artisans, merchants and farmers) by meticulously enforced laws. Occupations were mostly hereditary and movement from place to place was restricted.

Identity, security and often survival itself depended upon belonging to and supporting recognized social and economic groups, whether farming communities, handicraft shops, retail outlets or service facilities.

Each work unit, of whatever nature, was arranged and operated more or less like a family enterprise. Each individual had a vested family-type interest in the survival and success of the group.

In principle, at least, the youngest member of the group with the least seniority was just as important as the oldest and most senior member. With their lives so intimately integrated into their economic group, the Japanese identified themselves with their group first, and as individuals second.

When the country was industrialized in the 1870s and 1880s this pattern of thought and behavior was carried over into the modern company concept. The place of one's employment became *uchi no kaisha* (uu-chee no kie-shah), which is usually translated as "my company," but has much deeper implications than are indicated by these English terms.

The basic meaning of *uchi* is "inside." Long ago this meaning was extended to include the idea of home and then family—in the sense of "my home, my family." And it is this meaning that is expressed in the term *uchi no kaisha*.

To understand the true nature of a Japanese company it is essential that one understand the traditional Japanese concept of family, with each company employee bound by and motivated by the ties, obligations and responsibilities associated with a closed, Confucian-oriented group.

怨む

Uramu

(Uu-rah-muu)

"Instant Hostility"

The Japanese were traditionally conditioned by very specific, absolutely detailed cultural molds to behave in a certain way and to expect exactly the same kind of behavior from other people.

This carefully and precisely prescribed style of behavior was based on an ethic that demanded mutual dependence and cooperation founded on selflessness, infinite trust and loyalty.

Any deviation from this institutionalized and sanctified style of behavior was instantly obvious to the Japanese and grated on their sensibilities. If the situation involved non-family members or strangers, the typical reaction ranged from irritation to extreme hostility, depending on the circumstances.

The centuries-long cultural homogenization of the Japanese went beyond attitudes and behavior to include the appearance of individuals and other physical things. It was not enough to "act" Japanese, one had to "look" Japanese as well. The Japanese automatically distinguished between Japanese-made and foreign-made products.

Japaneseness was thus defined as an exclusive state that covered the mental as well as the physical world.

When typical Japanese are met by un-Japanese-like behavior, whether from another Japanese or from foreigners, it is upsetting to them and automatically results in *uramu* (uu-rah-muu), or "hostile feelings," that may be expressed in a variety of ways, from withdrawal and silence to indirect verbal criticism or some form of aggressive action.

It is especially difficult for Japanese to quickly develop close, trusting relationships with foreigners because they cannot predict how foreigners are going to react, and have no culturally validated basis for trusting them or depending upon them.

For this reason, and others, foreign businessmen wanting to do business with the Japanese must prepare a foundation for any business arrangement, making a special point of developing close personal relationships with as many of the Japanese principals as possible.

Overcoming the innate hostility of the Japanese toward consorting with and dealing with non-Japanese requires an extraordinary and never-ending investment in time and emotion.

If the reasons for the investment are understood, and if the foreign businessman concerned knows how to relate to and commune with his Japanese counterparts, the experience can be very rewarding in both a cultural and monetary sense.

There are several ways foreign businessmen can prepare themselves for more successful encounters with the Japanese. The best initial step is to read several books on the cultural history of Japan to gain as much insight as possible into why the Japanese think and behave the way they do.*

The next best step is to spend time in Japan, carefully observing and participating in the rituals of daily life and work with all senses operating fully, in order to pick up on the subtle nuances that set the tone and essence of Japanese expectations and behavior.

*More detailed advice can be found in several of my other books on Japan, including: *Behind the Japanese Bow—An In-Depth Guide to Understanding and Predicting Japanese Behavior; Japanese Etiquette & Ethics in Business; How to Do Business with the Japanese; Business Guide to Japan—Opening Doors & Closing Deals!; Etiquette Guide to Japan; Everything Japanese—An Encyclopedic Reader on Things Japanese.*

わ び

Wabi

(Wah-bee)

"A Secret Japanese Thing"

Traditional Japanese products have a special quality about them that attracts the viewer on both a conscious and subconscious level. This magnetic appeal is both sensual and spiritual, and therefore affects, at least to some degree, people who have had no training at all in aesthetics and are not known for their sensitivity to·beauty.

It is this below-the-surface appeal of Japan's arts and crafts to the libido and the soul, combined with the order of Japanese society, that causes first-time visitors to Japan to be so impressed, and lavish in their praise of Japanese things.

And it is this same attraction that keeps many foreigners in Japan even after they have experienced some of the equally common unpleasant and sometimes infuriating elements that are the flip-side of Japanese culture.

For those who are seduced by the positive side of things Japanese, there is nothing quite like a purely Japanese home, with its sliding paper doors, tatami floor mats, beauty alcove, wall scrolls, lacquered tables, and other representative arts and crafts that make up the traditional decor and furnishings. It imparts a sense of peace and tranquility that is also sexually stimulating—perhaps because it is impermanent and fragile, like pleasure.

Part of the sensual-spiritual appeal that has traditionally been built into Japanese homes and products of all kinds is bound up in the word *wabi* (wah-bee), which translates as "quiet" or "tranquil," with a strong connotation of refined simplicity.

One of the most important words in the aesthetic vocabulary of the Japanese, *wabi* is an essential element in anything Japanese—whether a scene, a shape, size, accessory, decoration, tool, utensil or whatever, and Japanese know instantly if an object has the *wabi* look.

Until the 1970s, the Japanese carefully distinguished between Western-type and traditional Japanese-type products, and did not relate the *wabi* concept to non-Japanese things. But when they began designing original Western-type products on their own, their cultural instincts led them to incorporate the *wabi* element into their creations.

By the 1980s, Japan's upscale consumers had begun to expect the *wabi* element in all of the products they bought, whether made in Japan or imported—and in some cases to demand it.

While growing numbers of young Japanese consumers totally ignore the *wabi* factor and buy foreign-made products because they look foreign, this market tends to be volatile and faddish, and the least profitable.

As these younger Japanese consumers mature and become a part of the Establishment, both their tastes and their buying habits change. They join the *wabi* crowd.

This revolutionary change in the attitudes of the more affluent Japanese naturally had special significance for foreign manufacturers selling or wanting to sell their merchandise in Japan. It meant they had to deal with the high-end marketplace on a much deeper cultural level than in the past.

At this point, European manufacturers have been more successful than American companies in understanding and taking advantage of the *wabi* tastes of the Japanese, and this advantage will probably continue for several more decades.

The *wabi* element is not something that is uniquely Japanese. It is a universal concept that is one of the ingredients found in any product that has been refined down to or near its essence—and is equally appreciated by anyone who has sophisticated tastes.

やぶへび

Yabu-Hebi
(Yah-buu-Hay-bee)

"Leaving Snakes in the Bushes"

In the samurai-run government system that prevailed in Japan from 1192 until modern times, common people had few rights that were protected by law. Too often the stance of the law was that suspects were guilty until proven innocent—and there were few if any restraints on how the authorities exercised their power.

This situation led ordinary Japanese to go to extremes to avoid breaking either government edicts or social taboos, including confrontations among themselves, because doing so would attract the attention of the authorities. People did their best to blend in with the crowd.

Some of the attitudes and behavior resulting from centuries of this kind of conditioning have remained characteristic of most Japanese down to present times. An outspoken, aggressive, individualistic approach is still taboo, even in politics.

In the 1950s, there was an interesting saying in Japan's business world in reference to young managerial candidates that was a direct carry-over from this early cultural conditioning. It was reminescent of "hear no evil, see no evil, speak no evil," but with a typical Japanese twist.

The saying was, *Yasumazu; okurezu; hatarakazu* (Yah-suu-mah-zuu; oh-kuu-ray-zuu; hah-tah-rah-kah-zuu), or "Never take a holiday; never be late for work; never do any work." The implication of this adage was that young men who came to work every day but kept such a low profile that they were practically invisible could depend on seniority to gradually carry them up the promotion ladder to success. (In other words, the more one did, the worse.)

One never hears the saying anymore, but the attitude has not totally disappeared from the scene because it derived from the ongoing reluctance of typical Japanese company employees to attract personal attention to themselves, add to their responsibilities, or get on anyone's bad side.

This concern is sometimes referred to in terms of *yabu-hebi* (yah-buu hay-bee), or "snake in the bush"—the connotation being that disturbing a snake in the bush can be bothersome or dangerous, depending on the situation.

There are numerous situations in the Japanese context that can result in someone warning, *Yabu hebi ni narimasu yo!* (Yah-buu hay-bee nee nah-ree-mahss yoe!), which means "That will turn into a snake in the bush!" It is especially used when someone contemplates taking some action for which the results cannot be predicted.

The Japanese reference to "snake in the bush" is a bit different from the Western saying of "snake in the grass," which refers to someone who is thought to be sly and treacherous. In the Japanese context, "snake in the bush" generally refers to results that might turn out to be unpleasant, if not disasterous, to the individual who "disturbs the snake."

Japan's *yabu-hebi* syndrome frequently impacts on foreigners wanting to do business with Japanese companies because the foreigners often do not approach them in an acceptable manner—that is, through carefully arranged introductions, with detailed proposals in writing, including comprehensive product and company profiles, business plans, and unhurried time-tables that give the Japanese side ample time to study the ideas <u>and amend them</u>.

Most Japanese companies are always on the lookout for new products and new ideas. One of the best scenarios is to make intended contacts aware of your product or technology through advertising, coverage in the news media or a direct-mail campaign, thereby inducing them to contact you.

横 飯

Yoko Meshi
(Yoe-koe May-she)

"The Ordeal of Eating Sideways"

Despite the fact that virtually all of Japan's international affairs—diplomacy as well as business—are conducted in English, the Japanese are not good linguists. In fact, they have more trouble with foreign languages than most people.

Although almost all Japanese are exposed to several years of English-language study while they are in school, only a very small percentage ever develop even modest skills in the language, and this only after extraordinary personal effort.

Over the years, many of my Japanese friends and acquaintances who speak fair to very good English have commented to me that having to speak English to foreign visitors in Japan or when they are traveling abroad leaves them physically and mentally exhausted.

I have also been asked many times by these same people if the same situation exists in reverse when I and other foreigners speak Japanese—if it is especially tiring and stressful for us.

The fact is, I have never been conscious of being stressed-out from speaking Japanese. I am regularly frustrated because my Japanese language vocabulary is mostly limited to ordinary conversational topics, but I am bugged because I cannot speak <u>more</u> Japanese—not by the speaking of what I know.

The stress problem associated with speaking foreign languages (not just English) is so common and so serious in Japan that someone coined a special term for use in referring to the syndrome—*yoko meshi* (yoe-koe may-she).

Translated literally *meshi* means "boiled rice," and by extension, "food" or "meal," and in very familiar usage, "lunch" or "dinner." *Yoko* means "horizontal" or "sideways." When put together you have a "sideways meal."

The figurative meaning of *yoko meshi* is a meal (breakfast, lunch or dinner) that is eaten with a foreigner and requires the Japanese participants to speak a foreign language.

Yoko is used in a humorous reference to the fact that the Japanese language is normally written in vertical lines, while English and other foreign languages are written in horizontal lines. A "horizontal meal" is a meal with someone who writes horizontally—i.e., with a foreigner.

According to Japanese scientists who specialize in how the brain works, the problems that Japanese have with English and other foreign languages is organic—not intellectual. They say that the Japanese brain works differently than the brains of non-Japanese, and that this difference makes it especially difficult for Japanese to "process" the sounds of foreign languages.

There is, of course, widely accepted evidence that the right and left halves of the brain perform different functions. Some Japanese authorities claim that the Japanese language is processed by the right side of the brain, while English and other foreign tongues are processed by the left side.

This difference, they add, creates emotional stress that is constant as long as a Japanese is thinking and/or speaking in a foreign language, and that the longer the Japanese speak in a foreign tongue, the longer it takes for them to recover and return to normal.

I have commented at length on this theory in my book, *Japan's Secret Weapon: The Kata Factor*,* but suffice to say now that the effects are there regardless of their cause.

Foreigners who do not speak Japanese, and depend upon their Japanese counterparts to speak English or some other foreign language, should keep this syndrome in mind and take care not to overtax them.

*Since republished as *Behind the Japanese Bow*.

───────────── 227 ─────────────

幽 玄　　妙

Yugen / Myo

(Yuu-gane / M'yoe)

"The Mystery of Beauty"

The first Westerners to set foot in Japan were particularly impressed with the refined beauty of virtually everything made in the country—from the art and decorative handicrafts to the utensils used in ordinary homes.

There was a character about Japanese-made things that gave them a look that was distinctive and different from similar things made in Korea and China, from where the original technology came.

This special quality of Japanese-made things was so commonplace that the Japanese themselves did not consider it anything unusual. The story of how Japanese-made woodblock prints first arrived in Europe is indicative of their casual attitude toward such things.

When the earliest Western traders in Japan began to buy ceramics, lacquerware and other Japanese-made items for shipment to Europe, the Japanese makers sometimes used woodblock prints as wrapping paper.

It was not until European art collectors and others of high station began making a fuss over the prints and other Japanese arts and handicrafts that the Japanese themselves began to view them as anything more than ordinary goods.

Japan's arts and handicrafts owed their refined quality to a combination of factors, beginning with the master-apprentice system of training artisans and craftsmen for many years, sometimes even decades, before they went out on their own.

The distinctive element in Japanese arts and crafts that caught the eyes of more discerning Westerners was apparently something that came from a merging of the Shinto concepts of cosmic harmony and spiritualism. The Shintoist concept of harmony included the size and shape of things, how they were to be used, and their relationship with people.

The spiritual element incorporated the essence and the spirit of the materials used, and was based on both respecting and revering these inherent qualities.

After generations of refining their designs and techniques, Japan's master artists and craftsmen achieved a level of beauty that transcended the obvious surface manifestations of their materials—a level that was described by the word *yugen* (yuu-gane), meaning "mystery" or "subtlety."

Yugen beauty referred to a type of attractiveness, beneath the surface of the material but in delicate harmony with it, that registers on the conscious as well as the subconscious of the viewer. It radiates a kind of spiritual essence.

Another aspect of the special character of Japanese products was described by the term *myo* (m'yoe), which by itself means "strangeness, queerness, mystery," plus "skill."

Japan's famed Zen master Daisetsu Suzuki said that the concept of *myo* expressed the essence of what is unique in Oriental arts and crafts. He called it an unconscious expression of "something" in Japanese life that goes beyond technique and comes from tapping into the cosmic spirit.

Suzuki added that it is impossible to achieve *myo* beauty through conscious effort; that it is something that must flow through the craftsman or artist, unimpeded by ego. He added that the reason few Westerners ever achieve the *myo* level of beauty is that their criterion for beauty is based on conscious realization, with the result that their ego prevents them from transcending mechanical skill.

Japanese designers, engineers and manufacturers today may not consciously think in terms of *yugen* and *myo*, but all that they do is significantly influenced by these powerful cultural elements.

融合化

Yugo Ka

(Yuu-go Kah)

"The Value of Fuzzy Thinking"

As soon as the severe restrictions of Japan's long feudal age ended in 1868, people began to mix Japanese and Western things and ideas, with results that ranged from wonderfully practical to funny. One example: when the first train service began in Japan between Tokyo and Yokohama in 1872, passengers boarding the train at Shimbashi Station in Tokyo left their shoes and sandals on the platform because it was taboo to wear them inside a living area.

But for a country that spent almost one thousand years treading water, and even had government regulations that prohibited change, the Japanese have obviously come a long way. One of the reasons why they came so far so fast was that once the taboo against change was lifted, they had no preconceived notions that certain things shouldn't be done or couldn't be done.

It was after the introduction of democracy and a form of government-sponsored capitalism in Japan following World War II, however, that the Japanese truly became free to innovate and change, and another decade was to pass before their latent imagination and talents began to show themselves.

I remember clearly when the shoe industry began to develop in Japan in the mid-1950s. Designers seemingly went wild. There were shoes on the market that no American or European shoemaker could have dreamed up, much less manufactured. There were no restraints because there were no precedents; no ingrained concepts of what was acceptable or possible and what was not.

Another factor that contributed greatly to the almost instant rise of inventiveness among the Japanese was their ability to discern—better than many others—the essence of a new product or concept; to see it unencumbered by cultural baggage, and improve on it by a process of reducing or eliminating the non-essentials.

The Japanese had also been endowed by their culture with the propensity and ability to look at things holistically—taking into consideration variables and things that are often not obvious or visible to linear thinkers. This led them to be especially adept at mixing technologies to create totally new products.

In 1986, Japan's Ministry of International Trade and Industry (MITI) introduced the concept of *yugo ka* (yuu-go kah), or "the <u>fusion</u> of ideas and technologies," as opposed to just mixing them. The technology-fusion concept was contained in a white paper that suggested directions and methods of research for Japan to create the most desirable society in the 21st century.

The white paper explained that while combining two technologies does not change the essence of their individual nature, the <u>fusion</u> of different technologies results in their transformation into something totally new. MITI foresaw that other technologies from many fields, from biology to electronics, could be fused to create new fields and new industries.

Some of the *yugo ka* work now going on in Japan involves six or more fields, including attempts to fuse optical, mechanical and electronic engineering into a new technology called optomechatronics; and using parallel optical computers with Trinitron-like switch guns to transmit laser beams from one grid of fiber-optic cables to another grid, in a process called optocube computing.

There is no doubt that *yugo ka* will play an increasingly important role in Japan, and have a direct long-term economic, political and social impact on the world at large. It is therefore a good word to add to your vocabulary.

善処します

Zensho Shimasu
(Zen-show She-mahss)

"When a Promise Is Not a Promise"

I have often noted that what you see and hear in Japan is just as often not what you get. One of the primary facets of Japanese culture is its emphasis on creating and maintaining facades that give a desired impression, but in fact do not represent reality.

This compulsion for facades evolved from an even deeper compulsion to maintain surface harmony, to present the world in an idealized state where there are no imperfections—or where the imperfections are perfect in their representations of nature and the human condition and are therefore in harmony with the cosmos.

It is not too much of an exaggeration to say that the Japanese have traditionally been obsessed with perfection—beginning naturally with form and proceeding to function and processes—in everything that makes up Japanese culture.

This obsession helped make Japan formidable in war and in commerce, but at the same time it is also an Achilles' heel that frequently trips up the Japanese in their relations with foreigners.

One aspect of this harmony/perfection syndrome is its effects on the Japanese language and how it is used. Linguist Ken Butler has written that the Japanese language is primarily designed—and typically used—to impress; not to communicate.

Until recent decades, one's ability to use the Japanese language and to draw the complicated ideograms with which it is written were equated not only with educational level, but morality and worth.

When the language was used verbally it often, in fact, was meant more to impress than to communicate, so one had to be able to divine the meaning of what was said from nonverbal cues and from a common knowledge of the conditioned behavior of the individuals concerned.

Still today, the majority of adult Japanese use the language more in the sense of a cultural transmitter than as a pure communications system. Many words used in social and business situations cannot be extracted from their cultural content.

The foreigner who learns the language but not the culture—not the way it is used—cannot communicate on the right cultural frequency, and comes across as an outsider, an alien, who does not "fit" in Japan, and more than anything else is a curiosity.

Because of the overpowering cultural content of Japanese, the language can be very hard to translate. If it is translated directly into English it can range from incomprehensible to quaint, and therein lies much of the trouble the Japanese have in interacting with outsiders.

Zensho shimasu (Zen-show she-mahss) is a good example of how confusing and troublesome Japanese can be when translated. *Zensho shimasu* is always translated into English as, "I will do my best," or "I'll take care of it," or "Leave it to me," and so on—with very positive connotations.

In the Japanese context, *zensho shimasu* means to cope with something, to make the best of some adverse situation, to take whatever steps one feels would be best. This is altogether different from the promise that is inherent in the normal English translation of the expression.

Zensho shimasu is one of the most used phrases in the vocabulary of Japanese politicians and diplomats, with the result that foreigners who hear the expression or see it written are misled. They take the meaning as embodying a promise or commitment. A much more accurate meaning is, "I will do what I think is best from my position/my viewpoint."

族

Zoku
(Zoe-kuu)

"Taking the Tribal Test"

Japanese businessologists, anthropologists and others typically say that the Japanese think and behave differently from Westerners because they are still primarily driven by tribal rather than rational instincts, and that Japanese society today is made up of thousands of *zoku* (zoe-kuu), or "tribes," that control their patterns of thought and behavior.

While tribalism disappeared from most advanced Western nations hundreds to thousands of years ago, it flourished in Japan in the form of clan fiefdoms until the fall of the Tokugawa shogunate government in 1868.

The end of the clan and shogunate system of government did not mean the end of the tribal instincts of the Japanese, however. Tribalism had been the foundation for all social and political organization since the dawn of their history, and was such an intimate part of their mores that it was inseparable from the only lifestyle they knew.

There have, of course, been many fundamental changes in Japanese thinking and behavior during the one hundred-plus years since the downfall of the country's last great tribal dynasty, but enough of the tribal culture remains to be easily recognizable in the institutions and conduct that exist in Japan today.

In today's language, however, *zoku* is translated as "group" instead of tribe, and is applied to every recognized grouping in the country, from political factions and motorcycle clubs to teams of co-workers in companies.

The overwhelming majority of Japanese, in fact, belong to some identifiable and functioning group. An individual not in a group (not a tribal member) is regarded as a maverick at best and un-Japanese at worst.

Political and professional groups in particular function as very exclusive clubs that are dedicated to protecting their turf and privileges, perpetuating their existence and advancing their cause. They exercise monopolistic power over their special area of interest and brook no interference from outsiders.

These modern-day tribes are territorial in the sense that their "domains" are limited to specific locations, such as in a single ministry or on one university campus. They are closed circles in that new members gain entry, usually at the bottom, only through precise rituals of passage.

Each of the *zoku* is hierarchical in structure, with advancement up the ladder of power and influence generally based on seniority. "Tribal" heads are naturally inclined to be autocratic. Those in the medical and scientific professions tend to run their "fiefdoms" as if they owned them.

Chief research professors at universities are particularly notorious for controlling all grants, research, and promotions, and taking credit for discoveries made by their associates.

Professors in charge of academic departments at their universities generally control job offers that come in for graduating students, parceling out students of their choice to companies from which they receive consultant fees or other favors.

Generally speaking, the main effect of Japan's lingering tribal heritage is that in any given situation, whether political, social or economic, the natural tendency of the Japanese involved is to consider the matter from a subjective rather than objective viewpoint.

This still deeply ingrained Japanese habit of reacting subjectively to business and political matters often results in misunderstandings, friction and conflict when they are dealing with objective-minded Westerners.

NTC'S FOREIGN LANGUAGE DICTIONARIES
The Best, By Definition

Spanish/English
Cervantes-Walls Spanish & English
Diccionario Básico Norteamericano
NTC's Beginner's Spanish & English
NTC's Dictionary of Common Mistakes
in Spanish
NTC's Dictionary of Spanish False
Cognates
The Dictionary of Chicano Spanish
NTC's Easy Spanish Bilingual Dictionary
Vox Compact Spanish & English
Vox Everyday Spanish & English
Vox Modern Spanish & English
(Thumb-indexed & Plain-edged)
Vox Super-Mini Spanish & English
Vox Traveler's Spanish & English

Spanish/Spanish
Diccionario Practico de la Lengua
Enspañola del Nuevo Mundo
Vox Diccionario Escolar de la Lengua
Española

French/English
NTC's New College French & English
NTC's Beginner's French & English
NTC's Dictionary of Canadian French
NTC's Dictionary of Faux Amis
NTC's Dictionary of French Faux Pas
NTC's Easy French Bilingual Dictionary
NTC's French & English Business

German/English
NTC's Easy German Bilingual
Dictionary
Klett's Modern German & English

Klett's Super-Mini German & English
NTC's Beginner's German & English
NTC's Dictionary of German False
Cognates
Schöffler-Weiss German & English

Italian/English
NTC's Beginner's Italian & English
NTC's Easy Italian Bilingual Dictionary
Zanichelli New College Italian & English
Zanichelli Super-Mini Italian & English

Other Foreign Languages
NTC's Bulgarian & English
NTC's Compact Korean & English
NTC's Compact Russian & English
NTC's New College Greek & English
NTC's New Japanese-English Character
NTC's Romanian & English
NTC's Vietnamese & English
The Wiedza Powszechna Compact
Polish & English
Easy Chinese Phrasebook & Dictionary
Languages of the World on CD-ROM

For Juveniles
French Picture Dictionary
German Picture Dictionary
Spanish Picture Dictionary
Let's Learn French Picture Dictionary
Let's Learn German Picture Dictionary
Let's Learn Hebrew Picture Dictionary
Let's Learn Italian Picture Dictionary
Let's Learn Portuguese Picture
Dictionary
Let's Learn Spanish Picture Dictionary

NTC Publishing Group
4255 West Touhy Avenue
Lincolwood, Illinois 60646-1975 U.S.A.